# Living Water

## Volume 2

D. MARTYN LLOYD-JONES

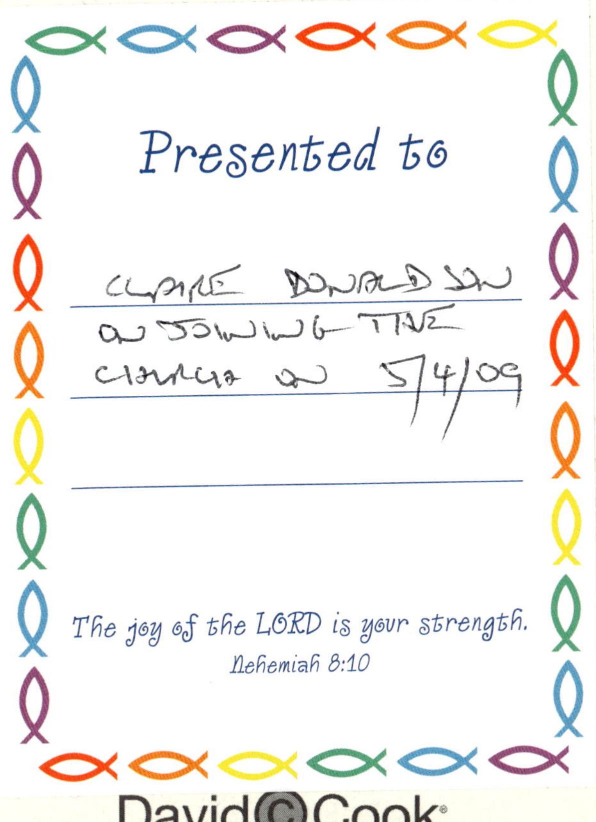


David C Cook

Published by David C. Cook
Kingsway Communications Ltd
26–28 Lottbridge Drove, Eastbourne BN23 6NT, UK

David C. Cook and the graphic circle C logo
are registered trademarks of Cook Communications Ministries.



ISBN 978 1 84291 4113 (Vol 1)

ISBN 978 1 84291 4120 (Vol 2)

Cover design by PinnacleCreative.co.uk

Cover photo © Manray | Dreamstime.com

Printed in Italy

# Contents

# *Note*

These sermons, which were preached in 1967 and 1968, are the last Sunday morning sermons preached by Dr Lloyd-Jones as the Minister of Westminster Chapel, before illness caused him to retire.

They have been edited lightly – enough to avoid repetition but not so much that his 'voice' cannot be heard through the printed pages. Over the years many people have commented on how they can hear him speaking as they read.

We owe a particular debt of gratitude to Rhona Pipe of Watermark, who for many years has worked tirelessly on the final edit of our father's books.

*Elizabeth Catherwood and Ann Beatt*

30

# The Coming of the Holy Spirit

*Jesus answered and said unto her, Whosoever drinketh of this water shall thirst again: but whosoever drinketh of the water that I shall give him shall never thirst; but the water that I shall give him shall be in him a well of water springing up into everlasting life. (John 4:13–14)*

We have seen that it is the teaching of the Bible everywhere that God's people are meant to enjoy full heart satisfaction, this complete satisfaction in the realm of their emotions, and we have seen that the subsequent history of the church illustrates the truth of this teaching. It is also our fundamental postulate that unless we have known a measure of this heart satisfaction, there is something seriously wrong with our whole Christian position. So at the moment we are considering how our Lord gives this satisfaction to the heart and to the emotions. He says: Take the water that I am offering and you will never thirst again – your heart will never be empty, you will never know that fundamental thirst.

But how does our Lord do this? Fortunately for us, he answers this question, and he does so in a very particular way in this

Gospel according to John, where we find the fullest teaching with regard to this whole matter. Some teaching is given in the statement from John 4 that we are considering, and we find it put still more explicitly in the seventh chapter, where we read:

*In that last day, that great day of the feast, Jesus stood and cried, saying, If any man thirst, let him come unto me, and drink. He that believeth on me, as the scripture hath said, out of his belly shall flow rivers of living water.*

And the apostle John adds:

*(But this spake he of the Spirit, which they that believe on him should receive: for the Holy Ghost was not yet given; because that Jesus was not yet glorified.) (John 7:37–39)*

Then in chapters 14, 15 and 16 of this great Gospel, there is extensive treatment of this very theme. Our Lord has begun to tell the disciples that he is going to leave them, and they are completely downcast, so he says to them: 'Let not your heart be troubled: ye believe in God, believe also in me' (John 14:1). And he goes on to give them comfort, and this is the real comfort:

*I will pray the Father, and he shall give you another Comforter, that he may abide with you for ever; even the Spirit of truth; whom the world cannot receive, because it seeth him not, neither knoweth him: but ye know him; for he dwelleth with you, and shall be in you. I will not leave you comfortless: I will come to you. (John 14:16–18)*

There our Lord tells the disciples that he is going to come to them through the Holy Spirit. Indeed, he goes so far as to say this to them:

*It is expedient for you that I go away: for if I go not away, the Comforter will not come unto you; but if I depart, I will send him unto you. (John 16:7)*

And he tells them:

*He [the Spirit] will guide you into all truth. (John 16:13)*

He also says that he will give them his joy (John 15:11), and peace such as the world can never give (John 14:27). That is the great teaching that our Lord gives us in this Gospel. In other words, it comes to this: Our Lord gives us heart satisfaction supremely through sending and giving to us the Holy Spirit and through the work of the Holy Spirit.

Now there is nothing more appropriate that we can consider together this morning – Whitsunday, the day on which we remember the mighty event that took place in Jerusalem as recorded in Acts chapter 2. Here is this notable event, the last of the great series of events recorded in the New Testament – the descent of the Holy Spirit upon the infant church and the astounding results to which it led. This is the way above all others whereby our Lord gives us this fullness of satisfaction, especially in the realm of the heart and the affections.

The coming of the Spirit had been prophesied many times in the Old Testament. That is why Peter, in preaching on that Day of Pentecost, immediately adduces Old Testament Scripture in order to explain and to expound to the people what is taking place. The crowd is aware that something strange and unusual has happened to these men, these ordinary men, these apostles. They are but fishermen, ordinary workmen, and yet here they are, something outstanding has occurred. Everybody comes crowding together, and the question is: What is this? And Peter says: 'This' – this event that you are seeing – 'is that which was spoken by the prophet Joel' (Acts 2:16). And then he proceeds to quote that prophecy.

A similar great prophecy concerning the coming of the Holy Spirit is in Ezekiel 36, where the prophet says, 'I will take away the stony heart out of your flesh, and I will give you an heart of flesh' (Ezekiel 36:26). There it is in very explicit and specific terms. One of the great effects of the coming of the Spirit into a human being is that the heart is changed from a heart that is stone-like and hard and unresponsive, to a heart of flesh that feels, that can be profoundly disturbed with tremendous consequences.

Now this is characteristic of the prophecies in the Old Testament with regard to the coming of the Holy Spirit. Indeed, all of the prophets deal with this in some shape or form. A familiar statement by the prophet Isaiah expresses it perfectly: 'Ho, every one that thirsteth, come ye to the waters, and he that hath no money; come ye, buy, and eat; yea, come, buy wine and milk without money and without price' (Isaiah 55:1). And, again in chapter 35 of Isaiah, we read: 'The wilderness and the solitary place shall be glad for them; and the desert shall rejoice, and blossom as the rose . . . And the parched ground shall become a pool, and the thirsty land springs of water' (Isaiah 35:1, 7). This is a typical prophecy of the coming of the Holy Spirit and the effect he will have upon men and women. Or in another and very glorious prophecy, God said, 'I will be as the dew unto Israel' (Hosea 14:5). Think of the dryness and the hardness of the land – and God says he will be as the dew.

Indeed, there is a sense in which the whole of the Old Testament is just looking forward to the Holy Spirit's coming, and the point that it is establishing is that this will be the great difference between God's people under the new dispensation and his people under the Old Testament dispensation. The Jews were, after all, the people of God, they had knowledge and understanding; yet they were being promised that something bigger, something greater, was coming. In the Old Testament, the Spirit came on occasional people. He would give ability and understanding, for instance, he would enable them to prophesy, or he would give ability to make the tabernacle (Exodus 35:31). But a promise was given that a day was coming when the Spirit would be poured out with great profusion, even upon young men and young women, 'upon the servants and upon the handmaidens' (Joel 2:29). It would be general, and would be common to all people. In many ways, the great difference between the Old Testament saints and those of the New Testament would be the coming of the Holy Spirit in this remarkable manner. The whole of the Old Testament is looking forward to this astounding event.

Now the last of the great prophets, John the Baptist, said exactly the same thing: 'I indeed baptize you with water unto repentance: but he that cometh after me is mightier than I, whose shoes I am not worthy to bear' (Matthew 3:11). Because John was unusual and a remarkable preacher, the people thought that he was the Messiah. No, said John, I am not the Messiah. He is the one who is to come after me. And the great characteristic of his coming and of his dispensation, said John, is that 'he shall baptize you with the Holy Ghost, and with fire' (verse 11).

And then we come to the Day of Pentecost and the Holy Spirit, as promised, was shed forth upon the apostles and the members of the early church, the 120 who were gathered together. And what happened to them? The record makes it quite plain and clear – there was an obvious transformation in them, something astonishing, something hitherto not known. And that was the phenomenon that created that great stir of excitement in Jerusalem. You see the typical picture there in the second chapter of Acts, and you find it, in a sense, still more strikingly at the end of the chapter, not among the apostles but among the common people. This is what we read:

*Then they that gladly received his word were baptized: and the same day there were added unto them about three thousand souls. And they continued stedfastly in the apostles' doctrine and fellowship, and in breaking of bread, and in prayers . . . And they, continuing daily with one accord in the temple, and breaking bread from house to house, did eat their meat with gladness and singleness of heart, praising God, and having favour with all the people. And the Lord added to the church daily such as should be saved. (Acts 2:41–42, 46–47)*

Now that is the typical picture of the New Testament Christian, that is how we are all meant to be. Our Lord says here in John 4, 'Whosoever drinketh of the water that I shall give him shall never thirst; but the water that I shall give him shall be in him a well of water springing up into everlasting life.' This is the message of Pentecost; this is the way in which the Lord gives this fullness of satisfaction to the heart of the one who receives the life that he has come to bring us.

So the coming of the Spirit on the Day of Pentecost should engage our most careful scrutiny. Here we see the measure of our Christianity: Do we conform to the picture and to the pattern given in Acts 2? That is what our Lord offers, and the question for us is: Have we received this? Do we know this fullness of satisfaction? In order to help this examination of ourselves, let me point out to you how the apostles take up this same theme. Let us look, for instance, at the apostle Paul, who puts this in a very interesting way when writing to the Romans:

*For as many as are led by the Spirit of God, they are the sons of God. For ye have not received the spirit of bondage again to fear; but ye have received the Spirit of adoption, whereby we cry, Abba, Father. The Spirit itself beareth witness with our spirit, that we are the children of God: and if children, then heirs; heirs of God, and joint-heirs with Christ; if so be that we suffer with him, that we may be also glorified together.*

And the mighty words that follow:

*For I reckon that the sufferings of this present time are not worthy to be compared with the glory which shall be revealed in us. (Romans 8:14–18)*

That is the Spirit. But what I am emphasizing is this: notice how the apostle defines the condition of the Christian by a negative as well as a positive. 'For', he says, 'ye have not received the spirit of bondage again to fear' – that is not the spirit you have received – 'but ye have received the Spirit of adoption, whereby we cry, Abba, Father.'

And the apostle makes exactly the same point in writing to Timothy. Timothy, obviously, by temperament and by nature, was a young man who was somewhat given to depression and to despondency. Whenever things went wrong, Timothy lost hope. He had been hearing rumours that the apostle Paul was about to be put to death by the Roman emperor so he held up his hands in horror, and said, 'How can we go on? What is going to happen to the churches?' And Paul reprimands him. This is how he puts it:

*Wherefore I put thee in remembrance that thou stir up the gift of God, which is in thee by the putting on of my hands.*

Then listen –

*For God hath not given us the spirit of fear; but of power, and of love, and of a sound mind [discipline]. (2 Timothy 1:6–7)*

Now here, too, the negatives are tremendously important. The apostle is saying, both to the Christians in Rome and to Timothy, something like this: You know, your condition is inconsistent with your profession of faith. You claim to have believed the gospel but

you are in a spirit of bondage, you are fearful, you are unhappy –
this is wrong. Our Lord said, 'Whosoever drinketh of the water that
I shall give him shall never thirst,' but you appear to be thirsting,
what is the matter with you? You do not realize what spirit you are
of. You have no right to be despondent and heavy and lethargic.

So what does this mean? Paul is saying that the Christian
character is produced in us by the Spirit – and this is what we
should all be concerned about. Our Lord has sent the Spirit in
order to give us this particular character, and we are examining it,
in particular, in terms of the satisfaction that we receive in the
realm of the heart and the emotions. Very well, then, let us have a
look at the Christian in order to see whether or not we conform to
this pattern. What are Christian people to be like? What does
Christianity do to us? In the light of the Day of Pentecost, what
should we be like, we who are members of the Christian church?

First of all, the negative teaching tells us that we are not merely
to be religious people. There is a great difference between being
religious and being truly Christian. As Christians, we are religious,
but we are not only religious. In other words, our religion is not
merely a matter of duty. The saints of the Old Testament were
religious people. They were under the Law and obeying the Law
was a matter of duty; they went to their services and offered
sacrifices in a legalistic manner because they were commanded to
do so by the Law. But we are not to be merely like that.

Neither, secondly, are we to be merely good, moral people. Of
course, we are to be moral, but the people were moral under the old
dispensation. While that is included, we do not stop there. That is
not the dominant feature of Christian people as the result of drinking this water, as the result of receiving the fullness of the Holy Spirit.

Or another negative is this: Christians do not merely hope to
be saved. That is not Christianity. Christians are not merely in

the position of hoping that some time before death they will know that their sins are forgiven, hoping that they *may* go into heaven. That is not the Christian, that is someone from the Old Testament. Christians, therefore, are not always struggling and striving; they are not fearful, full of problems and perplexities. They are not the sort of people who give the impression that the main effect their religion has had upon them is to create problems in their lives that they never had before. Now there are many people like that, are there not? They used to do what everybody else in the world did, but now, because they are Christians, they must stop and think about everything and they are burdened. They would like to do the things they used to do, but they feel that they should not. Either way, they are fearful. So here they are, in a spirit of bondage, hesitant and doubtful, not quite knowing what to do.

My dear friends, that is not Christianity, though there are many people who think that it is. And I believe that that is why the Christian church is as she is today, and why the masses of the people in this country are outside the Christian church. We have given the impression that our Christianity is a task to be performed, a burden. Many of us have been brought up in this way and have never thought enough about it even to consider changing. Others of us, in a spirit of fear, are a bit afraid to do anything but continue as we are. We do not have absolute certainty yet, so we keep on hoping. But our Christian life remains a matter of duty; and we seem to be filled with problems and difficulties and perplexities. We are carrying this great load upon our backs, hoping that somehow, some time or another, everything will be all right. That is the picture that has so often been given. To use the language of Milton, the Christian is often someone who 'scorns delights and lives laborious days': the miserable Christian.

And the world has reacted against this; it says it wants to be happy, it wants to live a full life, it wants freedom and enjoyment. 'Ah,' it says, 'fancy sitting in your miserable chapels, singing your miserable hymns, afraid to do this and that. You are narrow little people, you are to be despised.'

My dear friends, such Christians are nothing but a travesty of the picture given of the Christian in the New Testament, a travesty of what our Lord promises that we should be. 'God hath not given us the spirit of fear'; 'Ye have not received the spirit of bondage again to fear.' Do you go to worship God as a matter of duty? Are you rather pleased with yourself when you come out once on a Sunday? Is that your conception of Christianity? You have done your duty, now you can go and do what you want to do. Is coming to church against the grain? If it is, then it is the spirit of bondage, you are in a spirit of fear, you are a legalist, you are in the Old Testament. That is not Christianity.

What, then, is the picture? Well, here it is in the Bible, put before us plainly and clearly. Look again at Acts 2 – something has happened to these disciples and the others, and the whole of Jerusalem is listening to them. Some phenomenon has occurred. What is it? Well, all I know is that some people thought that these disciples were drunk! That is what they said: 'These men are full of new wine' (Acts 2:13). I know they said it mockingly, but even a mocker has some reason for speaking as he does. There was something about these people that justified this remark. Indeed, the apostle Paul justifies the remark, because in writing to the Ephesians, he puts it like this:

> *And be not drunk with wine, wherein is excess; but be filled with the Spirit; speaking to yourselves in psalms and hymns and spiritual songs, singing and making melody in your heart to the Lord.*
> *(Ephesians 5:18–19)*

The apostle there is making a comparison very similar to that which struck the members of the crowd in Jerusalem as they looked at the apostles. Here were men who had suddenly been filled with the Spirit and it was obvious that it had produced a great transformation in them. It was not merely the speaking in other tongues, though that was remarkable enough: here were men able to speak in other languages that they had never learned. There is no doubt about that. But that was not the only thing. The whole aspect, the whole demeanour, of these men was astonishing and challenging. What was it? Well, they were obviously released. New wine does that; it knocks off inhibitions and restraints and sets people at liberty. And that is obviously something that is done by the Spirit. Not the spirit of fear. That goes. There is a release, a freedom.

But there was more. There was not only an abandon and a freedom, there was happiness. There is no question but that there were smiles upon the faces of these men, that they were radiant. There was a joy that was expressing itself outwardly in their physical appearance. Indeed, one must not hesitate to say this: there was obviously an ecstatic element. They were men who in many ways were beside themselves They were so thrilled, so filled with joy and happiness that they were out of themselves and beyond themselves. You see the comparison with the new wine? They manifested an entire independence of their circumstances. In the past, these men had been very much afraid of the authorities. Peter had even denied his Lord because he had been so afraid. After the crucifixion they had all met in an upper room and had locked the doors because they were afraid of the Jews. But now here they were, standing in the streets of Jerusalem and in the Temple, oblivious of the presence of authorities or anybody else – unafraid, released, filled with a sense of power and of 'joy unspeakable and full of glory'.

And the other thing that characterized them was the way in which they kept on speaking about these 'wonderful works of God' (Acts 2:11). They did not speak of anything else. A kind of amazing generosity of spirit had come upon them. They wanted everybody to hear, they wanted everybody to know, they wanted to share all that had happened. They were free men, they seemed to possess the whole universe, and they were offering it to everybody. There was abandon and generosity and happiness. Indeed, you remember how our Lord had prophesied that what would happen to these people would be that out of their innermost parts there would flow 'rivers of living water' (John 7:38). And that was the very thing that had happened to them. Out of them was now pouring forth this ecstatic joy, this abandon, this freshness, and this desire that all should participate in their great blessing and that everybody should come and share 'the wonderful works of God'.

Now that is Christianity, that is what we are meant to be like. You do not take yourself by the scruff of the neck and drag yourself to your place of worship. No, no – 'daily'!

*They continued stedfastly in the apostles' doctrine and fellowship, and in breaking of bread, and in prayers . . . And they, continuing daily with one accord in the temple and breaking bread from house to house did eat their meat with gladness and singleness of heart, praising God . . .*

This was their life; this was everything to them.

This, then, is the special work of the Holy Spirit, this is the great difference between the New Testament saint and the Old Testament saint. Here are men and women who are filled with rejoicing and happiness and praise of God. Their religion is no longer a task imposed upon them, but is the delight of their lives, the centre of their whole being, what they live for.

How does the Spirit do this? Here is a subject that is so large that I can but deal with one aspect of it now, and that very briefly. But I needs must do this as it is Whitsunday, the anniversary of the Day of Pentecost. How does the Spirit produce the kind of Christian character that we have been talking about? I divide the answer into two: the first method is direct and the second is indirect. I am looking at the direct method this morning, because that is obviously what happened on the Day of Pentecost It is very important for us all to realize that the Spirit does deal with us directly, as well as indirectly. By indirectly, I mean the Spirit's continuous dealing with us through the teaching of the Scriptures; that is the normal, the usual method. But we must never confine the Spirit to that. The Spirit of God operates directly upon the heart and upon the will and also upon the mind, illuminating and opening it.

Now I am concerned about this and I am stressing it because I know that there are many people in the church today who are so afraid of excesses, so afraid of the ecstatic, that they go to the other extreme and 'quench the Spirit'. This, too, is one of the main troubles with the Christian church at the present time – with all sections of the church, evangelicals quite as much as others. We are so decent, so controlled, and everything is ordered and perfectly organized. All is under our control from beginning to end.

Now you cannot fit that into Acts 2. I repeat that we are so afraid of the excesses that have been manifested by certain people that we have undoubtedly become guilty of quenching and resisting the Spirit. We are not the only ones – the apostles have to say the same sort of thing. In their epistles they remind people who seem to have temporarily lost this happiness and peace that they are in error and have forgotten what they have received, and they must 'stir up the gift of God' (2 Timothy 1:6) and realize that this is how they should be.

The apostle Paul writes to the Thessalonians and says, 'Rejoice evermore. Pray without ceasing. . . Quench not the Spirit. Despise not prophesyings. Prove all things; hold fast that which is good' (1 Thessalonians 5:16–17, 19–21). The balance is still there, but, says Paul: In your fear of excesses, do not quench the Spirit. Of course, you must 'prove all things' and 'hold fast that which is good', but you must not carry that so far that you never allow the Spirit to have freedom. Do not so control your meetings that the Spirit has no opportunity at all. Do not be so mechanically, perfectly correct in your preaching and teaching and your sermon preparation that the Spirit can never come upon you and suddenly raise you up and use you in a manner that you have never understood – do not do that. Leave room for the freedom of the Spirit; leave room for revival; leave room for the unusual; leave room for the direct action of the Spirit.

This is clear New Testament teaching and, I repeat, I feel that it is very badly needed at the present time. Here in this second chapter of Acts, the matter is quite plain, is it not? The disciples were meeting together in the upper room: 'And suddenly there came a sound from heaven as of a rushing mighty wind.' They had done nothing new; they had been praying like this for ten days and they were just going on with what they had been doing. But, 'suddenly' the Spirit came upon them.

And it is exactly the same in the fourth chapter of Acts. The church is praying. They are in dire straits; they do not know what is going to happen. So they pray to God to have mercy, and this is what we read:

*And when they had prayed, the place was shaken where they were assembled together; and they were all filled with the Holy Ghost, and they spake the word of God with boldness . . . and great grace was upon them all. (Acts 4:31, 33)*

Now that is it. *They* do not do it. No, the Spirit comes, he falls upon us. And this can happen, and should happen, to the individual. This is how Paul puts it in Romans 5:

*We glory in tribulations also: knowing that tribulation worketh patience; and patience, experience; and experience, hope: and hope maketh not ashamed*

– why not? –

*because the love of God is shed abroad in our hearts by the Holy Ghost which is given unto us. (Romans 5:3–5)*

Or take again Romans 8:15:

*Ye have not received the spirit of bondage again to fear; but ye have received the Spirit of adoption, whereby we cry, Abba, Father.*

Or take a final passage in Galatians 4:6:

*And because ye are sons, God hath sent forth the Spirit of his Son into your hearts, crying, Abba, Father.*

Now all these verses are saying the same thing. If only we had the time to analyse them, we would find that each of them says that God pours forth his Spirit and he sheds abroad in our hearts in great profusion and abundance – what? His love! His love to us. This is something that happens to us. This is not the result of our study and our preparation and our careful anticipation. We do all that, but we do not determine what happens. 'Suddenly', unexpectedly, he visits us! He pours forth his Spirit, he sheds his love abroad in our hearts. And this is what moves and melts the heart and makes us realize that his love to us is overwhelming and creates a corresponding love to him in our hearts. The stony heart is taken away and we are given hearts of flesh.

This, my dear friends, is the height of Christian experience in this world; this is what is possible to us all. And if we know nothing about this, then we are falling very short of what our Lord offered to the woman of Samaria – a heart lifted up and out of itself, a heart overflowing with 'joy unspeakable and full of glory', a delight in the Lord, a rapture, an ecstasy – something beyond understanding.

Let me give you but two statements from men who experienced this. I take the first – old Henry Venn, a godly clergyman who lived towards the end of the eighteenth century. He lost his wife but this is how he wrote to a friend afterwards – and notice how he puts it:

> Did I not know the Lord to be mine, were I not certain his heart feels even more love for me than I am able to conceive; were not this evident to me, not by deduction and argument, but by consciousness, by his own light shining in my soul as the sun's light doth upon my bodily eyes, into what a deplorable situation should I have been now cast.

Or take Charles Simeon:

> This is a blessing which though not to be appreciated or understood by those who have not received it, is yet most assuredly enjoyed by many of God's chosen people. We scarcely know how to describe it because it consists chiefly in an impression on the mind occasioned by manifestation of God's love to the soul.

That is it. It is the direct action of the Holy Spirit upon the heart. You cannot understand it – it is beyond understanding. But he visits us, he manifests his love to us, he 'sheds it abroad', and we are 'lost in wonder, love and praise', our hearts fully satisfied. That is what the Holy Spirit was sent to do. That is what he did to those men on the Day of Pentecost. That is what he repeated to them the next day as recorded in Acts 4. That is what he has been doing throughout the running centuries. The testimony of the saints, the testimony of our hymn writers, the testimony of most ordinary people in revival, and even apart from revival, is that the love of God has suddenly overwhelmed them, that it has been shed abroad in their hearts, and they have been lifted up and out of themselves, unable even to express their feelings, it is so glorious, so marvellous and so wonderful.

> Jesus, thou joy of loving hearts,
> Thou fount of life, thou light of men,
> From the best bliss that earth imparts,
> We turn unfilled to thee again.
> *Bernard of Clairvaux*

My dear friends, do we know anything about this? This is what our Lord offers us. Not a correct, mechanical religion and morality; no, no! There is a fullness, there is freedom, an abandon, there is a joy, there is an ecstasy! Have you been taken out of yourself? Have you been lost in your love of him? Do you know anything about these visitations of his blessed Spirit, the Son himself coming down through the Spirit and melting and warming and moving your heart and letting you know his love to you, and creating in you a love to him? That is what our Lord offered to the woman of Samaria. That is how every Christian should be. That is how the church should be. And when she is like that, the world no longer despises her, it no longer laughs at her or feels sorry for her. When this happens, the world comes crowding, looking on and listening and saying, 'What is this?'

So here is the question: Are you such a person that your next-door neighbours are amazed at you and find it difficult to understand you because of the joy that is yours, because of the happiness they see in you, because of the way you stand up to your trials and your tribulations, because of the way in which you are more than conqueror, because you do not have a spirit of fear, 'but of power, and of love, and of a sound mind'? This is what he offers to us freely – 'Whosoever drinketh of the water that I shall give him shall never thirst; but the water that I shall give him shall be in him a well of water springing up into everlasting life.'

31

# *The Fruit of the Spirit*

*Jesus answered and said unto her, Whosoever drinketh of this water shall thirst again: but whosoever drinketh of the water that I shall give him shall never thirst; but the water that I shall give him shall be in him a well of water springing up into everlasting life. (John 4:13–14)*

Last time, as we looked at the disciples on the Day of Pentecost, we saw that there was something about the quality of their lives, their joy, their abandon, their assurance, their loss of the fear of death – all that accompanies this great experience of the work of the Holy Spirit – that astonished everybody. I am emphasizing this because it seems to me to be abundantly clear that nothing but this will have any influence upon the modern world. That is where it is so vital to see the distinction between the joy, the true joy, and happiness that we read of in Acts, and the kind of artificial joviality and cheeriness that at the present time is doing so much duty for the real thing.

The world can always recognize the psychological. It is not taken in by that. The world in its understanding and wisdom can see how certain effects are produced. We can read about these techniques in books on psychology and even in popular articles, and there is no difficulty at all in explaining how emotions are worked up. The world is not impressed at all. Such methods may have an influence upon certain less intelligent types, but they are of no value to the kingdom of God, and, in any case, this is not what our Lord is speaking about to the woman of Samaria. He is talking about another realm altogether, because, as we have seen, he is talking about that which is produced by the Holy Spirit, who is the special agent who has been sent to bring about true joy in the life of believers.

We have also seen that the Holy Spirit works in a number of ways. We have dealt so far with only one way, which is the *direct* way. Obviously, we had to do that on Whitsunday, the anniversary of the Day of Pentecost. We must never forget that the Holy Spirit can come upon us directly and immediately, and we must never exclude that. If we do, we are quenching the Spirit. But we must now go on and look at other ways in which the Holy Spirit produces this same joy and love, this same deep satisfaction to the heart and all within us that cries out to be loved and to love, to know joy and peace and so on. In addition to the immediate and direct method, he also works indirectly, and one of the ways in which he does this is by producing 'the fruit of the Spirit', which is a term used by the Scriptures themselves.

As Christians, the Spirit is in us: 'Now if any man have not the Spirit of Christ, he is none of his' (Romans 8:9). It is impossible for us to be Christians without the Holy Spirit being in us. This is of vital importance. Again, it is where the whole doctrine of regeneration is most important and it is why it is possible for all of us to know this joy. We do not all have a happy type of nature but, as I have already shown, this joy is offered to us all, and whatever we are by nature and temperament, we are all meant to experience it. I am not going into this in detail because we have already done so, but it is essential that we should carry it in our minds. Look at it this way – the Christian is not merely someone who has taken up a teaching and decided to live according to it. That is not Christianity, though it often passes as such. That is religion and, as we have seen, there is no more important distinction than that between religion and Christianity.

You can take up religion, you can take up other teachings. You like a teaching, so you decide to accept it, and, having adopted it, of course, you try to put it into practice. That is the basis of all morality and ethical conduct. People face life, they see the consequences of certain actions, they read books, biographies and direct teaching on morality, and so they solemnly decide that they will adopt a moral teaching. Similarly, people take up one of the religions, as they are called – Buddhism, Hinduism, Confucianism, Islam and so on. There are people in this country who have not been brought up in those religions, but, having read about them, they have decided to take one of them up, and they try to live a life in conformity with this teaching.

But Christianity is not a teaching that we take up with the mind and adopt, and then try to conform to. There is that element in it, but that is not the main thing. Primarily Christianity happens to us, something is done to us, something we could never do ourselves, something that God alone can do. And that is the particular work and function of the Holy Spirit; it is the third Person in the blessed Holy Trinity who does this for us. It is he who gives us a new birth.

The trouble with religious and moral men and women is that they are still essentially the same people before and after they take up a teaching. What they are trying to do is to affect and to influence, to change and to mould, their personalities. But they cannot, though they do their best. They can modify their personalities up to a point, they can restrain themselves, they can push themselves forward, but essentially they are the same person. But here in the gospel, everything is entirely different, and that is because of this blessed doctrine of regeneration. It is the differentia of Christianity and of the very essence of our position. That we are 'born again' is the most vital and central doctrine of all. We are not what we were, each of us has received new life, a new nature, a new heart.

The New Testament emphasizes this teaching everywhere. It is the whole point of our Lord's conversation with Nicodemus in John chapter 3. Nicodemus comes to our Lord as a teacher, almost as an equal; he recognizes a certain element of superiority in our Lord, and he is coming to have a discussion, what is called today a 'dialogue'. But our Lord does not have dialogues with people. He turns to Nicodemus and says, 'Verily, verily, I say unto thee, except a man be born again, he cannot see the kingdom of God' (John 3:3). What is a Christian? Christians, says Peter, are 'partakers of the divine nature' (2 Peter 1:4).

The fact of regeneration is absolutely crucial to our understanding of how our Lord is able to give us complete satisfaction in the realm of the heart. Without this new birth, he could not do it. You cannot suddenly make a phlegmatic type out of a mercurial individual; you cannot take a melancholic type and suddenly persuade him to become jovial. And there is nothing more ridiculous than to see people of those various types trying to make themselves something that they are not. But that is not what

Christianity does. It puts this seed of new life in us, there is this new element, there is this 'partaking of the divine nature'. Now let me show you this, because it is the only way whereby it becomes possible for someone who may, by nature, be the most miserable creature ever born, to rejoice, to be happy, and to be filled with a spirit of assurance and praise. The glory of the gospel is that nothing is impossible to it because of this miracle of the new birth.

What is the object of Christianity? Paul says, in writing to the Romans – this is only one of many statements but it is one of the greatest – 'For whom he did foreknow, he also did predestinate to be conformed to the image of his Son' (Romans 8:29). That is what we are to be like. We are to be 'conformed' to the image of the Son of God. Or take that other great statement of the apostle Paul in his letter to the Galatians: 'I live; yet not I, but Christ liveth in me . . .' (Galatians 2:20). There it is perfectly – 'I; yet not I'. Christians are not the people they were. There is this 'new man'. We must get rid once and for ever of this notion that Christians are men and women who are trying to make themselves something. That is a contradiction of the very basis of the Christian position. It is God who makes a soul. It is the re-creative action of Almighty God himself. This is the point – it is this life-giving water, this well that he puts within us. So we now can say that there is a sense in which the life we are living in the flesh is not so much our living as his.

*I live; yet not I, but Christ liveth in me: and the life which I now live in the flesh I live by the faith of the Son of God, who loved me, and gave himself for me. (Galatians 2:20)*

Again, in Galatians 4:19, Paul says, 'My little children, of whom I travail in birth again until Christ be formed in you.' This is Christianity. Not that we are changing and modifying our selves.

No, no! It is Christ being formed in us, until eventually he will fill us altogether.

Or, again, take the great and glorious statement at the end of Ephesians 3. The apostle tells the Ephesians that he is praying for them, and praying without ceasing, and his prayer is:

> *That [God] would grant you, according to the riches of his glory, to be strengthened with might by his spirit in the inner man*

– what for? –

> *that Christ may dwell in your hearts by faith; that ye, being rooted and grounded in love, may be able to comprehend with all saints what is the breadth, and length, and depth, and height; and to know the love of Christ, which passeth knowledge, that ye might be filled with all the fulness of God. (Ephesians 3:16–19)*

But you see how the apostle puts it? 'That Christ may dwell in your hearts by faith . . . that ye might be filled with all the fulness of God.' It is God coming in, not this modification or adaptation of the self. That is where the difference between religion and Christianity is absolute. The greatest enemy of the Christian faith has always been religion and morality, whatever form they may happen to have taken.

We see this again in Ephesians 4, where Paul, in dealing with the ethical behaviour of the Ephesians, tells them that they must not go on living as they used to live and as their fellow countrymen are still living. He says:

> *But ye have not so learned Christ; if so be that ye have heard him, and have been taught by him, as the truth is in Jesus: that ye put off concerning the former conversation the old man, which is corrupt according to the deceitful lusts; and be renewed in the spirit of your mind; and that ye put on the new man*

– notice –

*which after God is created in righteousness and true holiness.*
*(Ephesians 4:20–24)*

A 'new man' created within us, 'in righteousness and true holiness'. This is the action of God in us.

Now there is the Christian, and it is because this is true of the Christian that it is not only possible for all of us to know the heart satisfaction that our blessed Lord gives, it is also our duty to know it, and we are sinning if we do not. Miserable Christians should not only be ashamed of themselves, they should also realize that in many ways they are contradicting the essential teaching of the New Testament. I know the dangers of the false but nothing is so tragic as that people should be so afraid of the false that they never realize the true. I once listened to a man who was preaching on the text, 'The rainbow in the cloud'. That man was so afraid of false joy that after three-quarters of an hour he sent us out under the cloud and there was nothing about the rainbow!

But that is the ridiculous position in which we can arrive. I have said – I say it again – I am not talking about emotionalism or sentimentalism but about the joy of the Lord, about 'joy in the Holy Spirit'. Paul says, 'The kingdom of God is not meat and drink' – there were those silly little people in the church of Rome arguing about meats and days, details and minutiae – 'but righteousness, and peace, and joy in the Holy Ghost' (Romans 14:17). That is it! And, again, we read in 1 Peter 1:8, 'In whom, though now ye see him not, yet believing, ye rejoice with joy unspeakable and full of glory.' That is what our Lord is offering. That is what he is telling this woman of Samaria.

Now the Holy Spirit, let me remind you, sometimes immediately pours his joy into our hearts, but we are now considering his indirect

– his regular – way of working. He has given us the new birth, he has begun to form Christ in us, we are partakers of the divine nature. So now we are to live the kind of life that our blessed Lord himself lived, and we are to show the characteristics of the life that was so evident and so obvious in him. But how does this happen?

These are mysterious matters, we cannot finally understand them, but we know this: that as Christians a seed of divine life is put into us, that Christ dwells in our hearts by faith and that the Holy Spirit is resident in us: 'Know ye not that your body is the temple of the Holy Ghost which is in you' (1 Corinthians 6:19). And he gives us this heart satisfaction partly by producing in us 'the fruit of the Spirit': 'But the fruit of the Spirit is love, joy, peace, longsuffering, gentleness, goodness, faith, meekness, temperance' (Galatians 5:22–23).

Now that is a very wonderful way, it seems to me, of expressing this great truth that the Holy Spirit is in us, and is working in us. I say again, you cannot be a Christian unless this is true. He is producing in us the characteristics of our blessed Lord himself, who was the Son of God and was filled with the Spirit. 'God giveth not the Spirit by measure unto him' (John 3:34). There you see him in all the glory of his perfection. The Holy Spirit works in us and, of course, there is much work to be done. Though we are born again, the old nature is still here – not the old man but the old nature. We are not rid of that. But the Spirit works, and what he does is produce this new life in increasing abundance. So the apostle uses this comparison of 'fruit'.

What are the characteristics of this fruit produced by the Spirit? Well, you notice that Paul mentions nine, which fall quite naturally into three groups of three, and it is important that we should consider them. Look at the first group of three – 'the fruit of the Spirit is love, joy, peace'. Now you can describe those three as positive: there is positive fruit of the Spirit. When the Spirit is having his way in us, we are of necessity filled with love. He is the Spirit of love as well as of truth, and his action, always, is to produce love. God is love. God the Father is love. God the Son is love. God the Holy Spirit is love. There would be no salvation, there would be no gospel to preach and there would be no church, were this not true. So the Spirit works in us to produce a loving disposition.

And this is our only hope because remember what the apostle Paul – this same man who writes about this 'fruit of the Spirit' and puts love in the first position – says about every one of us by nature. I do not know whether you recognize yourself, but this is the truth about you:

> *For we ourselves also were sometimes [at one time] foolish, disobedient, deceived, serving divers lusts and pleasures, living in malice and envy, hateful, and hating one another. (Titus 3:3)*

Or, as he says to the Galatians, 'if ye bite and devour one another . . .' (Galatians 5:15). That is what we were, every one of us, and that is the old nature still. But Paul adds:

> *But after that the kindness and love of God our Saviour toward man appeared, not by works of righteousness which we have done, but according to his mercy he saved us, by the washing of regeneration, and renewing of the Holy Ghost; which he shed on us abundantly through Jesus Christ our Saviour. (Titus 3:4–6)*

And what the Holy Spirit does in this process of renewal is to produce this fruit, and the first is *love*. As the Spirit operates in us, we become less and less hateful, and we hate one another less and less; we are filled positively by a spirit of love. You cannot make yourself love, but the Spirit makes us love. He produces in us this love that is in God himself.

And the second fruit is *joy*. You cannot argue with these facts. If the Spirit is in you, there must be love in you and there must be joy. Now I know that some of you want to say, 'Ah, but if you only knew what I do, and don't do, and how I fall into sin, and how I am this, that and the other . . .' But that is true of everybody. None of us is perfect. Yet the Spirit produces joy. And, as we have seen, the tragedy is that there are some people who, because of false teaching, will not allow themselves to have this joy. It is there but they try to crush it; they are afraid of it. They are afraid of 'animal spirits' or of false joy, and they say, 'Ah, but look at this . . .' But these people are putting themselves back under law. They are trying to say that they have no right to be joyful until they are perfect, until by their own actions and efforts they are fully satisfactory to themselves and to God. The idea is monstrous, it is ridiculous! Allow the Spirit to do his work, my dear friend. Do not resist him, do not stand in his way, do not be afraid. He will produce joy, he is bound to. It is a part of the divine character.

Love and joy – and the third fruit is *peace*. This is a heart rest, the condition of true peace, the peace the world can never give us (John 14:27), the peace that the world is ever robbing us of in so many different ways. 'Peace, perfect peace, in this dark world of sin?' It is impossible apart from the Holy Spirit, but he can give us peace.

These, then, are positive productions of the Spirit. This is the outworking of the seed of life that he has implanted in us; and he tends it, he waters it, he deals with it in his own mystical manner. Come, let me put it to you in a very experiential and practical manner. Have you not sometimes been surprised at yourself, surprised at the fact that you are able to love in the way you do? Have you not been amazed at it? Have you not been amazed at times at this joy that is also in you; you are surprised at it but you find it is there? The same is true of the peace. The old restlessness seems to have gone and you have arrived at a place where at times you know 'perfect peace' – you are quite sure of it. This is the firstfruit of these known aspects of the fruit of the Spirit.

But now look at the second group – it is very interesting to see how the apostle classifies them – 'longsuffering, gentleness, goodness'. How do these constitute a group? Well, as the first three were essentially positive and active, these are negative; but they are tremendously important. Here are Christian men and women, they have this new life and the Spirit is in them, and the Spirit is producing 'love, joy, peace'. But still they have got to live in the world. As long as they are alone in their rooms, all is well, but the difficulty arises when they come out of their rooms and mix with other people; and in a moment, but for this second group, they would lose the first three. Why? It is because people are what they are. People are so difficult, are they not? *We* are all right, it is always other people. They annoy us, they irritate us, they are slow, stupid and dull. How trying people are! You have found that, have you not? Of course you have! And they have found exactly the same about you! That is why it is so extremely difficult to maintain this love, joy and peace. The old nature is still here and it reacts.

But now here is *longsuffering*. It is a quality. It is not active or positive as love, joy and peace are. I find it difficult to describe this quality, and yet you are familiar with what it means. Perhaps you can look at it like this: longsuffering puts the brake on so that you do not react immediately. Longsuffering takes an edge off you, it takes off a tendency to irritability and to annoyance and to over-reaction. This is profound psychology; this is biblical, spiritual psychology. Thank God for it, it is all so essential. God knows us perfectly and the Spirit understands us perfectly, so he realizes that in addition to creating the positive qualities, he must do something about the old nature, and this is what he does: he puts this brake on so that we become more longsuffering. He will speak to you; he will remonstrate with you. He will point out to you how unlike our Lord this irritability is, how wrong it is in any case, how foolish it is, how it does harm, and how it has made you lose your joy. There you were – you were enjoying communion with the Lord and experiencing his love, then some triviality made you lose it all in a moment. What a tragedy!

And the Spirit agrees, so he works in us negatively, and produces within us a spirit of longsuffering, which means that we can suffer long. What a difficult lesson to learn! And yet if you want to know the joy of the Lord and the joy of the Holy Spirit, you must be longsuffering, otherwise people will rob you of your joy every time. And a joy that is only experienced in God's house or when we are alone, is not the real thing. This is a joy that persists wherever we are and whatever is happening – and that is the glory of it.

What else? *Gentleness.* Go back to Paul's words in Titus 3 and in many other places and you will see the fruit that we need – gentleness. How difficult it is to be gentle in a world that is full of arrogance and aggressiveness, and yet if you are not gentle, you will not be able to maintain your joy. It is so wonderful to me that the Spirit not only sheds the love of God abroad in our hearts, but also safeguards it. He wants it to be perpetual, a permanent condition within us, and not spasmodic as it tends to be – and we are seeing the ways in which he does this. He creates within us longsuffering and then this spirit of gentleness.

It is wonderful, and it has been my privilege many times – I say it as a pastor to the glory of God – to watch the Spirit producing gentleness in people known to me. They were people with strong characters – we all have different battles to fight in this world, that is where these distinctions are so important – and this was one of their battles. But there is nobody who is truly gentle by nature. There are some people who seem to be nicer than others but I have found that the nicest people are often the most irritable. Have you ever thought about how the Spirit knows us all and how he alone can produce this true gentleness? He does it by reasoning with us.

The Spirit says, 'Now look here, you have lost what you had, that glorious experience, and here you are cast down and unhappy. Why? Well, simply because you did not speak to that person in the right way. It was wrong, in any case. Why should you speak to another in that harsh, brusque manner?' Gentleness – and the Spirit produces it. Again, it is a way of putting on the brake, a way of mortifying and getting rid of that old nature that is in us.

And then the third fruit in the second group is *goodness*. And goodness here means a kind of goodness of heart, a good disposition, so that we are well disposed towards other people. The whole problem of life is, in a sense, the problem of relationships – one is constantly seeing it. That is why the world, of course, is on the brink of war – failure in relationships is the cause of every war. But this problem is also found in the church and in missionary societies; it is a problem everywhere. The curse of life is that man cannot get on with man. But the Spirit helps us by producing this goodness in us, this 'good nature', which is not natural to any of us.

We now understand other people because we understand ourselves. We do not merely see what they do, we see that they are sinners, as we are, 'saved by grace', that the old nature is still there, that they have a fight and a problem, and we make allowances. So we develop a good disposition. Our whole attitude and outlook upon people becomes changed. And this is not only good and right in and of itself, but the point that the apostle is making, and I am trying to repeat, is that this is the way in which you and I can preserve the love and the joy and the peace. Without these three negatives, we would very soon lose the three positives.

And then take the last group – 'faith', which really should be translated 'faithfulness', 'meekness, temperance'. How do we classify these? I have called the first group positive, the second negative. This group is more akin to the first than to the second. And yet the apostle puts them last, and I think I begin to understand his reasons. Here is the Spirit working in us, and he positively produces 'love, joy, peace'. Then, in order to preserve that, he is doing this other work, which is partially negative, but also has its positive element in producing a good disposition within us. Then we come to the last three, and I can simply say that these are qualities that in and of themselves promote joy.

*Faithfulness* means stability of character. It is not faith in the sense of 'saving faith', nor faith in the sense of its being a gift, as in 1 Corinthians 12. This is a quality of the Christian's whole character. A faithful person is someone who can always be relied upon, someone who has a kind of equability, a balance and steadiness. How vital this is! Oh, how the world lacks reliable people! If you are reliable, you are happy. The person who is not reliable is always changeable. Not only can you not depend upon unreliable people, they cannot depend upon themselves. And because of this, they are constantly in trouble and are always trying to get out of it, and so they lose their joy. But as you become dependable and steadfast and faithful, so the love and the joy and the peace can continue.

And then the second quality in this third group is, of course, absolutely essential – *meekness*. 'Blessed are the meek,' says our Lord (Matthew 5:5). One of the causes of trouble in life is an aggressive personality – someone who talks about 'my rights'. That is the exact opposite of meekness. Our Lord says that he himself was meek. 'Come unto me,' he says, 'all ye that labour and are heavy laden, and I will give you rest. Take my yoke upon you, and learn of me; for I am meek and lowly in heart' (Matthew 11:28–29). Read the records in the Gospels and you will see our Lord's meekness. Or take Moses – he was the meekest of men (Numbers 12:3). Then as I read the writings of the great apostle Paul, and read, too, about his gifts and his ability, there is nothing that I find more astonishing than his meekness. What a meek man he was, what a humble man!

And the Spirit produces this meekness in us. The Spirit shows us that horrid 'I' for what it is. He reminds us that the old self has been crucified with Christ. Thank God! But the old nature, the way in which it used to manifest itself, is still here, and the Spirit deals with this by producing this essential quality of humility. 'I live; yet not I' (Galatians 2:20). I have nothing at all whereof to boast. The more we know about grace, the meeker we will be. And so this quality of meekness is developed within us.

And finally: *temperance*. This is nothing but self-control; this is discipline; this is continence and orderliness – and it is absolutely essential. It is not that you become negative or repressive; that is not what is meant by temperance at all. Temperance is very wonderful. It is like a spirited, active, powerful horse under your control. He may still be galloping, and he may be jumping fences, yes, but he knows that you are there, that you are the master and that you are holding the reins. That is temperance. Temperance is not weak, it is a very strong, a very powerful quality. It is these tremendous, active qualities and propensities harnessed, disciplined, held in the right position and the right way so that there is no dissipation of energy, no wasteful manifestation of power.

Now temperance is a great source of joy and a great guarantee of the maintenance of love and joy and peace. The apostle Paul puts this once and for ever in 2 Timothy 1:7: 'God hath not given us the spirit of fear' – what has he given us? – 'but of power, and of love, and of a sound mind [discipline, temperance, self-control, the ability to deal, as it were, with yourself].' And so you are an equable person, you are a controlled person, and you are thrilling and vibrating with the energy of life, the life that has been put into you by the Spirit of God. But it is all under such wonderful control that you are not up and down, you are not happy and miserable and you are not always correcting yourself. You are a complete person, a balanced person. And because of that, you will go on enjoying love and joy and peace.

There, then, is another way in which the Holy Spirit works in us. (There are others, and we must consider them.) We thank God for the occasional visitations and for the periods of revival: but they are not his only method of operation. There is this constant work that goes on and it all leads to the same end. There have been revivals that have not been the blessing they should have been to the church, because the church abandoned herself to the enjoyment of the unusual and the exceptional and failed to harness it all to this continuous work of the Spirit in producing his own blessed truth within us. When a revival comes, you cannot help yourself, you are filled with joy, you are lost, you are carried away. But, my dear friend, by the grace of God, it is possible for us, even as things are now, to know a joy that is 'unspeakable and full of glory' – and this is one of the ways in which the Spirit helps us to know and to experience that.

32

# The Purpose of the Scriptures

*Jesus answered and said unto her, Whosoever drinketh of this water shall thirst again: but whosoever drinketh of the water that I shall give him shall never thirst; but the water that I shall give him shall be in him a well of water springing up into everlasting life. (John 4:13–14)*

The point we are considering at the moment is that 'joy unspeakable and full of glory' is given to us mainly as the result of the work of the Holy Spirit. That is why he in particular has been sent and given to us. He does this partly by coming upon us directly. There are visitations of the Spirit. This can happen to the individual and it happens to numbers together in periods of what we call revival. That is what revival is: it is another descent of the Spirit, another baptism of the Spirit, an 'outpouring' of the Spirit. It always has this same effect of filling people with joy and assurance and happiness and certainty.

But now we are considering the indirect operation of the Holy Spirit upon us. We have seen that this takes place not only in regeneration, but particularly as the Spirit produces what Paul calls 'the fruit of the Spirit'. This is a more gradual work. The Spirit is forming Christ in us; he is reproducing in us the character, the life, of the Lord Jesus Christ himself, and that life is always characterized by what Paul calls 'the fruit of the Spirit: love, joy, peace, longsuffering, gentleness, goodness, faith, meekness, temperance' (Galatians 5:22–23). But that does not exhaust the way in which the Spirit gives us this joy, this heart satisfaction.

The Spirit also works – and I would say that, from the practical standpoint, this is his chief method – through the Scriptures. Why have we got the Scriptures at all? There is really only one answer: it is that we may know the character of this salvation that is given to us. John, in writing his first epistle, says quite plainly: 'These things have I written unto you that believe on the name of the Son of God; that ye may *know* . . .' (1 John 5:13). In other words, the object of the Scriptures is really to give us assurance. That is why they were even written – they came into being by the work of the Holy Spirit.

The Scriptures are not ordinary writings. They did not come about because a man sat down and decided to write certain things. No – the Scriptures are the result of the fact that certain men were taken hold of and dealt with by the Spirit, who gave them, first, a revelation of the truth and, second, an understanding of it. No man can do this in and of himself, as the apostles are very careful to say. The apostle Paul keeps on saying this. 'A dispensation of the gospel', he says, 'is committed unto me' (1 Corinthians 9:17). He means that the revelation has been given to him. Take, for instance, what he says about the Communion Table: 'For I have received of the Lord that which also I delivered unto you, That the Lord Jesus the same night in which he was betrayed . . .' (1 Corinthians 11:23). This was all by revelation and the apostle constantly repeats that it came to him 'by revelation'. In writing to the Galatians, he says, 'I certify you, brethren' – and this is a most important statement – 'that the gospel which was preached of me is not after man. For I neither received it of man, neither was I taught it, but by the revelation of Jesus Christ' (Galatians 1:11–12).

Our Lord illumined the minds of these men through the Spirit, he gave them the truth and he gave them the power to grasp it and understand it. But then, in addition to that, he gave them the ability and the power to write it, and he controlled them in the writing of it. That is what we call 'inspiration'. There is a difference between revelation and inspiration. Inspiration is the power and capacity that the Holy Spirit gave to record in an accurate manner the revelation that had been given. Now if these men had been left to themselves, though they had had the true revelation, they might, somehow or another, have made a mistake in the recording of it. So inspiration is as essential as revelation.

Here it is, then: the Holy Spirit had taken hold of certain men – these apostles, but also those who were under their influence. Apostolicity is always the test of canonicity, of what is truly inspired. And the result is that you and I have the Scriptures – the work of the Spirit. Our Lord had promised this. He had said, 'Howbeit when he, the Spirit of truth, is come, he will guide you into all truth' (John 16:13), and he said that the Holy Spirit would explain to them the things that he had been telling them, and bring them to their remembrance.

But if the Holy Spirit had stopped at that, it would not have led to this result of joy in us. Something further is necessary, and here it is: the Bible. It is translated into our own language; it is before us all. You can buy a Bible whenever you like and there are thousands, millions, of Bibles in this country. And yet we know that the vast majority of people of this country do not believe the Christian message; they have not drunk of this water that Christ offers them. By now, I am told, the figure is down to 8 per cent – even with all the Bibles, only 8 per cent of the people in this country claim to be Christian. Why is this?

The obvious explanation is that they cannot understand the Bible. It is quite impossible for the 'natural man' to understand it. People may be familiar with the words, they may give you their meaning, but it does not follow that they understand the meaning of the sentence, of the verse. They can tell you what the *letter* is, but they know nothing about the *spirit*. That is why, though people have their Bibles, that does not make them Christians. And that is why, though people are constantly writing in books and articles and journals, and talking on the television and the wireless, about the Bible, they twist it completely. They have missed the whole point, which is the spirit. Why? I say again that it is because they are 'natural men', they do not have the Spirit, and without the Spirit, no one can understand these things at all. So Paul says: 'But the natural man receiveth not the things of the Spirit of God: for they are foolishness unto him: neither can he know them, because they are spiritually discerned' (1 Corinthians 2:14).

People listen to the preaching of the gospel, but see nothing in it. They read the Bible and see nothing in it at all. It does not matter how able they are, they may be geniuses, but it does not help them. To be able to understand English literature or philosophy or science, does not help at all when you read the Scriptures. Indeed, it may be a hindrance because you are bringing your natural understanding to something that is not open to natural understanding.

There is only one way whereby any one of us can ever understand the Scriptures that have been produced through men by the Holy Spirit: it is by the same Holy Spirit, who does in our minds from the standpoint of reception, what he has already done in the minds of the writers from the standpoint of writing the words. Now this is marvellous, and at the present time we ought perhaps to be able to understand it more easily than our forefathers did, because we are helped by the illustration of radio. You have your transmitter, yes, but you have to have the receiving apparatus and you need the same electric power for the reception as for the transmission. Both are absolutely essential. Many people fail to grasp this point and seem to think that a mechanical distribution of the Scriptures is, in and of itself, going to do something. It cannot. The Scriptures are essential but the Scriptures alone are not sufficient, as the world proves to us.

This is how John puts it in his first epistle to these early Christians, who were a little bit confused because there were false teachers among them. There have always been false teachers. The modern heresies are not modern; they are old heresies repeated in different forms. So there were these so-called 'antichrists', and John says:

*They went out from us, but they were not of us; for if they had been of us, they would no doubt have continued with us: but they went out, that they might be made manifest that they were not all of us. (1 John 2:19)*

How, then, were those early Christians to know who was the right teacher and who was the wrong teacher? How were they to be saved from heresy? This is part of John's answer:

*But ye have an unction from the Holy One, and ye know all things. (verse 20)*

John says this again later in the same chapter:

*These things have I written unto you concerning them that seduce you [with false teaching]. But the anointing which ye have received of him abideth in you, and ye need not that any man teach you: but as the same anointing teacheth you of all things, and is truth, and is no lie, and even as it hath taught you, ye shall abide in him. (verses 26–27)*

It is this 'anointing' that is absolutely essential before we can derive any benefit at all from the Scriptures. And the first thing we must realize, therefore, is that when we come to read the Scriptures, we are reading something that is beyond ourselves. We do not rely on human ability, human understanding or any gift we may have. We need this 'unction', this 'anointing'. That is why we should never read the Scriptures without praying. That is why we should never read the Bible without realizing that we are doing something exceptional – and we offer a prayer. We do not just pray mechanically, but we ask God to illumine and enlighten our minds and our understanding in order that we may be enabled to receive what is contained in the Scriptures.

What is it that is contained in them? John, again, expounds this in a very wonderful way: 'And these things write we unto you, that your joy may be full' (1 John 1:4). And my whole contention is that one of the ways in which the Holy Spirit gives us this joy, this assurance and certainty, this extra plus quality that makes us more than conquerors over everything that is set against us, is by giving us the Scriptures:

*These things have I written unto you that believe on the name of the Son of God; that ye may know that ye have eternal life, and that ye may believe on the name of the Son of God. (1 John 5:13)*

So here is the whole question: Do you know that you have eternal life? Is this joy in you? Do you have in you this well of water springing up into everlasting life? This is full satisfaction to the heart. This is 'joy unspeakable and full of glory', and you get it through the Bible. Sometimes, as I have said, he pours it in our hearts; perhaps when we are seated alone without a Bible, he suddenly does it. But not always. The regular, the usual way is through the Scriptures. They have been given in order that we might have this great joy and rejoicing.

But how do the Scriptures do that? These are the truth that we take for granted, and I suppose our main trouble as Christians is that we so often miss the wood because of the trees. We are so concerned about details and minutiae that we miss the big grand thing itself. The Scriptures give us this joy and assurance by unfolding to us the Lord Jesus Christ himself and what he has done for us. Have you noticed how so often the apostle Paul puts it like this: 'Rejoice in the Lord alway: and again I say, Rejoice' (Philippians 4:4). Yes, but: 'Rejoice *in the Lord.*' Or again, he says, 'For we are the circumcision, which worship God in the spirit, and *rejoice in Christ Jesus*, and have no confidence in the flesh' (Philippians 3:3). This is the key to the whole subject.

John in his first epistle tells the Christians that he is writing to them in order that their joy may be full and he tells them quite plainly at the very opening of the epistle how he is going to give them this fullness of joy:

> *That which was from the beginning, which we have heard, which we have seen with our eyes, which we have looked upon, and our hands have handled, of the Word of life; (For the life was manifested, and we have seen it, and bear witness, and shew unto you that eternal life, which was with the Father, and was manifested unto us;) that which we have seen and heard declare we unto you, that ye also may have fellowship with us; and truly our fellowship is with the Father, and with his Son Jesus Christ. And these things write we unto you that your joy may be full. (1 John 1:1–4)*

The emphasis is always the same. Look at John's Gospel: 'In the beginning was the Word, and the Word was with God, and the Word was God' (John 1:1). Why did John ever write that Gospel?

There is only one answer: he was writing it in order to confirm the faith of the early Christians. That is why the Gospels were ever written. People were Christians before the Gospels or the Epistles were written. Christ was preached and the Spirit gave the people power to believe, and they were added to the church. Why, then, were the Scriptures necessary? They were necessary to confirm Christians in the faith. The Scriptures are really for believers. Their original intent and design was to establish believers in the truth. Heresies were coming in saying that our Lord was only God and not man, or that he was only man and not God; and so all the Scriptures were written. They are all about him and what he has done for us and our relationship to him; and as we grasp their teaching we should be filled with joy.

Now this is a most important matter in that it helps us to see very clearly the nature of the Christian's joy. It also enables us to differentiate between this joy and all mere superficial excitements and passing emotions. Nothing is more pathetic than the church's attempts to make people happy and to produce joy. It is very sad because it is a denial of the gospel. But that is done — aesthetic and psychological methods are used, certain types of music, clapping, different coloured lights, all in order to stimulate people. And then there is a psychological 'pep talk', as it were, all to make people bright and happy. Oh, what a contradiction of the New Testament joy! No, no; we must realize that the character of the joy that the New Testament speaks about, and that our Lord speaks about, is in a category on its own. It is entirely different from all mere passing emotional excitement and titillation of the feelings. True joy and happiness are not superficial but are always profound and always have a solid foundation in the understanding. That is the great message of the New Testament.

Let me work that out in a number of propositions. First, the Christian should never seek for joy as an end in itself. Never! That is a great fallacy. And if we do that, if we do seek it directly, immediately, in and of itself, then the joy will be a spurious joy. That, of course, is what the cults do. They deliberately set out to give us what we want. They know that we are unhappy, that we are troubled by the world, and that we want joy and peace. And they will give it us, they have the agency, they have developed a form, a kind of ritual, a technique – that is the word – to give us this feeling that we want, and, of course, they do give a temporary satisfaction, like drinking that water out of the well. But it does not last, it is not solid, it is not true.

Secondly, and this follows, of course, Christian joy is always a by-product of something else – our relationship to the Lord. 'Rejoice in the Lord alway; and again I say, Rejoice.' In other words, the New Testament never comes to us and says, 'Be happy! You ought to be happy; make yourself happy. Come along, let us all be happy together.' That is the flesh, that is exactly what the world does with its song leaders, its bands and so on. But that is remote from the New Testament, it is really almost the exact antithesis of New Testament teaching.

Or let me put it in this way: the joy that Christians have is based on the realization of what they are, and, therefore, to Christians, what they are is much more important than what they may feel like, it is much more important than what may be happening to them. Now this, again, is a basic, central, foundational principle of the whole Christian position. The emphasis of all the New Testament writers, from the very beginning of the book of Acts onwards – and it is particularly the theme of the Epistles and, of course, is implicit in the Gospels as well – is for us to realize who and what we are. It is the failure to realize this that, more commonly than anything else, robs us of this joy and happiness that our Lord offers us.

Let me give you an example of how this joy is lost. Take the apostle Paul's words in Romans 8: 'I reckon that the sufferings of this present time are not worthy to be compared with the glory that shall be revealed in us' (verse 18). Now he says that, and all that follows in that chapter, because these early Christian were in trouble, they were suffering and being persecuted, things were going wrong, and some of them, because of this, had lost their joy. Indeed, some were even beginning to doubt whether their faith was real and whether the gospel was true.

Why was this? It was because they had obviously got a false notion, which was: Believe the gospel and you will be happy ever afterwards. If you believe on the Lord Jesus Christ, you will walk down the road of life with head erect and will never have any more troubles. What nonsense it is – what utter nonsense! It is putting the wrong emphasis. No, no; the apostle writes to get the Christians to realize that their joy must not be dependent upon what is happening to them, or on how they feel, but is to be based upon what they are, their relationship to the Lord Jesus Christ and what that is going to lead to.

But how does Paul know that? He has already told us:

*The Spirit itself beareth witness with our spirit, that we are the children of God: and if children, then heirs; heirs of God, and joint-heirs with Christ; if so be that we suffer with him, that we may be also glorified together. (Romans 8:16–17)*

Our joy is all dependent upon our relationship to him, and the way to preserve joy, therefore, is not to be controlled and governed by our feelings and moods and states, nor by what is happening to us. If we are, we will be miserable because this is an evil world and there are evil people in it; and because there is illness and accident and death and sorrow. So the way of the New Testament is not seeking joy but having certainty and assurance with regard to who we are, what we are, our relationship to him and all that is implicit in that.

And so my third proposition about the character of true joy and happiness is that the way to obtain it, therefore, is not to look into myself or to try to produce joy – never. It is always the result of 'looking unto Jesus the author and finisher of our faith' (Hebrews 12:2). And that is the message of the entire New Testament – look unto Jesus. He himself said, 'In the world ye shall have tribulation: but be of good cheer; I have overcome the world' (John 16:33). Our Lord never promised us an easy time in this world. He never taught a kind of jovial back-slapping Christianity. People have this foolish notion that you cannot be happy and serious at the same time. That is where the trouble comes in. But you can. The only joy worth having is a serious joy, it is a sober joy, it is a deep joy, it is a solid joy.

> Solid joys and lasting treasure
> None but Zion's children know.
> *John Newton*

It is the element of solidity that is important, and that is always the outcome of our relationship to the Lord Jesus.

Are you a depressed Christian? Are you dejected? Do you feel that all things are against you to drive you to despair? Are you having a hard time in your Christian and your spiritual life? Have you come to this service this morning hoping for something? What are you hoping for? How do you think it is going to come to you? Is it my business to make you happy? No, no, my friend. I am not a psychologist, I am a preacher of the gospel. It is not my business to make you happy. If it were, then I would bring a supply of drugs, or drink, or I would have some orchestra here – I would do a thousand and one things. But that is not my calling and the outcome would not be Christian joy.

No, my business is not to make you feel happy while you are here and then let you go back and face the tragedy and the problem of life exactly as you left it. That is a cheat, a lie. That is an artefact. It is not true, it is not clean, it is not honest; above all, it is not Christian. No, no; all I must do is tell you about him. My business is to try to do what the apostle John did. He wrote, 'These things write we unto you, that your joy may be full' (1 John 1:4), and he brought this about by telling them about him whom he had 'heard', 'seen', 'looked upon', 'handled' (verse 1). He was bearing witness! And this is the only way in which we can have this joy and heart satisfaction that our Lord talks about. In other words, you do not look into yourself, you look out from yourself and forget yourself, and you look at him.

This is, again, a great kind of watershed between the true Christian message and what passes in general under the name of mysticism. There is a Christian mysticism, but that is the only true mysticism. Every other type is bad because it starts by telling you, 'Look for the "divine spark" that is in you.' It says, 'Do not look at the world; the world is against you. Look into yourself. You have it all there if you could only see it and let it come out.'

But that, again, is the antithesis of the gospel. I say again that the only way to go through the world triumphantly and happy and joyful is to keep your eyes steadfastly upon him. But when you look at him, what do you look at? Well, let me show you. You start by realizing who he is. He says this himself to the woman of Samaria: 'If thou knewest the gift of God, and who it is that saith unto thee, Give me to drink; thou wouldest have asked of him, and he would have given thee living water.'

This meeting at the well is one of the greatest dramas in all literature – can you not see it? Here is a woman in desperate need, living in adultery at the moment. Oh, the poor woman! Her need is tremendous and here is the one who can satisfy every need. But there is one thing that is absolutely essential: he can only give this living water as she realizes who he is. If she does not realize that, she will remain as she is.

This is always the starting point. If you are in trouble, if you are unhappy, if circumstances and trials are pressing upon you, the method of the New Testament is not to deal with your problems and troubles directly, it is to ask you to look at him. He will never deal with these things directly, but only if you are in the right relationship to him. The benefits of Christianity only come to those who believe the message concerning him. So you see the fallacies that come in at this point. People want the benefits of Christianity – they want peace, joy, healing, and they do not get them, and they say, 'There's nothing in it.' No, no; they have misunderstood; they think they can get the results and the benefits without the faith that is the first essential.

In other words, as I have often put it, the first thing the New Testament tells every one of us is this: the real trouble with you is what you are. It is not your circumstances, it is not your illness, it is not your accident, it is not your surroundings, it is not other people; the real trouble is you, yourself. The New Testament convicts us of our sin. And this is always the beginning. So it confronts us with him. It does not deal with the situation as we think it will; it has its own method and it is a radical one – it tells us that what we are is more important than anything else. And then what we are is immediately put into the relationship that is absolutely essential, namely, our relationship to him. So you start by looking at him.

'This is hard. I'm in trouble.'

 ...t, it is because you are in trouble that I'm telling you to look ... ...im. The woman of Samaria is in terrible trouble and she goes on arguing and disputing until our Lord nails her down, and she has to realize who he is – then she gets the help. Never until then. And it is always like this. All our troubles arise from the fact that we are estranged from God, that we are under his wrath and that we are not his children. So the New Testament does not try to tinker with our problems and put a patch here and a patch there. No, no; it says: 'You must be born again.' The whole thing must start afresh, and you do this by looking at him.

I could give you endless illustrations of what I am saying. Let me give you what is, perhaps, one of the most striking of all. Take the great Epistle to the Hebrews; there it is, a long epistle of 13 chapters. Why was it ever written? The answer is the same: the Epistle to the Hebrews was written to Hebrew Christians who were in a state of unhappiness. They were dejected, many of them were even threatening to give up Christianity altogether and to go back to the old Jewish religion and the Temple, with the priests and the high priests and all the animal sacrifices. That was their actual position. That is why the writer had to give them such terrible warnings about turning away from the gospel.

But why were the Hebrews in that position? It was because of all that had been happening to them, as the writer reminds them. He says:

*But call to remembrance the former days, in which, after ye were illuminated, ye endured a great fight of afflictions; partly, whilst ye were made a gazing-stock both by reproaches and afflictions; and partly, whilst ye became companions of them that were so used. For ye had compassion of me in my bonds, and took joyfully the spoiling of your goods, knowing in yourselves that ye have in heaven a better and an enduring substance. Cast not away therefore your confidence, which hath great recompence of reward. (Hebrews 10:32–35)*

He reminds them that when they first believed the gospel, they were filled with joy, in spite of the fact that they were being persecuted. But all the things that were happening to them had made them unhappy. Some of them, he says, were even being robbed of their goods and were being maltreated, persecuted by their own relatives, the Jews, who hated them because they had become Christians. So these people were in a really pathetic position. But how does the writer deal with them? Here they are – keep the picture in your mind – full of unhappiness, rejection, trials, troubles, tribulations, persecutions. And this is the remedy:

*God, who at sundry times and in divers manners spake in time past unto the fathers by the prophets, hath in these last days spoken unto us by his Son, whom he hath appointed heir of all things, by whom also he made the worlds; who being the brightness of his glory, and the express image of his person, and upholding all things by the word of his power, when he had by himself purged our sins, sat down on the right hand of the Majesty on high. (Hebrews 1:1–3)*

That is what is supposed to make them happy. Does it make you happy? How do you view the Epistle to the Hebrews? Have you sometimes said something like this: 'Oh, well, of course, those people had time to be interested in great statements like that – that's theology. It's just doctrine. I want something practical, I want something to help me. I'm in trouble, life is very hard. I don't have time to try to understand these great statements, these great theological propositions. I want some immediate practical help.' I know you do, and that is why you are what you are.

No, this is the only help, there is no other, and that is why the writer of this epistle starts with it. There is no easy comfort offered in the Epistle to the Hebrews. What he is really saying is this: Look here, you are unhappy, and you are miserable, and you are threatening to go back. Why? Because you have failed to realize the truth about him. So he starts with it. Come back, he says, and realize the truth about him, and all your troubles will leave you for the nonce. They will still be there but they will not get you down. You will be filled with joy in spite of them.

It is the only answer – 'looking unto Jesus' (Hebrews 12:2). The way to get joy is to contemplate the glory of this blessed person. He is 'the brightness of his [God's] glory, and the express image of his person'. He is God the eternal Son. He is the one whom we are concerned about. He is the one who has come into this world in order to put us right with God. Whatever you may feel, whatever is happening to you, do not look at these things; look at him and realize that he has it in him to give you all you need and infinitely more. He looks at you as you are now, in your situation, however desperate it may be, and do you know what he says to you? He says what he said to the woman of Samaria. She had said to him: 'How is it that thou, being a Jew, askest drink of me, which am a woman of Samaria?' And he replied: I am not just a Jew, I am not just a man among men, I am not just a philosopher, I am not just a pacifist, I am not just a politician. Look at me! 'If thou knewest . . .'

And that is what he is saying to you: If you only knew who I am and what I have got to give you. 'Whosoever drinketh of the water that I shall give him shall never thirst; but the water that I shall give him shall be in him a well of water springing up into everlasting life.' *I* – this is the point. 'The water that *I* shall give.'

Look at him again. Look into his eyes, look into his face, realize that this is the Son of God – 'the brightness of his [God's] glory, and the express image of his person', and he has come to supply your every need.

33

# *The Ultimate Test*

*Jesus answered and said unto her, Whosoever drinketh of this water shall thirst again: but whosoever drinketh of the water that I shall give him shall never thirst; but the water that I shall give him shall be in him a well of water springing up into everlasting life. (John 4:13–14)*

We have seen that Christians are aware of a joy in their hearts that is 'unspeakable and full of glory', and we have seen that this is the work of the Spirit. We have considered together the direct influence of the Spirit, and have also seen that he works indirectly by giving us new life, and producing within us the fruit of the Spirit. Then in our last study, we saw that the Spirit also works indirectly through the Scriptures. This is the normal way in which he works. He works in us directly, yes, but he also works in us indirectly to enable us to understand the Scriptures. He is the author of the Scriptures, and they have been given in order that we may have assurance. Above all, they point us to Christ, so that we may know what it is to rejoice in Christ Jesus.

As we read the Scriptures, we look at our Lord. That is the only way to get this full heart satisfaction and that is what we come together to consider. I am not going to talk this morning about the problem in the Middle East. That is not Christian preaching. The Christian message is much bigger, much greater. I have a message to offer you in terms of this statement of our Lord to the woman of Samaria, and it is this that can enable people this morning, in the acute tension and crisis of the Middle East, to have 'a joy unspeakable and full of glory'. That is what matters. It is a tragedy that the Christian church should waste her time in talking about things that she is not competent to deal with. This is our message: 'In the world ye shall have tribulation: but be of good cheer; I have overcome the world' (John 16:33). Here is a message that comes to us whatever the conditions in the world round and about us, and this message is always the call to look at him.

How do we get this joy as we look at him? I ended last week by saying that you just look at his person: 'Who being the brightness of his glory, and the express image of his person . . .' (Hebrews 1:3). Have you not noticed how the New Testament keeps on just describing him? 'In the beginning was the Word, and the Word was with God, and the Word was God' (John 1:1). 'Who is . . . the firstborn of every creature' (Colossians 1:15). 'And he is before all things, and by him all things consist' (Colossians 1:17).

Do you want to have Christian joy? Well, meditate on him, think about him; try to think about the glory of this person, this incomparable person. The New Testament is constantly dealing with this. Our Lord told us that the Holy Spirit has been specially given in order to glorify him: 'He shall not speak of himself . . . he shall glorify me' (John 16:13–14). And the way to test whether or not our experiences are the work of the Spirit is always to ask what view they give us of him.

This is a most thorough test and I want to apply that now. We need to examine ourselves. Perhaps we are living on services, on meetings, perhaps we are living on excitement, or on organizations. That is not living on him. No, the ultimate test of our position, every one of us who claims to be a Christian is this: Do we find our joy, our peace, our contentment in him – I mean in him himself, the person of our Lord. Think of him in his own eternal glory, think of him as he is, as he is revealed to us in the Scriptures.

The only way to get real, solid, lasting joy is to know the truth about him and it is amazing that people have lost sight of this. This modern objection to doctrine and theology is not only fatal from the standpoint of truth, it is particularly fatal in the matter of experience. It is because people have ceased to be concerned about understanding doctrine that they are having to turn to various other expedients. Have you not noticed how the element of entertainment is coming more and more into our meetings and how it is increasingly similar to the entertainment offered by the world? Christianity is having to fall back upon the world and its methods to make people happy and joyful in its meetings. It is so tragic. It is such a contradiction of what we have in the Bible. No, no; you do not borrow anything from the world to make Christian people happy. What you do is state the doctrine concerning the person of the Lord Jesus Christ.

Do you ever sit down and contemplate him? Do you think of him – the effulgence of the everlasting and eternal God, who was born as the babe of Bethlehem? Does that move you? Does it thrill you? If it does not, I take leave to ask the question: Are you a Christian? This is most important. Let me tell you what a friend from Africa once told me. He had had experience of revival in Africa, and he and others had come over to this country on a visit. He had gone round telling people about the revival, and everyone had greatly enjoyed listening to him. But then, a year later, he came back again and he began going round the same churches. But he had a feeling, indeed, he felt certain, that it was the leading of the Holy Spirit that this time he should preach the gospel about the Lord Jesus Christ, and he began to do so. And he told me that this is what happened: people used to come to him at the end of the meeting, good, evangelical Christian people, and say, 'Thank you very much for the message, but we did hope you would have told us some more about the revival.' He said, 'You see, they did not want to hear about Jesus, they wanted to hear about the thrills and the excitements of revival.' How devastating that is!

Does our Lord give you joy? Does he give you happiness? Does he give you peace? Let us be distrustful of any joy that we may have that is not directly related to him. Start with the glory of the person and meditate on him. Look at him, think about him. Like the writers of the hymns, consider him – 'Jesus, Lover of my soul'; 'Thou Son of God and Son of man, beloved, adored Immanuel'. That is the way to know true joy. And unless these things move us, we must examine the very foundations of our faith. But then we go on from there. Our Lord was in the everlasting and eternal glory – 'In the beginning was the Word' – but also – 'the Word was made flesh, and dwelt among us' (John 1:1, 14).

Now you say, 'But I know all about that, I thought I was going to have something that I didn't know.'

I know. And it is because you think you know it that you are as you are. You are not applying it. You spend the whole of your Christian life in going over these things. If you think you know all about the Gospels, you will just continue to be what you are. You are merely displaying your ignorance of spiritual things. If you think you have got it all taped, as it were, and that you have read the passages and know all about it – what a tragedy that is! The apostle Paul, having spent so many years in contemplating him, says to the Philippians that his deepest desire and ambition is 'that I may know him' (Philippians 3:10). You get to know more and more as you contemplate him.

So I now ask this question: Why was the Word made flesh? Why did the Word ever dwell among us? And then we come to one of the most amazing and glorious aspects of the gospel. You cannot ask that question without at once being driven to the only answer: it was the result of God's eternal plan and purpose. I must confess that I find it the most staggering thing that I ever contemplate – that before the world was created at all God had planned this redemption that you and I are sharing. What are we doing this morning? Well, we are considering this: 'We speak the wisdom of God in a mystery, even the hidden wisdom, which God ordained before the world unto our glory' (1 Corinthians 2:7). 'Before the world'!

Or take it as Paul puts it again in Ephesians chapter 1:

*Having made known unto us the mystery of his will, according to his good pleasure which he hath purposed in himself: that in the dispensation of the fulness of times he might gather together in one all things in Christ, both which are in heaven, and which are on earth; even in him.* (Ephesians 1:9–10)

This is the great plan and purpose of God, conceived and planned even before the foundation of the world. This is the source of Christian joy. Look at the world; look at all that is happening in it; look at all the failure and the misery and the shame and all that is involved. How can anyone be happy in a world like this? Is it possible? How can one have peace? 'Peace, perfect peace, in this dark world of sin?' Is it possible? And there is only one answer to this – and this is that the Christian can 'Rejoice in the Lord alway' (Philippians 4:4).

I look at the modern scene, I see the world as it is. I do not waste your time or mine in talking about that or in telling the statesmen what to do about it. That is just a sheer waste of breath and time and energy; it is folly. Again, I say that I have something much more glorious to tell you. I am here just to tell you that God's ultimate purpose is to restore all things in perfection and glory in Jesus Christ. All that we see in the world is the result of the Fall, of man's rebellion; and man will never be able to put it right. Anyone who still has confidence in statesmen or in Leagues of Nations or United Nations or anything else, is just a sheer spiritual ignoramus. There is only one hope for this world: it is in this person. And I know that for one reason only, and that is that God has planned all this and that is the only real source of joy, therefore. So you do not look at your circumstances and surroundings, you look at God and his great plan and purpose that he has put into execution in Christ Jesus, the babe of Bethlehem.

And as you meditate on these truths, you find your joy. This is 'rejoicing in tribulations', of course it is, because you are seeing the ultimate. And the purpose itself, the very fact that God has ever planned it or even thought of it, is so glorious. We do not deserve it, we deserve hell, we deserve damnation. You should not complain about the state of the world. Man has produced it and he deserves what he is getting; it will get worse unless he humbles himself and repents. That is the Christian message. And to blame God, to say, 'If there's a God, and God is a God of love, why does he allow . . .?' is not to see that the amazing thing is that God has not blotted us all out to everlasting destruction. We deserve nothing but what we are getting, and infinitely more, and worse.

No, the astounding fact is that 'God so loved the world' – this wretched, evil world – 'that he sent his only begotten Son' into it, and he planned to do it before the very foundation of the world. Does the contemplation of that not move you? Does it not thrill you that the everlasting God whom we have so insulted, should be doing this for *us*? You are not thinking of your own little aches and pains now, are you, and the little pin pricks and what somebody has said or done? Ah, what a tragedy it is! Look away from it all, look to him, contemplate this, and you will know 'a joy unspeakable and full of glory'.

And then go on: consider the way in which he came. Try to consider what it meant to him. Do you do this? This is Christianity. You do not sit passively and wait for something to make you happy, or go to a meeting because you think, 'Ah, they're having great happiness there!' Oh, how false that is! No, this is the method.

Then let me give you another illustration in terms of the way in which he came. Why do you think we have these accounts of our Lord's birth, why were they ever written? They were written, of course, to establish us in the truth, but they were also written to give us comfort and consolation. The heresies had already started to come in and John had to write his Gospel in order to show that Jesus of Nazareth is the eternal Son of God, the everlasting Word. Some people said that he was only a man, that he was only Jesus. The Gospel's emphasis is: no, no; he is God the eternal Son. But then John writes his first epistle with the exact opposite objective. There were other people who were saying that the Lord Jesus Christ was God and did not really have a true body, only a phantom body, an appearance. So then John had to write to show that he had truly come 'in the flesh'.

But in both cases, the ultimate objective was to establish the believers in the faith and in the truth as it is in Christ Jesus, in order that they might go on rejoicing in him. The false teaching had shaken them and it had made them lose their joy. So we are given these details about his coming and what it cost him. There is no greater account of this than the one that is to be found in Philippians chapter 2. Here, again, Paul is dealing with a most practical subject. If I do nothing else, I do hope I am showing you the method of the Scriptures. There were people who were quarrelling with one another in the church at Philippi, so Paul says:

*Fulfil ye my joy, that ye be like minded, having the same love, being of one accord, of one mind. Let nothing be done through strife or vainglory; but in lowliness of mind let each esteem other better than themselves. Look not every man on his own things, but every man also on the things of others.*

A most practical, ordinary problem, is it not, but this is how the apostle deals with it.

*Let this mind be in you*

– what mind? –

*which was also in Christ Jesus: who, being in the form of God, thought it not robbery to be equal with God*

– he was in the form of God; he is God the eternal Son, co-equal, co-eternal with the Father. He has all the insignia and manifestations of everlasting divine glory. But he did not regard those as a prize to be held on to, to be clutched on to. He did not say, 'Well, now, whatever happens, I'm not going to let go or to forgo my privileged position, and all the privileges that belong to it' – that is the real meaning of 'thought it not robbery to be equal with God' – but far from doing that –

*he made himself of no reputation*

– our very imaginations are affected by the Fall, are they not? Can you feel the content of that statement? He had made men: 'For by him were all things created . . . and for him' (Colossians 1:16); 'upholding all things by the word of his power' (Hebrews 1:3), he, of whom all that is true, 'made himself of no reputation' –

*and took upon him the form of a servant, and was made in the likeness of men: and being found in fashion as a man, he humbled himself, and became obedient unto death, even the death of the cross. (Philippians 2:2–8)*

Now if the contemplation of that does not move us to the depth of our being, there is something radically wrong with us as Christians. That is what it comes to. That is how Paul deals with a practical problem; this is the only way to know the joy of the Lord. You just look at him and consider what he did. This was planned before the foundation of the world, but the time came, the appointed time, 'the fulness of the time' (Galatians 4:4) arrived and this eternal Son of God was born as a helpless babe in the stable in Bethlehem, and his little body was put into the manger. Can you imagine what it meant for him to divest himself of his everlasting and eternal glory? He put it off, as I put off this gown; he laid it aside. He did not empty himself of Godhead, he could not have done that, but he laid aside all that belonged externally to the glory of heaven.

You say, 'But I've always known that. I've known it since I was a child.'

All right; I accept your statement, but I will convict you out of your own mouth. You say you have always known that, and yet you are miserable. How do you reconcile these two things?

Can you know all that and what it really means, and be miserable or selfish, or wounded, or slighted, and all the rest of the things that get us down and make us so wretched? There is something wrong somewhere, is there not? No, no; there is all the difference in the world between being aware of a thing and really knowing it. Oh, 'Let this mind be in you'! Realize what happened, realize what it meant. He who owns the universe was born into abject poverty; Mary and Joseph could not even afford a lamb to present at the Temple after his birth, they had to use two turtle doves because of their poverty. The Lord of glory, the creator of the universe, born in a stable – that is it. The author of life, helpless as a babe. The poverty and the lowliness of it all!

But, oh, the glory of it all! This was so tremendous that the angels were singing in heaven. That is what the shepherds heard, is it not, as they were watching their flocks? They heard a choir, the heavenly choir, a choir of angels singing, 'Glory to God in the highest, and on earth peace, good will toward men' (Luke 2:14). This was so tremendous that the angels burst forth into song, and they have been singing ever since and will go on singing to all eternity. Turn to the book of Revelation and you hear them singing the song of 'the Lamb that was slain': 'Blessing, and honour, and glory, and power, be unto him that sitteth upon the throne, and unto the Lamb for ever and ever' (Revelation 5:12, 13). It is all because they realize something of the glory of the way in which he came into this world.

And then go on; look at him as he was in this world. That is why we have the four Gospels. They were not written that you and I might pass scriptural examinations; they were not just written that you and I might read daily portions, they were written to enable us to see him and to know him and to rejoice in him. How are we reading our Scriptures, I wonder? Oh, we become so mechanical, self-righteous, even, about it! Forget your 'systems' and begin to read the Scriptures, and to meditate upon them, and to pray over them, and to be filled with the Spirit as you do so. If your reading of the Scriptures does not fill you with joy, you are misreading them. You are using this book as a text book, which it is not. Its purpose is to feed the soul, and to bring us into this knowledge that leads to the joy that is beyond description. So look at him as he was in this world, look at his lowliness, 'the meek and lowly Jesus' – nothing much to look at. He passed among men, and often they did not even notice him. He took upon him the form of a servant – he humbled himself to that extent.

But, oh, look at his compassion and his sympathy! This is what I want to emphasize before we leave this matter. Are you in trouble?

> Art thou weary, art thou languid,
> Art thou sore distressed?
> *John Mason Neale*

You are getting old, you are losing your health, your memory is going, you are finding evidences of decay – you are bound to, it happens to us all. Or you have lost someone who is dear to you, or someone has disappointed you, or you have had some other loss, or some anxiety about your husband or about your wife, or about your children, and you are in trouble and cast down, and nobody seems able to help you?

My dear friend, do you know that the four Gospels were written because you are like that? That is why we have them. We do not merely have a doctrine, we have a person. We have a picture of a person there in those four portraits of him. And what do you see as you look at them? Well, it is always his pity, his compassion: 'When he saw the multitudes, he was moved with compassion on them, because they fainted and were scattered abroad, as sheep having no shepherd' (Matthew 9:36). He never missed a case of suffering. You remember what happened when he was on his way to heal the daughter of Jairus? Jairus was an important man, an official, and he had come to ask him to go and heal his daughter. So our Lord went with him and there was a great throng. But there was a poor woman there with a desperate need. Nobody knew anything about her at all but she knew her own suffering: 'the heart knows its own bitterness'. And she said to herself: 'If I could only touch the hem of his garment I am sure I would get something' – and she was so right. She did touch the hem of his garment, she got her healing and infinitely more. Why? Well, though he was on an official errand, in a sense, he always had time for a suffering, lonely, forgotten individual (Luke 8:41–48). His compassion!

Our Lord was often reprimanded by his own followers because he would see and stop for a blind man or a beggar, and be with tax collectors and sinners. 'Ah!' they said, this is not consistent with your position and the greatness of your teaching, and the miracles that you are performing – why do you do this sort of thing?' But he never failed.

Then there he was on the cross, dying in shame and in agony, but he still had time to talk to the penitent thief, to this poor fellow who was also dying and realizing his sin and his hopelessness. Our Lord in his agony had the time to talk to him and to give him the word of consolation and of help.

That is the picture we see of him. Listen to his teaching, listen to what he has to say, it is always the same – love and mercy and compassion. Look at what he says to this poor woman of Samaria, the adulteress who is ostracized by the polite and respectable people who would not be seen talking to such a woman. He not only talks to her, he holds before her all the blessings that he has come into the world to give, even to her. That was his teaching, that was his practice, and he had the power to do it. He could say, 'Son, be of good cheer; thy sins be forgiven thee' (Matthew 9:2). He was able to forgive; it was not merely talk, he had the power.

So there in the four Gospels, when you look at him, that is what you see. And then you must apply all you see and understand. You do not stop merely at reading – reading your daily portion of Scripture – all right, do that but do not stop there, that is all I am saying. The whole art is application. Preaching that does not apply the message is no good, and reading the Bible without applying the message is no good either. So here is your application. There he is, you see him as he was on earth, and then in the depth of your need, in the agony of your condition, you say to yourself: he is still the same, still 'touched with the feeling of our infirmities' (Hebrews 4:15). He sees us, and he is still the same compassionate, loving, piteous person. Turn to him and he will tell you, 'I know all about you' – and you will find your relief, you will find your peace, you will find your joy. That is how you do it. You do not seek peace and joy directly, you always go to him.

But then you say, 'Well, what is he like? If he is now in the glory everlasting, is he still concerned?' He is. 'I am he that liveth, and was dead; and, behold, I am alive for evermore' (Revelation 1:18). Jesus Christ, the same yesterday, and to day, and for ever' (Hebrews 13:8). Look at him, therefore, as you see him living his life in this world, in this contradictory, evil, sinful world, as you and I are having to do. Look at him there in the pages of the Gospels and then – go to him! You will not be miserable very long, you will not be unhappy for long. I do not care what your circumstances or your position may be, he is still the same and is ready to do for you what he did for those who were in need and suffering while he was in this world. And he will say to you, 'Peace be with you'; 'Rise'; 'Walk'; 'See' – whatever it is – and he will send you on your way rejoicing.

## 34

# 'Looking unto Jesus'

*Jesus answered and said unto her, Whosoever drinketh of this water shall thirst again: but whosoever drinketh of the water that I shall give him shall never thirst; but the water that I shall give him shall be in him a well of water springing up into everlasting life. (John 4:13–14).*

The whole object of the whole of the New Testament is 'looking unto Jesus' and we have been trying to do that. We have looked at him in the glory of his person: 'the brightness of his [God's] glory, and the express image of his person' (Hebrews 1:3), and we have considered why he ever came into the world, the way in which he came, the humiliation that was involved, the self-abnegation and the laying aside of the signs and the marks of his eternal glory. Finally, we have looked at him as he walked here in this world with his eye of compassion.

And now let us go on – this is the way to get happiness and peace and joy, not in some kind of psychological service that makes a direct attack upon the emotions. That is wrong. The way to have the joy of the Lord is to know the Lord. So let us continue to look at him. Here he is in the world, he is walking about the world, he sees the need and he deals with it; but look at what he himself endured, look at what he suffered while he was here. Are you unhappy because of people or circumstances, or because of something you are having to endure? Are you unhappy because you are beset by temptations or surrounded by trials and by problems? These are the things that make us miserable, the things that are so constantly robbing us of our joy. But our Lord says, 'Whosoever drinketh of the water that I shall give him shall never thirst.' It does not matter what the circumstances may be, we are not disturbed by them; he delivers us.

And this deliverance is partly because of what our Lord endured and suffered while he was here, and that is why the Gospels were written. There were people who said, 'Ah, yes, he is eternal God and only had a kind of cloak of flesh, a kind of phantom body, he never really suffered anything at all.' And the Gospels were written partly to establish the fact that that view is heresy; he did suffer, he was truly 'made flesh', he really did 'become man'. He added manhood on to his Godhead, and he lived his life in this world as a man. Now this is most important and there is no greater comfort and consolation than to realize it.

James says to us, very rightly: 'Let no man say when he is tempted, I am tempted of God: for God cannot be tempted with evil, neither tempteth he any man' (James 1:13). By definition, God cannot be tempted; God cannot lie. There are certain things that are impossible to God because he is God. The presence of evil in the mind of God is unthinkable: 'God is light, and in him is no darkness at all' (1 John 1:5). He hates evil with the whole intensity of his eternal being, so God cannot be tempted. But we look at

Jesus of Nazareth and we see that '[He] was in all points tempted like as we are, yet without sin' (Hebrews 4:15). We read the accounts of the temptations for forty days and forty nights in the wilderness, but that is only a specimen, an example. And the tempter was not some underling but the devil himself, tempting him at his most sensitive points, yet he did not fall into sin.

But the point for us is that our Lord has been tempted, that he has endured this. Not only that, look at the trials he suffered – what the author of the Epistle to the Hebrews calls 'such contradiction of sinners against himself' (Hebrews 12:3). How difficult it is for us to realize what our Lord endured while he was in this world! We tend to read our Scriptures so superficially that we forget that these are facts; we tend to read the Bible as fiction. But it is all so true, it actually happened – the Son of God was in this world; and look at the way he was treated. His own mother misunderstood him; he even had to rebuke her. His own brothers completely misunderstood him, even taunting him and jeering at him. We read:

> *His brethren therefore said unto him, Depart hence, and go into Judaea, that thy disciples also may see the works that thou doest. For there is no man that doeth any thing in secret, and he himself seeketh to be known openly. If thou do these things, shew thyself to the world.*

And John adds:

> *For neither did his brethren believe in him. (John 7:3–5)*

You are in trouble, you are having a hard time, people are misunderstanding you and are cruel to you, and you are losing the joy of your salvation. You are defeated, you are down, you wonder whether there is anything in Christianity after all. You are thinking of giving it up. 'What is the point of it? The people in the world seem to be so happy. Is it true, are these promises true?' That is what you are feeling, that is what the devil is suggesting to you. And there is only one answer to all that: it is to look at him who endured 'such contradiction of sinners against himself', in his own family and in his own home.

Yet even worse was to come. Our Lord had chosen twelve men to be specially his people, his disciples, and he had paid much attention to them, giving them considerable teaching and instruction, and some very high privileges. He had let them into secrets that 'the wise and prudent' knew nothing about at all (Luke 10:21). He had given them more knowledge and information than was possessed by all the Pharisees and scribes put together. Here they were, the inner circle. But at the end of the three years, when the plans of the enemy came to fruition, we are told this: 'And they all forsook him, and fled' (Mark 14:50). He was left alone, forsaken, completely misunderstood, even by his own innermost circle of followers. And then, of course, there was the scoffing and the jeering and the mocking of the ignorant crowd. My dear friends, the Son experienced and endured all this.

This is how the Scriptures give us comfort and consolation. They say to us:

*Consider him that endured such contradiction of sinners against himself, lest ye be wearied and faint in your minds. Ye have not yet resisted unto blood, striving against sin. (Hebrews 12:3–4)*

He did. For the end of all that betrayal and forsaking and all the rest of it was death upon the cross.

Now I must not stay with these things, though we could so easily. I am trying to give you a method, a picture; I am trying to show you how you are to deal with yourself when you tend to be losing your joy. This is the method:

*Looking unto Jesus the author and finisher of our faith; who for the joy that was set before him endured the cross, despising the shame, and is set down·at the right hand of the throne of God. (Hebrews 12:2)*

When you are hard pressed and tried, when the devil tempts you to your foundations, and when everybody else seems to be against you to drive you to despair, do you just give in? If you do, then it is entirely your own fault that you are unhappy. Our Lord says, 'Whosoever drinketh of the water that I shall give him shall never thirst.' How do you drink that water? Well, this is part of it – you just go straight to him, you see what he went through for you and you realize you are not alone; indeed, you realize that you have been given a very great and a very high privilege. Peter works that out like this when he is telling us to be obedient:

*Servants, be subject to your masters with all fear; not only to the good and gentle, but also to the forward. For this is thankworthy, if a man for conscience toward God endure grief, suffering wrongfully. For what glory is it, if, when ye be buffeted for your faults, ye shall take it patiently? but if, when ye do well, and suffer for it, ye take it patiently, this is acceptable with God. For even hereunto were ye called: because Christ also suffered for us, leaving us an example, that ye should follow his steps: who did no sin, neither was guile found in his mouth: who, when he was reviled, reviled not again; when he suffered, he threatened not: but committed himself to him that judgeth righteously. (1 Peter 2:18–23)*

And if you do the same, why, whatever is happening to you, you will still have 'a joy unspeakable and full of glory'. Work that out for yourselves.

But we must go on; all that our Lord endured ended in the death on the cross. Here, of course, is the central theme of the Christian faith. But our danger is to say, 'Oh, yes, I know all about the cross, I've got that taped. Oh, yes, I understand exactly about the death of Christ.' Is not that our tendency? But listen to what Isaac Watts tells you:

When I survey the wondrous cross

– you cannot take a hurried glance at the cross. It is to be contemplated, to be meditated upon for the rest of your life. You *survey* it, and you begin to see its depth and height, its breadth, its length. You see that there is no end to it, that it is the most amazing thing that has ever happened. Look at it, and the more you do, the more you will find comfort, consolation, peace, joy – everything you stand in need of. And you will discover this: that he came into the world in order to go to the cross.

Why be influenced by the thinking of the secular world that has come so much into the church? The death of Christ is not an accident, it is not pacifism. No, he came from heaven in order to die – he kept on saying so. 'The Son of man', he said, 'came not to be ministered unto, but to minister, and to give his life a ransom for many' (Matthew 20:28). The Son of man must be lifted up, he said, 'as Moses lifted up the serpent in the wilderness' (John 3:14). Or, again, in the Epistle to the Hebrews, we read: 'We see Jesus, who was made a little lower than the angels for the suffering of death, crowned with glory and honour; that he by the grace of God should taste death for every man' (Hebrews 2:9); and in Revelation: 'The Lamb [of God] slain from the foundation of the world' (Revelation 13:8). The death of the Lamb of God was in the eternal mind as the only way of salvation. What I am emphasizing is that our Lord came for this purpose. He offered himself. You will find it set out in the tenth chapter of the great Epistle to the Hebrews:

*Wherefore when he cometh into the world he saith, Sacrifice and offering thou wouldest not, but a body hast thou prepared me: in burnt offerings and sacrifices for sin thou hast had no pleasure. Then said I, Lo, I come (in the volume of the book it is written of me,) to do thy will, O God. (Hebrews 10:5–7)*

He volunteered, he came deliberately. 'He stedfastly set his face to go to Jerusalem' (Luke 9:51). His friends tried to dissuade him, they warned him that Herod and others were waiting for him. But he rebuked them. His object, in other words, was 'to give his life a ransom for many' (Mark 10:45). The Son of God came into this world specifically to take your sins and mine upon himself, to bear our guilt, to receive our punishment: and he has done so to the full. He has paid the penalty, he has made full satisfaction for sins. 'This man, after he had offered one sacrifice for sins for ever, sat down on the right hand of God' (Hebrews 10:12). Here is one who was able to say, 'It is finished' (John 19:20).

Are you troubled and unhappy about your sins? Tell me, you who do not have the joy of salvation, you who do not have the assurance of salvation, what is robbing you of it? You who, when you are on your knees praying to God, find yourselves uncertain and troubled, having to spend the whole of your time pleading for forgiveness, why are you like that? You are not meant to be. The Son of God came from heaven to earth and did all he did, especially the death on the cross, in order that you may never be like that again. He has once and for ever borne the punishment of your sins; they are 'blotted out'; they have already received their punishment.

*There is therefore now no condemnation to them which are in Christ Jesus . . .*

– you will never get joy and assurance by just looking into yourself and examining yourself. Of course not. There is only one way to get it –

> *for the law of the Spirit of life in Christ Jesus hath made me free from the law of sin and death. For what the law could not do, in that it was weak through the flesh, God sending his own Son in the likeness of sinful flesh, and for sin, condemned sin in the flesh: that the righteousness of the law might be fulfilled in us, who walk not after the flesh, but after the Spirit. (Romans 8:1–4)*

You have no right to be miserable, you have no right to be lacking in joy. If you do not have the joy of salvation – I am speaking to Christians – there is only one reason. It is because you are deliberately listening to the devil rather than to the word of God. You need to look again at the one on the cross, and you must ask questions. What is he doing there? Was it an accident or was it deliberate? If it was deliberate, why was he there? What was the object? Listen to what he says: 'I came not to call the righteous, but sinners to repentance' (Mark 2:17).

You say, 'But I can't be happy because I'm a sinner.'

But he says he has come to call sinners to repentance. 'They that are whole have no need of the physician, but they that are sick' (Mark 2:17). By your lack of joy you are denying his teaching. You think, perhaps, that it is because you are such a sensitive soul that you lack joy. It is not! It is because you are ignorant, because you do not believe the word of God, because you will not exercise your senses. You have as a Christian, I say, no right to be under condemnation. You are detracting from the glory of God's salvation. He came not only to purchase pardon for his people, but also that we might know it and might rejoice in it. 'Rejoice in the Lord alway: and again I say, Rejoice' (Philippians 4:4).

Now I say again that you will not get this joy by trying to work up a feeling. I often watch people in the Communion service, and I see their struggle and agony, and know that they are trying to feel something. Don't you do that any more! Look at him and consider who he is and what he has done; that is how you receive joy. Don't try to work up feelings, it is always fatal. Look unto Jesus. Look at him dying on the cross and realize something of the depth of its meaning.

There, then, is our Lord on the cross. And he dies, and they take down the body and lay it in a tomb, and they roll the stone in front and seal it and put soldiers to guard it. But you and I would not be here now if it had stopped at that!

So you then begin to look at the glory of the resurrection, and it is here everywhere in the New Testament. The Gospels all record it, and what was the preaching of the apostles in the book of Acts? 'Jesus, and the resurrection' (Acts 17:18). They were witnesses to the resurrection. The records are so honest and so true and they make it quite plain and clear that all these apostles would have gone home and would have given up in despair but for the glorious fact of the resurrection. Peter, we are told, was so miserable at the death of our Lord that he did not know what to do with himself. So, typically the fisherman, he said, 'I go a fishing' (John 21:3) – to get a bit of relief, to do something, to get away. He had not understood it, though he had had the teaching. Blinded by sin! But you remember what happened: the Lord appeared and kept on appearing. He spoke to the apostles and taught them.

There is something wrong with us, my dear friends, and we know what it is, do we not? It is sin remaining in us, and it is the indolence that sin leads to, and the lack of application. If you and I only lived in the light of the fact of the resurrection, we would never be downcast again. Its meaning is endless. Its first meaning is that God is fully satisfied – that he has accepted the offering made by his own Son: '[He] was delivered for our offences, and was raised again for our justification' (Romans 4:25). God raised his Son publicly, as it were, in order that we might have the joy and the comfort and assurance of knowing that our sins are forgiven.

And for us it means, as Paul puts it in writing to Timothy, 'Our Saviour Jesus Christ, who hath abolished death and hath brought life and immortality to light through the gospel' (2 Timothy 1:10). You and I need not dabble in spiritism, or with the cults and sciences, so called, which are not sciences at all. We *know*. He has opened the gates of heaven, he has brought life and immortality to light, we have this certain, sure fact.

But not only that, by our Lord's resurrection, we know that he has conquered all our enemies – every one of them. He conquered the devil when he tempted him, and he has conquered that 'last enemy': 'The last enemy that shall be destroyed is death' (1 Corinthians 15:26). He has taken the sting out of death; it is no longer there; for the Christian, it has gone.

So once again we see that what we need is to know how to study our Scriptures. Look at Timothy. He is the type of individual who is always ready to be cast down, always wondering what is going to happen – problems in the churches, people misunderstanding him. And then he hears the news that Paul is in prison and that the Emperor Nero has decided to put him to death, and poor Timothy says: The end has come, Paul is going, what can we do? Look at the churches, the old, the young, look at the opposition. Oh, it's terrible!

So Paul writes to Timothy, and says this:

*I put thee in remembrance that thou stir up the gift of God, which is in thee by the putting on of my hands.*

Pull yourself together, man, Paul says. Don't sit down and mope and whimper and cry and commiserate with yourself.

*For God hath not given us the spirit of fear; but of power, and of love, and of a sound mind [discipline, self-control].*

And then the apostle goes on to make this tremendous assertion, which is the essence of the Christian position:

*For the which cause I also suffer these things*

– because he is preaching the gospel, he is suffering and is in prison facing death –

*nevertheless I am not ashamed: for I know whom I have believed, and am persuaded that he is able to keep that which I have committed unto him against that day. (2 Timothy 1:6–7, 12)*

'Don't be worried about me,' Paul says, in effect, 'don't commiserate with me, don't offer me your sympathy, I don't need it. I'm not cast down, I'm not ashamed, I'm not frantic and I'm not in trouble at all. "I know whom I have believed, and am persuaded that he is able to keep that which I have committed unto him" – my soul and its eternal destiny – "against that day," the Day of Judgement, the day of his second coming.' Of course, Paul was always saying this. He says exactly the same thing to the Philippians when they were worrying about him:

*For I know that this shall turn to my salvation through your prayer, and the supply of the Spirit of Jesus Christ, according to my earnest expectation and my hope, that in nothing I shall be ashamed, but that with all boldness, as always, so now also Christ shall be magnified in my body, whether it be by life, or by death. For to me to live is Christ, and to die is gain. But if I live in the flesh, this is the fruit of my labour: yet what I shall choose I wot not. For I am in a strait betwixt two, having a desire to depart, and to be with Christ; which is far better: nevertheless to abide in the flesh is more needful for you. (Philippians 1:19–24)*

This is the way in which one obtains this full heart satisfaction from him and will 'never thirst' even in such circumstances. This man Paul 'surveys' him. He says: It is true, I am not ashamed, of course not, in fact, I am exulting.

We rejoice even in the midst of tribulations. And, as you know full well, this rejoicing is not confined only to some outstanding persons such as the apostle Paul, but was true of the most ordinary early Christians. These were the people who counted martyrdom the final crown of glory. These were the people who considered it a great honour to suffer shame for his name's sake, the people who had such joy in the Lord that nothing could rob them of it. Have you got that? Have you got this joy? Have you been rid of fear? Are you able to rejoice in the Lord always?

So look at the resurrection; contemplate the fact, realize something of the content of its meaning. But go on. He rose from the dead, he manifested himself for 40 days to chosen witnesses, then he ascended into heaven in the presence of some of them. And where is he now? This is how you deal with these subjects, and I do not know what you feel, my friends, but the more I study these Scriptures, the more wonderful they become to me, and the less I feel I know about them.

Consider that man, the author of the Epistle to the Hebrews. In three verses he tells you everything you can ever know, and then he goes on for 13 chapters! This is the scriptural method and it means that you have got to know it all and then you must grasp it in portions and parts.

*God, who at sundry times and in divers manners spake in time past unto the fathers by the prophets, hath in these last days spoken unto us by his Son, whom he hath appointed heir of all things, by whom also he made the worlds; who being the brightness of his glory, and the express image of his person, and upholding all things by the word of his power, when he had by himself purged our sins, sat down on the right hand of the Majesty on high. (Hebrews 1:1–3)*

The writer could not get over that, and repeats it again in the tenth chapter:

*But this man, after he had offered one sacrifice for sins for ever, sat down on the right hand of God; from henceforth expecting till his enemies be made his footstool. (Hebrews 10:12–13)*

Here is something glorious and tremendous. Here we are, a handful of people in a gainsaying world, wars and troubles, higher criticism, people worshipping science and other gods, and we are cast down and wondering how we can keep going. Has the church any future? What is the matter with us? I repeat, the trouble with us is that we do not know the Scriptures because, if we feel like that, a reply is given to us. Here are the last words in Matthew's Gospel:

*And Jesus [who is about to ascend to heaven] came and spake unto them, saying, All power is given unto me in heaven and in earth. Go ye therefore, and teach all nations, baptizing them in the name of the Father, and of the Son, and of the Holy Ghost: teaching them to observe all things whatsoever I have commanded you: and, lo, I am with you alway, even unto the end of the world. (Matthew 28:18–20)*

Is that not enough for you? Do you not get up on your feet and shout and defy all your enemies? You would, if you understood what that means, and you would never be cast down again. He is 'seated at the right hand of God', which is the position of honour, the position of power, and he says that all power has been given unto him. It has. As Paul reminds the Ephesians, God has 'raised him up' because of what he has done:

*[God] raised him from the dead, and set him at his own right hand in the heavenly places, far above all principality, and power, and might, and dominion, and every name that is named*

– yes, Nassau, Israel, Soviet Russia, United States, Great Britain, all these powers we are hearing so much about –

*not only in this world, but also in that which is to come: and hath put all things under his feet, and gave him to be the head over all things to the church, which is his body, the fulness of him that filleth all in all. (Ephesians 1:20–23)*

There he is, he has it all and you belong to him, and you are dear to him. What is he doing there? Paul, in writing to the Romans who were also in great trouble because the sufferings of this present time had got them down, says this:

*Who shall lay any thing to the charge of God's elect? It is God that justifieth. Who is he that condemneth? It is Christ that died, yea rather, that is risen again, who is even at the right hand of God, who also maketh intercession for us. (Romans 8:33–34)*

This, again, is the great theme of the author of Hebrews. In contrasting the old dispensation – the ritual of the Jewish Temple – and the Christian faith in Christ, he says:

*By so much was Jesus made a surety of a better testament. And they truly were many priests, because they were not suffered by reason of death*

– your priests and your high priests come and go, your popes come and go, and all your earthly priesthood –

*but this man, because he continueth ever, hath an unchangeable priesthood. Wherefore he is able also to save them to the uttermost that come unto God by him, seeing he ever liveth to make intercession for them. (Hebrews 7:22–25)*

Not only can you pray to God, the Lord Jesus Christ is praying for you, he is representing you. He is your great High Priest; he is taking your feeble cries and prayers, and transmitting them and transmuting them unto God. There he is seated at the right hand of God, and he is there for you and for me.

Now these are not idle tales, these are sheer, solid facts. This is the Christian faith, the faith you think you know already. Well, if you know it, I say again, why are you miserable? Why are you defeated? Why are you filled with fears and forebodings? This is the way to have this joy and this peace and heart satisfaction. So consider what he has already done for you. He has reconciled you to God, you have forgiveness of sins, you are regenerate, you have new life in you, you have been adopted into the family of God, you are special objects of God's concern. You are 'heirs of God, and joint-heirs with Christ' (Romans 8:17). How did you go through the last week when you thought it might be the beginning of the third world war – how did you feel? How do you stand up to these possibilities? Christians see beyond all this; they know they are heirs of God, and joint heirs with Christ. They say, 'The sufferings of this present time are not worthy to be compared with the glory which shall be revealed in us' (Romans 8:18). Do you only hear the news? Do you only see literal countries in a material sense? Or do you see beyond it all to the glory? This is the question.

But you are still in this world, and you are still fighting the world, and the flesh, and the devil – remember, the Lord Jesus Christ is there, at the right hand of God, and he is 'touched with a feeling of our infirmities' (Hebrews 4:15). He has been through it all. He became man in order that he might be a merciful and faithful High Priest. He did it all in order that he might sympathize with you. He understands. There is nothing that has happened to you but that he has been through it. Go to him, look to him, he will immediately give you peace. As he conquered it all, he will enable you to conquer it. You are not alone, he is with you. Having been tempted himself, 'He is able to succour them that are tempted' (Hebrews 2:18). And he tells you this – 'I will never leave thee, nor forsake thee' (Hebrews 13:5). Never! Remember this: 'Jesus Christ the same yesterday, and to day, and for ever' (Hebrews 13:8). Look at him in the Gospels, see his sympathy, his understanding, his tenderness, his humility. He cannot change because of his eternal nature. All that he suffered and experienced here in this world is still there in his mind and heart, and he looks down on you, and he is ready and willing to help you and to succour you in all your need.

And, lastly, consider what he is yet going to do. 'Yes,' says the writer to the Hebrews:

*[He] sat down on the right hand of God; from henceforth expecting till his enemies be made his footstool. (Hebrews 10:12–13)*

*As it is appointed unto men once to die, but after this the judgment: so Christ was once [and for all] offered to bear the sins of many; and unto them that look for him shall he appear the second time without sin [not in connection with sin, but] unto salvation. (Hebrews 9:27–28)*

I do not know what the future of Palestine is to be; you do not either. The Scriptures are not clear on this. I hope you have not been spending the week just trying to work out times and seasons. What you and I have to consider is this:

> Jesus shall reign where'er the sun
> Doth his successive journeys run;
> His kingdom stretch from shore to shore
> Till moons shall wax and wane no more.
>
> *Isaac Watts*

'Whosoever drinketh of the water that I shall give him shall never thirst' – never, whatever happens, whatever calamities, whatever wars, whatever pestilences. These will come, he has prophesied that: there shall be 'wars and rumours of wars' (Mark 13:7) and pestilences, earthquakes and people's hearts failing them – it does not matter. He will come, and he will receive his own unto himself, and where he is they shall be for ever and for ever.

My dear friends, 'looking unto Jesus, the author and finisher of our faith', you will have the 'joy of the Lord', and it will become increasingly 'a joy unspeakable and full of glory'.

35

# 'Loved with Everlasting Love'

*Jesus answered and said unto her, Whosoever drinketh of this water shall thirst again: but whosoever drinketh of the water that I shall give him shall never thirst; but the water that I shall give him shall be in him a well of water springing up into everlasting life. (John 4:13–14)*

We have been seeing that ultimately the way to the heart satisfaction that our Lord gives and offers here so abundantly is really to know him. The Spirit was sent to glorify him. And the Spirit may give this joyful assurance directly – there are spiritual manifestations of the Son of God. But the normal method is through the Scriptures, and we have been seeing that and working it out together. The Scriptures are simply concerned to give us a portrait of him, to make us look at him. Their statements, all of them, can be summed up in the words: 'Looking unto Jesus'.

We have been looking at this joy objectively – as an objective fact – and have seen that we become happy by the indirect working of the Spirit as we look at our Lord in the Scriptures, as we contemplate him and meditate upon him and realize the truth concerning him. But now, having looked at this joy objectively, I think it will be most helpful to us if we also look at it subjectively. We must always take these two approaches. We must start with the objective because if we do not, we will soon be going astray. The trouble with the cults, with mere emotionalism, is that they do not start with the objective, they start with the subjective. Instead of starting with the gospel and the revelation of God in Jesus Christ, they start with man, and human needs and desires. You must never do that, it is always a false approach. You start with him and contemplate the fullness that is in him, and then you see the application and the relevance of that to your particular needs.

So, having started with the objective, we come now to the subjective. In other words, we are being very practical and we come down to the level where we ask: What are the desires and the needs and the demands of our hearts? That is the purely subjective or experiential way of looking at it, and it is perfectly legitimate. I suggest that we can do this along two main lines. There are certain legitimate desires of the heart and there are certain wrong or illegitimate desires and I think we will be able to show that our Lord deals with both.

First, then, Christ satisfies the deepest *legitimate* desires of the heart. What are these? I think we will all agree that the heart cries out for rest and for peace and for joy and happiness. Now there is nothing wrong with that. It is very wrong to think that a human being should not desire rest. Man was meant to enjoy rest and peace, he was never meant to be restless. So the desire for rest and peace is good and right. It is a part of the protest that even fallen human nature makes against itself and against sin, which man as the result of his rebellion and listening to the devil has brought into the universe. So these are perfectly legitimate desires.

And likewise with joy. Just as it is wrong to think that we should always be restless or ill at ease, so it is wrong to think we should be miserable. It is right to desire to be joyful. There is no merit in being miserable. I know some people who twist and pervert themselves. You are familiar with masochism, and some people have at times foolishly thought that that is the height of spirituality, and that Christians are only truly functioning as Christians when they are unhappy. They think that the right thing to do is always the thing you do not want to do. What a perversion of Christianity that is! What a denial of the truth of the Fatherhood of God. No, no; the desire for rest and for peace, for joy and for happiness is perfectly legitimate. The point I am making, however, is that these cannot be given to us by the world. Our Lord said, 'Whosoever drinketh of this water shall thirst again', and is not that the simple truth?

Now I could put this to you in many ways but two illustrations in particular have come within my reading comparatively recently. Lord Snow – C. P. Snow – has recently written a most interesting and fascinating book called *Variety of Men*.[1] In this book, he writes of a number of great men whom he has known and of one whom he has never met. These men are some of the outstanding figures in the life of the world during the present century – not only statesmen and politicians, but also men who were leaders in the realm of science, great men, such as Einstein. But what emerges so significantly in every single case is their failure to find rest and peace and true joy and happiness. Now Lord Snow is not a Christian and he is not concerned to bring out this point, but in being truthful and in analysing these characters, that is what he shows – and there is nothing new about this.

---

[1] C. P. Snow, *Variety of Men*, Macmillan 1967.

And then I read of the famous author of the Maigret detective stories, Georges Simenon. Here is a man who has made a fortune out of writing books – he has published 191! He has built himself a house in Switzerland above Lausanne. From the house there is a magnificent panorama stretching from the Italian Alps to Mont Blanc, including a wonderful view of the lake right down to Geneva. This is how Simenon describes his aim in building it: 'I have tried to build a kind of perfection here,' and, of course, it has everything that can be desired. It has wonderful windows – double glazing with gas between the two sheets of glass so that there should be no noise. He claims that 'even though 50 children should be playing and shouting together outside at the same time, you would not hear a sound'.

This is the way the world seeks for peace and for rest, for happiness and for joy. It is a marvellous house! We are given a list of the contents: 21 telephones, 7 bathrooms, 7 refrigerators, 7 television sets, immaculate sick room, a laundry with 3 washing machines, a kitchen like the galley of a liner, 4 or 5 paintings in every sitting room, in the main study 11 pictures by some of the masters! So there it is, but this is his confession:

> I have only one ambition left: to be completely at peace with myself; I doubt if I shall ever manage it. I do not think it is possible for anyone. It is not a question of money for that kind of happiness must come from within yourself. I do not know any man, however successful, who is completely happy.

Now that is something that should make us stop and think. There is a man who has everything that money can give but he has one ambition left – 'to be completely at peace with myself'. Here is the great problem, the great task. How easy it is to talk cleverly. Simenon can do it, he can write brilliantly. So can the others to whom I have referred – they are possessors of great power, great money, great influence, of every conceivable thing that thought and money can provide, yet still peace and joy elude them, they cannot find it. 'Whosoever drinketh of this water shall thirst again.' Read the end of the lives of the great men of the world and that is what you always find. There is something very sad, very tragic even, about the declining years of these men: the biggest thing of all they know nothing about. To the very end it eludes them.

One of our hymn writers puts it so well. Here is the craving, the longing, and the desire of the human heart:

> I ask thee for a thoughtful love,
> Through constant watching wise,
> To meet the glad with joyful smiles,
> And wipe the weeping eyes;
> A heart at leisure from itself

– that is the problem –

> To soothe and sympathize.
> *Anna L. Waring*

You cannot truly 'soothe and sympathize' and help others unless you have 'a heart at leisure from itself'. Self is the trouble, how to find peace with oneself. Here is the great quest.

Now all great literature really treats just this one subject. The greatest drama is always tragedy; great biographies and auto-biographies – it all comes to this. Here is the great problem of the human race, and our Lord's constant claim is that he, and he alone, can satisfy this longing and deep desire of the heart – and how abundantly does history record the truth of that claim. 'Peace I leave with you,' he said, 'my peace I give unto you: not as the world giveth, give I unto you. Let not your heart be troubled, neither let it be afraid' (John 14:27).

And, of course, we see this promise and assurance running right through all the writings and the teachings of the Epistles: 'Grace unto you, and peace, from God our Father and the Lord Jesus Christ' (2 Thessalonians 1:2). That is a very common form of salutation at the beginning of the various Epistles. You also find it actually put into practice in the book of Acts. This is what stands out at once about those early Christians: they found a place of rest, a place of peace.

And this is not confined only to the early Christians. This comes out so wonderfully and so gloriously in the subsequent history of the church and is celebrated in such an amazing manner in all the great hymns. Take this one, for instance, by Philip Doddridge:

> Now rest, my long-divided heart,
> Fixed on this blissful centre, rest:
> With ashes who would grudge to part
> When called on angels' food to feast.

That is it – the thing that the poor writer of literature cannot discover – 'a heart at leisure from itself', peace and rest within. Here is a man who can address his heart and say, 'Now rest, my long-divided heart.'

Now as we have found, there is a sense in which you cannot make too sharp a distinction between the intellectual aspect and the emotional heart aspect of the Christian life, the two go together; and Doddridge, in those words, is addressing his mind as well as his heart; it is true of both. The mind comes to the end of its quest and so he can address his heart – 'Rest, my long-divided heart.' You remember the famous words of Augustine. This scintillating, brilliant philosopher could not find rest and peace;

when at last he found it, he could but burst out and say, 'Thou hast made us for thyself, and our hearts are restless until they find their rest in thee.' But they do find it there.

One of the most glorious aspects of this blessed gospel is that men and women really do come to a place where they find quiet. We do not need to resort to mechanical devices, we do not need to get the bricks of our houses made of glass, and we do not need double glazing with the gas in between to keep out the sounds. When Christ is in your heart, you do not hear them, you are hearing him. You have a place of rest in spite of the noise. It is said that at the very centre of every hurricane there is a point of complete rest, and that is the Christian in this life, in a world like this.

And so Christians find that by our Lord they are given rest and peace: peace with God – 'Therefore being justified by faith, we have peace with God through our Lord Jesus Christ' (Romans 5:1) – and until men and women find peace with God, they will never know true peace. They cannot. That is the cause of their restlessness. That is really what Augustine was saying, in his way. It is because they are at enmity with God and have lost the peace that they originally had with him, that they are restless and unhappy and lacking in peace in every other realm of their lives. It is because they are out of the right relationship with God that they are in the wrong relationship even to themselves as well as to other people. This is the law of man's being.

Men and women have been made in the image and likeness of God, they are made for God. God has put such laws into human nature that they can only really function, even physically as well as mentally and spiritually, when they are obeying the laws of their nature – and obeying these laws means that they are in the right relationship with God. The mechanism cannot work otherwise, and without the oil of the Spirit there will be grindings, cracklings, noise, disturbance, an absence of a smooth, harmonious working. This is the message of the entire Bible. Those great men of the world who are honest all admit that there is no peace to be found in the world. It is all very well to make statements, to talk cleverly and brilliantly and to use wonderful terms that people do not understand, but the question is: Are they really happy? How do they face death? How do they face their declining years? How do they face disappointment? That is the test. And all the great people of the world fail at this point. I am referring to those, of course, who are not Christians. The moment you drink of this water that Christ has come to give, the whole situation changes. You are put right at the centre, you are put into the true relationship. You feel that the command has come and everything drops into position.

Now, of course, this must be worked out, but there it is, the big change has happened. And then that immediately means that you are put right with yourself, and as these men admit, self is the great problem. We find other people difficult because we find ourselves difficult. It is because you are quarrelling with yourself that you tend to quarrel with other people. I was listening to a musician talking the other afternoon about the great conductor Toscanini, who was notorious for his tantrums and his bad temper. On one occasion, when this musician was playing in the orchestra, the Maestro lost his temper and fumed and raged and walked off. The man walked out after him to apologise, and said, 'What were we doing wrong, Maestro? What was the matter?'

And Toscanini replied, 'You were doing nothing wrong, it was I who was wrong.'

You see the trouble? He could not conduct to his own satisfaction, he was ill at ease with himself, he was fighting and quarrelling with himself, so he was unpleasant to other people and quarrelled with them. And this is the whole trouble in life, is it not? Man will never be at peace with himself until he is at peace with God. Why? Because until he has the right view of himself in his relationship to God, he will always see himself in the wrong way. We are ambitious, we have jealousies and rivalries – all these take our rest and peace from us. But the moment we get into this 'peace with God', we are at peace with ourselves, we have a true view of ourselves and an object and purpose in life and in the world: we see everything in a different way. 'A heart at leisure from itself' – do you have that?

My dear friend, it is not your opinions on evolution or on creation that matter, they are irrelevant, that is a lot of camouflage. The problem for you is not to understand how human beings have evolved but to know why you do not have rest and peace with yourself. Are you in the position of George Simenon: 'I have only one ambition left, to be completely at peace with myself'? What is your answer to him? Has your self fallen into the right place and do you know this rest? Are you able to say with the apostle Paul, who has put this perfectly to the Christians in Corinth:

> *But with me it is a very small thing that I should be judged of you, or of man's judgment: yea, I judge not mine own self. For I know nothing by myself; yet am I not hereby justified: but he that judgeth me is the Lord. (1 Corinthians 4:3–4)*

He has ceased to be concerned about himself – 'a heart at leisure from itself'.

And then it follows, obviously, that if you have peace with God, and peace with yourself, you are in a position to have peace with other people. But it is the only way, it is the inevitable order. Our Lord, in giving an account of the great commandments, was very careful about the order:

*Thou shalt love the Lord thy God with all thy heart, and with all thy soul, and with all thy mind. This is the first and great commandment. And the second is like unto it, Thou shalt love thy neighbour as thyself.* (Matthew 22:37–39)

The foolish world starts with the neighbour, and people come to church saying, 'What is the Christian church going to do about these problems?' – expecting that we can tell the statesmen what to do. That is starting with the neighbour and it is hopeless. But if you drink of this water that our Lord is offering, you will find that it will work from above downwards – God, self, others, and you find peace. And so you find joy.

We have already considered this in dealing with the fruit of the Spirit as outlined by Paul in the fifth chapter of the Epistle to the Galatians. These things are quite inevitable. Your heart, my heart, we are all of us by nature longing for rest and peace and joy. He offers it and he gives it. This is the testimony of the saints of the centuries.

The next thing, I think you will agree, that the heart always cries out for is love. I need not describe this, you are familiar with it. We are so made and constituted that we all long to be loved. If you do not, you are an abnormality, a monstrosity. The feeling of being unloved is a prolific cause of the agony and the strain and the unhappiness in the world. Now our Lord says, 'Whosoever drinketh of the water that I shall give shall never thirst.' Whatever you and I may know of human love, it will never fully, finally satisfy. He alone can do that, and he does.

How does our Lord satisfy this longing for love? Let me give you some of the great statements in the New Testament:

*For when we were yet without strength, in due time Christ died for the ungodly. For scarcely for a righteous man will one die: yet peradventure for a good man some would even dare to die. But God commendeth his love toward us, in that, while we were yet sinners, Christ died for us. Much more then, being now justified by his blood, we shall be saved from wrath through him. For if, when we were enemies, we were reconciled to God by the death of his Son, much more, being reconciled, we shall be saved by his life. (Romans 5:6–10)*

Now this is the love of God to us, and God commends it. Indeed, Paul has told us in the fifth verse, 'Hope maketh not ashamed' – why? – 'because the love of God is shed abroad in our hearts by the Holy Ghost which is given unto us.' The Holy Spirit makes God's love real to us. We have a longing to be loved, and here we have an assurance that God himself loves us. But listen to Paul later on in the Epistle to the Romans, and you will find that he rises to some of the greatest heights, even judged by Paul's standards:

*We know that all things work together for good to them that love God, to them who are the called according to his purpose. For whom he did foreknow, he also did predestinate to be conformed to the image of his Son*

– there are some people who argue about predestination. Predestination is not something to be argued about, it is something to be gloried in!

*that he might be the firstborn among many brethren. Moreover whom he did predestinate, them he also called: and whom he called, them he also justified: and whom he justified, them he also gloried. What shall we then say to these things?*

It is the inevitable question.

*If God be for us, who can be against us?*

This is the great logic, is it not?

*He that spared not his own Son, but delivered him up for us all, how shall he not with him also freely give us all things? (Romans 8:28–32)*

Here is a man who knows that God loves him, that God loved him 'before the foundation of the world' (Ephesians 1:4), and set his affection upon him, and predestined him for this glory. He knows he is loved with an everlasting love. The apostle Paul never tires of saying this, and this is just his way of telling us his experience of what Christ said to the woman of Samaria.

Before he became a Christian, Paul had been a very unhappy man, struggling, striving, sweating, trying to keep the Law. His life had been hard, it had been rigid, it had been cold. He was a genius at all times, a giant intellect, but he had known nothing about *love*. Then he met this blessed Christ and he began to love. Why? Because he knew Christ's love to him. He says:

*For I through the law am dead to the law, that I might live unto God. I am crucified with Christ: nevertheless I live; yet not I, but Christ liveth in me: and the life which I now live in the flesh I live by the faith of the Son of God, who loved me, and gave himself for me. (Galatians 2:19–20)*

'The Son of God, who loved me': this is what broke Paul's heart and really enabled him to feel deeply for the first time in his life. He realized on the road to Damascus that that blessed Lord of glory whom he had dismissed as a carpenter and as a 'fellow' had loved him even while he was blaspheming against him and persecuting him, and trying to destroy his church. Paul knew he had been loved and he was being loved, and would be loved for ever and for ever, and he could not get over it. That was why he constantly found that he had to burst out into hymns of praise and thanksgiving. Listen to him trying to express this love in Ephesians 2. He says we were dead in trespasses and sins (verse 1):

*But God, who is rich in mercy, for his great love wherewith he loved us, even when we were dead in sins, hath quickened us together with Christ, (by grace ye are saved;) and hath raised us up together, and made us sit together in heavenly places in Christ Jesus: that in the ages to come he might shew the exceeding riches of his grace in his kindness toward us through Christ Jesus. (Ephesians 2:4–7)*

Paul does not know how to express it. Later on, he says, in effect, 'You know, you Ephesians, I thank God for you. I have been thanking God for you but you have not understood it all, yet I am praying for you. What I am pleading for you is this:'

*That he would grant you, according to the riches of his glory, to be strengthened with might by his Spirit in the inner man.*

What for?

*That Christ may dwell in your hearts by faith; that ye, being rooted and grounded in love, may be able to comprehend with all saints what is the breadth, and length, and depth, and height; and to know the love of Christ*

– the love of Christ to you –

*which passeth knowledge. (Ephesians 3:16–19)*

There is no end to this love. 'Whosoever drinketh of the water that I shall give him shall never thirst.' And Peter, in his simple manner, says, in one of the most moving passages in the whole of the New Testament: 'Humble yourselves therefore' – he is writing to people who are in trouble – 'under the mighty hand of God, that he may exalt you in due time: casting all your care upon him'

– why? – '*for he careth for you*' (1 Peter 5:6–7). Do you know, the whole of the heart of God is in that. God's fatherly love to you, it is all there – 'he careth for you'. He is watching over you, he is loving you with such a love. He has numbered the hairs of your head, he knows them all. He cares for you, and nothing will ever happen to you apart from him. This is the glorious promise that our Lord is making to the woman of Samaria.

And then John, too, knows it – they all know it – it is what made them the men they were. 'And we have known and believed the love that God hath to us.' There is a better translation of that: 'We know the love that God hath to us, and we confide in it' (1 John 4:16). That is it; we rest in it, we are happy in it. We know it; it has been given to us.

So here it is in the New Testament, but we are always in danger, are we not, of saying, 'That was all right, perhaps, in those days and times. But is this sort of thing still true?' Well, the hymn book is the answer to that question, and not only the hymn book, but also the history of the church and the biographies of God's people. Listen to one of them bursting out and putting it like this:

> Loved with everlasting love,
> Led by grace that love to know,
> Spirit, breathing from above,
> Thou hast taught me it is so.
> O this full and perfect peace!
> O this transport all divine!
> In a love which cannot cease,
> I am his, and he is mine.
> *George Wade Robinson*

This is the language of love. You need not read novelettes to know about love. Read the Scriptures, read the hymn books, read the lives of the saints and you begin to learn something about a love that the world knows nothing whatsoever about.

> Come, thou fount of every blessing,
> Tune my heart to sing thy grace!
> Streams of mercy, never ceasing,
> Call for songs of loudest praise.
>
> Teach me some melodious measure,
> Sung by flaming tongues above:
> O the vast, the boundless treasure
> Of my Lord's unchanging love.

This man knows he is loved.

> Here I raise mine Ebenezer;
> Hither by thy help I'm come;
> And I hope, by thy good pleasure
> Safely to arrive at home.
>
> Jesus sought me when a stranger
> Wandering from the fold of God;
> He, to rescue me from danger,
> Interposed his precious blood.
>
> *Robert Robinson*

And on they go, there is no end to this.

> I've found a friend, O such a friend!
> He loved me ere I knew him;
> He drew me with the cords of love,
> And thus he bound me to him.
>
> I've found a friend, O such a friend!
> He bled, he died to save me;
> And not alone the gift of life

But his own self he gave me.
Nought that I have my own I call,
I hold it for the giver:
My heart, my strength, my life, my all
Are his, and his for ever.

I've found a friend, O such a friend!
So kind, and true, and tender,
So wise a counsellor and guide,
So mighty a defender.
From him, who loves me now so well,
What power my soul can sever?
Shall life, or death, or earth or hell?
No; I am his for ever.

*James Grindlay Small*

I have often commended the reading of the journals of George Whitefield and I commend them once more. Read them just for this one element, if for nothing else. Read about how he was so exhausted one day that he could scarcely speak and went to lie on a bed to have a bit of rest and leisure and to sleep. But he could not sleep. Why? Oh, because Christ was pouring transports of his love into his heart. Read the early years of Howell Harris – this also happened to him. And all this is but a confirmation of our Lord's words: 'Whosoever drinketh of the water that I shall give him shall never thirst.' Your desire for love will be more than satisfied for ever. 'Loved with everlasting love!' That is it.

But let me say just one other thing. The heart not only longs to be loved, but it also wants to love, it wants an outlet for its love; and here, again, is a need that can only be fully satisfied in Christ, nowhere else. 'We love him, because he first loved us' (1 John 4:19). I have been quoting to you the statements of the apostle Paul about his realization of the love of God and the love of Christ to him, but he is equally eloquent in his descriptions of his love to them – he is lifted up by it. 'To me to live is Christ, and to die is gain' (Philippians 1:21). This is it – 'to be with Christ; which is far better' (verse 23). Read this man's epistles and you will find that ever and again he bursts forth into some great apostrophe, some great hymn of praise and of thanksgiving and worship and of adoration.

What makes Paul do it? Well, he has just mentioned the word 'Christ' and that thrills him, so off he goes, his love pours forth. Once it was shut up, as it were, corked down by legalism, pharisaism. There is nothing that will ever give an outlet to the heart and its love so much as this blessed and glorious gospel. And so at the very height of Paul's experience you will find him saying this, again in one of his most moving passages, a bit of autobiography. He has been describing what he was by nature, not boasting but saying how he once did boast:

> *But what things were gain to me, those I counted loss for Christ. Yea doubtless, and I count all things but loss for the excellency of the knowledge of Christ Jesus my Lord: for whom I have suffered the loss of all things, and do count them but dung, that I may win Christ.*

Paul will give everything to possess Christ. Nothing else is of value; this is what he wants.

> *And be found in him, not having mine own righteousness, which is of the law, but that which is through the faith of Christ, the righteousness which is of God by faith: that I may know him . . .*
> *(Philippians 3:7–10)*

That is the language of love again. The apostle wants to know the Beloved more and more. This is what is called the Christ mysticism, the Christ intoxication, of Paul. Christians are people who are Christ intoxicated. They love him with the whole of their being; they are 'the bond-slaves of Jesus Christ'.

But, again, you may want to say, 'Ah, but that's only New Testament, is that normal for us?'

Of course it is. The whole of the New Testament is normal for us. The book of the Acts of the Apostles and the Epistles are all normal for us; that is why we have them. And this is verified in the subsequent history of the church. I could keep quoting hymns to you endlessly, and this, too, is preaching, is it not? What is preaching? Quoting Scriptures and hymns! They do it better than I do. God forgive me for having spoken so much. Perhaps the best thing I can do is just to quote Scripture to you, and if that does not move you to the depth of your being, I tell you – go home and find out whether or not you are a Christian. And these hymns; not the tunes, it is the words. The tunes are all right kept in their right position, but people get drunk on tunes and do not realize the words. I am quoting to you, I am not singing. Here they are:

> Jesus, Lover of my soul,
> Let me to thy bosom fly.

Do you know this?

> Thou, O Christ, art all I want,
> More than all in thee I find.
> *Charles Wesley*

Is that true of you?

> Jesus, the very thought of thee,
> With sweetness fills the breast;
> But sweeter far thy face to see,
> And in thy presence rest.
> *Bernard of Clairvaux*

Object of my first desire,
Jesus crucified for me;
All to happiness aspire,
Only to be found in thee.
Thee to please, and thee to know
Constitute my bliss below;
Thee to see, and thee to love,
Constitute my bliss above.
　　　　　*Augustus Toplady*

Oh, yes, says Charles Wesley:

O for a thousand tongues to sing
My great Redeemer's praise . . .
　　　　　*Charles Wesley*

Jesus, these eyes have never seen
That radiant form of thine;
The veil of flesh hangs dark between
Thy blessed face and mine.

I see thee not, I hear thee not,
Yet I am oft with thee;
And earth hath ne'er so dear a spot
As where I meet with thee.
　　　　　*Ray Palmer*

Yes, says Count Zinzendorf, 'I have one passion; it is he, and he alone.' The whole of his heart was taken up.

'Whosoever drinketh of the water that I shall give him shall never thirst.' You will know that you are loved, and you will love with the whole of your being.

36

# The Longing of the Heart, Mind and Will

*Jesus answered and said unto her, Whosoever drinketh of this water shall thirst again: but whosoever drinketh of the water that I shall give him shall never thirst; but the water that I shall give him shall be in him a well of water springing up into everlasting life. (John 4:13–14)*

We have seen that our Lord satisfies completely what I have described as the legitimate desires of the heart – rest, peace, happiness – to give us 'a heart at leisure from itself'. He alone gives that. We have also seen that our desire to be loved is fully satisfied. He lets us know that he has 'loved us with an everlasting love'. And then we ended by showing how he gives us an outlet for our love. There is that within us that makes us feel the desire to love, it is a part of our very nature as God has made us. And we have seen that this, again, is primarily expressed in terms of our attitude to him.

But our Lord's love does not stop there. Not only do we now love him, but also he so deals with us that we have an outlet for our desire to love others. This is equally important because the notion that a Christian is a kind of monk or anchorite, someone who chooses to be separate from the world, and to live in lonely, isolated contemplation and meditation, is quite foreign to the New Testament. That is one of the fallacies of Roman Catholicism and all that type of piety, but that is not New Testament Christianity and it is not Protestant.

No, no; one of the grand discoveries made by Martin Luther was that the servant girl sweeping the floor could be as assured of God's love as the monk or the anchorite in a cell; and therefore we find that one of the great marks of New Testament Christianity is that people begin to love one another. You see the relevance of this to the age and the times in which we live. The world is torn asunder, and not merely the world in terms of nations and countries, but even within nations, classes, groups and so on. Everything is divided – 'middle wall[s] of partition' – and there is no love.

Now our Lord satisfies that need, too. John in his first epistle puts it in a memorable phrase: 'We know that we have passed from death unto life, because we love the brethren' (1 John 3:14). In other words, we have been brought into the fellowship of God's people – and we rejoice in this. We have come into a great family. We find that we are now interested in and love people in whom before we had no interest at all. Here is this extraordinary one-ness – 'to make in himself . . . one new man' (Ephesians 2:15) – and so the fellowship of Christian people is always a great characteristic of the Christian life. It is not surprising, therefore, that in one of the first accounts that we have of the early Christians, this element is brought out very prominently.

*Then they that gladly received his word were baptized: and the same day there were added unto them about three thousand souls. And they*

*continued stedfastly in the apostles' doctrine and fellowship, and in*
*breaking of bread, and in prayers. (Acts 2:41–42)*

It happened immediately; they were taken out of the world and were drawn together. They wanted to spend all their time with the apostles and with the company of Christians; they wanted the teaching, the doctrine, but also the fellowship. This is always one of the first signs of the rebirth. The one who is born again is anxious to be with such people – birds of a feather flock together. You are aware of this common interest, common life, common expectation, common everything. And so I go on and read this:

*And fear came upon every soul: and many wonders and signs were done*
*by the apostles. And all that believed were together, and had all things*
*common; and sold their possessions and goods, and parted them to all*
*men, as every man had need. And they, continuing daily with one accord*
*in the temple, and breaking bread from house to house, did eat their*
*meat with gladness and singleness of heart, praising God, and having*
*favour with all the people. (Acts 2:43–47)*

Now that is a lyrical picture, is it not? But that is what our Lord had promised, that is what he does. He gives an outlet to this gregarious instinct, if you like, this longing for fellowship and for friendship and for community, for being together. You can express it and make your contribution and give to others.

This is one of the themes of the New Testament. Again, our Lord, in that great statement that he made on the last day of the feast at Jerusalem, put it like this: 'If any man thirst, let him come unto me, and drink. He that believeth on me, as the Scripture hath said, out of his belly [out of his innermost parts] shall flow rivers of living water' (John 7:37–38). Christian men and women are a blessing and a benediction to other people, it does not matter where they are – among Christian people especially, but also everywhere. These blessings flow out, and so the land is fructified, as it were.

Now our Lord, and he alone, enables us to love in this way. This desire to love is there in us, though it has been blunted, of course; sin has perverted and twisted everything. Humanity was never meant to be fighting as it is, we were meant to love one another and to work together and to help one another; and though sin has marred it, there is still that in us that cries out for this. And our Lord gives a full outlet to this longing to love in a way that nobody else does. And that, as I said, is the striking feature and characteristic of the life of the early church, as it has been of the church in every period of revival and reformation.

Read the history; this fellowship is one of the wonderful characteristics of the work of the Spirit. It is his special work: 'the communion [the fellowship] of the Holy Ghost' (2 Corinthians 13:14) – and not only fellowship with him and with the Father and the Son, but fellowship with one another. The great characteristic of those little groups before the Protestant Reformation, was the way they kept together and enjoyed one another's society and talked about Christian things; and it was again the mark of the early Protestants, Puritans and early Methodists. They did not believe in isolation and only occasionally coming together. No, no! There was a blending and a unity and an outlet for the love that was within them.

> Blest be the tie that binds
> Our hearts in Jesu's love;
> The fellowship of Christian minds
> Is like to that above.
>
> *John Fawcett*

There it is – this one-ness, this unity, and it is given its full scope by this blessed life that he is ready to give us so freely.

That, then, we should think about and rejoice in and, at the same time, we should examine ourselves. Do you love the brethren? Would you sooner spend your day with Christian people than with the greatest people in the world who are not Christians? That is the sort of test we apply. 'We know that we have passed from death unto life, because we love the brethren' (1 John 3:14). We know that we belong together, we are related, we are 'fellowcitizens with the saints, and of the household of God' (Ephesians 2:19), we are 'children of the heavenly King'.

But then let me go on to another aspect, which is equally important, perhaps even more so. He gives us an outlet for our desire to be *glorying*. I think you will agree, again, that this desire is very powerful in human nature – the desire to glory in various things. Human beings by nature like to glory in themselves, they like to glory in other people, certain outstanding people, and they like to glory in their country. I need not elaborate on this, we are all aware of it. History teaches it very plainly. Ultimately, it is the cause of most wars: My country right or wrong. My country can do no wrong. This is a part of us, is it not? We are hero worshippers and we are ever ready to glory in this or that, and we spend so much of our time in praising people, praising countries, praising institutions, praising different events.

You notice that I am putting this under the heading of the 'legitimate' desires of the heart, and I want to show you why. We have perverted this desire – man in sin has perverted everything. But we must be very careful that we do not condemn something in and of itself because we have perverted it. The instinct for food must not be condemned because some people are gluttons. The desire for drink, likewise, must not be condemned because people drink too much. So with sex, so with everything. You must not dismiss or condemn instincts because people abuse them and become their slaves. And I feel that this principle also applies to the whole question of glorying. Glorying is a part of human nature – badly misused, of course, and as a result, productive of human tragedy. But when our Lord deals with us and when he gives us of this water and we drink it, this particular desire also is given full scope and an outlet, and it becomes one of the most wonderful things of all for the Christian.

Let me show you something of what I mean. The apostle Paul particularly emphasizes this in all his writings. Read his epistles and keep your eye on the word 'glorying in', which really should be translated 'boasting'. It is his great word, he constantly uses it, and, of course, it is not surprising. Before his conversion, Paul was a man who knew a good deal about glorying. He was not backward in that respect. He was a man of outstanding gifts and he was aware of them, as such men usually are. He said:

*Though I might also have confidence in the flesh. If any other man thinketh that he hath whereof he might trust in the flesh, I more: circumcised the eighth day, of the stock of Israel, of the tribe of Benjamin, an Hebrew of the Hebrews; as touching the law, a Pharisee; concerning zeal, persecuting the church; touching the righteousness which is in the law, blameless. (Philippians 3:4–6)*

That is glorying. Paul says, in effect, 'If you want to start talking about boasting, I am ready to take you on. If you think you have anything to boast about, listen to this, here is my record, here is my position. Look who I am, take my ancestry, take my nation, take the blood that is in me. Talk about ability, talk about morality, talk about religion, come along, I am ready to meet you.' Boasting! It was his characteristic, not only as a Pharisee but as a quite exceptional man in so many respects; and there is nothing more wonderful to me about this man than the way in which all that is, as it were, taken hold of and sublimated and transformed and transfigured by the Lord Jesus Christ and made one of the most wonderful things of all.

And so it is not at all surprising that the apostle keeps on talking about glorying, and referring to it in so many ways. He glories in the Lord himself. Take these words from the First Epistle to the Corinthians:

*Ye see your calling, brethren, how that not many wise men after the flesh, not many mighty, not many noble, are called*

– that is what the world glories in, is it not – wise man, mighty, noble –

*but God hath chosen the foolish things of the world to confound the wise; and God hath chosen the weak things of the world to confound the things which are mighty; and base things of the world, and things which are despised, hath God chosen, yea, and things which are not, to bring to nought things that are*

– why? –

*that no flesh should glory in his presence. But of him are ye in Christ Jesus, who of God is made unto us wisdom, and righteousness, and sanctification, and redemption: that, according as it is written, He that glorieth, let him glory in the Lord. (1 Corinthians 1:26–31)*

That was Paul's position. Again, he says to the Philippians: You are being troubled by certain Judaizers who are telling you that it is not enough to believe in Christ, that you must be circumcised, that you must belong to the circumcision. What are they talking about? 'For we are the circumcision' – who are 'we'? – 'which worship God in the spirit, and rejoice in Christ Jesus, and have no confidence in the flesh' (Philippians 3:3). That is it – 'rejoice in Christ Jesus'.

But I suppose we will all agree that one of the most moving statements that the apostle ever made in this respect is in his Epistle to the Galatians. He is dealing, again, with the people who are trying to get others to become Jews, to 'add on' this or that to their Christian faith, saying that keeping the Jewish Law was essential, in addition to believing in Christ. But the apostle is impatient with it all and this is how he puts it:

*But God forbid that I should glory, save in the cross of our Lord Jesus Christ, by whom the world is crucified unto me, and I unto the world. For in Christ Jesus neither circumcision availeth any thing, nor uncircumcision, but a new creature. And as many as walk according to this rule, peace be on them, and mercy, and upon the Israel of God. From henceforth let no man trouble me. (Galatians 6:14–17)*

That is the position: 'God forbid that I should glory, save in the cross of our Lord Jesus Christ.' In whom are you glorying? About whom are you talking? Are you talking about men? 'Let no man trouble me,' says Paul (Galatians 6:17). Do not talk to me about men. He does not want to talk about anybody except the Lord Jesus Christ. He glories in him, and in him alone.

Now this desire to glorify was always there in the apostle but it was wrong before, it was under sin. Now it is in Christ, and all the intensity of this noble, majestic nature, this desire to praise and to glory in and to glorify, has its full outlet. Here is a theme that can never be exhausted. Here is one who is worthy to be praised. And, of course, Paul not only says this about the Lord himself, the Saviour, but he glories equally in the salvation that we have in the Lord, and he is never tired of saying this. He writes to the Romans that he has been longing to come to Rome to preach the gospel to them, as he has in other places:

> *I am debtor both to the Greeks, and to the Barbarians; both to the wise, and to the unwise. So, as much as in me is, I am ready to preach the gospel to you that are at Rome also. For I am not ashamed of the gospel of Christ*

– now that is a figure of speech, which is called litotes. Paul puts the point he is making negatively in order to emphasize it yet more. When he says, 'I am not ashamed of' he means 'I am very proud of', 'I glory in', 'I exult in', 'I triumph in', 'it is the biggest thing in my life', 'I will lay aside everything else for this.'

> *I am not ashamed of the gospel of Christ*

– he is writing to Christians in Rome, the imperial city, home of the emperors, seat of government, centre of learning, art, literature – the centre of the world. 'I am not ashamed of my gospel,' says Paul. I am not ashamed to come to Rome, I do not care where I am. I have preached it in the villages and the hamlets of Asia, I am equally ready to come to the great imperial city because, in the last analysis, what does it have with all its pomp and show? –

> *for it is the power of God unto salvation*

– greater than all your imperial powers put together and multiplied –

> *to every one that believeth; to the Jew first, and also to the Greek. (Romans 1:14–16)*

A universal gospel! The power of God! He is not ashamed. Of course not. He glories in it. And in the same way, Paul says to the Ephesians:

*For by grace are ye saved through faith; and that not of yourselves: it is the gift of God: not of works, lest any man should boast. For we are his workmanship, created in Christ Jesus unto good works, which God hath before ordained that we should walk in them. (Ephesians 2:8–10)*

Oh, I could keep you endlessly in just quoting these magnificent statements that the apostle makes! Here is another and, again, one that is very moving:

*We preach not ourselves, but Christ Jesus the Lord; and ourselves your servants for Jesus' sake. For God, who commanded the light to shine out of darkness, hath shined in our hearts, to give the light of the knowledge of the glory of God in the face of Jesus Christ. But we have this treasure*

– and what a treasure it is –

*in earthen vessels, that the excellency of the power may be of God, and not of us. (2 Corinthians 4:5–7)*

And then there is the grand climax of it all in the Epistle to the Romans. Paul has been working out the mighty argument concerning the gospel. He deals with every problem, even the problem of the Jews – who were not believing the gospel but rejecting it, and had crucified their Messiah, and of the Gentiles – who were crowding into the kingdom. People were saying, 'How do you reconcile all this? What about the promises of God to the fathers in the Old Testament? Do the promises cover all this?' And the apostle has worked out the great argument in chapters 9 and 10 and the bulk of chapter 11. Then, having said it all, he stops and stands back, and there is only one thing to do, it is to break out into a great hymn of adoration and of praise, a mighty apostrophe:

*O the depth of the riches both of the wisdom and knowledge of God! how unsearchable are his judgments, and his ways past finding out! For who hath known the mind of the Lord? or who hath been his counsellor? or who hath first given to him, and it shall be recompensed unto him again? For of him, and through him, and to him, are all things: to whom be glory for ever and ever. Amen. (Romans 11:33–36)*

There it is. Paul glories in the Saviour, the Lord, and he glories in the mighty salvation. Oh, yes, you can talk about 'the simple gospel'. It is, in a sense – it can save a child. But it is not simple in an ultimate sense, it is profound – 'the depth of the riches' – the treasures of God's wisdom and knowledge, all in this blessed person.

But the apostle's glorying is not confined to what he thinks and says about the Lord and about the great salvation, it goes as far as this: he is ready to die for it. This is it: hero worship; he is ready to die for him. He has already suffered, and is prepared to suffer endlessly for him.

But this was not confined to the great apostle, it was true of all the apostles, and of other Christians. There is a wonderful statement at the end of Acts chapter 5. The apostles had been arrested and thrown into prison, and they had escaped in a wonderful manner. Then they were arrested again and brought before the high court, the Sanhedrin, and had it not been for the pleading of a certain man, whose name was Gamaliel, they would all undoubtedly have been killed, and they knew that perfectly well. But they were sent out of court and were commanded not to speak in the name of Jesus. They were allowed to go free on condition that they stopped preaching and teaching about this blessed person. Then this is what I read:

*And they [the apostles and the company] departed from the presence of the council, rejoicing that they were counted worthy to suffer shame for his name.*

They gloried in the fact that they were suffering. Their greatest honour was to suffer dishonour for him. That is the test of the true Christian. And so we read:

*And daily in the temple, and in every house, they ceased not to teach and preach Jesus Christ. (Acts 5:41–42)*

And, I repeat, the same is true of the apostle Paul. He gives that great list of the things in which he can boast, and then he turns on it all and says: 'But what things were gain to me, those I counted loss for Christ. Yea doubtless, and I count all things but loss for the excellency of the knowledge of Christ Jesus my Lord' (Philippians 3:7–8).

Then here he is, an old man now, writing his last letter, probably, the Second Epistle to Timothy, knowing that he can be put to death at any moment. And this is how he puts it:

*I am now ready to be offered, and the time of my departure is at hand. I have fought a good fight, I have finished my course, I have kept the faith: Henceforth there is laid up for me a crown of righteousness, which the Lord, the righteous judge, shall give me at that day: and not to me only, but unto all them also that love his appearing. (2 Timothy 4:6–8)*

This is the characteristic of the New Testament Christians: 'They loved not their own lives unto the death' (Revelation 12:11). They so gloried in him that they considered it the supreme honour of their lives to be martyred. Martyrdom, to the early Christians, was the final crown of glory, the accolade that was given to the soldier in the army of the living God.

Now this is a part of our Lord's claim. He says, 'Whosoever drinketh of the water that I shall give him shall never thirst.' All this longing that is in us to give glory has its full outlet in him.

And it is a theme that will last throughout eternity. Here is a wonderful and thorough test that we can apply to ourselves. Are we glorying in him? Are we glorying in this great salvation? Are we ready, if necessary, to lay down our lives for him? Like these early Christians, would we account it the greatest honour to suffer dishonour for his name's sake? Like the apostle, can we say 'To me to live is Christ, and to die is gain'? Here it is: glorying in him and in his cross, in his great salvation, ready to forsake the world and all it has, if needs be life itself, rather than cease to glory in him, and in him alone.

Then let me just mention one other matter. This theme is endless, you will never exhaust it. But let us not forget that he deals with these desires of the heart not only positively but also negatively. He does it by getting rid of and delivering us from the false and the wrong ideas that we have in our hearts. He not only gives us a positive theme to draw out all that is legitimate within us, but he also gets rid of that which is wrong and illegitimate – selfishness, ambition, lust, jealousy, envy, pride. It is these that lead to dissatisfaction, unhappiness and restlessness. He shows us how wrong all that is.

When we look at him, how ashamed we feel when we think of selfishness! 'Let this mind be in you, which was also in Christ Jesus: who, being in the form of God, thought it not robbery to be equal with God' (Philippians 2:5–6). He did not hold on to that; he laid it aside for our sake. So are we going to hold on to our rights or claims, our birth, our country or anything else? The idea is monstrous! 'The meek and lowly Jesus' – and he shames us. He makes us feel that to do that is despicable, so unworthy, so unlike him. We look at him and we get to know him, and these evil desires are made so ugly and foul and vile that we long to get rid of them and be delivered from them. And he can do that.

But our Lord also gives an equal satisfaction to the conscience and to the will – if he failed at this point, again, his claim would not be justified. Of course, as I have already indicated, you must not make these divisions too absolute. There are distinctions but each merges into the other. What I am trying to say is that he deals with our failures. 'Whosoever drinketh of the water that I shall give him shall never thirst.' What! Even when I fail, even when I fall into sin, even when I do wrong? Oh, what a prolific cause of dissatisfaction and of unhappiness! How often does the pastor have to deal with this! 'I have fallen into sin. I have failed. I have been unworthy.' The devil comes in and I am cast down.

Now here is a tremendous need that we all know from experience. Who can give us satisfaction at this point? Of course, morality cannot, neither the old morality nor the new morality. The old morality cannot help us because it just condemns us and tells us that we should not have failed. The new morality cannot help us either because it tells us that it does not matter at all what we do, and we know that that is not true because our conscience is telling us that we have done wrong. But can our Lord help us? He is the Son of God; he never sinned. Is it possible that he can help me when I fail? Surely, he who never failed at all, who was without sin and who was so pure, cannot help me here? Surely, he is the last person to whom I can turn when I fall?

But to think that is terribly wrong. This is one of the glories of this gospel. It is to him above all that you can go when you fall or when you fail. Look at him. This is what we are told about him, this was the prophecy concerning him before he ever came: 'A bruised reed shall he not break, and the smoking flax shall he not quench' (Isaiah 42:3). And when he came, he turned out to be like that. Who was he? He was the pure, holy Son of God, yet what I read is: 'Then drew near unto him all the publicans and sinners for to hear him' (Luke 15:1). This is one of the glories of the gospel; it is a paradox. It is the holy that attracts the publicans and sinners. They were never attracted by the Pharisees. The Pharisee in his self-righteousness drew his skirts up, he kept apart, he despised, he looked down upon. Oh, but here is the blessed Son of God and publicans and sinners 'drew near unto him'. The poor man of Gadara with a legion of devils in him, he 'ran' to him (Mark 5:6).

Look at his dealing with people in sin. There is a woman caught in the very act of sin, and the self-righteous bring her forward, saying, 'Now, what is your judgement?' He begins to write on the sand, on the dust, and they all slink out. Then he says, 'Where are those thine accusers?. . . Neither do I condemn thee: go, and sin no more' (John 8:10–11). His compassion, his pity, his readiness to forgive, his encouragement to the failures. This was his greatest characteristic.

But I suppose the supreme example is the apostle Peter himself, the impulsive, self-confident Peter. He says: Though all men should deny you, I will never deny you. I will walk with you through hell. There is nothing I will not do for you.

But you remember what happens. Our Lord is arrested, he is on trial. Peter, out of curiosity and also affection, slips into the courtyard. When he is recognized and challenged by a maid, he denies it, and says, 'No, I know nothing about him.' He denies his Lord with oaths and curses. And we are told one of the most tremendous things, I sometimes think, in all the accounts of our Lord: 'And the Lord turned, and looked upon Peter' (Luke 22:61). Ah, there was a rebuke in it, but it was not only rebuke, it was pity, it was sympathy, and it was understanding.

And so we find in the last chapter of this Gospel of John, in that lyrical scene by the lakeside, that our Lord takes Peter over this very failure, and he does not merely condemn him. He makes him realize that he must not trust in himself and in the flesh, but he also gives him his commission: 'Feed my lambs . . . feed my sheep' (John 21:15–16). Peter is restored. He is not dismissed; he is not condemned. Our Lord sees that he is humble and penitent and contrite, and he forgives it all, renews the commission and sends him on his way rejoicing. Our Lord is like that always. And this is the truth on which we rely, in which we glory and which keeps us going. He is still the same! 'I am he that liveth, and was dead; and, behold, I am alive for evermore' (Revelation 1:18).

> Though he ascended up on high,
> He bends on earth a brother's eye;
> Partaker of the human name,
> He knows the frailty of our frame.
>
> Our fellow-sufferer yet retains
> A fellow-feeling of our pains,
> And still remembers, in the skies,
> His tears, and agonies, and cries.
> *Michael Bruce*

He was, while he was here, 'in all points tempted like as we are' (Hebrews 4:15). He knows the force, the power, of the devil and of hell, and so when he sees you faltering and falling, he sympathizes, and not only that: 'in that he himself hath suffered being tempted, he is able to succour them that are tempted' (Hebrews 2:18).

Then, in addition, we read in the first chapter of John's first epistle:

*If we say that we have fellowship with him, and walk in darkness, we lie, and do not the truth*

– we have often done that –

> *but if we walk in the light, as he is in the light, we have fellowship one with another, and the blood of Jesus Christ his Son cleanseth us from all sin.*

Listen!

> *If we say that we have no sin, we deceive ourselves, and the truth is not in us. If we confess our sins, he is faithful and just to forgive us our sins, and to cleanse us from all unrighteousness. (1 John 1:6–9)*

And that is still true.

> *My little children, these things write I unto you, that ye sin not. And if any man sin*

– do not trade on this, but remember it; do not let the devil keep you grovelling on the ground, condemning yourself and feeling you are not a Christian –

> *we have an advocate with the Father, Jesus Christ the righteous: and he is the propitiation for our sins: and not for ours only, but also for the sins of the whole world. (1 John 2:1–2)*

That is what happens when you sin. And what about your weakness? Well, it is the same: he is always there, it is his strength. We look at the task and at the world, the flesh and the devil and the glory of our calling and we say, 'Who is sufficient for these things?' (2 Corinthians 2:16). And there is only one answer: 'Our sufficiency is of God' (2 Corinthians 3:5). We look at him; it is his strength, not ours. 'Come unto me,' our Lord said, 'all ye that labour, and are heavy laden, and I will give you rest. Take my yoke upon you, and learn of me . . . my yoke is easy, and my burden is light' (Matthew 11:29–30). Be yoked with him, so, whatever the task, he is with you and he is bearing it with you. Look at his power, the infinity of his power; he gives you new life and he does not leave you to yourself.

> *The law of the Spirit of life in Christ Jesus has made me free from the law of sin and death. For what the law could not do, in that it was weak through the flesh, God sending his own Son in the likeness of sinful flesh, and for sin, condemned sin in the flesh: that the righteousness of the law might be fulfilled in us, who walk not after the flesh, but after the Spirit. (Romans 8:2–4)*

You must 'mortify the deeds of the body' – how can you do that? 'If ye *through the Spirit* do mortify the deeds of the body' (Romans 8:13). Oh, yes, we are 'earthen vessels': 'We have this treasure in earthen vessels, that the excellency of the power may be of God, and not of us' (2 Corinthians 4:7). So however weak you may feel at this moment, the word that comes to you is the word that tells you, 'Put on the whole armour of God' (Ephesians 6:11); 'Be strong in the Lord, and in the power of his might' (Ephesians 6:10). It is the only way that even Paul could keep on going and preaching. This is how he puts it:

> *Whom we preach, warning every man, and teaching every man in all wisdom; that we may present every man perfect in Christ Jesus: whereunto I also labour, striving*

– how? –

> *according to his working, which worketh in me mightily. (Colossians 1:28–29)*

And undergirding it all is just this: 'When I am weak, then am I strong.' Why? Well, because, 'My grace is sufficient for thee' (2 Corinthians 12:10, 9), and it always will be.

So, you see, he satisfies every desire, not only of the mind and of the heart, but also of the conscience and the will. 'Whosoever drinketh of the water that I shall give him shall never, no, *never*, thirst; but the water that I shall give him shall be in him a well of water springing up into everlasting life.'

37

# In Trials and Tribulations

*Jesus answered and said unto her, Whosoever drinketh of this water shall thirst again: but whosoever drinketh of the water that I shall give him shall never thirst; but the water that I shall give him shall be in him a well of water springing up into everlasting life. (John 4:13–14)*

We have made an extensive review of the supreme excellency of the gospel and all that our Lord has to give us. We have looked at it from all aspects and all angles. But I imagine that there is still one question that is left in our minds and in our hearts. This is typical of unbelief, typical, particularly, of the suggestions that the devil is ever ready to insinuate into our minds. The question is this: All right, you've displayed the gospel, you've unfolded it, and we must agree that it does seem at the moment to satisfy the various demands of our hearts and wills and minds, but will it always? Will it in all circumstances and under all conditions?

Now this question arises because this is the result of our experience. There are many ideas that have interested us and attracted us and have seemed to us to be very good. We were quite well at the time and our circumstances were very favourable, and this teaching, whatever it was, seemed eminently satisfactory. But a time came when we lost our health, perhaps, or had some disappointment or sorrow, or circumstances went against us, and we suddenly found that these ideas about which we had thought so much did not help us, and in fact were of no value to us at all. This was a teaching, a philosophy, that was quite all right when, in a sense, we did not need any help, but just at the moment of our greatest need and trouble, it let us down.

This is a very common experience. You trust teachings, you trust people, you trust things, but sooner or later you find that just when you need them most of all, they fail you completely – they are fair-weather friends that desert you in the hour of your trial. So it is not a bit surprising that this kind of questioning should arise within us and we want to know: Does the gospel *always* give satisfaction?

And our Lord's claim is that it does, so we must examine it again. We are living in a world such that trials and tribulations are inevitable. There is the whole strain of living, the contradictions of life, the contradictions within ourselves, the contradictions of people, the difficulties that seem to arise in various ways all around us. To refuse to face this is to show folly. Of course, that is the folly of the world; it does not like facing problems and difficulties. The world says, 'Let's eat, drink, and be merry, let's enjoy the moment.' But the Bible, while it tells us not to worry about the future, nevertheless does encourage us to think about it and to make sure that we have a view of life that covers every conceivable eventuality.

So this is the great question: Does this gospel, does this life that our Lord is offering to give us so freely, does it really still satisfy us even when all things seem against us to drive us to despair?

This is obviously a most important matter. It is important from the standpoint of our experience and our happiness and joy and peace in the Christian life and from the standpoint of facing the future. It is also extremely important from the standpoint of testing us and of making sure that we really are Christians. The Bible teaches us, and we know from experience and from the history of the church in particular, that it is quite possible for people to think they are Christians when they are not Christians at all. Again, we are faced with the subtlety of the devil, who can turn himself into an 'angel of light' (2 Corinthians 11:14), so that we imagine that we are Christians and are perfectly happy until we suddenly find that we are not. We have the authority of our Lord himself for saying that we can be deceived in this way, and may be just using Christian terminology without having any real life within us.

Now our Lord has put this once and for all in a very clear way in the parable of the Sower. In this parable, the sower goes out to sow and casts his seed on different kinds of ground, but only some of the seed produces grain. After telling the parable, our Lord goes on to analyse its meaning. He says:

> *Hear ye therefore the parable of the sower. When any one heareth the word of the kingdom, and understandeth it not, then cometh the wicked one, and catcheth away that which was sown in his heart. This is he which received seed by the way side. But he that received the seed into stony places, the same is he that heareth the word, and anon with joy receiveth it*

– he thinks he has become a Christian –

> *yet hath he not root in himself, but dureth for a while: for when tribulation or persecution ariseth because of the word, by and by he is offended.*

He thought he was a Christian, he appeared to be, but persecution tests him and it soon shows that he is not a Christian at all, there was never any root there. There was some temporary reaction to the gospel but not a real response. Then our Lord goes on:

*He also that received seed among the thorns is he that heareth the word; and the care of this world, and the deceitfulness of riches, choke the word, and he becometh unfruitful.*

Again, he is not a Christian, though there was an immediate, temporary response. And then the contrast:

*But he that received seed into the good ground is he that heareth the word, and understandeth it; which also beareth fruit, and bringeth forth, some an hundredfold, some sixty, some thirty. (Matthew 13:18–23)*

Now in many ways the point of that parable is that it is the coming of trials and troubles, whether persecution or the cares of life in this world, that ultimately test us. They not only show the value of the gospel, but test us at the same time and reveal very clearly whether we have this well of water within us 'springing up into everlasting life', or whether we have just made some temporary, superficial reaction to the gospel.

So this is a most important matter from every standpoint and it is a very prominent teaching in the New Testament. Our Lord himself deals with this very often and it is his claim that the gospel never fails. On the question of persecution, he says this:

*Blessed [happy, to be congratulated] are ye when men shall revile you, and persecute you, and shall say all manner of evil against you falsely, for my sake. Rejoice, and be exceeding glad: for great is your reward in heaven: for so persecuted they the prophets which were before you. (Matthew 5:11–12)*

Far from being offended by persecution and drying out and proving that you had no root at all, you rejoice – you are in a blessed, in a happy, position. That is our Lord's teaching. And later on, he says, 'In the world ye shall have tribulation: but be of good cheer [cheer up]; I have overcome the world' (John 16:33). He warns his followers to expect trouble: 'If they have called the master of the house Beelzebub, how much more shall they call them of his household?' (Matthew 10:25). He warns that the world will be against us. The world is always against the true Christian. Christianity is not popular with the world. Our Lord says: The world hated me before it hated you.

This teaching is not confined to our Lord himself; we find it also in the book of Acts. The apostle Paul, going around the churches, warned the Christians that 'we must through much tribulation enter into the kingdom of God' (Acts 14:22). And he is quite explicit about this in the Epistle to the Philippians: 'Unto you', he says, 'it is given in the behalf of Christ, not only to believe on him, but also to suffer for his name's sake' (Philippians 1:29).

We find the same teaching in James: 'My brethren, count it all joy when ye fall into divers temptations', which means trials (James 1:2). And Peter is equally explicit in his first epistle, where he puts it like this:

*Beloved, think it not strange concerning the fiery trial which is to try you, as though some strange thing happened unto you: but rejoice, inasmuch as ye are partakers of Christ's sufferings; that, when his glory shall be revealed, ye may be glad also with exceeding joy. If ye be reproached for the name of Christ, happy are ye; for the spirit of glory and of God resteth upon you: on their part he is evil spoken of, but on your part he is glorified . . . judgment must begin at the house of God. (1 Peter 4:12–14, 17)*

So the teaching of Scripture is quite clear; that is one of its glories. It does not say, 'Believe in the Lord Jesus Christ and you will never have another problem or trouble, all is going to be wonderful.' It tells you the exact opposite. It tells you that, by becoming a disciple of his, the world will be against you in a way it has never been before, and you will be tried and tested; and, of course, history proves that this is what happens in practice.

I have reminded you of that marvellous statement at the end of Acts chapter 5, when the apostles departed from the presence of the council, 'rejoicing that they were counted worthy to suffer shame for his name' (Acts 5:41). And we find the same theme of suffering for Christ in the wonderful story in Acts chapter 12, where we read of how the apostle Peter was arrested. James had already been arrested and put to death, and Peter was now arrested and thrown into prison. It happened to be just before Easter and there was a rule that no man should be killed at that time (Acts 12:3–4), so Peter was allowed to languish in prison, the intention being to bring him out after Easter and to put him to death. And a most extraordinary thing is said in that story. Peter was there in prison, and, as a Jew, he knew perfectly well that he was alive only because this was the time of unleavened bread. Then we come to the very last night of the days of unleavened bread, and this is the marvellous thing we are told:

> *Prayer was made without ceasing of the church unto God for him. And when Herod would have brought him forth, the same night Peter was sleeping between two soldiers, bound with two chains: and the keepers before the door kept the prison. (Acts 12:5–6)*

Now do you get the significance of that? Here is a man who is chained to two soldiers, one on each side, and who knows that in a few hours he is to be brought out and executed, and yet what we are told about him is that he is soundly asleep! Do you think you would be able to sleep under such circumstances? This is the gospel, here it is in operation. Our Lord says that whoever drinks the water that he will give will never thirst. Though Peter knows his life is to be taken in a few hours, he sleeps like a newborn babe.

And then there is another equally remarkable and lyrical example in the sixteenth chapter of Acts. Paul and Silas were badly maltreated at Philippi, their backs were scourged, they were thrust into the innermost prison and their feet were fastened in the stocks. But this is what I read: 'And at midnight Paul and Silas prayed, and sang praises unto God' (Acts 16:25). It is not merely that they were not grumbling and complaining, they were singing praises to God, though their backs were aching as the result of the lashing and the scourging and their poor feet were fastened in the stocks. Now there we see this rejoicing in practice.

So what does it all mean? It means that our Lord not only promises to enable us to bear our troubles and trials and tribulations without fainting or faltering, but he promises also – and all his apostles and teachers promise this after him – that we shall not only be able to bear them but that we shall glory in them, that we shall rejoice in them, that we shall be more than conquerors. Not just conquerors, but *more than* conquerors. There is a plus here.

Now this is one of the most marvellous and glorious aspects of the gospel and this is where it differs from every other teaching. Our Lord is right: 'Whosoever drinketh of this water shall thirst again.' The world at its very best and highest knows nothing at all about this. Oh, I know the world can rise to the great heights of Stoicism but that is the limit of its rising; it has never gone beyond that. There is something very wonderful about Stoicism, I know. People sometimes talk about 'the Roman'; a certain statesman is regarded as 'the last of the Romans'. I suppose it is all right but it is all negative, it is resignation. There is a kind of nobility about the person who can stand when everybody is whimpering and crying and falling or running away and disappearing. It is rather heroic to see someone just standing and refusing to give in or to give up. I agree. But such people are not singing praises, are they? They are not rejoicing, they are not smiling, they are not 'more than conquerors'. No, no; they just refuse to give in, they just have grit, they are sticking at it, just holding on, just standing, and no more. But here there is an entirely different atmosphere, there is an overplus, there is a triumph, a joy: 'shall never, no, never, thirst as long as the world stands'. In other words, they are filled with the spirit of rejoicing and of victory and of exultation.

So here is the great question: How does the gospel do this? Or let me put it still more accurately: How does our Lord do this to us? What is this water that he gives us? How does it work? What is there about it and how does it so operate that it brings us to this position that we are more than conquerors when everything is against us?

Many answers are given to this question in the New Testament. There is no better one than the passage from 2 Corinthians 4 where the apostle Paul deals extensively with this subject. He starts off by saying, 'But we have this treasure [this gospel] in earthen vessels, that the excellency of the power may be of God, and not of us' (2 Corinthians 4:7). He then goes on to say that this is true of him and then he gives a list of the trials, troubles, tribulations, the bombardment of the world, the flesh, the devil, evil forces and powers, everything set against him to get him down. Yet Paul tells us that he has not been got down, and in this passage he lets us into the secret.

And 2 Corinthians 4 is by no means the only passage. The end of the eighth chapter of the Epistle to the Romans, where the apostle gives us his great teaching concerning time and life in this world, is equally important in this respect. So let us consider what the teaching is because the end of Romans 8 is a good summary of our Lord's own teaching, and of the teaching of all the other apostles. Paul says that he is more than conqueror in spite of all that is happening to him because the gospel, this Christian view of life, this life that is in him, enables him to see everything differently. He repeats this in 2 Corinthians 5:17: 'If any man be in Christ, he is a new creature [new creation]: old things are passed away; behold, all things are become new.' And that is a literal fact. The Christian sees everything in a different way from the non-Christian. Do not forget the list that Paul has given in 2 Corinthians 4 – it is so important. He says:

> *We are troubled on every side, yet not distressed; we are perplexed, but not in despair; persecuted, but not forsaken; cast down, but not destroyed; always bearing about in the body the dying of the Lord Jesus, that the life also of Jesus might be made manifest in our body. For we which live are alway delivered unto death for Jesus' sake, that the life also of Jesus might be made manifest in our mortal flesh. So then death worketh in us, but life in you. (2 Corinthians 4:8–12)*

And yet, looking at all that together, Paul says: 'For our light affliction, which is but for a moment, worketh for us a far more exceeding and eternal weight of glory' (2 Corinthians 4:17). 'Our *light affliction*' – can you picture this? Consider what was happening to this man, and yet he looks at it all and he says, 'our light affliction'! Is this just some sort of self-hypnotism, some refusal to face the facts? Of course not. There is something profound here; any other teaching only deludes you – you are not facing the facts. But here is a man who is facing them, he gives the list, he puts it all down, and there it is. Yet he says, 'light affliction'.

But in what way can Paul possibly say that all this is but a light affliction? And there is only one answer. He is a man who has an entirely new view of the whole of life and of himself. Before his conversion, he used to think of himself as a man who always deserved the best. He thought that he deserved happiness, joy and peace; never should any problem come his way. That is what the natural person always thinks and expects, and when things go against him, of course, he is annoyed, he is upset, he goes down. But here is a man who has become a Christian and he realizes now that he deserves nothing good, that if he really had his deserts, he would be in a much worse position than he is. But, above all, he now thinks of himself as a soul. Before he only thought of himself in his relationship to the world: success, making money, getting on, popularity, a thousand and one things. But not any longer. He knows now that the one thing that matters is that he has a soul, an eternal soul, and that he is a pilgrim of eternity.

Then add to that Paul's whole view of the meaning of life. What is life for? What is its meaning and purpose? Is it just to have enjoyment, just to get a kick? Are we here merely to eat and drink and indulge in sex – is that the whole of life? Obviously, thousands think it is, and when they are deprived of these in any shape or form, they go down, they have no resources, nothing at all to fall back on. But Christians see that the world is not their home; it is a kind of preparatory school, and their destiny is elsewhere. This is not the only world, this is not the only life. 'Our light affliction,' says the apostle. These things do not touch him very much. He is human, he is not unnatural, he does not, like the Christian Scientist, say that there is no pain or there is no difficulty, because that is not true. There is pain, there is difficulty, there is disease. But what he says is that if the world does everything that it can, if it kills him, so what? It is the soul that matters; and the soul is ultimately beyond the reach of these problems.

And then there comes in the tremendously important element of time: 'Our light affliction, *which is but for a moment.*' Now here is a very good way of testing whether or not you are a Christian. Here is a list of troubles and trials and it seems that they are going on for ever, that Paul has no way of escape, and yet he says that they are 'but for a moment'. Why does he say that? It is because he has the Christian view of time. He does not measure time in seconds and minutes and hours and days and weeks and months and years and decades and centuries. That is what the man of the world does, and that is why man is a victim of time. Time seems so long, does it not? Will there ever be an end to all this!

Oh, let me put it like this to you. Imagine a father and a mother who lost their only son in the last war. Their immediate feeling was this: 'How can we possibly go on living?' They were fairly young, how could they go on facing life? It is so long. Many people commit suicide for that reason. Everything that you held dear in life has gone and you have this awful stretch ahead – how can you bear it? But the apostle says that it is only for a moment.

The Christian views everything in the light of eternity, not in the light of time. It is because we will persist in judging everything from the standpoint of time that we get depressed and defeated. What is time, then? Well, time is really 'but a moment'. You think of it in the human, ordinary, earthly manner and you say, 'Seventy years! How long it seems!'

Yes, but now take that 70 years and put it into the context of eternity. What is eternity? Well, there is no end to it. Can you think of a million years? Of course not. But then think of a billion years. Of course you cannot. But think of that going on and on and on for ever and for ever, what is 70 years in that context? It is a moment, a flash. 'What is your life?' says James. 'It is even a vapour' (James 4:14). Like a breath of air, it has come, it has gone. So the apostle Paul is able to say that our light affliction is 'but for a moment' because he has this whole new Christian view of time, and as soon as you have this, you are already more than conqueror over everything that is set against you. You say, 'It doesn't matter what's happening to me now, it doesn't matter how long it's going to last in calendar terms, as far as I'm concerned, eternity is before me.'

This is how Paul deals with these afflictions. But then he adds another most fascinating phrase: 'Our light affliction, which is but for a moment, *worketh for us*.' The apostle makes the same point in the Epistle to the Romans: 'And not only so, but we glory in tribulations also: knowing that tribulation worketh patience; and patience, experience; and experience, hope' (Romans 5:3). And James has taken hold of exactly the same idea – it is an essential part of Christian teaching. James puts it in these words: 'My brethren, count it all joy when ye fall into divers temptations; knowing this, that the trying of your faith *worketh* patience' (James 1:2–3).

Now what does this mean? What is this 'working'? Let the apostle Paul tell us. Here, he says, is the process: A Christian is someone who has been justified by faith:

*Therefore being justified by faith, we have peace with God through our Lord Jesus Christ: by whom also we have access by faith into this grace wherein we stand, and rejoice in hope of the glory of God. And not only so, but we glory in tribulations also: knowing that tribulation worketh patience. (Romans 5:1–3)*

So how does the process operate? The answer seems to me to be this: tribulation deals with the defects in us and replaces them by good qualities, by virtues. Tribulation, says Paul, is a good experience for Christians because it produces something that was not there before – patience. You see what he means? Why are we unhappy? Why do we get defeated? It is very often because we are impatient. I say, 'Why should this happen to me? I can't stand it. I can't possibly go on.' The cause of much of our trouble and failure in life is our hasty spirit, our tendency to feel disappointed, our inconsistency, our reliance upon circumstances and upon conditions, and, therefore, our readiness always to grumble and to complain. We want everything to be perfect and if anything goes wrong, we are at once annoyed, we are 'het up', as we say, and we are full of stress and strain.

Tribulation is a very good treatment for all that. The way to get rid of that kind of spirit is to let tribulation work in you, and it does a wonderful work. It gets rid of all that impatience, it makes you think, it makes you face things instead of just reacting to them, and the result is that it produces constancy, a spirit of 'patient endurance', a spirit of reliability; and all this is the result of having a deeper view of ourselves, a deeper view of the Christian life and a deeper view of our whole relationship to God. The trouble with children, always, is that they want quick results, they want things immediately, they cannot wait. But as you get older, you have to learn, do you not, that things do not come like that. You have to learn to be patient and to bear with things.

Now this is something that life does to all of us, but the gospel does it in a most amazing manner; it immediately produces patience. It makes us ask questions: Why should I always want things immediately? Why should I always want to have an unruffled kind of existence? What right have I to ask for these things? And so it makes you more patient. And once you develop this patient endurance and reliability and steadfastness, you are already well on the road to being more than conquerors over all these things that are set against you.

And then patience, in turn, leads to experience (verse 4). Now unfortunately 'experience' is a bad translation. Patience leads to proof or trial, approvedness, or, as one translation puts it, 'patience leads to maturity of character'. This is why tribulations do good to Christian men and women – they make them mature. Peter has a wonderful way of putting this. Dealing with people who are having trials and troubles, he says that they are 'kept by the power of God through faith unto salvation ready to be revealed in the last time'. And he continues:

*Wherein ye greatly rejoice, though now for a season, if need be, ye are in heaviness through manifold temptations: that the trial of your faith, being much more precious than of gold that perisheth, though it be tried with fire, might be found unto praise and honour and glory at the appearing of Jesus Christ. (1 Peter 1:5–7)*

This is what trials do for us. Though we are born again and there is the pure gold of eternal life within us, there is still a lot of dross. And it is the admixture that gets us down, it is that which makes us complain and feel unhappy and whimper when things go against us. But trials purge us of the dross, they purify the gold, and so they work in us, creating patience, which produces maturity of character. So we are not children, just reacting quickly, violently, superficially. There is a depth about us and a steadiness and a solidity, a maturity of character.

There is a specific treatment of this subject in chapter 12 of the great Epistle to the Hebrews. We tend to forget this, but it is most important for us to realize it. The writer says there:

*Ye have not yet resisted unto blood, striving against sin. And ye have forgotten the exhortation which speaketh unto you as unto children, My son, despise not thou the chastening of the Lord, nor faint when thou art rebuked of him: for whom the Lord loveth he chasteneth, and scourgeth every son whom he receiveth. If ye endure chastening, God dealeth with you as with sons; for what son is he whom the father chasteneth not? But if ye be without chastisement, whereof all are partakers, then are ye bastards, and not sons. Furthermore we have had fathers of our flesh which corrected us, and we gave them reverence: shall we not much more rather be in subjection unto the Father of spirits, and live? For they verily for a few days chastened us after their own pleasure; but he for our profit, that we might be partakers of his holiness. (Hebrews 12:4–10)*

Tribulations enable us to see and to understand that God is at work within us purifying the gold. And that, in turn, leads to hope (Romans 5:4). We do not feel hopeless because things are against us. No, no! We have this bigger, deeper understanding. We see the ultimate end and objective, and in the light of that we are able to continue.

That, then, is one way in which tribulation and trial work in us and that is why we should rejoice. That first way is most important because though we are born again, much work needs to be done in us, a work of sanctification, purification, the work of purifying the gold. But in addition to that direct way of working, tribulation also does another wonderful thing. As the apostle puts it here in 2 Corinthians 4:17: 'For our light affliction, which is but for a moment, worketh for us *a far more exceeding and eternal weight of glory*' – it drives us to consider the glory that is awaiting us. This is one of our greatest lacks as Christian people and where we go wrong; we will think of salvation in terms of this world and this world alone. Thank God for all salvation does do for us here, but what it does for us in this world is a mere, almost infinitesimally small fraction of what it is going to do for us.

So many people say, 'I became a Christian and I thought that now I would never have any more trouble.' But then troubles come and down these people go. What is the matter? Their real trouble, above all else, is that they have not considered what is awaiting them. There is 'a far more exceeding and eternal weight of glory'. Or listen to Paul putting it perhaps still more clearly in Romans chapter 8:

*If [we are] children, then [we are] heirs; heirs of God, and joint-heirs with Christ; if so be that we suffer with him, that we may also be glorified together. For I reckon that the sufferings of this present time are not worthy to be compared with the glory which shall be revealed in us. For the earnest expectation of the creature waiteth for the manifestation of the sons of God . . . Because the creature itself also shall be delivered from the bondage of corruption into the glorious liberty of the children of God. For we know that the whole creation groaneth and travaileth in pain together until now. And not only they, but ourselves also, which have the firstfruits of the Spirit, even we ourselves groan within ourselves, waiting for the adoption, to wit, the redemption of our body. (Romans 8:17–19, 21–23)*

That is the glory that is coming, and that is what tribulation makes us consider. While all things are going well with us, we tend just to enjoy them. We take the Christian life more or less for granted, and we hardly ever think about what we are going to, what awaits us, what God has prepared for us, and what Christ is reserving for us. He said, 'Let not your heart be troubled: ye believe in God, believe also in me . . . I go to prepare a place for you' (John 14:1–2). How often do we think of that? And that is why we are so defeated, and often so unhappy, and tend to go to pieces when things are against us. 'Oh,' we say, 'now look at what's happening to me! Everything's against me. I'm losing everything.' Losing everything? What about the place that he is preparing for you? You see, you had forgotten all about that.

Now the value of tribulation is – and this is how Christian men and women become more than conquerors – that tribulation makes them think of that place. At last they realize that they have been living too much in this world, this life, the present, the seen, the temporary, and have been forgetting the other. When you have lost your health, or your loved ones, or your money, when everything seems to be taken from you, you are left alone, paralysed, helpless, as it were. There is nothing that you can look forward to in this world and that drives you to look for what God is preparing for you. What a wonderful thing tribulation is! It 'worketh for us a far more exceeding and eternal weight of glory'; it makes us think of the marvel and the glory of heaven, and the certainty of it. It is beyond description! That place will be 'with Christ'; it is a mansion that he is preparing; it will be glory everlasting. Even your very body will be glorified with no defect whatsoever.

We have so concentrated on this life that we have forgotten the glory that is coming. What we have here, says Paul, is 'the firstfruits of the Spirit' (Romans 8:23) – only the firstfruits, the foretaste, the mere 'earnest'. The great harvest is awaiting us, and tribulations drive us to contemplate it. So they are of value to us as they do this work within us. And the result of all this is that Christian people learn contentment. They are contented because their needs are fewer, and their needs are fewer because they live a life in the soul and in the spirit. The needs of the non-Christian are endless. They must have more and more – more money, more cigarettes, more drink, more drugs, more sex – they are never satisfied. Oh, how difficult it is, and everybody is short of money because their needs are so prolific. But when people become Christians, their needs are greatly reduced. I must not say that they have no needs, or that they are satisfied, but that they are so satisfied by what they have that they do not need anything else.

Listen to how Paul puts it. The Philippians had sent him a gift and he thanks them for it. Then he says:

*Not that I speak in respect of want: for I have learned, in whatsoever state I am, therewith to be content. I know both how to be abased, and I know how to abound: every where and in all things I am instructed both to be full and to be hungry, both to abound and to suffer need. (Philippians 4:11–12)*

It does not matter what Paul's circumstances are, he is satisfied. Wherever he is, he has a satisfaction in Christ. He is writing to the Philippians from prison, remember, and he is an old man. He has been told that Nero has suddenly decided to put him to death. What does it matter? It does not matter at all!

On another occasion when Paul is in prison, he is brought out to speak before King Agrippa and the Roman proconsul Festus, and he says a marvellous thing to them. He is standing there with the prison chains hanging heavily from both his wrists and he is probably tied to a soldier on each side. He looks at these people in authority and with great power, who have everything that can be desired. They are in a bantering mood and King Agrippa says to him, 'Almost thou persuadest me to be a Christian.' Then Paul replies, 'I would to God, that not only thou, but also all that hear me this day, were both almost, and altogether such as I am, except these bonds' (Acts 26:28–29). He is saying: I do not wish you to become prisoners, I do not wish evil upon you, but you know, I wish you were like me.

Is this conceit? Is this just a man boasting or being egotistical? Of course not. Paul means: 'You know I am a prisoner and you have deprived me of everything. You think you have a lot and I have nothing, but it is I who have everything and you who have nothing.' That is how tribulation gives contentment and renders us immune to circumstances. It does not matter what happens, you have inner peace, inner rest, you have Christ in your heart and 'the hope of glory' also. It does not matter what people may do, what circumstances may do, they cannot touch that.

And the result is that you even rejoice in your tribulations because it is tribulation that has brought you to the realization of the truth of salvation. You realize that regeneration is not little or superficial. It is profound and ends in that glory, the vision of God and the sharing of eternal bliss with God the Father, God the Son, God the Holy Spirit, and 'the spirits of just men made perfect'.

So Christians are not merely able to put up with the things that happen to them without collapsing, but they also rejoice in them. They do not rejoice in spite of them, they rejoice in them, they thank God for them. 'It is good for me that I have been afflicted,' says the psalmist, because 'before I was afflicted I went astray' (Psalm 119:71, 67). It is afflictions that wean me from the world and drive me to consider him and the glory that he is preparing for me, and the joy that is around the throne of God in the eternal bliss. 'In all these things we are more than conquerors through him that loved us' (Romans 8:37).

Do you know this, my friend? How do you react to trials and tribulations? How do you respond to adverse circumstances? Have you got patience? Do you have maturity of character as a Christian? Are you dependable, are you reliable? Are you immune to circumstances and chance. Are you able to say, 'All things' – whatever they are – 'work together for good' – that is my experience? Even things that are against me are good for me. Why? They drive me to him.

*For our light affliction, which is but for a moment, worketh for us a far more exceeding and eternal weight of glory; while we look not at the things which are seen, but at the things which are not seen: for the things which are seen are temporal; but the things which are not seen are eternal. (2 Corinthians 4:17–18)*

And they are my things because I belong to eternity.

38

# All in Christ Jesus

*Jesus answered and said unto her, Whosoever drinketh of this water shall thirst again: but whosoever drinketh of the water that I shall give him shall never thirst; but the water that I shall give him shall be in him a well of water springing up into everlasting life. (John 4:13–14)*

We are, let me remind you, considering this great and wonderful statement at some length because it is one of these perfect summaries of the gospel that we find scattered about here and there in the Scriptures, especially in the Gospel of St John. What our Lord is offering here, and what he claims is the essential character of the Christian life, is its all-sufficiency, its fullness, its completeness, as John tells us in verse 16 of chapter 1: 'And of his fulness have all we received, and grace upon grace.'

This is Christianity. Christianity is not merely an intellectual belief, it is not merely moral living. It includes all that but to stop at that is tragic. It is life, and life more abundant, life in all its fullness, life that gives complete and entire satisfaction, and here is our Lord setting it forth again in an interesting pictorial manner to this woman of Samaria at the side of a well. And the great question for every one of us to address at this very moment is this: Is this our experience? And it is because this is not true of so many of us that the Christian church is as she is today – weak, ineffective, giving people outside the impression that the Christian faith is small, cramped and confined, a duty to be performed, a burden that we carry, instead of this glorious life that is here indicated by our blessed Lord.

We have been examining Christianity, therefore, in the light of the full teaching of the Scriptures, particularly, of course, the New Testament, and we have seen that it really does do what our Lord claims – it gives complete intellectual satisfaction, it gives complete heart satisfaction and it deals with the will and all the problems that confront us. In the last study, we saw that this is true in practice, it really does work when circumstances are against us and when we are surrounded by trials and troubles and tribulations, and we can, therefore, rejoice in tribulations – not in spite of them but in them.

In the light of all this, I would say that we are entitled to make this assertion: this life that our Lord gives us enables us to face the future, whatever it may be, without any fear or foreboding: 'The LORD is my shepherd; I shall not want' (Psalm 23:1). That follows of necessity. Or we can put it in the language of the apostle Paul, that man who suffered so much because he was a Christian – and let us make no mistake about this, if we are Christians, we shall suffer. 'Yea,' says Paul to Timothy, 'and all that will live godly in Christ Jesus shall suffer persecution' (2 Timothy 3:12); and as he puts it to the Philippians: 'For unto you it is given in the behalf of Christ, not only to believe on him, but also to suffer for his sake' (Philippians 1:29). If ever a man suffered, it was Paul – imprisoned, maltreated, maligned – and yet here he is writing probably his last letter, the Second Epistle to Timothy, and saying:

*For the which cause I also suffer these things*

– these indignities and imprisonments and so on, and then, so typical and characteristic of Paul –

*nevertheless I am not ashamed*

– why not? –

*for I know whom I have believed, and am persuaded [certain] that he is able to keep that which I have committed unto him*

– my soul and its eternal salvation and destiny –

*against that day. (2 Timothy 1:12)*

And that, it seems to me, sums up this great statement of our Lord concerning the gospel and its fullness. It does not matter what may come, there is no shame, there is no faltering, there is no failing. Paul is rejoicing, he is glorying.

But I would also emphasize that not only does fullness of life come immediately, it continues and increases. We worked out earlier that it really does become a well of water springing up into everlasting life, but now I particularly want to emphasize that one of the great glories of this Christian life is that it increases and becomes more and more glorious to us and more and more wonderful; it must do if we follow through our Lord's teaching here in John 4. That, again, is one of the great differentiating points between the gospel and any philosophy or cult you may happen to take up. You get as much as you are going to get out of them at once, and you do your best to hold on to that, but when you need them most of all, they will fail you most of all. They are fair-weather friends, as we have seen. They do not have life in them. Ultimately, they all depend upon us. They are mere ideas and you have to keep the idea going.

But the glory of the gospel is that it is life, life from God, and because it is life it grows and develops. Life does not remain stagnant but goes on growing and manifesting itself within us and we experience it in an ever deeper and more mature manner. This is what is wonderfully true about this life. I have never understood Christians who always talk about their conversion. When I find such a person, I am saddened. I remember such people very well in my early days in the ministry, particularly in Wales. They would come to me and always tell me the same thing. It was the revival[1] and it was 'marvellous', especially their own conversion. I remember that I heard this so often from one particular individual that I once looked at him and said, 'Tell me, has nothing happened to you since then? Did God finish dealing with you then? What has happened in the intervening 23 years or so?' This is very sad and it is something to which evangelical people are particularly prone. My dear friends, it is all wrong.

Thank God for the beginning, without that, of course, we have nothing; but, oh, the marvellous thing is the growth and the development, the increasing understanding. Do you not rejoice more in your Christian life today than a year ago? If not, then there is something very wrong with you and there is something very wrong with me as a preacher. If you do not marvel at it more than ever, if you are not moved by it more than ever, if it does not thrill you more than ever, there is something seriously wrong. This life is a 'well of water' that goes on springing on and up into everlasting life.

We must test ourselves by this. Do you not find that as you go on in this journey, the scenery becomes more glorious, with unexpected things coming to meet you as God reveals yet further examples of

---

[1] The 1904–5 revival in Wales.

what he has provided for you? This is an essential part of the description that is given here by our blessed Lord of this wonderful life that he has to give us. God grant that we all may be able to say, 'The beginning? Well, it was all right but it was but the beginning.' 'When I was a child,' says Paul, 'I spake as a child, I understood as a child, I thought as a child: but when I became a man, I put away childish things' (1 Corinthians 13:11). Can you say that? Is your knowledge increasing? Is your heart being more and more warmed? Are you more and more amazed at the wonders of his ways and the increasing unfolding of his purposes with regard to you and with regard to the church, and with regard to the whole world?

Now all this is implicit in the definition of this life, but what I want to leave with you as the great final thought concerning this matter is that the secret of all this, of course, is the Lord himself. 'Whosoever drinketh of the water that I shall give him' – and that really means himself. That is what is meant by drinking this water, that is what is meant by possessing this well: it is 'Christ in you, the hope of glory' (Colossians 1:27). Paul's great prayer for the Ephesians was 'that Christ may dwell in your hearts by faith' (Ephesians 3:17). It is he. Life is in him. 'We receive of him, the fountain head.' 'He is the head of the body, the church' and in him 'all fulness' dwells (Colossians 1:18–19), and it is because he is in us that this fullness is in us.

And, therefore, it all comes to this: to drink of this water means getting to know him more and more and the fullness that is in him. This is what makes this life so wonderful. The moment we regard it in this way, we have a deeper understanding of it. We have been considering different aspects of this life and thinking of it as it is expounded as doctrine, but now look at it as it is all in our Lord and who he is. It is because he is who he is that he is able to satisfy our every need.

I was sorely tempted – if it is, indeed, a temptation, but that is how we speak, is it not? – to spend this morning in just reading hymns to you because these writers are expressing their experience and they tell us what they know of him. The apostle Paul puts it in his way, again in Ephesians 3, when he says he wants the Ephesians to know 'what is the breadth, and length, and depth, and height; and to know the love of Christ, which passeth knowledge, that ye might be filled with all the fulness of God' (Ephesians 3:18–19). That is it.

And this is all in Christ! Paul says to the Colossians, 'In whom are hid all the treasures of wisdom and knowledge' (Colossians 2:3). It is all there in him and we receive it from him, and he is everything to us. Now I think that Charles Wesley has probably excelled over everybody in expressing just this aspect in what I have increasingly come to regard as the greatest of his hymns, greater even than 'Jesus, lover of my soul' because it goes further, though there is a wonderful beginning to that hymn and though at the end of it he goes on to say:

> Thou of life the fountain art,
> Freely let me take of thee;
> Spring thou up within my heart,
> Rise to all eternity.

But this is even better:

> Thou hidden source of calm repose,
> Thou all-sufficient love divine,
> My help and refuge from my foes,
> Secure I am if thou art mine;
> And lo! from sin, and grief, and shame,
> I hide me, Jesus, in thy name.

We have worked that out. We have seen how our Lord satisfies the accusations, indeed, the demands, in a sense, of our consciences:

> And lo! from sin, and grief, and shame,
> I hide me, Jesus, in thy name.

But on he goes:

> Thy mighty name salvation is,
> And keeps my happy soul above;
> Comfort it brings, and power, and peace,
> And joy and everlasting love:
> To me, with thy dear name are given
> Pardon, and holiness, and heaven.

It is magnificent poetry, but look at the sentiment, look at what Charles Wesley is saying:

> Jesus, my all in all thou art;
> My rest in toil, mine ease in pain;
> The medicine of my broken heart;
> In war, my peace; in loss, my gain;
> My smile beneath thy tyrant's frown;
> In shame, my glory and my crown.

> In want, my plentiful supply;
> In weakness, mine almighty power;
> In bonds, my perfect liberty;
> My light in Satan's darkest hour;
> My help and stay whene'er I call;
> My life in death, my heaven, my all.

That is everything, is it not? Charles Wesley has covered it. In a world like this we face weakness, temptation, war, tyrants' frowns, all these many things – we are familiar with them. But as Wesley says in the second line of that great hymn:

Thou all-sufficient love divine.

He is everything. My dear friend, you can be sure of this: nothing can ever happen to you but that he will be able to help you. Nothing – that is a simple statement of fact. It does not matter what happens to you, he is sufficient: 'My all-sufficient love divine'. And what matters is our realization of this. Have you found him to be: 'In want my plentiful supply'? Can you use the language of the apostle: 'I have all, and abound: I am full' (Philippians 4:18)? Can you say, 'I know both how to be abased, and I know how to abound (verse 12)? The whole essence of this matter is to know him. As you know him, you find this *fullness*. He knows all; he is able to do all. There is nothing that you can ever need or desire, nothing that can ever happen to you, but that he is able to deal with it, and deal with it with this amazing fullness. He will reverse everything and he will fill you with rejoicing in the midst of your tribulations.

Now that is one way of looking at the 'well of water springing up' and in many ways it is the most important of all. You must look at him and you must consider him. This takes time but you must do it. You must seek his face; you must get to know him. And the more you know him, the more you will be amazed at the fullness that is in him.

But I want to add to that, and thank God for what I am going to say. It is not only what is in him that explains this fullness of life, it is also what he does, what he does to us. We go to him but there is nothing more wonderful than the fact that he comes to us. I am referring now to what some of the saints in the past have called 'visitations' or 'manifestations' of the Son of God, intimations that he gives of his loving interest in us.

Now this is wonderful because there are times when, perhaps because of illness, tiredness, weakness, age or various other factors, we find ourselves dull and lethargic and not able to do anything, as it were, and we cannot even contemplate. And it is just then that he comes and makes all the difference to us. There are wonderful examples of this in the Scriptures themselves. Look at it in connection with the apostle Paul. He was in Corinth and he was having a particularly difficult time there, everything had gone against him, and Paul obviously went to bed one night feeling somewhat dejected and discouraged, but this is what I read in Acts:

*Then spake the Lord to Paul in the night by a vision, Be not afraid, but speak, and hold not thy peace: for I am with thee, and no man shall set on thee to hurt thee: for I have much people in this city. (Acts 18:9–10)*

Now that is a vision. It is all right, I am not suggesting that you should all be seeking visions! No, no; we must not do that. But what I am saying is that our Lord, in his infinite love and mercy and compassion, chooses to visit us when we are going through times of great stress and crisis. He may visit us not in a vision, but in our spirits. We will see nothing, we will not hear an audible voice, but we will know that he is there; there will be no uncertainty.

Or take another example. The apostle Paul, again, was in a very difficult situation and he says:

*And it came to pass, that, when I was come again to Jerusalem, even while I prayed in the temple, I was in a trance*

– all right, this again is exceptional. You will never experience a trance, perhaps. It does not matter, you can know the very experience that the apostle had –

> *and saw him saying unto me, Make haste, and get thee quickly out of Jerusalem: for they will not receive thy testimony concerning me. And I said, Lord, they know that I imprisoned and beat in every synagogue them that believed on thee: and when the blood of thy martyr Stephen was shed, I also was standing by, and consenting unto his death, and kept the raiment of them that slew him. And he said unto me, Depart: for I will send thee far hence unto the Gentiles. (Acts 22:17–21)*

Or take a dramatic illustration, again from the book of the Acts. Paul was in a ship on the way to Rome to appeal to Caesar, and a shipwreck took place. The terrible time endured by all those on board is one of the most dramatic descriptions of a storm at sea that has ever been written; but this is what interests us:

> *But after long abstinence Paul stood forth in the midst of them, and said, Sirs, ye should have hearkened unto me, and not have loosed from Crete, and to have gained this harm and loss. And now I exhort you to be of good cheer: for there shall be no loss of any man's life among you, but of the ship.*

How does Paul know this?

> *For there stood by me this night the angel of God, whose I am, and whom I serve, saying, Fear not, Paul; thou must be brought before Caesar: and, lo, God hath given thee all them that sail with thee. (Acts 27:21–24)*

Or, in a less dramatic manner than that, and perhaps a little nearer to the kind of thing we are likely to experience, listen to this in 2 Timothy 4:16–17. Paul, under arrest and awaiting trial, writes to Timothy and says:

> *At my first answer no man stood with me, but all men forsook me: I pray God that it may not be laid to their charge. Notwithstanding the*

*Lord stood with me, and strengthened me; that by me the preaching might be fully known, and that all the Gentiles might hear: and I was delivered out of the mouth of the lion.*

'The Lord stood with me'! And this is what he promises to us all.

These are illustrations, not of the apostle going to the Lord and finding this fullness, but of Paul in terrible trouble and the Lord coming to him just when he needs him. This is a part of Christian experience, an essential part of the Christian life. Listen to William Cowper saying the same thing:

Sometimes a light surprises
The Christian while he sings;
It is the Lord who rises
With healing in his wings.

He comes suddenly, 'to cheer the soul after rain', as Cowper goes on to say. When you are down, when you are discouraged, when the clouds are there, 'sometimes a light surprises'. You are amazed at it. It is he who comes; he visits you. He gives you a manifestation of his nearness, his fullness, and the glory of his presence.

Now we modern Christians have strangely neglected this teaching. Oh, how we have robbed ourselves of the riches of his grace! I am afraid some of us are so busy and have so emphasized our activity, our decision, our effort, that we do not give him an opportunity to come to visit us. Let me give you a taste of this. I could give you many examples, as I have done in the past, out of the journals of George Whitefield, but now I am just going to give you something out of the diary of Augustus Toplady, the author of 'Rock of Ages' and other great hymns. Here it is:

To have a part and lot in God's salvation is the main thing; but to have the joy of it is an additional blessing which makes our way to the kingdom smooth and sweet. Here let me leave it on thankful record for my comfort and support if it please God in future times of trial and desertion, that I was never lower in the valley than last night, nor higher on the mount than today. The Lord chastened me but did not give me over unto death, and he never will. He may indeed for the small moment hide his face from me, but with everlasting kindness will he have mercy on me.

From morning until now (that is to say, eleven at night) I have enjoyed a continual feast within. Christ has been unspeakably precious to my heart, and the blessed Spirit of God hath visited me with sweet and reviving manifestations.

Now Augustus Toplady was a great Calvinist and a great controversialist, but that is what kept this man going, that is what enabled him to write those incomparable hymns. You notice how he puts it: 'manifestations'. He himself did not do this. If you read his diaries, and those of other people, you find that they all say that it is the Lord who comes to them.

My friends, we are not worshipping a theology, we are not worshipping an orthodox belief, we are worshipping a living person, and he manifests himself, he has promised to do so. In John chapter 14, verse 1, we read, '[I] will manifest myself to him', and in verse 23: 'My Father will love him [the one who keeps his words] and we will come unto him, and make our abode with him.' As we read the biographies and autobiographies of saints throughout the centuries, we find a repetition of this. And let me make this clear – this is not confined only to outstanding Christian people, to great poets and preachers. No, no; our Lord manifests himself to some of the most 'ordinary' people, so called. A Christian cannot be ordinary, but we use these distinctions. Some of the most ordinary Christians have testified to these inexpressible experiences. That is why Christians will never thirst. Even when they can scarcely do anything, the Lord comes to them.

Do you know these visitations of his? Does he come to you? Do you know what it is to be turned suddenly from the depth of anguish to heights of rejoicing? Do you know what it is to be overwhelmed by his love, to weep tears of joy and of rapture? He promises this. It is a personal relationship and it is an essential part of this whole Christian teaching. And it is all in him. Thank God that our Lord comes to us even when we cannot go to him.

But then another, and a most comforting and consoling thought, is this: our Lord's unchangeableness. Not only do we rejoice in the inexhaustible riches that are in him, but we also rejoice in the fact that they will never diminish, they will never change, they will never become small; he is 'a never-ebbing sea'. Again, the apostle Paul has given expression to this and it gave him great comfort. Here was this man, a great man of God, a preacher, evangelist, builder of churches, contender for the faith, but, oh, the troubles he had, the persecution and the trials, people leaving him and forsaking him, rejecting the doctrine! In his second epistle to Timothy, he puts it like this when dealing with people who are denying the doctrine of the resurrection:

*Remember that Jesus Christ of the seed of David was raised from the dead according to my gospel: wherein I suffer trouble, as an evil doer, even unto bonds; but the word of God is not bound. Therefore I endure all things for the elect's sakes, that they may also obtain the salvation which is in Christ Jesus with eternal glory.*

And then:

*It is a faithful saying: For if we be dead with him, we shall also live with him: if we suffer, we shall also reign with him: if we deny him, he will also deny us: yet he abideth faithful: he cannot deny himself.*

Is that the sheet anchor of your whole position? Is that the truth on which you are resting? Paul then goes on and says:

*Nevertheless the foundation of God standeth sure, having this seal, The Lord knoweth them that are his. And, Let every one that nameth the name of Christ depart from iniquity. (2 Timothy 2:8–13, 19)*

The New Testament is full of this. These people lived on it. They were having such a trying, terrible time, death was always staring them in the face simply because they were Christians, so the writer of the Epistle to the Hebrews tells them that this is the way to deal with these tribulations:

*Seeing we also are compassed about with so great a cloud of witnesses, let us lay aside every weight, and the sin which doth so easily beset us, and let us run with patience the race that is set before us, looking unto Jesus the author and finisher of our faith; who for the joy that was set before him endured the cross, despising the shame, and is set down at the right hand of the throne of God. (Hebrews 12:1–3)*

And then, summing it up, he says: 'Jesus Christ the same yesterday, and to day, and for ever' (Hebrews 13:8).

And that is our only final comfort. You read of it in the four Gospels. You see who our Lord was. You see the love, the mercy, the compassion, the patience, everything that was so true of him. And you and I must realize that now, in the glory, he is still the same. In the book of Revelation, John tells us of how he had a great vision of our Lord, and then John says:

*And when I saw him, I fell at his feet as dead.*

But John adds the most wonderful words:

*And he laid his right hand upon me, saying unto me, Fear not; I am the first and the last: I am he that liveth, and was dead; and, behold,*

*I am alive for evermore. Amen; and have the keys of hell and of death. (Revelation 1:17–18)*

That is what immediately put John right: 'He laid his right hand upon me.' How often had our Lord done that in the days of his flesh! And he still does that, he does not change. So read the Gospels, you will get to know him there, and, as you read, remember that he is still the same:

> In every pang that rends the heart,
> The Man of Sorrows had a part.
> *Michael Bruce*

Though he is there in the glory everlasting, he has not forgotten all that he suffered and endured while he was here. And so, in the glory, he comes and he will put his hand on you, and you will feel the touch, and you will know that all is well. When you are agitated, when you are liable to fall, just the touch of his hand and you are well, you are strong. He comes, and he remains ever always the same.

Is not this a glorious comfort and consolation for us? We are all so changeable and so are our circumstances. We have no idea what we will feel like tomorrow morning. We have no idea what is going to happen to us. That is the characteristic of this world in which we find ourselves, and things that bring us relief suddenly fail us. We tend to lean on things that cannot hold us; we lean on one another. But we must not. We are all here in the flesh, we are 'here today and gone tomorrow'. We must not depend upon anybody or anything, or sooner or later we will find ourselves bereft, with nothing. But this is the glorious reality:

> When all created streams are dried,
> Thy fullness is the same.

When the drought has come, the spiritual drought, and things are failing us everywhere, to the right and left, he will never become dry: droughts do not affect him. He is from everlasting to everlasting, and all the fullness of the Godhead dwells in him bodily.

> May I with this be satisfied,
> And glory in thy name.

Of course!

> He that has made my heaven secure,
> Will here all good provide;
> While Christ is rich, can I be poor?
> What can I want beside?
>> *John Ryland*

That is the simple truth. He is eternally rich and he will never change. In the glory there will never be any diminution of his power and his ability – never. He abides ever, always, everlastingly the same.

> Change and decay in all around I see,
> O thou who changest not, abide with me.
>> *Henry Francis Lyte*

And he will, he has promised to. He has said, 'I will never leave thee, nor forsake thee' (Hebrews 13:5). Never! Whatever happens. He has given his word and he will never break it.

And that brings us to the conclusion concerning this aspect of the matter, and that is the glory of his power, guaranteeing that nothing will ever be able to separate us from him. It is not only that he will never leave us or forsake us, but nothing will ever be allowed to come between us and him. This is the most comforting and consoling truth: not my holding on to him, but his strong grasp of me. If I felt that my eternal future depended upon me and my stability and strength and understanding, I would be lost; so would you, every one of you. It is his strong grasp of us that saves us. That is the only certainty and it is an absolute certainty. 'He that spared not his own Son, but delivered him up for us all, how shall he not with him also freely give us all things?' (Romans 8:32). 'Who shall separate us from the love of Christ?' That is it. The apostle throws out this tremendous challenge at the end of that eighth chapter of Romans:

> *Who shall separate us [who can separate us, who ever will be able to separate us] from the love of Christ? shall tribulation, or distress, or persecution, or famine, or nakedness, or peril, or sword? As it is written, For thy sake we are killed all the day long; we are accounted as sheep for the slaughter. Nay, in all these things we are more than conquerors through him that loved us.*

And then this tremendous conclusion:

> *For I am persuaded [I am absolutely certain], that neither death, nor life, nor angels, nor principalities, nor powers, nor things present, nor things to come, nor height, nor depth, nor any other creature*

– can you think of anything else? Put it in if you can and still I say that none of them, nor all of them together –

> *shall be able to separate us from the love of God, which is in Christ Jesus our Lord. (Romans 8:35–39)*

We are safe!

> Safe in the arms of Jesus,
> Safe on his gentle breast.

That is where he has put you. He has embraced you, he has enfolded you with the arms of his love, and he will never let you go – never. And nothing will ever be able to separate you from his love and the love of God in him and through him by the Holy Spirit; it is impossible.

'Whosoever drinketh of the water that I shall give him shall never, no, never, thirst as long as the world standeth.' What does he mean? He means this: I will always be surrounding you; you will always be in the embrace of my eternal love.

And so Jude, in his doxology, puts it like this:

*Unto him that is able to keep you from falling, and to present you faultless before the presence of his glory with exceeding joy, to the only wise God our Saviour, be glory and majesty, dominion and power, both now and ever. Amen. (Jude 25)*

So I leave you with a question: Is this true of you? What a difference there is between being religious and being a Christian! I am not asking if you are religious; you would not be here if you were not. What I am asking you is this: Have you found your sufficiency in him? You have known all created streams going dry at times, have you not? Have you known at such times that his fullness is still the same? Have you ever gone to him in vain? Have you ever found him to disappoint you? Or let me put it in a better way: Have you not always found everything in him? Oh, nothing matters but this! Nobody knows what the future is to be, internationally, nationally, family, individual. But the point is that it does not matter. If your position, if your happiness, depends upon things that are going to happen to you, then, in a sense, you are of all people the most miserable. The glory of this message is that it does not matter what happens. He will be with you – in life, in death, throughout eternity. Do you know him?

And our Lord tells you that all you need to do is to drink. 'Whosoever drinketh of the water that I shall give him' – he has got it, he is standing there, he is saying that to you and all you must do is drink of it.

What does that mean? Well, that might have occupied us for weeks and months, but let me just tell you what it means in its essence. It means that you realize your need, your utter bankruptcy, your complete helplessness and hopelessness. You will never know this as long as you are relying on anything in yourself. It is to this poor woman of Samaria, who has nothing, who does not have a character or chastity, who has lost everything, that he offers everything. And if you are holding on to your religion, your religiosity, your morality, your understanding, your will power, you will not know this living water; it is a blessed gospel for paupers. This water is offered to people who are dying of thirst and who know it, those who have finished, who have come to the end, who are bankrupt. That is the first and the most important thing of all. Let me put it in the words of that verse out of the hymn of Horatius Bonar:

> I heard the voice of Jesus say,
> Behold, I freely give
> The living water; thirsty one,
> Stoop down, and drink and live.

There is a fountain here. You are dying of thirst, you are staggering about the world. But here is everything you need, it will slake your thirst, it will put you on your feet, it will give you life; but you cannot drink from a fountain standing erect. Stoop down! Lie prostrate on the ground.

> I came to Jesus, and I drank
> Of that life-giving stream;
> My thirst was quenched, my soul revived,
> And now I live in him.

Come to the end of all your abilities and self-confidence and trust, all your self-defence, all your rationalizing of your imperfections and failures: 'Stoop down, and drink and live.' Tell him the truth about yourself, tell him about your lack of love, your lack of joy, your lack of whatever it is. Tell him that you are like this, you can do nothing about it, that you have tried and tried and tried, and you have constantly failed. Just go to him as you are, tell him all and say, 'I want to know this. I want to have this life springing up within me. You can give it to me and you alone.' Cast yourself utterly upon him, and say, as Jacob said to him, 'I will not let thee go, except thou bless me' (Genesis 32:26). And I can assure you that as certainly as you do that, he will give it you, for he has said, 'Him that cometh to me I will in no wise cast out' (John 6:37).

My dear friend, go to him and drink, and you will never thirst, no, never, as long as the world stands and you will be aware within yourself of a well of water springing up into everlasting life.

39

# The Work of Christ

*And upon this came his disciples, and marvelled that he talked with the woman: yet no man said, What seekest thou? or, Why talkest thou with her? The woman then left her water pot, and went her way into the city, and saith to the men, Come, see a man, which told me all things that ever I did: is not this the Christ? Then they went out of the city, and came unto him. In the mean while his disciples prayed him, saying, Master, eat. But he said unto them, I have meat to eat that ye know not of. Therefore said the disciples one to another, Hath any man brought him ought to eat? Jesus saith unto them, My meat is to do the will of him that sent me, and to finish his work. Say not ye, There are yet four months, and then cometh harvest? behold, I say unto you, Lift up your eyes, and look on the fields; for they are white already to harvest. And he that reapeth receiveth wages, and gathereth fruit unto life eternal: that both he that soweth and he that reapeth may rejoice together. And herein is that saying true, One soweth, and another reapeth. I sent you to reap that whereon ye bestowed no labour: other men laboured, and ye are entered into their labours. (John 4:27–38)*

I want now to take a general look at the teaching that stands out in the whole of the section that runs from verses 27 to 38 of John chapter 4. We are working through this Gospel of John, not in the sense of a verse by verse exposition, but rather we are picking out what is, after all, the great theme of this Gospel. The apostle makes that theme perfectly clear in the first chapter. It is that the Lord Jesus Christ, the Son of God, has come into this world to give us the right and the authority to become the children, the 'sons', of God, and that we may be filled with all his fullness: 'And of his fulness have all we received, and grace for [upon] grace' (John 1:16).[1]

Our Lord constantly repeats this promise. He says, 'I am come that they might have life, and that they might have it more abundantly' (John 10:10). And, as we have been seeing at great length: 'Whosoever drinketh of the water that I shall give him shall never thirst; but the water that I shall give him shall be in him a well of water springing up into everlasting life' (John 4:14). This 'fullness', this 'abundant life', is the great theme of this Gospel and we are concerned to find out how it is to be obtained. In the various incidents that are recorded in John's Gospel, we are given an account of the difficulties, the obstacles, to receiving this fullness. Can we all say, 'Of his fulness have I received, and grace upon grace'? Can I say of a surety that I have this 'well of water' in me, and that it is 'springing up into everlasting life' so that I do not thirst? This is the great question.

Now in dealing with this passage in John 4 from verse 4 up to the end of verse 26, we have seen many of these difficulties and we are aware of them in our own lives. But we have also seen how

---

[1] D. Martyn Lloyd-Jones, *Joy Unspeakable* (including *Prove All Things*), Kingsway Publications, 1994.

our Lord enables us to overcome them, how he deals with us, and we have looked at this wonderful, positive teaching. And now we come to the stage at which we see the result in this woman's life. It is very important that we should consider this because in a sense it is always the same for everyone, and as we have tested ourselves in terms of the difficulties and the obstacles, so we can also test ourselves in terms of the result. This is a most practical matter and that is why we deal with it together.

But before we even do that, we must remind ourselves again of who it is who makes all this possible. A great danger confronting us all at the present time is to keep on talking about Christianity instead of talking about the Lord Jesus Christ. We start with ourselves, we start with our problems and difficulties, we start with the world as it is, and we end with that, and people are merely interested in the application of Christianity to this, that and the other problem. The whole emphasis today is upon the practical application. Now that is all right, that must be done, but the constant danger is that in the process we forget about him. And the devil, of course, seeks to make this happen.

There are others who seem to have lost the Lord in the doctrines concerning him. They approach the doctrines in a theoretical and purely intellectual manner. Again, of course, it is right to study the doctrines, but if we stop at all that, if we forget him, we shall soon be in trouble. And in any case, we are missing and failing to enjoy what is, after all, the greatest lesson of all, and that is our personal relationship to him. So we must concentrate on our Lord himself.

Why do we have these Gospels? Why were they ever written? Well, they have two main functions; one is, of course, to establish the facts concerning our Lord and to remind us constantly of who he is and what he is. But they have an additional function and that is to remind us that he is still the same, that as he was on earth, so he is now. Though high and exalted, at the right hand of God in the glory everlasting, he still remembers all that he suffered in this world. He is still the same one who spoke to the woman of Samaria by the side of the well; all that characterized him then characterizes him now.

Do we know him? Are we able to go to him? Are we able to speak to him as this woman spoke to him, as the disciples spoke to him? This, after all, is what matters. If our faith, if our Christianity that we talk about, is not of value to us in the ordinary circumstances and details of life, then there is something tragically wrong with us. The very heart and nerve of this message is to tell us that it is possible for us to know him, and to go immediately and directly to him. So we must look at him again. He dominates the situation, always. Even in the sequel to this incident, he is still the most important person.

So what do we find here? Let me just open out some of these truths for your consideration, for they are wonderful, they are most comforting and encouraging. The trouble is that the church, with its ceremonial and ritual, and by putting others between us and him, has so often hidden him from us. He is banished, put at some distance, and people do not derive the great benefits of the Christian life that are waiting for them. But here they are, open before us in the New Testament. Let us, then, above all else, realize the truth concerning our Lord.

Now I have taken this one paragraph – verses 27 to 38 – and have put all that we are told here under two main headings. There are certain general things that we learn about our Lord, and then there are certain things that are more particular, and that he himself brings out in his teaching. The first comment I would make concerns the opening of verse 27. It reads like this: 'And upon this came his disciples, and marvelled that he talked with the woman.' Now this expression, 'upon this', is not the best translation. A better way of translating these words is: 'just then'; or, better still, 'at that moment'. What moment? Well, obviously, the reference is to what has just gone before. Our Lord is instructing this woman and she says to him, 'I know that Messias cometh, which is called Christ: when he is come, he will tell us all things.' And Jesus replies, 'I that speak unto thee am he.' Then, 'at that moment the disciples came'. Just as he says that, the disciples arrive.

Now what is the significance of this? Well, this is to me one of those glorious things that we find so constantly in the Scriptures. A few years back, a man wrote a book that I think he called *Golden Nuggets in the New Testament*,[2] and he is quite right – there are 'golden nuggets' here. But you must seek them. If you take the trouble to look for them, you will find how wonderful they are. Now you must not suppose that the disciples interrupt the conversation. That is what we are tempted to think. You remember that they have gone to buy provisions; they are all very tired and they have not eaten. We are told that our Lord, 'being wearied with his journey, sat thus on the well', and then we think that just as he is talking with the woman, back they come. But to think that is to miss the glory of this particular teaching. It is not that the disciples return and interrupt the conversation, but that our Lord has finished saying to this woman what he intended to say. He has reached the climax: 'I that speak unto thee am he.' He has delivered his message, and immediately afterwards, or just as he is finishing, they come back.

This is one of these 'golden nuggets' that should give us such comfort and consolation. He is always in charge of the situation,

---

2 Kenneth S. Wuest, *Golden Nuggets in the Greek New Testament*. Reprinted 1973 by Eerdmans as one of a four-volume set, *Word Studies in the Greek New Testament* (ed.).

he knows everything, nothing is accidental. All his conversation with the Samaritan woman is so arranged that he finishes his statement and makes his declaration before the disciples come back. Nothing can interrupt his work. We tend to think that his work can be interrupted, but that idea is a fallacy, it is our self-importance that makes us think that. What he has purposed he will always do. He can control time, he can control persons, there is nothing that he does not do for them. He knows everything. We have already seen how he knows all about this woman. He knows about her immoral life, he knows that she has had five husbands. She does not understand this and is astonished, but this is simply the truth about him. Therefore, in chapter 2, we read:

> *When he was in Jerusalem at the Passover, in the feast day, many believed in his name, when they saw the miracles which he did. But Jesus did not commit himself unto them, because he knew all men, and needed not that any should testify of man: for he knew what was in man. (John 2:23–25)*

And John chapter 3 similarly tells us that he knew the exact position of Nicodemus and so could cut through his conversation.

Now here, it seems to me, is one of these great principles that we should always bear in mind. There is nothing about our circumstances that our Lord does not know, and he is the Lord of all circumstances. There can be no interruption, his plan is perfect and he will certainly carry it through. We are so self-important and put such emphasis upon our decisions, as if we can keep the Lord waiting. My dear friend, get rid of that notion; he is always in charge, he knows what he is doing.

> He knows the way he taketh,
> And I will walk with him.
> *Anna L. Waring*

Just at that moment! Not before, not after, just at the right moment the disciples come back. Do you realize that you are in the hands of this Lord, this blessed person, this one who is in charge and in control of the entire universe? He has said, 'All power is given unto me in heaven and in earth' (Matthew 28:18).

And then the next thing we notice is that he does surprising things. 'And upon this came his disciples, and marvelled that he talked with the woman.' They do not understand. Of course not: they are Jews and are creatures of tradition. It was the teaching of the rabbis – and had been made into an absolute law – that a man was not to speak to a woman in a public place. A husband should not even speak to his wife in public if they happened to meet accidentally on a street. So this is part of the disciples' difficulty. And not only that, the further reason, as we have already seen, is that she is a Samaritan, and, still more, there is her particular character.

We all have our preconceived notions, and we often get into trouble, both before and after we have come into the Christian life, because we are bound and fettered by our prejudices. But our Lord breaks through them all. This is one of the first things we must realize about him. He acts in ways that are utterly unexpected. He sometimes does the exact opposite of what we think he should be doing. But this just opens out to us, does it not, the utter folly of trying to dictate to him, of trying to tell him what he should do. We need to cultivate the attitude and the spirit of these disciples who, because they do not understand, behave in the right way. We are told, '[They] marvelled that he talked with this woman: yet no man said, What seekest thou? or, Why talkest thou with her?' They have enough sense to say nothing – and this is one of the lessons we learn in passing.

*For my thoughts are not your thoughts, neither are your ways my ways,
saith the LORD. For as the heavens are higher than the earth, so are my
ways higher than your ways and my thoughts than your thoughts.
(Isaiah 55:8–9)*

So the lesson you must learn is that you are dealing with this
great and glorious person and you must shed your prejudices,
your preconceived notions and ideas. You must not turn your
Christianity into something little that is just set and formal and
polite and respectable and so ordered. No, no; abandon yourself,
just look at him and watch what he does. Be open to his leadings.
You never know which way he is going to take you, you never
know what he is going to do. He does things that, to us, are
unusual and strange, and seem at times to be wrong.

Now this was the whole tragedy of the Pharisees and the scribes
when our Lord was in this world. Here were these people –
remember that they were godly, religious people – who were always
being stumbled by him. He seemed to them to be a law-breaker.
They were so narrow and rigid in their ideas of the Sabbath that
when they saw him healing a man on the Sabbath, they said, 'This
is breaking the Law.' They did not realize that 'The sabbath was
made for man, and not man for the sabbath' (Mark 2:27). These
are the sort of legalisms and prejudices that we tend to carry with
us into the Christian life and, therefore, at times we will be
shocked and amazed at his treatment of us, or at his handling of
some situation; we marvel and we also tend to grumble and
complain. So let us learn the lesson from these disciples and not
say anything. If we do not understand, we must remember that he
knows what he is doing. We must have faith in him and keep
silent. We must let him lead us. Our business is to follow him.

And that leads to the next general point that comes out here,
which is the fact that he is one who always commands respect. He is

always to be approached with reverence and with awe. Though the disciples do not understand him, though they 'marvel', they keep silent. Why? Well, there is something about him – and you find this running right through the Gospels. And how important it is for us, periodically at any rate, to stand back and just look at him again, to see him as he was here on earth, and to remember that he is the same one, but infinitely glorified, there above the heavens at the right hand of God! So we are delivered from the temptation to approach him with an easy familiarity.

Now there is a paradox here. I am going to tell you about his condescension and about how the woman of Samaria and the disciples can speak to him and put their questions; yes, but, at the same time, there is this about him that holds them back – 'Yet no man said, What seekest thou? or Why talkest thou with her?' Read the story concerning him in the Gospels and you will see how he could silence his enemies. When the very soldiers who came to arrest him saw him, they fell back. He was just a carpenter, he appeared to be an ordinary man, and yet there was this about him that created a sense of awe, a sense of respect, a sense of 'someone other'. As you read the stories and the miracles and his teaching, you will find that people were amazed. We read, 'And they were astonished at his doctrine: for he taught them as one that had authority, and not as the scribes' (Mark 1:22). They were filled with wonder; they praised God and worshipped God. They said, 'We have seen strange things to day' (Luke 5:26). So let us remember that here we are in the realm of the miraculous, the supernatural, the divine. Let us remember that we are dealing with the everlasting and eternal God in three Persons – Father, Son and Holy Spirit.

But, come, let us listen to his own teaching as we find it in this paragraph. You notice his self-revelation. He puts it in terms, as he so generally did, of 'I' and 'you'. 'My meat,' he says, in contradistinction to the food of the disciples – 'His disciples prayed him, saying, Master, eat. But he said unto them, I have meat to eat that ye know not of . . . My meat is to do the will of him that sent me, and to finish his work' (John 4:31–32, 34).

Here, again, is something that should be fundamental in all our thinking. It is a tragedy that I even have to mention such a point as this, but we are living in an age when people who call themselves Christians do not seem to believe any longer in our Lord's unique deity. They not only believe that he was a man, but they are capable of believing that he was a pervert. If there is any suggestion of such thinking in your approach to him, then do not be surprised if you do not know these great blessings and have not received of his fullness and grace upon grace (John 1:16).

This is the very beginning of it all. He is a man but he is not only a man. He stands among us as a man among men but he says 'I' – 'you'. He is not in a series with us; we must get rid of any notion that he is one of us in that sense. The devil is so subtle. I am not querying the motives of people who teach these blasphemous heresies, but they go wrong because they do not approach these issues in the right way. They say, 'If he is to help modern people, then he must be like them.' So they reduce him to our level and argue that he can help perverts by being something of a pervert himself and so on. The whole tragedy is that that is the wrong way round. You start with him! The only hope of our salvation is that he is not one of us; that he can say 'I'. He is the great 'I am that I am' (Exodus 3:14). He is the Lord Jehovah appearing in the flesh as the Son: 'I and you'.

Now I repeat that if there is any query in our minds with regard to his blessed person, there is no hope of any blessing. We immediately reduce him to the level of an earthly human teacher, making him just one in a series with the great men of the ages.

But that is a lie, it is wrong. This is what these disciples have grasped. They are still unlearned and are lacking in their understanding of him and of his way, but they have already felt something that keeps them quiet.

But then our Lord puts the truth of who he is plainly and clearly to the disciples, as he had put it to the woman when he said, 'I that speak unto thee am he.' He says: 'My meat is to do the will of him that sent me' (verse 34). By nature, he does not belong to this world. He has come *into* the world, he has been sent *into* the world. This, of course, is just another way of summing up the whole of what we read in the prologue of John's Gospel. This is just another way of saying, 'In the beginning was the Word, and the Word was with God, and the Word was God' (John 1:1), and, 'And the Word was made flesh, and dwelt among us' (John 1:14).

Now, again, this is a basic Christian truth. Unfortunately I have to say these things because of this foolish age in which we live, which talks about 'tolerance' and says that though you may not believe the truth about the person of Christ, you can still be a Christian if you do good and so on. But there is no Christianity if that is true. This is one of the subjects about which there can be no discussion. There is no 'well of water springing up into everlasting life' if Jesus of Nazareth was only a man. These infidels have their own consistency. They say that he had not even got this fullness of life himself – that he was a fallible, ignorant man and a failure. So there is no hope for us and there was failure in him.

But, oh, how wrong this is! Our whole salvation depends upon the fact that God sent into the world his only begotten Son: 'The Word was made flesh.' Man, yes; but God the eternal Son taking upon himself human nature: 'I – you'. I am the sent one: 'I have come into the world.' That was what he kept on saying. He did not say, 'I was born', but, 'I am come.' He was a visitor. '[God] hath visited and redeemed his people' (Luke 1:68). If we are not clear about all this, it is not surprising that we do not know about the fullness. Let us realize, then, that what we have here is just another way of saying, 'When the fulness of the time was come, God sent forth his Son, made of a woman, made under the law, to redeem them that were under the law' (Galatians 4:4–5). 'I am come.' He is the sent one.

But let us go on: our Lord takes it upon himself to do this work. He says, 'My meat [my whole purpose] is to do the will of him that sent me, and to finish his work.' Do you see the content of that? There is the whole of Christianity in a nutshell. Why has this person come into this world? Why is this blessed Son of God speaking to the woman of Samaria? What is he doing here? And he tells us he has come to do the will of God, 'the will of him that sent me'. What does that mean? It refers to Christian salvation. He came to carry out God's plan of salvation. That is what he was doing in this world. He was not merely here to teach us – that is a part of it – but, oh, the plan of God is for the redemption of the world! This is the great plan conceived in the mind of God before the very foundation of the world, that 'hidden mystery' about which the apostle Paul so delights to write. He says:

> *We speak wisdom among them that are perfect: yet not the wisdom of this world, nor of the princes of this world, that come to nought: But we speak the wisdom of God in a mystery, even the hidden wisdom, which God ordained before the world unto our glory. (1 Corinthians 2:6–7)*

Or, as Paul puts it in writing to the Ephesians, God's purpose is:

> *That in the dispensation of the fulness of times he might gather together in one all things in Christ, both which are in heaven, and which are on earth; even in him. (Ephesians 1:10)*

We must not think of salvation only in subjective terms – what it means to us. That is all right, we must do that, thank God for it, we are to enjoy this personally. But let us see, I say, the whole grand, glorious purpose: 'the will of him that sent me'. Our Lord was a messenger, an envoy, one who had been given an allotted task, and the way to be delivered from so many of the shallows and miseries of the Christian life, that we should never be in at all, is just to look up and to look at him and to see this grand and glorious unfolding purpose.

And our Lord adds to that, to open it out still further: 'to finish his work'. What does this mean? Well, this is a summary of all that he came to do. He means that he came into this world to finish the work that God had sent him to do. And what is that work? It is your salvation, it is my salvation, but it is also the salvation of the world. This is an antidote to every form of spiritual depression. He did not merely come to experiment, he did not merely come to try to do something, he came to finish it. There were certain things that had to be done before you and I could be saved. My dear friend, how can you ever get this glorious Christian experience that the saints of centuries have always enjoyed? You can never get it until you are clear about the way of salvation.

Many people do not realize that our Lord came to finish the work of salvation, and that is why they spend the whole of their lives in seeking. This is the basic error of what is called 'mysticism'. There is a true and there is a false mysticism. The true mysticism is the mysticism of a personal relationship to the Lord Jesus Christ in the way that is indicated in the New Testament. The false mysticism bypasses the work he came to do, that work that he has finished. What that mystic does is this: he starts by saying, 'God is in you, and what you must do now is to seek the God that is in you.' So you go through a long process of meditation and contemplation – 'the dark night of the soul' – and at last you may get some sort of an experience. What it is one does not know. It can be purely psychological. It can make people happy at times – the very few who succeed in getting through the process. But my point is that it is not Christianity at all.

No, there is only one way to this blessed fullness of which our Lord speaks and that is to realize that it is only possible as the result of his finished work. So many people go to God in trouble. They pray and they are surprised that they are not answered; indeed, many Christians go to God and do not get satisfaction. Again, it is because they are forgetting the essential fact that there is a finished work. This subject could keep us, of course, for a great length of time. I am only mentioning it in passing because we are looking at our Lord as he is and as he enunciates these basic questions. You should always read what he says here in the light of his high priestly prayer in John chapter 17. He says:

> *Father, the hour is come; glorify thy Son, that thy Son also may glorify thee: As thou hast given him power over all flesh, that he should give eternal life to as many as thou hast given him. And this is life eternal, that they might know thee the only true God, and Jesus Christ, whom thou hast sent. I have glorified thee on the earth: I have finished the work which thou gavest me to do. (John 17:1–4)*

Now there our Lord sums up his work.

He gave himself to the death of the cross 'to finish the work'. What is this work? It is all that he gave in his teaching, it is all that he manifested in his person and power, but supremely it is what he went on to talk about in that seventeenth chapter of John: 'I sanctify myself' (verse 19). This work is to redeem us, to reconcile us to God. There is no hope for us until we are reconciled to him. It is no use seeking blessings from God until you are reconciled to him, until you realize, in other words, that you have sinned against him, that you are guilty before him, that his wrath is upon you, and that he will not bless a sinner. God may grant you certain temporal or general blessings, but he will never give you this intimate and greatest blessing of all, which is the knowledge of God and of his Son. That knowledge is eternal life and it is only given to those who are covered by the finished work of Christ, which means that the only way whereby we can be reconciled to God is by realizing that God has laid our sins upon his own Son. This is the finishing of the work: it is his going as a lamb to the slaughter, yielding himself passively, allowing the Father to lay our sins upon him, becoming the Lamb of God, and, without grumbling and complaining, being smitten by God. And there he finishes the work of this grand redemption and cries out, 'It is finished' (John 19:30).

And then he rose again to justify us, and 'ever liveth to make intercession for us' (Hebrews 7:25). That is what our Lord is saying here in John 4. This is what he has come to do. He has come to do the will of him that sent him and to finish the work. And he finished it, nothing could stop him. All the powers of hell arrayed against him could not stop him.

Have you realized this? When you go to him or when you seek him in prayer, do you always realize that the only way into the presence of God is 'by the blood of Jesus' (Hebrews 10:19)? Without the finished work there is no access. You will spend the rest of your life seeking, but you will never find the living water. This is the possession only of those who realize the truth concerning this finished work, God's plan in redemption, which is Jesus Christ, and him crucified. Without this atoning death, no blessing is offered us, and we have no right to expect it.

And then to complete this picture, notice our Lord's zeal in this work that he has been sent to do, this commission that has been given to him. Oh, what comforting words these are! 'My meat is to do the will of him that sent me.' The disciples do not understand this: 'I have meat to eat,' he says, 'that ye know not of.' They are pressing him to eat, but he does not. Why not? He says, in effect: 'For one thing, though I am a man, and though I need food, and though I know what it is to be weary, oh, these do not control me. I have hidden resources that you do not understand. I have sources of satisfaction beyond anything that you have ever imagined.'

He is saying: 'Yes, I stayed here, and I let you go to buy the provisions, because I was feeling tired, but now I do not need the food, I am absolutely refreshed.' Why? 'Because I have been doing the very work I was sent to do. I have been engaged in spiritual activity. I have been handling a soul. I have brought a woman to the place of understanding and of joy. I can live on this; this is my meat and this is my drink. These are the resources, these are the things by which I live.'

What a tremendous consolation it is for us that the Son of God not only came but came with delight, with pleasure, that he enjoyed doing this work for you and for me. And you can be certain that in exactly the same way he enjoys working for you now – 'ever living to make intercession for you', ever ready to listen to you. It is his meat and drink. This is what ravished his soul. This is what filled him with delight and glory.

But there is another truth hidden here in this same statement, is there not? That is our Lord's utter forgetfulness of himself, his readiness to sacrifice himself. He needs the food, in a sense, but when it becomes a question of handling this soul, and the possibilities of life for the Samaritans through this woman, he forgets food and drink, he is not interested in them for the time being. He gives himself. The disciples press him. We read here that they 'prayed him'. The

Greek word is very strong. It means that they try to persuade him, they bring pressure to bear upon him to make him eat. They say, 'You know, you're tired and you need food. You must eat. It will all be too much for you and you'll break down under the strain.' Our Lord's mother and his brothers did the same thing on a different occasion. They said, 'He is beside himself' (Mark 3:21) – he cannot go on like this, he will break down. Here, our Lord forgets everything, he sacrifices himself completely for the sake of this woman's soul and the souls of the others.

And our Lord is still the same, my dear friends; this is the very essence of the gospel; this is what we are told everywhere in the New Testament. It is stated supremely in that well-known passage in the second chapter of the Epistle to the Philippians. Here it is:

*Let this mind be in you, which was also in Christ Jesus: who, being in the form of God, thought it not robbery to be equal with God*

– in other words, he did not hold on to that, he did not say, 'Well, yes, I am prepared to help those people but I cannot give up the signs of my eternal glory.' He did not regard this as a prize that he was to hold on to at all costs. No, no; he laid it aside, he laid aside the 'signs' –

*but made himself of no reputation, and took upon him the form of a servant, and was made in the likeness of men: and being found in fashion as a man, he humbled himself, and became obedient unto death, even the death of the cross. (Philippians 2:5–8)*

This is it. Self-forgetfulness, self-abnegation, self-abasement. The insignia of the everlasting glory do not stand in the way. He puts them aside, as he puts the food and the drink aside here in order to help these people. For you and for me he put it all aside and humbled himself, and became a man, and was tempted and suffered – yes, 'even the death of the cross', and the shame accompanying it, and was laid in a tomb. This is his 'meat and drink'. This is his concern for you and for me. And the whole object of recording this is that you and I should remember it. As you go to him in your need, remember all this about him. Though there in that excellent and eternal glory, he still looks at you with a brother's sympathizing eye. He is aware of your need and he is with you. This is the whole point of this teaching. So remember the zeal that he displayed.

And then there is the joy that our Lord talks of, the joy of sowing and the joy of reaping – it gladdens his heart. Whenever a soul is saved, it gives him joy; there is joy among the angels of heaven, and you and I are to be participators, he says, in this joy.

And, finally, remember his glorious and amazing condescension – this one who does not hesitate to say 'I' in contradistinction to 'you', is not only ready to talk to a woman, but is ready to talk to this 'fallen' woman, this woman who is living in sin, and he allows her to speak to him and to put her fumbling questions and her clever arguments. Oh, the infinite condescension of the Son of God! And he is still the same, he is the same blessed person. Do not let your weakness keep you from him, do not let your sin keep you from him. His heart is the tenderest in the whole universe. Though high and exalted and pure and apart from sin, he will never refuse you, he will never reject you if you go to him penitent and repentant, humble and contrite, if you really seek his face.

Here he is – infinite in his glory, infinite in his condescension, infinite in his pity, his sympathy, his tenderness and his readiness to deal with us. He stands before the woman of Samaria and the disciples, and later the Samaritans, but, thank God, also before us now. That is who he is!

40

# *Conviction of Sin*

*The woman then left her waterpot, and went her way into the city, and saith to the men, Come, see a man, which told me all things that ever I did: is not this the Christ? (John 4:28–29)*

I want in particular to deal with the words spoken by the woman of Samaria when she hurries back to the town in which she lives and invites the men there to come out and see this strange and wonderful person whom she has just met herself, the Lord Jesus Christ, the Son of God. We have been seeing together that our great endeavour should be to know and to be certain that we have received, and are receiving, of his fullness and grace upon grace.

Last time we saw that we must always start with the Lord Jesus Christ himself. If we do not do that, we are inevitably doomed to go wrong because everything is in him. The apostle Paul likes to compare the Christian church to a body, of which we individually are members. Christ is the head and we all receive from that head. The fullness is in him: '[The church] is his body, the fulness of him that filleth all and in all' (Ephesians 1:23). Or, again, as Paul puts it in a pregnant statement in the Epistle to the Colossians – this, in a sense, is the great theme of all the Epistles:

> *I would that ye knew what great conflict I have for you, and for them at Laodicea, and for as many as have not seen my face in the flesh.*

What is the apostle concerned about? He continues:

> *That their hearts might be comforted, being knit together in love, and unto all riches of the full assurance of understanding, to the acknowledgment of the mystery of God, and of the Father, and of Christ; in whom are hid all the treasures of wisdom and knowledge.*

That is it.

> *For in him dwelleth all the fulness of the Godhead bodily. And ye are complete in him. (Colossians 2:1–3, 9–10)*

So we must start with him.

The great question, therefore, is, I repeat: Have we received of this fullness? If not, why are we lacking? What is the obstacle? What is the hindrance? Everything that was possessed by the greatest saints that the church has ever known was all derived from the Lord Jesus Christ. The saints were not what they were because of some natural powers and faculties. That does come in, in ministry and so on, but the experiences that they had came from nothing in them. If you read about them before their conversion, before they were born again, you see that they were failures like everybody else, in spite of their shining gifts. The whole secret was that they were in communion and fellowship with him; they were receiving this fullness from him. So what was possible to them is possible to us and, therefore, we must discover the obstacles that are preventing our experiencing this fullness.

We will find that we are given further instruction as we examine the case of this woman of Samaria. We have already seen many principles, but here is a fresh one, and we find it in this statement that she makes to the people of her city – 'Come,' she says, 'see a man, which told me all things that ever I did.' Now that is the first thing that she says about him. And I want to direct your attention to just that very point, and to ask a question: Why does she say that? Why is that the particular way in which she issues her invitation to come and see the Lord Jesus Christ? Why does she not talk about his personality or describe his physical appearance? Why not tell them some of these wonderful truths that he has taught her about worship?

What is this? It is what we call 'conviction of sin', and I want to show you the primacy of this – that if we are not clear about this, then it is not surprising that we know nothing else. There are certain rules in the spiritual life that must be observed. There are no shortcuts in the spiritual realm, there are certain absolutes, and unless we conform to them, we shall never know much about this fullness that is in him. And the first is conviction of sin – 'a man, which told me all things that ever I did'. This is what is uppermost in her mind.

Now you notice that there is on the surface what appears to be an element of exaggeration in this woman's words. She says that our Lord has told her 'all things' that she has ever done. That is not a lie, it is hyperbole. What our Lord actually told her, of course, was that he knew all about the immoral life she was living, and the fact that she had had five husbands and that the man she was now living with was not her husband. That is all he said about her life. When she refers to 'all things that ever I did', she means that as our

Lord revealed to her his knowledge of her present life and of what she was actually guilty, both at that moment and in the recent past, he made her feel that he knew everything. And though our Lord did not put it into words, he produced it, he resurrected it, and, as it were, she saw on a screen flashing past her eyes the whole of her life and all her misdeeds and sins.

This is frequently found in the testimonies that saints of God have left behind them; some people have testified to this kind of experience when their conversion has been due to some crisis or to some accident. I remember one man in particular who was converted as the result of a terrible accident, an explosion in a mine. He suddenly heard the noise and saw the flash, and he realized that his end might be at hand. He testified that immediately there passed before him the whole of his life, as it were, and his individual misdeeds.

Now it is difficult to understand or to accept this, is it not? And yet we know that even in the natural realm this whole problem of time is very strange; there can be a foreshortening that we do not understand. This kind of thing happens. We are so ignorant, we think so much in terms of clocks and watches, of seconds and minutes and hours, but there is this extraordinary capacity to see the whole, as it were, in a flash. This is, of course, still easier to comprehend in the spiritual dimension, and there is no doubt at all but that this is precisely what happened in the case of this woman. Our Lord only mentions one thing but that brings her face to face with herself and her life and her misdeeds. So she says, and says quite truly, therefore: 'Come, see a man, which told me all things that ever I did.' It is clear that this woman was more conscious of a conviction of sin than of anything else and it is in terms of this that she invites her fellow townspeople to come and see our Lord.

This is most important. If I were asked to say what, in my opinion, is most lacking in the life of the Christian church at the present time, without any hesitation I would answer that it is just this – it is a conviction of sin, a sense of our unworthiness and a sense of the glory of God. We are too healthy, we are too satisfied, we are too pleased with ourselves. When we contrast the state of the church today with what we read of in past ages (and I shall refer to this later, God willing) what strikes us immediately is that there is an absence of humility, an absence of repentance. This, of course, is vital and if we are to know individual or general revival, we must start here.

Let me give you one example of how this works out. Here we are – it is harvest thanksgiving. Is the world interested in harvest thanksgivings? Why doesn't the world thank God? Why do we not always realize our indebtedness to him? And the answer of the New Testament is that it is all due to the fact that we have never realized the truth about ourselves and the truth about God. This is the great argument of the apostle Paul in the second half of Romans 1. He says:

*For the wrath of God is revealed from heaven against all ungodliness and unrighteousness of men, who hold [down] the truth in unrighteousness; because that which may be known of God is manifest in them; for God hath shewed it unto them. For the invisible things of him from the creation of the world are clearly seen, being understood by the things that are made, even his eternal power and Godhead; so that they are without excuse: because that, when they knew God, they glorified him not as God, neither were thankful; but became vain in their imaginations, and their foolish heart was darkened. Professing themselves to be wise, they became fools, and changed the glory of the uncorruptible God into an image made like to corruptible man, and to birds, and four-footed beasts, and creeping things. (Romans 1:18–23)*

Now all that just means that the world does not realize the truth about creation, about daily life and living and the very means whereby we go on living. This is because of its 'ungodliness and unrighteousness'. In other words, you will never persuade men and women to realize the truth until they are in the right relationship to God, until they are godly and righteous. They need to be convicted of their sin, they need to repent, they need to turn to God. It is then, and only then, that they will be able to see things truly.

Now this is a most important point because there are those who think that you can persuade men and women about these things by sheer argumentation. You cannot. They cannot even see the universe and creation truly unless they have new life in them. The 'natural man', is incapable of this and sees the creature rather than the Creator.

> A primrose by a river's brim
> A yellow primrose was to him
> And it was nothing more.
> *William Wordsworth*

But a man or woman with a new nature and a mind illuminated by the Holy Spirit sees God in the flower. You can only truly see creation, and all things, as you have this 'mind', this 'eye' of Christ. So these things all hang together. And it is exactly the same with receiving his fullness and grace upon grace. The last people to receive it are always the people who think they are already full. You do not seek for fullness if you think you have it, that would be foolish. It is the people who have never gone down who never go up. It is the people who have never realized their emptiness and their woe, who never know very much about 'the exceeding riches of his grace' (Ephesians 2:7). And I want to show you that it is our failure to put conviction of sin in the first position that accounts for so many of our troubles and certainly accounts for the poverty of our Christian lives.

Why must conviction of sin be put first? Here are some answers. First, the great difference, in the last analysis, between the cults and the Christian faith is just this very point. Has that ever occurred to you? It is no use denying that the cults can help people. They do; they would not succeed but for that. Look at Christian Science and similar movements. Look at their buildings; look at their wealth. That is because of the numbers of their adherents. And listen to their testimonies. Yes, the cults can do many things for many people, but there is one thing that cults never do – they never produce in anybody a sense of guilt. And, of course, that is a part of their popularity. The cults always come to you and more or less tell you that you really are all right as you are, that it is circumstances or other people that are the problem, and all you need is a bit of help. They are most ingratiating and pleasant. They never disturb you; they never make you feel uneasy; you never come under any sense of conviction; they never make you feel that you do not deserve any blessing. No, no; they tell you that you deserve everything and can get everything.

And that is where cults differ so essentially from this Christian message; that is what makes Christianity unique. The trouble is that so many people approach the Christian faith as if it were but one in a series with the cults, and they come expecting that kind of teaching. But they do not get it. They say, 'I came for comfort and for help but you make me feel uncomfortable and I don't like it.' Exactly! But you will never know this blessing until you have been made to feel uncomfortable.

And, of course, this is equally true of the difference between all psychological treatments and movements and Christianity. This, again, must be emphasized because there are people who turn the

Christian faith into a psychological method of treatment. You are familiar with this. There are men well known in what are called Christian pulpits who do nothing but treat people psychologically. There are people flourishing at the present time who talk about the power of 'positive thinking', as if that were the Christian message. It is pure psychology – nothing else; psychology using Christian terminology.

How do you tell the difference? What right have I to say that that is not Christianity, that it is not even pseudo-Christianity, but a travesty of Christianity? I say it solely on the strength of this one particular: all that psychological misuse of the Scriptures never produces a conviction of sin. Indeed, you will find that the purveyors of those false teachings generally denounce the biblical doctrine of sin. They are the very people who talk about 'that God sitting on the top of Mount Sinai' in whom they do not believe. 'Ah,' they say, 'we don't believe in that God of the Old Testament, the God of law, the God of wrath.' They dislike that; they say, 'That's a travesty, don't accept it.' They believe in the God of Jesus, who is nothing but love.

That is their way of putting their whole case, and they go on to say that nothing has done so much harm to people as the preaching of the doctrine of conviction of sin. They say, 'You've given people complexes, you've made them lose confidence in themselves, you've kept them down. That's wrong, it's a perversion. The first thing you must do is get rid of the whole notion of sin, which has so depressed people and stood between them and all there is to enjoy.' But thereby they betray themselves completely. Nobody who has gone to them can come back and say, 'Come, see a man, which told me all things that ever I did.' Never! Because they never produce that effect. They never make us feel worse than we were, they never make us feel hopeless.

Now you see the vital importance of all this? If the Christian message has never made you feel worse than you were before you first heard it, you have never really heard it. If it has never made you feel hopeless, you do not know it. This is the very essence of the Christian faith, as one can illustrate so easily and in so many different ways. When old Simeon held our blessed Lord in his arms, he said, 'This child is set for the fall and rising again of many in Israel' (Luke 2:34). You notice the order? The fall! There is no rising without going down, there is no salvation without preliminary condemnation. People come to me as if they were coming to the cults – they want this, that and the other; and at first they are shocked and amazed – at least, they should be. If they are truly hearing the gospel, they always will be. They say, 'I know I have my problems but now I'm made to feel that I'm wrong, that I'm a worm,' and they dislike it. Exactly! This is always what our Lord does.

And we find all this in the case of the woman of Samaria. We saw how this woman with her glib argumentation is very ready to talk about this world and about worship – 'this mountain', 'Jerusalem' – oh, how easy that is! But then our Lord becomes personal: he puts his finger on the running sore of her life, he reveals her utter sinfulness, and that is essential before she can ever be led to this great and glorious salvation.

Then, secondly, conviction of sin is also the crucial point of difference between taking up religion and becoming truly Christian. Here, again, is a most important distinction. It is possible for us to take up religion, it is possible for us to take up what we regard as Christianity, and there are many who do that. God forbid that there should be any in this congregation this morning. There is a vital, essential difference between that and truly becoming a Christian.

What am I talking about? It is this. It is possible for men and women – the 'natural man' – to be interested in Christ. There are many who are. After all, he is a remarkable phenomenon of history. When you have always thought in terms of evolution and gradual development and progress, it is startling suddenly to find, very nearly two thousand years ago, this towering figure. And when people who are merely interested in history and in the processes of thought and in philosophy, confront him, they have been fascinated by him.

And then there is an interest in our Lord's teaching. People who are concerned about the state of the world and have made many attempts to find solutions, say, 'You know, what's really needed is the application of the Sermon on the Mount.' There are still many who say this – there used to be many more in the early years of this present century. It used to be the prevailing teaching: 'the social gospel', it was called. It was really believed that the Sermon on the Mount could be turned into acts of Parliament and that the world could thereby be put right.

Not only that, there are many who desire to live a good, a better life. Not every sinner is as bad as he can possibly be. There are great differences among sinners. Some poor sinners are just wallowing in the mire and the filth and the gutters of life; but there are others who are very concerned about living a good life, though they are equally sinners and are no more Christian than the man in the gutter. There is idealism and there are idealists. There are large numbers of people who really want to be good. They are troubled, they have consciences – every man and woman has a conscience and some are more sensitive than others. Some people have taken the trouble to read and are concerned about the whole problem of life in this world. They have studied ethical, moral systems, they have read not only the Greek philosophers, but also the maxims of Marcus Aurelius and other idealistic writings about life, and their whole desire is to be able to live that sort of life.

And then there are others who desire to do good. The world has large numbers of such people. We must never, as Christians, say that nobody but the Christian wants to do any good in the world. It is not so. These people are anxious to improve the world, to uplift the human race, to put an end to war. Our Lord is, to them, the great pacifist, and the Sermon on the Mount, they say, teaches that war is wrong. So they take up what they regard as Christianity and set about trying to do good.

And then at the top of the list, perhaps, we have the people whose great ambition in life is to imitate Christ. It is fascinating to trace the history of this idea in the long story of the Christian church; it has been one of the greatest snares for many an honest soul who has been seeking salvation. 'The imitation of Christ' – it sounds so good, does it not? These people are obviously anxious to be good, they are anxious to do good, and they go on to say, 'Here is one who has lived a perfect life in this world, he is the person I must emulate. I must go after him. I must follow him.' So they set out and they find books and manuals to encourage them in the imitation of Christ, and they are ready to make sacrifices; and this is regarded as the height of Christianity and the Christian profession.

Again, we must be very careful how we speak. There are people in the world today who quite genuinely and honestly have set out to imitate Christ. They have given up good posts and prospects in the world, they have made great financial and other sacrifices to follow him. We do not hear as much of this as we used to because the two wars have shattered people's belief in the ability to imitate Christ, but this teaching still often appears in different guises. I remember very well – I mention this simply as a typical illustration of what I am saying – attending a young people's rally over 40 years ago. There were three speakers and they had been given the same subject – 'The appeal of Christ to the enthusiasm and heroism of young people'. You see the idea? He was to be depicted as a young man, full of heroism, full of enthusiasm, full of idealism – here is the one for you to follow. Now this, it is said, is the way to win young people, this is the way to get hold of them. Young people always admire heroism, they are enthusiastic, they have it in them to do good. They want to follow Christ, so here he is, let us hold him before them and he will appeal to them.

But you see how this all betrays itself? All that teaching, all this interest in the person of our Lord, in his teaching, in the desire to be good, to improve the world and to imitate him, is based on one assumption: that we have it in us to be like him. So all we need to do is to be enthused, to rise up and follow him in this great crusade. This teaching has never made us feel uncomfortable, has it? Indeed, it has done the very opposite, it has made us feel we are rather wonderful, that we can do this. Indeed, we feel that there is something good in us or we would not be responding in this way. The person who has come under this kind of influence does not rush back and say, 'Come, see a man, which told me all things that ever I did.' No, no! It is, 'Come, see a man who has told me that I have it in me to live as he lived, that I can put the world right, that all we need to do is band together and march down this highway and the world will become paradise.' This teaching says: Believe in yourselves. Follow him – he is what you can be.

No, no; that is religion; you can take up that kind of teaching, and very many have done so. And, alas, is it not one of the great problems of the church that it regards this as Christianity? It is just calling upon people to take it up, to go into some great crusade. The world can be invited, of course. So the biblical doctrine of sin is denounced and people are appealed to in terms of the idealism of Christ, and the wonderful teaching and the possibilities he holds out.

But he does not do that. What he does is expose you to yourself and make you see yourself as you really are. It is horrible, and you feel you are unworthy to do anything. Now here, therefore, is something that we must obviously be very clear about. It is not surprising that people say they have tried Christianity and have found it wanting. Such people have started with the wrong conceptions. This is a message that first and foremost convicts us of sin.

Let me put it like this, and this is the third reason why conviction of sin must be put first. The New Testament teaching itself makes it perfectly plain and clear that it is impossible for us to be truly Christian without a conviction of sin. How does it show this? The first way is by giving this teaching priority.

Let us assume for a moment that we do not believe this message at all, but that we are approaching the Bible as literary critics who are going to make an analysis of the New Testament. We are given this question: What is the first teaching in the New Testament? I think you will have to agree that we will discover that it is always a message of repentance.

Who is the first preacher in the New Testament? The answer is, John the Baptist. We are told about his wonderful birth, and then about how he set out on his ministry. This is the introduction, this is the prologue. What did John preach about? There is no difficulty about this – he preached 'the baptism of repentance for the remission of sins' (Mark 1:4). Now there had been 400 years of silence, as it were, after the time of the prophet Malachi – not a word of prophecy. Then suddenly a phenomenon – a strange man preaching in a wilderness, clothed with camel's hair, with a leather belt about his loins, eating locusts and wild honey. A strange man with an extraordinary message – 'the baptism of repentance for the remission of sins'. And the people came crowding out to listen to him, the Pharisees included, and look at the reception he gave them. He did not say, 'I'm glad to see you. Are you ready to go forward in this great crusade I'm starting to put the world right?' No, he looked at them and said:

> *O generation of vipers, who hath warned you to flee from the wrath to come . . . And think not to say within yourselves, We have Abraham to our father: for I say unto you, that God is able of these stones to raise up children unto Abraham.*

Do not make any mistake about this, says John the Baptist.

> *The axe is laid unto the root of the trees; therefore every tree which bringeth not forth good fruit is hewn down, and cast into the fire. (Matthew 3:7, 9–10)*

'The baptism of repentance for the remission of sins' – the first message of the first preacher. 'I indeed baptize you with water . . .' (Matthew 3:11). There it is, nobody can dispute that.

The second great preacher, of course, was none other than our Lord himself. What did he preach about? The message is exactly the same:

> *Now after that John was put in prison, Jesus came into Galilee, preaching the gospel of the kingdom of God, and saying, The time is fulfilled, and the kingdom of God is at hand: repent ye, and believe the gospel. (Mark 1:14–15)*

Then in John chapter 3, we see Nicodemus, a ruler of the Jews, a teacher, a good man, a religious man, a moral man, who wanted to be arguing with our Lord on equal terms, as it were, and was ready to receive a little further information. But this is what our Lord said to him: 'Verily, verily, I say unto thee, Except a man be born of water and of the Spirit, he cannot enter into the kingdom of God' (John 3:5). 'Born of water' – that is repentance again; that is baptism again; that is acknowledgment and confession of utter sinfulness. To a man such as Nicodemus, who wanted to start from where he was and go on, our Lord said: No, no! Come, start again. You must be born again, you must go through the water, you must be baptized.

Repentance! Our Lord was constantly making this point, especially to the Pharisees. In one of the parables that he addressed to them, he said:

> *But what think ye? A certain man had two sons; and he came to the first, and said, Son, go work to day in my vineyard. He answered and said, I will not: but afterward he repented, and went. And he came to the second, and said likewise. And he answered and said, I go, sir: and went not. Whether of them twain did the will of his father? They say unto him, The first. Jesus saith unto them, Verily I say unto you, That the publicans and the harlots go into the kingdom of God before you. For John came unto you in the way of righteousness, and ye believed him not: but the publicans and the harlots believed him: and ye, when ye had seen it, repented not afterward, that ye might believe him. (Matthew 21:28–32)*

This is what determines our entry into the kingdom of God. You cannot enter the kingdom of God without repentance. It does not matter who you are, or how good you are – the tax collectors and harlots will go in before you. Why? Because they repented! It is the very essence of his teaching.

We find exactly the same teaching in the famous parable about the tax collector and the Pharisee who went up into the Temple to pray. What could be plainer and clearer?

*Two men went up into the temple to pray; the one a Pharisee, and the other a publican. The Pharisee stood and prayed thus with himself, God, I thank thee that I am not as other men are, extortioners, unjust, adulterers, or even as this publican. I fast twice in the week, I give tithes of all that I possess.*

'Here is a typical follower of Christ,' people think. 'Here is a man who has taken up Christ.' But it is all wrong.

*And the publican, standing afar off, would not lift up so much as his eyes unto heaven, but smote upon his breast, saying, God be merciful to me a sinner. I tell you, this man went down to his house justified rather than the other: for every one that exalteth himself shall be abased; and he that humbleth himself shall be exalted. (Luke 18:10–14)*

And this need for repentance is implicit in the whole of our Lord's teaching. Look again at the Sermon on the Mount, which the kind of person we are dealing with always admires and is ready to take up and to put into practice in order to follow Christ and imitate his example. Such a person says, 'This is what the world needs.' But what a complete misunderstanding of the Sermon on the Mount and its purpose! No, the Sermon on the Mount is nothing but an exposition of the Law. Our Lord did not preach it because he thought that men and women as they were could keep it; it was the exact opposite. He gave the Sermon on the Mount to convict those who felt they could keep the Law of God, and to show them that they could never do so. In effect, he said: 'The moment you really understand the Law, you will see how impossible that is.' Take the examples: take a man who says he has never committed murder. But, says our Lord, have you understood that? You say that because you have never murdered a man you have kept the Law in this respect, but have you? Have you ever said of your brother, 'You fool!'? Have you ever murdered him in your heart and in your mind? If you have, you are guilty of murder.

Now does that mean that the Sermon on the Mount is possible? No, no; it means that it is impossible. Is the Law possible? It is impossible. The Law is concerned with my motives, my desires, my hidden imaginations, and therefore the moment I see it, I am undone. The Sermon on the Mount was given to convict people of their utter helplessness and to show that our Lord had come to save them out of their helpless and their hopeless position.

And it is the same with the whole of our Lord's teaching. All along he shows men and women that they cannot save themselves. 'The things which are impossible with men', he says, 'are possible with God' (Luke 18:27). That is his reply to the question, 'Who then can be saved?' No, no; as Simeon prophesied of him, he casts down, he condemns. That is why the Pharisees hated him. And here, with this woman of Samaria, we see how he cuts across all the talk and the pleasant argument and immediately comes down to the question of sin and guilt – conviction of sin.

And as this is true of the teaching of our Lord, so it is equally true of the teaching of the apostles. Turn to the book of Acts and there you will find this theme at the very beginning and running right through. Here is Peter filled with the Spirit on the Day of Pentecost, and he is expounding the Old Testament Scriptures. He declares that God has raised Jesus from the dead and shows that this is what was prophesied of the Messiah because the body of David is in the sepulchre and remains there. And on Peter goes, expounding these Scriptures; he declares that God has at last sent the Deliverer, and that the coming of the Holy Spirit upon them is the absolute proof of this. Then Peter says: 'Therefore let all the house of Israel know assuredly, that God hath made that same Jesus, whom ye have crucified, both Lord and Christ.'

We are told that when all the people heard this, 'They were pricked in their heart, and said unto Peter and to the rest of the apostles, Men and brethren, what shall we do?' Here is the announcement of the gospel, the proclamation of the kingdom of God, and the first effect it has is that people say, 'Men and brethren, what shall we do?'

And Peter says, 'Repent' – repent! Acknowledge, confess your sin; you have felt a pricking in your hearts, you are aware of your guilt, it has been exposed to you for the first time, then acknowledge it, give up your defence, cast yourself at his feet – 'and be baptized every one of you in the name of Jesus Christ for the remission of sins' (Acts 2:29–38). That is Peter, the first preacher among the apostles.

And then look at the apostle Paul with his mighty ministry, what did he preach? There he is in Athens, what does he preach in this cultured, sophisticated society, to this gathering of Stoics and Epicureans? This is the message:

*Whom therefore ye ignorantly worship, him declare I unto you. God that made the world and all things therein, seeing that he is Lord of heaven and earth, dwelleth not in temples made with hands; neither is worshipped with men's hands, as though he needed any thing, seeing he giveth to all life, and breath, and all things; and hath made of one blood all nations of men for to dwell on all the face of the earth, and hath determined the times before appointed, and the bounds of their habitation; that they should seek the Lord, if haply they might feel after him, and find him, though he be not far from every one of us: for in him we live, and move, and have our being; as certain of your own poets have said, For we are also his offspring. Forasmuch then as we are the offspring of God, we ought not to think that the Godhead is like unto gold, or silver, or stone, graven by art and man's device. And the times of this ignorance God winked at; but now commandeth all men every where to repent. (Acts 17:23–30)*

For philosophers, idealists – repent! It is the universal message. And, finally, Paul takes his farewell of the elders of the church at Ephesus, and this is what he says:

> *When they were come to him, he said unto them, Ye know, from the first day that I came into Asia, after what manner I have been with you at all seasons, serving the Lord with all humility of mind, and with many tears, and temptations, which befell me by the lying in wait of the Jews: and how I kept back nothing that was profitable unto you, but have shewed you, and have taught you publickly, and from house to house, testifying both to the Jews, and also to the Greeks, repentance toward God, and faith toward our Lord Jesus Christ. (Acts 20:18–21)*

So if you merely take the New Testament teaching chronologically, in the order of priorities, there is no question but that the need for repentance is the first message. The gospel starts with this: 'Come, see a man, which has told me all things that ever I did' – a man who has made me see myself as I am, my guilt, my emptiness, my woe, my helplessness, my hopelessness. That is always the first effect that he has.

Has he had this effect upon you? There is no hope of receiving of his fullness, and grace upon grace, until you have known conviction of sin, and have realized your appalling need and your precarious position. Have you known this? Start with this, because without it he has nothing to give you; but having had this, he has everything to give you. Make certain that you start at the beginning.

41

# *The Essential First Step*

*The woman then left her waterpot, and went her way into the city, and saith to the men, Come, see a man, which told me all things that ever I did: is not this the Christ? (John 4:28–29)*

We are dealing, let me remind you, with the woman of Samaria's response to our Lord and to what he has been saying to her. We are looking at this whole incident because we are anxious to see what it is that hinders so many from knowing this final satisfaction, this sufficiency that our Lord has to give. We have seen that she is convicted of sin and we are trying to show that this conviction of sin is always essential for a true receiving of the well of water that springs up into everlasting life.

Now I have already given you some reasons for emphasizing this need and for putting it first. I suggested, first, that it shows us the difference between the teaching of psychologists and the cults, on the one hand, and the true Christian faith on the other, and, secondly, I pointed out that it is the difference between taking up religion and becoming truly Christian. Then, thirdly, I suggested that we must put this first because it always comes first in the New Testament itself.

But there are further reasons for putting conviction of sin first, and I want to consider them with you. Have you ever looked at it from this standpoint: if you read these four Gospels, at once you will be impressed by the opposition that our Lord received. It is extraordinary that he, the Son of God, who had come to bless humanity, should have had such opposition. Much space is given in the Gospels to the wranglings of the Pharisees, the Sadducees, the doctors of the Law, and all these other people. Why did they oppose him? What was it they objected to? I think you will agree that the answer is quite simple. They always hated the fact that he convicted them of their sin. This was the great trouble, especially with the Pharisees. It cut right across all their ideas. They had divided people up into Pharisees and sinners. The tax collectors were among the sinners, of course, while they, the Pharisees, were the godly, the self-righteous. We see this to perfection in our Lord's parable of the Pharisee and the tax collector who both went up to the Temple to pray (Luke 18:10–14).

The religious leaders finally crucified him simply because he made them feel that they were sinners. Indeed, he not only made them feel it by the general tenor of his teaching, he put it specifically to them: 'I am not come to call the righteous, but sinners to repentance' (Matthew 9:13). He is saying: All right, you reject my gospel, you say it is not for you; very well, 'They that be whole need not a physician, but they that are sick' (Matthew 9:12). In those words, he is simply telling them very plainly and directly that they are putting themselves outside the salvation that he has come to give. But perhaps one of our Lord's clearest statements is at the end of John chapter 9:

*And Jesus said, For judgment I am come into this world, that they which see not might see; and that they which see might be made blind. And some of the Pharisees which were with him heard these words, and said unto him, Are we blind also?*

That is it! 'Are you saying that we are blind?'

*Jesus said unto them, If ye were blind, ye should have no sin; but now ye say, We see; therefore your sin remaineth. (John 39–41)*

This was the explanation of the constant argumentation and wrangling of these Pharisees and scribes against our Lord. So it was obviously the aspect that stood out prominently in his teaching. The Pharisees saw it negatively and they reacted against it, but thereby they were giving proof that the first thing that he always did was convict of sin. The woman of Samaria saw it. The Pharisees felt it but hated it. So I repeat that we must put this in the first position.

Or take it in the way in which the apostle Paul puts it at the beginning of Romans chapter 7. Saul of Tarsus had been a man who was very satisfied with himself. As a Pharisee, he had resented this particular teaching. He puts it like this: 'I was alive without the law once' (Romans 7:9). He had thought he was all right, he had been perfectly satisfied, but then he had suddenly realized the meaning of the Law. You can know the letter of the Law, you can be very expert at keeping it, from a purely external point of view, and you will say, 'Touching the righteousness which is in the law, [I am] blameless' (Philippians 3:6) – and that had been Paul's position. In that third chapter of his letter to the Philippians and especially in verses 4 to 6, you find that he gives a list of all his reasons for being pleased with himself as a religious, moral man and an expert in the Law.

But then suddenly the Spirit came upon the apostle Paul, and he saw it all: 'I was alive without the law once: but when the commandment came' – by that he means, 'when the Spirit came upon it and came upon me, then it really did get me, it came to me' – 'sin revived, and I died' (Romans 7:9). He saw then that he was the chief of sinners – that is what he says about himself: 'This is a faithful saying, and worthy of all acceptation, that Christ Jesus came into the world to save sinners; of whom I am chief' (1 Timothy 1:15). That is the difference between someone who is religious and the Christian. Religious people are not aware that they are sinners at all. The determining factor that shows whether we are just religious, or whether we are truly Christians, is that the commandment comes to Christians with the enlightenment of the Spirit and we are convicted and undone.

Then Paul goes on in Romans 7:

*Was then that which is good made death unto me? God forbid. But sin, that it might appear sin, working death in me by that which is good; that sin by the commandment might become exceeding sinful. For we know that the law is spiritual: but I am carnal, sold under sin. (Romans 7:13–14)*

That is it! As a Pharisee, it was the last thing the apostle would ever have said, but the moment conviction came, this is what he found and he was ready to admit it. And so he goes on with this analysis, ending with the final cry:

*O wretched man that I am! Who shall deliver me from the body of this death? (Romans 7:24)*

So it is obvious that it is conviction of sin that always comes out first and most prominently in the whole of our Lord's ministry. The reactions of the self-righteous Pharisee and the religious person are proof of the fact that without conviction of sin there is no such thing as becoming a Christian.

But even apart from our Lord's teaching, is it not interesting to observe how his very presence, his person, and all that he was, so often produced this same effect upon people, even, at times without his saying a single word? This, again, is found right through the whole Bible. We are concerned about our relationship to God, and the Bible emphasizes that this is not intellectual, but is personal. There are some people who say, 'I've always believed in God. I was brought up to believe in him.' But thereby these people betray themselves. They argue about God and what God should and should not do, and so on, but that is not the atmosphere of the Bible at all.

Let me give you just one or two examples of what I mean. It is one thing to believe intellectually, but people who only believe intellectually know very little about the well of water springing up into everlasting life; they know nothing, practically, about this fullness that is in him. The moment you are in that realm there is a change in your whole demeanour, your whole attitude. There is a perfect example of this in the case of Jacob. Jacob had been brought up to believe in God, he was a religious man. But then he had an experience that changed his whole life and he never forgot it. It happened when he was running away from the wrath of his brother Esau after he had supplanted Esau and received Esau's blessing from their father. His mother had suggested to him that he had better go if he wanted to save his life; so off he went.

But here he is, troubled. He has been running and he is weary. So he puts himself down to sleep with a stone under his head as a pillow and there he has an extraordinary dream. Then he wakes up, and this is what we read:

*He said, surely the LORD is in this place; and I knew it not. And he was afraid, and said, How dreadful is this place! This is none other but the house of God, and this is the gate of heaven. (Genesis 28:16–17)*

That is it! You see, he is a man who believes in God; and he goes to sleep, he does not think, but something happens, and he has a direct, immediate experience of God.

We find many another example. When Moses had finished erecting the tabernacle in the wilderness for the people, and had furnished it perfectly, and everything was in position, then suddenly the glory of the Lord descended upon it all, and Moses, we are told, 'was not able to enter into the tent of the congregation, because the cloud abode thereon, and the glory of the LORD filled the tabernacle' (Exodus 40:35).

This personal experience of God's glorious presence is emphasized right away through the Bible. The same thing happened to Isaiah. It was a part of the very call of this man, a part of his commissioning:

*In the year that king Uzziah died I saw also the Lord sitting upon a throne, high and lifted up, and his train filled the temple. Above it stood the seraphims: each one had six wings; with twain he covered his face, and with twain he covered his feet, and with twain he did fly. And one cried unto another, and said, Holy, holy, holy, is the LORD of hosts: the whole earth is full of his glory. And the posts of the door moved at the voice of him that cried, and the house was filled with smoke.*

This was a wonderful vision given to Isaiah; what was its effect?

*Then said I, Woe is me! for I am undone; because I am a man of unclean lips, and I dwell in the midst of a people of unclean lips: for mine eyes have seen the King, the LORD of hosts. (Isaiah 6:1–5)*

You see the effect of having a vision of God! Do you see the result of coming anywhere near the presence of God? Isaiah had not seen God, 'For there shall no man see me and live,' God had said to Moses (Exodus 33:20). But he had had a vision, he had had a glimpse, and the immediate, invariable effect was: 'Woe is me! for I am undone; because I am a man of unclean lips.' No condemnation had come from the throne of God to Isaiah, the Law had not thundered at him, he had not been condemned in detail – there was no need. He had come into the presence of God. There was no defence, no self-defence. He saw the truth about himself and he was 'undone'.

Now all I am suggesting to you is this: we are not mere believers in God with our minds and intellects; we claim to know him, we say we are his people, but that is impossible without our knowing something of what Isaiah felt on that occasion. I agree that is an exceptional experience; yes, but it is only exceptional to indicate what is the norm. This is where we are supposed to be.

But let us go on and consider the New Testament teaching, and here, as one reads the Gospels, one is struck constantly by the way in which our Lord himself had this effect upon people, especially at moments when he had worked a miracle or had done something unusual and remarkable. Every time you read the accounts of the miracles, watch the effect upon the disciples and upon the people – the sense of marvel and amazement, or their worship of God for this strange power that he had given.

One of the most interesting occasions is in the case of Peter. The disciples had been out fishing all night long and had caught nothing. In the morning our Lord appeared and got into Peter's boat to preach from it. He later told Peter to go further out and throw the net into the sea, and they caught so many fish that the net broke. Those in the boat called James and John to help, and both boats were so full of fish that they began to sink. And it is interesting to read the effect that that had upon Peter. When he saw this tremendous haul of fish after a night of failure, he said, 'Depart from me; for I am a sinful man, O Lord' (Luke 5:8).

Why did Peter feel that? Our Lord had not rebuked him, he had not said that Peter was a sinner or read out a list of his particular sins. No, no! Our Lord had just given the word, 'Let down your nets for a catch,' and they had. But the effect upon Peter was to make him feel that he was a sinner, that he could not stand it, in a sense. What was this? Oh, he had just had a glimpse of the glory of the Son of God, and the power of the infinite and the eternal, and whenever one has that, it always has this effect. 'Come, see a man, which told me all things that ever I did: is not this the Christ?'

Here, I repeat, is something that is at the very heart and centre of the whole of the teaching of the Bible concerning our relationship to God. How can we say that we know God if we know nothing of this? And yet at the present time we are subjective, we are self-centred, we want blessings and we do this and that – and God himself is forgotten. The sense of awe and of reverence, the sense of sinfulness and of unworthiness and of vileness that should come first do not seem to be there at all.

Take another instance. In John chapter 18, we read the account of our Lord's arrest, and we are told:

*And Judas also, which betrayed him, knew the place . . . Judas then, having received a band of men and officers from the chief priests and Pharisees, cometh hither with lanterns and torches and weapons. Jesus therefore, knowing all things that should come upon him, went forth, and said unto them, Whom seek ye? They answered him, Jesus of Nazareth. Jesus saith unto them, I am he. And Judas also, which betrayed him, stood with them. As soon then as he had said unto them, I am he, they went backward, and fell to the ground. (John 18:2–6)*

They did not rush forward to arrest him, they 'went backward, and fell to the ground'. And all he had said was, 'I am he,' the words he had spoken to this woman of Samaria. Why did they fall to the ground? Oh, they suddenly realized something of the truth of this statement that he was indeed not only Jesus of Nazareth, but the everlasting Son of God. They were in the presence of his majesty, and they were humbled and alarmed, and they fell down.

We find this also after our Lord's resurrection and ascension. John tells us in the first chapter of the book of Revelation how he was given a vision of this blessed risen Lord:

*In the midst of the seven candlesticks one like unto the Son of man, clothed with a garment down to the foot, and girt about the paps with a golden girdle. His head and his hairs were white like wool, as white as snow; and his eyes were as a flame of fire; and his feet like unto fine brass, as if they burned in a furnace; and his voice as the sound of many waters. And he had in his right hand seven stars: and out of his mouth went a sharp twoedged sword: and his countenance was as the sun shineth in his strength.*

Listen!

*And when I saw him, I fell at his feet as dead. (Revelation 1:13–17)*

It is the glory, my friends. It is the glory of God. And Paul says that this is the truth about a Christian:

*For God, who commanded the light to shine out of darkness, hath shined in our hearts, to give the light of the knowledge of the glory of God in the face of Jesus Christ.*

That is what makes me a Christian, says Paul.

*But we have [received] this treasure in earthen vessels. (2 Corinthians 4:6–7)*

What I have received is: 'the glory of God in the face of Jesus Christ'; and the effect of that, invariably, is to humble, to subdue, to silence, to convict, to reveal to us our true state and condition, our emptiness and woe, our sinfulness, our unworthiness. You cannot be healthy in his presence, you cannot be self-satisfied and glib and slick; it is impossible.

You and I are not people who merely believe a number of propositions with our intellects. We do that, but what makes us truly Christian is that we know something of him, there is this personal fellowship and communion; and the moment this comes in, the effect is that: 'I fell down as one dead.' 'Come, see a man, which told me all things that ever I did: is not this the Christ?' Quite apart from his explicit teaching, his very person, his very presence does this.

But come, let us go on. This conviction of sin is always also, is it not, the primary work of the Holy Spirit? Our Lord has returned to heaven, and is seated at the right hand of God in the glory everlasting, but he had said to his followers, 'Let not your heart be troubled' – do not be distressed. I will send you another Comforter. I am not going to leave you orphans, I will send you another Teacher, one who will stand by your side. He will be with you, he will lead you, he will guide you into all truth, he will instruct you. You will be in a better position after I have gone than you are in now. 'It is expedient for you that I go away: for if I go not away, the Comforter will not come unto you; but if I depart, I will send him unto you' (John 16:7). And he did.

So what is the work of this Comforter, the Holy Spirit? There is no difficulty, is there? It is especially clear in this Gospel according to St John. This is how our Lord himself teaches his disciples about it:

*And when he is come*

– what will he do? What is the first work of the Holy Spirit? –

*he will reprove the world of sin, and of righteousness, and of judgment: of sin, because they believe not on me; of righteousness, because I go to my Father, and ye see me no more; of judgment, because the prince of this world is judged. (John 16:8–11)*

Now this, according to our Lord, is to be the first and essential work of the Spirit; the Spirit who is now in the church, the Spirit who is now the teacher, the one through whom the risen Lord himself is working and active among his people, and through them to those who are outside. This, he says, is to be the primary work, this will characterize his ministry – conviction of sin. And as our Lord prophesied, so it turned out to be.

In the second chapter of the book of Acts, we have the great account of the coming of the Holy Spirit upon the church in Jerusalem in a mighty baptism of power on the Day of Pentecost. And filled with this tremendous power of the Spirit to preach and expound, the apostle Peter stands up and expounds the Scriptures, preaching the first sermon, in a sense, under the auspices of the Christian church as we now know her. What effect does this have? It is no longer Peter, it is Peter filled with the Spirit, it is Peter being clothed with the Spirit, Peter as the vehicle of the Spirit and his power. What does the Spirit do through Peter? You remember what happened: 'When they heard this, they were pricked in their heart, and said unto Peter and to the rest of the apostles, Men and brethren, what shall we do?' (Acts 2:37).

What is this? It is conviction. These people listening to Peter are in trouble. They are unhappy, they are ill at ease, they are made to feel desperate. The Law has come, it has found them, and they cry out in their agony, 'Men and brethren, what shall we do?'

And Peter answers, 'Repent'! In a sense, he says: Go on, let it work in you; do not defend yourselves, give in to what you are feeling. You see how wrong you have been, and how unworthy you are; let it go on, do not resist the Spirit. 'Repent, and be baptized every one of you in the name of Jesus Christ for the remission of sins, and ye shall receive the gift of the Holy Ghost' (Acts 2:38). There it is, the very first instance of the operation of the power of the Spirit in the church. The Spirit does the very thing that our Lord had prophesied that he would do.

And as we work our way through the book of Acts, we find this same conviction everywhere. Take the ninth chapter, where we see Saul of Tarsus on the way to Damascus. The powerful, defiant Pharisee, who hates Christ and is going down to exterminate his church in Damascus, suddenly sees his Lord, and he falls to the ground and in his helplessness says, 'Lord, what wilt thou have me to do?' (Acts 9:6). He is finished; he sees his vileness and emptiness, his woe, his utter wrongness.

Then take the famous case of the Philippian jailor in Acts chapter 16. Here is a man who has carried out his instructions and has thrust Paul and Silas into the innermost part of the prison and put their feet fast in the stocks, having already scourged them. And Paul and Silas are praying and singing praises unto God at midnight when suddenly there is a tremendous earthquake, and this man, the keeper, wakes up thinking all the prisoners have fled. But we read: 'But Paul cried with a loud voice, saying, Do thyself no harm' – the jailor is on the point of committing suicide – 'for we are all here.'

What effect does that have upon the Philippian jailor? Well, these records are so wonderful in their detail; it is all here, perfectly simple and plain before us. 'He called for a light, and sprang in, and came trembling, and fell down before Paul and Silas.' He falls down before the men whom he has just been scourging, the men whom he has put into the innermost prison, whose feet he has fastened in the stocks! He falls down before them – what is the matter with this man? And he says, 'Sirs, what must I do to be saved?' But they have not preached to him, they have not condemned him, they have not tried to convict him of anything, so what is it?

Oh, this man has sensed the presence of God and he is convicted of sin. He does not mean: What must I do to retain my job? No, it is: What must I do to get myself saved? What must I do to be like you are? Where can I get this joy that you have, that makes you sing when you are in the innermost prison with your feet in the stocks? You are happier than I am as the keeper – what is this? He feels his sinfulness, he is convicted. That is the effect: trembling, falling down, even before the servants of the Lord. Everything about them and this tremendous action in the earthquake has convinced and convicted this man of sin, and, as in the case of the woman of Samaria, suddenly all that he is flashes before him on a screen, as it were, and he is horrified; so he says, 'What must I do?' (Acts 16:23–30).

And we cannot be Christians without something of this; it is impossible. It is here everywhere in the Scriptures. I say again that conviction of sin is one of the essential preliminaries to receiving of his fullness, and grace upon grace, to having this well of water springing up into everlasting life.

'But,' you say, 'this all belongs to New Testament times' – that is the argument today, is it not? All that was all right in the time of the apostles, but not any longer. The New Testament? You mustn't judge yourself by the New Testament, that was an exceptional period.

What a terrible lie that is! How dreadful to narrow the word of God down to the measure of our little understanding! That view is not even true historically. Read the history of the church, read the biographies of the saints, the stories of these outstanding men and women, and you will invariably find what you have found in the Scriptures. Start, if you like, with St Augustine of Hippo – read the story of his conversion. There was an increasing conviction of sin before he found peace and joy and release and happiness. There was desperation, unhappiness, struggling, knowing he was wrong, being convicted but resisting, and then at last the abandon. It is invariable.

Martin Luther! Next week we are hoping to commemorate that great day when he nailed the Ninety-five Theses to the door of the church at Wittenberg. What is the story of Luther? The essential story was conviction of sin. You do not understand the Protestant Reformation apart from this. It is not the result of a conference! We are living in an age of conferences and of ecclesiastics. They meet in conference and they decide this and that. You never get a Reformation like that! No, no; it happened in the soul of a man who was convinced and convicted of sin, who was in agony.

Perhaps one of the greatest classics in these matters is John Bunyan's *Grace Abounding*, or, if you like, *The Pilgrim's Progress*. It does not matter, read both books and you will find exactly the same depiction of conviction of sin. That mighty man, John Bunyan, tinker as he was, with his great soul, for 18 months passed through an agony of repentance, sensing the vileness of his own heart, seeing his utter helplessness and hopelessness.

Then go on to the next century and read about the conversion of Whitefield and the two Wesleys, John and Charles. These men felt such a conviction of sin that they became physically ill; there are points when you almost feel they were losing their reason. Why was this? Well, it was due to an agony of soul in these marvellous mighty men of God. This is the invariable rule; it is the work of the Holy Spirit. When the Holy Spirit deals with people, he invariably must produce conviction of sin. 'See a man, which told me all things that ever I did.' You see yourself for the first time in your life. The man of the world has never seen himself, that is why he goes on as he is.

But then read as well the stories of the great revivals in the long history of the church, and you will find, without a single exception, that in the early stages of every revival, the first effect was a terrifying conviction of sin. Now this happened to people who had been brought up in the church, who had been church members, perhaps for many years, and were highly respected and regarded as religious people. Suddenly the Spirit would come down and these very people would begin to feel they had never been Christians at all. This conviction could sometimes be so powerful that they would fall to the ground in a great spiritual agony and crisis.

Now I am not the one saying this – this is history and I am just commending you to read history. All I am trying to show you is that the Spirit always does what our Lord prophesied he would do – he starts by convicting us of sin. You do not start where you are, feeling nothing, and then suddenly accept Christ into your heart. No, no! 'See a man, which told me all things that ever I did, is not this the Christ?' Conviction of sin is invariable in all the great movements of the Spirit, whether in individuals or in masses of people at the same time.

And let me conclude with this argument: surely there is no meaning in the word 'salvation' apart from conviction of sin. Is Christ your Saviour? What do you mean by that? What is a saviour? What is salvation? Surely, by definition, a saviour is one who saves us from something, from a predicament, from trouble.

The Saviour! Salvation! What is it? And there is only one answer to all this in the whole of the Bible. Think of the angel who appeared to Joseph, the husband of Mary, the mother of our Lord. The angel made this quite plain to Joseph at the very beginning, putting it in explicit terms so that there should never be any misunderstanding. We read:

> *But while he thought on these things, behold, the angel of the Lord appeared unto him in a dream, saying, Joseph, thou son of David, fear not to take unto thee Mary thy wife: for that which is conceived in her is of the Holy Ghost. And she shall bring forth a son, and thou shalt call his name JESUS: for he shall save his people from their sins. (Matthew 1:20–21)*

That is why he is to be called Jesus; that is why he is called the Christ, the Messiah, the Saviour. There is no sense, there is no meaning to the word salvation, apart from this. He saves *from* – what? – from the condemnation of the Law.

It is all there in Paul's epistles, expressed in different ways. Paul in writing to the Galatians says: 'Wherefore the law was our schoolmaster to bring us unto Christ' (Galatians 3:24). What brings us to Christ? The schoolmaster, the pedagogue. How does he do it? He convicts us of our sin; he shows us our need. That is the whole business of the Law. All of the Old Testament is preparation for the New. The Law brings us to Christ by revealing our need to us, our emptiness, and our woe. And, indeed, this is what we are told of our Lord himself: 'When the fulness of the time was come, God sent forth his Son, made of a woman, made under the law' – what for? – 'to redeem them that were under the law' (Galatians 4:4–5). That was why he came.

And so when our Lord came, he said, 'The Son of man is come to seek and to save that which was lost' (Luke 19:10), and,

'The Son of man came not to be ministered unto, but to minister, and to give his life a ransom for many' (Matthew 20:28). Why do they need a ransom? Why do they need to be saved? What is it all about? And there is only one answer – it is to save us from sin, to save us from the condemnation of the Law. 'God was in Christ, reconciling the world unto himself, not imputing their trespasses unto them' (2 Corinthians 5:19). That is it! 'He hath made him to be sin for us, who knew no sin; that we might be made the righteousness of God in him' (2 Corinthians 5:21). We are under the Law: 'the whole world lieth in wickedness' (1 John 5:19).

There is no sense in the words 'Saviour' and 'salvation' unless we realize our guilt, our condemnation. And so the triumphant cry of the redeemed is, 'There is therefore now no condemnation to them which are in Christ Jesus' (Romans 8:1). And if you do not say that first of all, the question must be: Are you saved? Do you know what salvation means? The first thing is that we are saved from the guilt and the condemnation of sin.

And so, you see, the very terms that we use carry this essential principle. The first thing that any kind of contact with our Lord does, whether in his teaching, or in some experience of him, is to make us feel, as the woman of Samaria felt, that we are vile in his presence, that we are unworthy, that we are foul. Have you felt that? I am not asking you about the degree, the intensity, of your feelings, I am simply asking, as you think of him, whether the first thing that comes into your mind is that he has saved you from the guilt of your sin, from the condemnation of the Law; that he has revealed to you what you are, and your utter hopelessness and vileness, and has delivered you from it 'Come, see a man, which told me all things which ever I did: is not this the Christ?' That is the order, and it is the only order.

42

# *What Is Meant by Conviction of Sin?*

*The woman then left her waterpot, and went her way into the city, and saith to the men, Come, see a man, which told me all things that ever I did: is not this the Christ? (John 4:28–29)*

We are still dealing in particular with the words of this woman of Samaria. The first words she speaks reveal conviction of sin. I have been giving a number of reasons to show why this must always come first. First, this is the way in which we differentiate between the cults and Christianity, and, secondly, it differentiates between religion and Christianity. Thirdly, conviction of sin always comes first in the teaching of the New Testament. Fourthly, as I was trying to show you last time, we cannot come into God's presence without feeling our sinfulness, our utter unworthiness.

This is so vital that we cannot afford to be uncertain about it. Let us, therefore, make sure that we are clear as to the meaning of the term 'conviction of sin'. I am emphasizing this, not only because it is a tragedy that anybody should claim to be Christian and yet not enjoy this great fullness offered by our Lord, but also because I am convinced that the great cause of trouble in the Christian church today, including the evangelical section, is the absence of conviction of sin, the absence of humility, the absence of the godliness that runs right through the whole Bible. We are too healthy, we are too glib, we are too self-assured, too confident in ourselves and what we do. 'The fear of the LORD is the beginning of wisdom' (Psalm 110:10). How much of 'the fear of the Lord' is there among us and in the church in general at the present time? We must be clear about this.

So what is meant by conviction of sin? Let me put it negatively first – it is not enough to recognize that there are some things that are wrong. Some people think that conviction of sin means recognizing that there is right and wrong and that certain things in particular are especially wrong. Now that, obviously, is not conviction of sin because most people in the world are aware of this distinction. We all have a conscience within us that makes us aware of right and wrong. Pharisees always had that awareness, they were experts on this subject. Moralists are always perfectly clear, indeed, it is the one thing they are clear about and they never talk about anything else because it is generally the only thing that they do see. But conviction of sin is something quite different.

Neither is it enough to know that we sometimes do wrong. This, again, often passes for conviction of sin, for true repentance. People feel that as long as they occasionally realize that they have done something that is wrong and should not have done it, then they have experienced conviction of sin. But, again, for the same reasons, this cannot be accepted as a definition because 'natural' men and woman, especially those who are moral and religious, are aware of that. Their whole idea of Christianity is that you do not do certain things and you do others. So if they do the prohibited things, they feel they are wrong. But that is not of necessity conviction of sin.

I will go further. Somebody may say, 'Well, all right, I agree with all this, but, surely, if people are really annoyed with themselves when they do wrong, that must be conviction of sin?'

No, it is not. This, again, falls short of conviction of sin. We know something about this, do we not? We do something wrong and we feel we have let ourselves down and are annoyed with ourselves. But the natural person does that; religious people, especially, know that. It is a part of conviction, but in and of itself it is not sufficient. In other words – let me use the term – it is remorse; and remorse is not conviction of sin.

What is the difference between remorse and conviction of sin? Well, the person who is only conscious of remorse is one who has a temporary feeling of unhappiness, and a temporary desire to be delivered from this sin that gets them down. Remorse is concerned primarily with the consequences of sin. Men and women do something that is wrong and are unhappy afterwards. They feel they have been fools and have let themselves down. They should not have done it and are miserable. They dislike that feeling and say, 'Oh, I wish I could get rid of it.' All that is just remorse.

In 2 Corinthians chapter 7, the apostle Paul draws a distinction between 'the sorrow of the world' and 'godly sorrow' (verse 10). The world, I say again, knows what it is to be sorry because of having done wrong things. There are many people who are suffering remorse this morning because of having drunk too much or taken drugs last night, or because they have done something else that is wrong. This morning they are miserable, suffering the physical consequences, perhaps, and consequences in their spirits. But that is not repentance, that is not conviction of sin; that, again, is only remorse. These people regret the wrong because it caused these particular consequences, which they now want to get rid of. That does not come near to being conviction of sin.

What, then, is conviction of sin? Here is the vital question, and the answer is quite clear. The essence of conviction of sin is the realization that our very natures are sinful. It is the difference between particular actions and our condition. Those who are truly convicted of sin realize that their very nature is wrong and perverted and polluted. That is why this woman of Samaria's way of putting it is so interesting. Though our Lord only mentions certain particulars in her life, she says, 'all things that ever I did'. She realizes her nature; for the first time she sees herself for what she is. She knows that people, pharisaical types in particular, point at her and say, 'Look at her!' but she could always retort, 'I do these things, but they think them, miserable hypocrites that they are!' She has always been able to defend herself – people living in gross sin can always put up a marvellous defence. But now she realizes that her trouble is not so much that she does particular things that are wrong as that her heart is wrong, that her desires are wrong.

Now this is a profound understanding. Read Psalm 51, where David sees this so clearly. He had committed terrible sin, adultery and murder, but still he was perfectly happy until the prophet Nathan was sent by God to convict him, and then he saw it all. But what troubled David was not even the adultery and the murder, it was that he had ever desired to do these things. He saw his nature, he saw that there was something there that produced these desires, so he cried out in his agony, 'Create in me a clean heart, O God; and renew a right spirit within me' (Psalm 51:10). He had gone beyond the realm of actions to his condition, to his state, to his whole life; he realized that his very heart was black and foul and ugly and vile; his whole spirit was wrong.

This is of the very essence of conviction of sin, and this is where it is differentiated from the sorrow of this world that is merely remorse. In the seventh chapter of the Epistle to the Romans, the apostle Paul puts it in a similarly graphic way: 'For we know that the law is spiritual: but I am carnal, sold under sin' (Romans 7:14). That is the point. He is not talking about actions but about his whole state. He says, 'I see another law in my members, warring against the law of my mind, and bringing me into captivity to the law of sin which is in my members. O wretched man that I am!' (verses 23–24). People who experience remorse never know that. They feel that as long as they can put certain actions right, all will be well. They have not realized that it is their *nature* that matters. But Paul had: 'For I was alive without the law once,' he says, 'but when the commandment came, sin revived, and I died' (Romans 7:9). So here is the first point: you are convicted of sin when you are troubled not so much about the things you do as about what you are – your whole hopeless condition. 'Vile, and full of sin I am,' says Charles Wesley.

But let us go on. The second aspect, obviously – I am putting these as we experience them and as we feel them – that we must emphasize about true conviction of sin is that it always creates within us a realization that we have sinned against God. What a tremendous point this is. People of the world, and those who are moral or religious, are only concerned with themselves. They have let themselves down, they have done something they should not have done. What will people say? What will the consequences be? God does not come into it. But the moment they are convicted of sin by the Holy Spirit, their concern is that they have sinned against God and broken his holy laws.

Now you see again how David brings this out in Psalm 51:

*Have mercy upon me, O God, according to thy lovingkindness: according to the multitude of thy tender mercies, blot out my transgressions . . . For I acknowledge my transgressions and my sin is ever before me. Against thee, thee only, have I sinned, and done this evil in thy sight: that thou mightest be justified when thou speakest, and be clear when thou judgest. (Psalm 51:3–4)*

This is what now troubles David. He sees the enormity of his sin. By that I mean he is no longer concerned primarily about the wrong things he has done, but that he has done them against God, the God who gave him the honour and the dignity of being a human being, created in the image and likeness of God himself, who made man for his own pleasure, that he might have a companion.

God made man the lord of creation, and set him in authority over everything in creation. That is the dignity that God has given us; and God looked upon it all and he saw that it was good. But we have let God down, the God who has made us like this, the God who has been so kind, the God who has been so loving toward us. We have deliberately flouted his laws, we have wounded him, we have hurt him, we have violated what he intended us to be. We see now that sin is not merely a matter of wrong actions, but is lawlessness, it is arrogance, it is pitting ourselves against God, rebelling against him. Having some realization of the character and the being of God, we see the enormity of it all and are appalled that we should thus offend a holy God and a loving and a righteous God. 'Against thee, thee only, have I sinned, and done this evil in thy sight.'

This is the response of the Prodigal Son after he has come to himself (Luke 15). He has been a fool, he has squandered his money, he has allowed his fair-weather friends to take his money from him for entertainment and so on, and now here he is, he has lost everything and even finds himself in the field with the swine and the husks and the degradation and the shame of it all. That is what would have worried him if he had only felt remorse, but now that he has truly come to himself, what does he realize? He sees that he has sinned against his father, sinned against the one who showered his love upon him and did so much for him; this is what seems to him to be unforgivable. 'I have sinned against heaven, and in thy sight, and am no more worthy to be called thy son' (Luke 15:21). He now sees his actions in the true way.

It is the question of this personal relationship to God that is the very essence of the conviction of sin. Whatever we may feel about our actions, however acute the remorse may be, however violent our reaction, it is not conviction of sin, it is not repentance, until we have seen it in terms of our rebellion against God, our violation, not only of his laws, but of his fatherly relationship to us. So that is the second point.

And then I must emphasize a third element, which is feeling. Now this, again, is most important. True conviction of sin never stops at mere intellectual apprehension. That comes in, of course, but conviction does not stop at that; and, as I have said, it does not even stop at annoyance. An essential part of conviction of sin and repentance is a feeling of true sorrow, what the apostle calls *godly* sorrow. Now godly sorrow is very difficult to define, and yet once one has ever known it, there is no difficulty at all. It is unique to the Christian. It is not irritation, it is not that you are annoyed with yourself, no, it is much deeper. You are troubled, you are grieved; it is a deep sorrow in the heart, in the centre of your being, that you are what you are, that you should ever have been guilty of such behaviour against God.

And godly sorrow is not transient. It is always very deep. It cannot easily be healed. This, too, is widely expounded in the Old Testament. The charge that God always brought against the false prophets of Israel was that 'they have healed the hurt of the daughter of my people slightly, saying, Peace, peace; when there is no peace' (Jeremiah 8:11). That is always the characteristic of the false prophet and false teaching. Ah, yes, you have got a bit of sorrow, but you are quickly over it and you have soon forgotten it. But you cannot do that when you are truly convicted of sin; you do not get over it so quickly; this sorrow is deeper than a surface emotion, some temporary feeling.

And that, in turn, leads, of course, to this: people who have been convicted of sin always have a realization that their first need is the need of mercy, the need of forgiveness. Now I emphasize that for this reason: you are well aware that this element is missing in so much of today's evangelism. Salvation is represented as something that can help us conquer particular sins or give us peace, happiness and joy. The need for mercy and forgiveness is often not even mentioned, and that is why true conviction of sin is so largely absent at the present time. But once we are convicted of sin, then more than anything else whatsoever, we are aware of our need of the compassion of God. This awareness is either there or it is not there. It is not enough that you feel, 'I wish I didn't do these things. I wish I could be free of this thing that gets me down.' That is all right, that comes into the Christian life, but if that is first, and if you have never known the need of forgiveness, if you have never realized that, in a sense, you do not deserve forgiveness and that God perhaps cannot even forgive you, then you have never known true conviction of sin.

Let our Lord say it himself. In his picture of the Pharisee and the tax collector who go up to the Temple to pray, he tells us about the poor tax collector, who is at the back and cannot even lift up his head. He is smiting his breast and all he can say is, 'God be merciful to me a sinner' – be propitiated towards me. He is so aware of his sin that his greatest needs are for forgiveness, mercy, pity, compassion. Can God forgive me? Is it possible? Is it possible that such a wretch as I am, such a vile creature, can be forgiven even by God? (Luke 18:10–14). That is what he needs above everything else. It is inevitable when there is a true conviction of sin. But you can be highly religious and never know that at all, and that is one of the differences between being religious and being a Christian.

Or let me put it like this. Another feeling experienced by those truly convicted of sin – and we put these true feelings over against the false – is that the desire to be holy is altogether greater than the desire to be happy. Of course, by nature we all want to be happy: the real explanation of remorse is that we do not like to be unhappy. If only we could sin without suffering, if only the consequences did not follow, we would have a wonderful time. And that is the problem with people who feel remorse. They are miserable, and will promise anything for the time being in order to get rid of the unhappiness. But that is not the effect of conviction of sin. Someone who is convicted of sin has a great desire to be free from sin. 'Create in me a clean heart, O God; and renew a right spirit within me' (Psalm 57:10).

> O for a heart to praise my God

– I am praising with my lips –

> A heart from sin set free.
>
> *Charles Wesley*

Once we see the true nature of sin, we realize that it is a pollution of the very nature, that it is not merely a matter of doing wrong things or a problem of the will – that is the fatal teaching that came in with Finney above all others, and has been so popular – but is a matter of the nature. So this is a way whereby we can test ourselves as to whether we know true conviction of sin. 'Though he slay me,' says Job, 'yet will I trust him' (Job 13:15). And anyone who is truly Christian says, 'I don't care what I may have to suffer, I don't care what tribulations I may have to go through, as long as I am clean, as long as I am holy, as long as I am worthy of him, as long as he is well pleased with me.' Holiness comes before happiness. We desire not merely to be delivered from things, but to be like God, to be worthy of him. We have heard his command: 'Be ye holy; for I am holy' (1 Peter 1:16). Our supreme desire is to be holy because God is holy and because it is the will of God – 'For this is the will of God, even your sanctification' (1 Thessalonians 4:3).

Now these are vital matters, are they not? Have you been convicted of sin? Have you, like this woman of Samaria, felt that your heart is opened, and have you been astounded at what you have seen? Have you got beyond the realm of being interested only in conduct concerned with the state, the plague, of your own heart, the pollution of your own spirit? Have you ever seen that?

Do not misunderstand me – I do not hold the view that the test of Christian people is that they are always miserable about themselves. It is not. All I am saying is that they should have passed through that stage some time or another. No, no; the Christian knows about this 'well of water'. But this sorrow is not glib, it is not superficial or intellectual; it is much deeper. There is a kind of paradox in the Christian. One of the great statements made by Martin Luther is that the Christian is a man who is at one and the same time a great sinner and a great saint; he is extremely miserable and he is extremely happy.

But now let me come to a question. I am sure there are many who are saying to themselves, 'Are you saying that all should feel this conviction of sin? Are you laying this down as a universal rule?' Now this is being asked very freely at the present time. There are people who maintain that what I am saying here is quite wrong. Some go as far as to say that repentance was only for the Jews at the time of our Lord. This is the teaching of the ultra-dispensationalists. 'Oh, yes,' they say, 'of course John the Baptist and our Lord preached repentance, but they only preached it to the Jews.' These people have divided God's plan of salvation into 'dispensations' – periods of time – and say repentance was only for the Jews, and nobody need repent after that. But, to start with, they are utterly unscriptural, denying what we are plainly told in the book of Acts and the Epistles where we see that the apostle Paul preached repentance to the Gentiles. They evade the need to repent by saying that all you need to do is accept Jesus and take him into your heart. This is being taught today. More than once I have had friends from another part of the country consulting me in my vestry because this is the prevailing teaching in the assembly to which they belong.

Then there are others who feel that surely teaching about conviction of sin and the need to repent is only for people who are guilty of some gross sin – a drunkard or a drug addict or a prostitute. Someone who holds this view will say, 'You've quoted David, and of course he committed adultery and murder. If I'd been guilty of sins like that, then I'd see the need of conviction of sin, but I've not done any of those things.'

Then, thirdly, there are those who say, 'That may be all right for people who've been brought up in godless homes and were never taken to a place of worship; people who really did not know any better. But we've been brought up in Christian homes and have always gone to a place of worship and Sunday school. You surely are not saying that we ought to experience this kind of thing? Surely,' they say, 'what you are talking about – this conviction of sin – oh, yes, your woman of Samaria – exactly. She had five husbands and the man with whom she was living was not her husband – we can understand all that: but what has that got to do with us?'

This is how the devil comes in. What is the answer? It is very plain: the facts are entirely opposed to that argument. There is no such distinction, there is nothing in the Scripture that says that repentance is to be confined to the Jews only or to certain other people only. The fact of the matter is that in the history of the church, the people who have known most intensely what I have defined to you as conviction of sin have been people who have been brought up in a most godly manner. I refer again to Martin Luther. If ever a man knew conviction of sin, it was Martin Luther. But what a godly young man he was, brought up in an entirely religious home. He had never committed what we call gross sins, yet look at the conviction of sin that he experienced. It was while he was a monk that he endured an agony of repentance.

I could keep you for hours telling you about such people. Look at the two Wesleys, If ever two men were brought up in a Christian home it was John and Charles Wesley, yet these two men knew such intense conviction of sin that they became desperately ill, both of them. The same was true of George Whitefield. Is it not amazing how we can do things without thinking? We all like Charles Wesley's great hymn, do we not: 'Jesus, lover of my soul'. But remember, it was Charles Wesley, this man brought up in a rectory, with an exceptionally godly father and mother, who had given his life to godliness, who says, 'Vile and full of sin I am.' And this is not a poet's rhetoric, this is not hyperbole created by a poetic imagination. The man meant it. He had been through agony and felt that he was beyond forgiveness.

And, indeed, I go further and say, in the second place, that there can be no question at all but that such people have felt conviction of sin and grief and godly sorrow more than anybody else. You have simply got to read the biographies to see what I mean. These people have experienced it much more intensely than your ex-drunkards, ex-adulterers, ex-murderers, or anyone else.

And, thirdly, you will generally find – and this is a part of the paradox I am referring to – that as saints go on in the Christian life, their awareness of the rottenness of their natural self becomes greater and greater. Again, do not misunderstand me. The saints are not people who are therefore always moaning and groaning. No, no; they have the well of water in them, but at the same time, they know the truth about the old nature that is still in them – and it is this that troubles them. I was reading again the other day of Daniel Rowlands, the great Methodist father in Wales 200 years ago. He was dying and knew he was dying. Some of his brethren went to see him and asked him how he felt. He said: 'I am an old sinner, but saved by the grace of God.' That is the way. Oh, yes, he was rejoicing in his salvation, but on his deathbed he knew that he was an old sinner still. It was all right, he went through triumphantly and gloriously, but the other consciousness was still there.

I can prove all this in another way. When a revival breaks out, the first effect of the falling of the Spirit of God upon a people, a congregation, a group of churches or a nation, is invariably conviction of utter sinfulness. It always happens, it has always happened. People who have been members of a church perhaps for 50 years begin very seriously to doubt whether they have ever been Christians at all, and they are in real trouble. The revival is in the church – not outside. We are all so clear about the outsider, but these are the people inside. They feel they are nothing. So you see how utterly wrong it is to argue that conviction of sin is only for certain people, for notorious sinners, or for Jews only.

But let me wind this point up by putting it like this: Why is it so wrong to argue that we respectable people, as it were, do not need to feel conviction of sin, that it is only for the flagrant sinner? Oh, here is the final reason. That argument is based on an entirely wrong position. What matters is not the number of sins we have committed, nor their character or quality. What matters, and what matters alone, is our relationship to God. Of course, if it is a matter of the number of sins, or the quality of the sins, then it is perfectly all right to say, 'Look at that man! He has a full page of sins while I've only a few at the top of the page. Look at the quality of his sins – they're scarlet, they're vile, they're foul, they're bloody! Mine aren't! I've done wrong things, but thank God I've not done those things!' That is how it works, is it not? And that is the devil. It is the devil who teaches us to keep ledgers and account books. God does not; Christ does not. I say again that it is not the number of your sins, it is not the character of your sins, it is your relationship to God that counts.

When you come into God's presence, you realize the truth about yourself, and it does not matter who comes into his presence, there is no difference when you are face to face with him. You have your comparisons, your contrasts, then you come to him, the burning light! 'God is light, and in him is no darkness at all' (1 John 1:5). And all your differing shades are nothing – they are all black! 'There is none righteous, no, not one' (Romans 3:10); 'The whole world lieth in wickedness' (1 John 5:19). The greatest sin of all is the failure to see your need of salvation; that is much worse than murder. To feel that you can stand in the presence of God because you are who you are and what you are and what you have not done, is the greatest of all sins because it means that you do not need the death of the Son of God on the cross on Calvary's hill. And that is the greatest insult you can ever offer to God. The nearer you get to him, the more you are aware of your guilt, your unworthiness and your foulness. Conviction of sin is positive, it is not negative.

What is it that makes a good young man like Charles Wesley say, 'Vile and full of sin I am'? Well, read the hymn again or think of it at this moment and you will see how it works. This is always the argument and the only true argument.

Just and holy is thy name.

You do not start with yourself. If you start with yourself, you will never know conviction of sin because you will always see that you are better than somebody else and you will always be able to square the books. Charles Wesley does not start with himself.

Just and holy is thy name.

And in the light of that, and that only, he says:

I am all unrighteousness;
Vile, and full of sin I am.
Thou art full of truth and grace.

This is the only way whereby you will ever be convicted of sin. So people who talk about 'big sins' and 'being brought up respectably and religiously' and so on have missed the whole point. To speak like that is a denial of the doctrine. You are interested in actions and in their number and character? But you must not be.

Just and holy is thy name.

It is 'thou' and 'I'. It is 'he' and 'I'. It is only when you are in his presence that you see it; and if you have not seen it, it means you have never been in his presence. It comes to that. So if you have never felt your vileness or if you object to preaching that tells you that you ought to feel vile, you are entirely on the human level. Oh, numbers and categories are irrelevant, they are madness, they are folly, they are the devil.

> Thou art full of truth and grace.

And as I look at him, there is only one thing that I can say about myself at my best:

> I am all unrighteousness;
> Vile, and full of sin I am.

But blessed be his name, he said, 'They that be whole need not a physician, but they that are sick . . . I am not come to call the righteous, but sinners to repentance' (Matthew 9:12–13). And the men and women who go to the greatest heights in their knowledge of the Christian life and the receiving of his fullness, are those who have been deepest down in the depths under conviction of sin and a realization of their utter hopelessness. Before I ask you whether you have been raised to the heights, I ask: Have you been down in the depths of your own vileness?

# 43

# Salvation and Sanctification

*The woman then left her waterpot, and went her way into the city, and saith to the men, Come, see a man, which told me all things that ever I did: is not this the Christ? (John 4:28–29)*

I have been demonstrating to you from the Scriptures the centrality of the teaching that forgiveness of sins follows a sense of guilt and unworthiness: the first message is a call to repentance. Repentance is the key that leads to all the treasures and riches of the Gospels. And I have shown you also the central and vital place of this teaching in the experience of Christian people throughout the centuries. Indeed, beyond any question at all, it can be laid down as a law that the greater the saint, the greater his appreciation of his sinfulness and guilt.

I once stayed with a man who was an expert in growing sweet peas and had won prizes many times at the Royal Horticultural Society shows. I noticed the extraordinary length of the stalks and asked him the secret. He said, 'There's only one secret to having a long stalk like this and a wonderful bloom. You must dig as far down as you desire the plant to be high. Many people,' he said, 'do not seem to realize this, but if you want great height, you must dig a deep trench.' It is exactly the same in the spiritual life, and I am suggesting that very many fail to realize the importance of the fact that it is only as we truly see our need that we shall ever receive of this fullness and satisfaction. I trust that I was able to demonstrate to you last time that this applies to all people, whatever their background.

I am anxious to make it clear, however, that I am not suggesting that we should all experience conviction of guilt in exactly the same way and to the same degree. Nor am I saying that it is bound to come at exactly the same point in the experience of each Christian. What I am asserting is that it is an invariable rule that at some time or another there has to be a consciousness of guilt and of unworthiness. Furthermore, I postulate that the closer we draw to God, the more likely we are to be convicted of our guilt. Let me illustrate this.

George Müller was a man who exercised an astounding ministry in the nineteenth century, particularly in connection with orphanages in Bristol. He was a man who was given a very unusual gift of faith, a man whose faith was unshakeable. In his autobiography he writes that as a young man he lived a dissolute, unworthy and immoral life, yet, he says:

> In the midst of all this I had a desire to renounce this wretched life, for I had no enjoyment of it and had sense enough to see that the end one day or another would be miserable, for I should never be able to get a living. But I had no sorrow of heart on account of offending God.

In other words, Müller felt remorse, as I have defined it. He was miserable; he was living a life of sin but he was not really enjoying it and he could see the consequences. But notice his emphasis: 'I had no sorrow of heart on account of offending God.' Then in 1825 he was taken by a friend to a little gathering of Christian people who met together to pray, to read the Scriptures and to read sermons — the law of Prussia, where he grew up, did not allow anybody unordained to preach so that they had to read sermons. And he writes that in that little meeting he began to enjoy great peace and happiness, which continued when he went home. And then he adds:

> though if I had been asked how I was happy, I could not clearly have explained it. This shows that the Lord may begin his work in different ways, for I have not the least doubt that on that evening he began a work of grace in me, though I obtained joy without any sorrow of heart and with scarcely any knowledge.

God does this work and bring us to this experience in different ways. We must not stereotype the work of salvation. I remember a man who was very worried about his son. He had no need to be, but he was a man with a rigid mind. He kept on shaking his head and saying, 'My son has never had the Damascus Road experience.' But, as Müller shows here, we must not postulate that God can only work in one way. Though Müller had little understanding, and no deep sorrow of heart with respect to sin, he was confident that God had started a work in him.

That was in 1825. Then we come to 1829, four years later. Müller was very ill, and this is what he says:

> The weaker I got in body, the happier I was in spirit. Never in my whole life had I seen myself so vile, so guilty, so altogether what I ought not to have been as at this time. It was as if every sin of which I had been guilty was brought to my remembrance

— 'a man, which told me all things that ever I did'; it is the same —

> but at the same time I could realize that all my sins were completely forgiven. The result of this was great peace; I longed exceedingly to depart and be with Christ.

He was still a young man; but what is important is that this was four years after the event that he himself regards as his conversion. He certainly had been living an entirely different life from 1825 onwards and I have no doubt, as he says, that he was truly a Christian – but you would never have heard of George Müller if it had not been for this experience in 1829. It was from there on that he became this exceptional, unusual man of God who enjoyed such peace and tranquillity, such joy in the Lord, and was given such outstanding faith, which enabled him to do mighty things to the glory of God.

But you notice that the essential part of this experience was: 'Never in my whole life had I seen myself so vile, so guilty, so altogether what I ought not to have been as at this time.' It was as if every sin he had ever committed flashed in front of him as some terrible, horrible panorama and he saw his utter emptiness and woe. And it was as the result of that that he truly saw the fullness that is in Christ, and saw it to such an extent that, as he says, he did not want to live. And he says that when later he was told by his doctor that he was beginning to get better, he was truly disappointed. He had already come to the state in which he could say with the apostle Paul, 'To me to live is Christ, and to die is gain' (Philippians 1:21). Not that he wanted to get out of this world, but he wanted to be 'with Christ' whom he had now come to know in this manner, and whose love was filling his heart.

Now there is a perfect illustration, and it really is, I repeat, a universal law – I do not know a single exception. People such as Müller who have had exceptional experiences of the love of God and who have consequently been used in an exceptional manner, invariably have had the deepest view of their sinfulness, their guilt, their emptiness, their woe. And this, I say again, is not confined to these outstanding people. We happen to have their biographies and autobiographies, but it is equally true of others who we read of in connection with the lives of great people, but whose names one does not remember.

So, then, the great question for us is: Do we know anything about this conviction? To me, this is one of the most urgent questions facing the church today – every section of the church. It is obvious that the church is not counting as she should, but are we as individuals exemplifying the New Testament picture of people with this well of water within them springing up into everlasting life? And if we are conscious of not knowing much about this fullness, we must face this question: Why, then, is this sense of guilt so absent today? Different periods in the history of the church have different characteristics, and there is no doubt at all but that this present age to which we belong, with all its activities, is an age that is lacking in this depth of the realization of guilt and of sin; correspondingly, it knows very little about the profundities and the heights of the Christian life. Why is this? I think that there are certain answers to that question.

The first answer, surely, is that somehow or another we must have a wrong view of salvation. What is our conception of salvation? I think that we will find that often many of us have been concerned only about particular blessings. We were after happiness; we were miserable for various reasons. Perhaps, like George Müller, we were living a wrong life, which brought us into a miserable state of remorse. The one thing we wanted was to be delivered from all this, and then we were told that the Christian faith would give us happiness. So we turned our attention to Christianity, and our sole purpose was to obtain this happiness. It may be that in our unhappiness we were in a Christian meeting, or we met someone who had been like us and we heard of an experience that had been given to that person as a result of believing this message. And we wanted that experience.

So often people seem to take a decision, as they put it, 'for Christ' with no thought of God at all – all they have done is think about themselves. They want what somebody else has got. And then they adopt a formula and seem to have 'got it', but the idea of offending God has never been present. That was what Müller, in writing his autobiography, and looking back across his life, was able to see so clearly. So he said, 'I had no sorrow of heart on account of offending God.' You simply cannot accept that as a true view of salvation if you are guided by the Scriptures as to what salvation really means. Everywhere in the Scripture salvation is described in terms of being 'reconciled to God'. Reconciliation to God is the beginning and the end of salvation.

Why did our Lord Jesus Christ come? Why did he die? Well, according to Peter, he did all this 'to bring us to God' (1 Peter 3:18). Or, as Paul puts it: 'God was in Christ, reconciling the world unto himself, not imputing their trespasses unto them' (2 Corinthians 5:19). This is salvation. The Old Testament comes before the New, the Law precedes the gospel. It is wrong, it gives us a false view of salvation, to ignore the Old Testament, to ignore the Law, to start just where we are and to 'come to Christ', as it is put. Salvation means being reconciled to God, and if we have no awareness of having offended God, if we are in no sense concerned about the fact that we have rebelled against him and offended him and wounded him and transgressed his laws, and done so deliberately, indeed, if we are not aware of the fact that the most terrible sin of all is to be so self-centred that we are not concerned about God and our relationship to him, then we do not know what salvation means.

This is a most solemn matter. Of course, it shows itself in many ways. For instance, there are many Christian people who always pray to the Lord Jesus Christ, and to him alone, and who never talk about anybody else – and thereby they betray themselves. This just shows that they have never understood what salvation means. The Lord Jesus Christ is the mediator – he brings us to God. We do not stop with him. He was sent by God, and was sent to reconcile us to God. It is through him that we enjoy access to God.

Now it is most extraordinary, but I think you will agree that if you examine yourselves and examine many whom you know, you will find that probably the greatest danger of all is to be purely subjective and to fail to realize that the first principle of salvation is our relationship to God. How can we be truly godly? How can we, indeed, be truly Christian in any deep sense, without being aware that we have offended God and are guilty before him?

But, further, it seems to me that there is also in this matter very clear evidence of a lack of a true belief in the Holy Spirit and his work, and especially a lack of faith in him and in his work. I was able to show you earlier that our Lord himself, in telling his disciples about the coming of the Spirit, said, 'He will reprove [convince, AV margin; convict] the world of sin, and of righteousness, and of judgment' (John 16:8). And when he came on the Day of Pentecost that is precisely what he did. The Holy Spirit has been sent primarily to apply the finished salvation that has been obtained for us by the Lord Jesus Christ in all his work on our behalf, in his death and burial and resurrection and ascension. It is the Holy Spirit who 'mediates' that to us, that is his particular work. There it is, the completed salvation – how does it come to me? Primarily by the Holy Spirit's work of conviction.

But must we not agree that far too often in connection with evangelism there is no ultimate reliance upon the Spirit? Now this shows itself in many ways, and I think it accounts for the absence in so many today of the sense of guilt that is so characteristic of the saints. The very atmosphere of evangelistic meetings is often quite contrary to everything we read of in the Scriptures and would expect when the Holy Spirit is operating. It is no part of my business to say that Christian preachers should be solemn: they should not be; they should not be mournful. But there are also certain other things that they should not be: they should never be light, they should never be flippant, they should never indulge in what the Scriptures refer to as 'foolish talking' and 'jesting' (Ephesians 5:4). In other words, if we really have met together to consider the everlasting and eternal God and our relationship to him, it is he who should dominate the meetings. When we realize that we are in the presence of God, then what happens to us is what happened to Jacob who, when he was at Bethel, was filled with fear as he said, 'Surely the LORD is in this place; and I knew it not' (Genesis 28:16).

Now I am not concerned about motives – I know that the motive is to attract people, and to give the impression that Christianity is bright and happy and so on. But, my dear friends, need we do that? Is it not the work of the Holy Spirit to attract people? We are talking about souls, immortal souls and their eternal destiny; we are talking about people who may go to hell and eternal misery. This is the most solemn thing in the whole universe. We are very serious, are we not, if somebody is dangerously ill? Life-threatening illness immediately sobers everybody. There is a danger of a person dying, there is no levity, no jocularity then. But apparently when we are dealing with the danger to a soul of eternal death, we must become like the world. Do you not see that this already is a quenching of the Spirit? The motive may be excellent, but surely the method is desperately and dangerously wrong, and militates against the operation of the Spirit? He is a dove, he is gentle, he can be grieved, he can be quenched.

Is it not extraordinary that we are starting with people, instead of starting with God? And then, because we are starting with people, we are anxious to ingratiate ourselves, we are anxious to make the gospel palatable and nice and acceptable. But that is not our business. All we are told to do is to 'preach the word', to 'declare' the gospel of salvation; we are 'ambassadors for Christ', and speak and act in his name. As we are so often reminded these days, ambassadors and foreign secretaries and others have the reputation of the country, and the king or the queen whom they represent, in their hands, and their conduct must correspond to those whom they are representing.

Very well, there it is in general. But it seems to me that that then leads to our Lord himself being presented in the wrong way. He is offered as someone who will make us happy, someone who will take all our problems from us. Now, of course, he does do all this, but I am concerned about the way in which he is presented, which is as a friend, or as a companion, someone who will put everything right, someone who will lead to blessing if we but come to him. But that is not the way in which he is presented in the New Testament. Surely the great emphasis here is always the same: he is the only one who can save us from the wrath of God and eternal destruction. That is who he is. He died – he had to die – his body was broken, his blood was shed. It was as tremendous as that. He is the Saviour, 'the Lamb of God, which taketh away the sin of the world' (John 1:29). If this is not central in the whole of our thinking, we are already wrong.

What is he to you, my friend? This is the question. You say you have believed in him, but why did you believe? How did you believe in him? What did you believe concerning him? We must examine ourselves in the light of the prominence of the teaching about this need for a sense of guilt and of sin – 'a man, which told me all things that ever I did'.

Then, further, so often an appeal is made to us 'to take Christ', or we are urged to 'decide for Christ', or 'follow Christ', or 'give ourselves to Christ', or 'give our hearts to Christ'. But, again, I think we must examine this. Is it scriptural? Does the Scripture put it in that way? Surely the Scripture does not ask, 'Will you take Christ?' but, 'Will Christ take you?' Is it possible for him to take me in view of my sinfulness, my vileness, my guilt, my hopelessness? This idea that I can take Christ or not, or that I should be pleaded with or cajoled, that pressure should be brought to bear upon me, to 'take Christ' or 'follow him' is wrong – it is 'I' all along. Miserable worm! Wretch!

No, here is the most terrifying question: Can he possibly look upon me? That is what the poor tax collector felt in our Lord's parable of the tax collector and the Pharisee going up to the Temple to pray (Luke 18:1–14). Look at this man striking his chest: Is it possible? He pleads for mercy. There is nothing else to plead for. He does not say, 'Well, now then, I think I'll decide for Christ; I'll take this up and I'll follow him.' Dear me, no! He is desperate. The New Testament does not exhort us to 'take Christ' but to believe on him. Then, when we see our guilt, our unworthiness, our emptiness and our woe, when we see that we are perishing, it says, 'Though that is true of you, he has died for you. Believe that! Believe on him and what he has done for you, and you will be rescued.' That is how the gospel is presented everywhere.

And so it is in our hymns:

Foul, I to the fountain fly:
Wash me, Saviour, or I die.

This idea that we can weigh up the gospel and balance out the arguments and decide . . . and . . . yes, take a decision . . . is remote from everything we have here in the Bible and in all our great hymns and in all the biographies, as I am showing you.

> Nothing in my hand I bring,
> Simply to thy cross I cling:
> Naked, come to thee for dress;
> Helpless, look to thee for grace.

That is it! And it is that always.

> Rock of Ages, cleft for me,
> Let me hide myself in thee.
> *Augustus Toplady*

Can we truly come to Christ unless we are desperate, unless we see our utter hopelessness and helplessness? Our whole conception of salvation has gone astray, it is subjective, it is always seen in human terms. Salvation is never understood in terms of our ultimate relationship to God, this holy God, who has manifested himself in his Law, and Christ as the only way, at such a cost.

And so the last observation I would make under this heading is that the moment you look at salvation in this biblical way, you see that any pressure for a quick decision is of necessity a form of 'quenching the Spirit'. There are terrible phrases that people use that have always alarmed and frightened me. They talk about 'getting people through', and the impression they give is that they push them through. My dear friends, you can push people to make a decision but you can never push them to true conversion. This is the work and the prerogative of the Holy Spirit. You need not be over anxious, I know the motive is excellent, always. I am not querying motives. It is this over-anxiety that results from a false way of understanding that leads to all the trouble.

Of course, we are anxious that people should be saved, but let the Spirit work in his own way, let him convict. We are very anxious for people to be happy, but there is something more important than that, and it is that they should be truly regenerate, that they should be truly reconciled to God. The Spirit does not need your help, and we must certainly not try to go ahead of him or hurry the work, as so many do. The result of trying to take over the Holy Spirit's work is that not only are there reactions, with only a very small percentage of decisions being accepted as true conversions, but even among those there are often tragedies. No, the Holy Spirit alone can convict, he alone can apply the Law, he alone can bring us to see our utter emptiness and vileness, and it is he alone who can reveal the Lord Jesus Christ to us in the plenitude of his divine Saviourhood. Let the Spirit do his law-work.

Again, I could give you endless examples – people such as Müller, who were familiar with the statements of the gospel and had attended gospel services, but who nevertheless had to pass through a process of conviction. I am not standardizing this. It is possible for men and women to be converted the first time they hear the gospel, but it does not always happen like that. The Spirit has his different methods and knows us one by one. We must leave the work to him. We state the truth, we pray for people, we do everything we can, but no decision must ever be produced by human pressure. It is not surprising that today there are many people who know nothing about a sense of guilt and sin, and correspondingly know practically nothing about the higher reaches of the Christian life. These all belong indissolubly together. If the birth has been wrong or faulty, it will tend to show itself throughout the life. This is a most serious and solemn matter. Have we known much about a sense of guilt? If not, why not? Let us examine it.

But not only is there a lack of faith in the power of the Holy Spirit in the matter of evangelism, the same lack of faith is also evident in the whole question of sanctification. I do advise you to read the history of the church, especially the great revivals of history, the great tides and movements of the Spirit. If you do, you will find that during the last hundred years or so something new has come in, something different from what had always obtained previously. Before then, we read of men and women undergoing terrible periods of conviction – groaning in agony, doubting whether they can ever be saved, almost desperate, indeed, becoming desperate. But that seems to have gone; everything is so slick and easy and can be done quickly. And there is a corresponding absence of godliness and sobriety, of all that is depicted of Christians in the New Testament itself.

Now why is this? Well, I am suggesting that it is partly the type of evangelism that is found today, but it is equally the whole teaching with regard to sanctification. For some reason or another, the idea has come in that sanctification is mainly negative. People are taught that it just means getting rid of certain sins. Conventions are held that are described as casualty clearing stations. People are told, 'Here you are, you're a Christian but you keep on falling into sin. Now you want to get rid of that, don't you? Come along, we'll be able to deal with this, we can help you.' And then it is put in terms of victory. 'We'll give you victory. We'll teach you how to live the victorious life.' This has been the popular approach for the last hundred years. The emphasis is on getting rid of particular sins. Again, this type of holiness teaching always starts with *me*: Are you happy? Are you victorious? If you're not, this is how you can be put right.

And then the steps that need to be taken are spelled out, and they are consistent with the essential fallacy. These teachings are always consistent with themselves. Having found out that I am unhappy because of my failures and because of certain things that get me down – and these are specified – they go into details: Have you answered that letter that you should have answered? Have you made this apology? There will be a whole list of things that you are guilty of not having done, and you are told, 'Now, then, you must get rid of all this.'

How do you get rid of it?

Well, pressure is brought upon you to make a 'crisis decision'. This is essential. You must come to a crisis decision in which you surrender all these things and yourself, too. And if you do that, you have had this great experience that is now going to release you, and will lead to victory and to the rest of your life being spent 'abiding in Christ'. A man who was a great exponent of this teaching used to describe his experience in a very graphic manner. He had been a Christian and truly converted and he was enjoying much assurance of salvation and much usefulness in the Christian life as a preacher, but still something was lacking. Then he went to a certain gathering and there he was convicted because in one pocket he had a pipe and in the opposite pocket a pouch. In that meeting he went through agony over the pipe and the tobacco pouch. And at last he felt he must go and get this right, so he climbed up the side of a hill near the place where the meeting was held, and there this tremendous struggle took place. But at last out came the pipe and the pouch, and from there on all was different.

Now do not misunderstand me. I am not here to say that particulars do not matter: they do, details do count. But that is not New Testament holiness and sanctification. From the standpoint of sanctification, a man can be in as bad a state after he has thrown the pipe and the pouch away as he was before, indeed, he may even be worse because he is tending to rest upon this action. This whole view is negative, it is getting rid of particular things. And then formulae come in, techniques, to enable you to do this. Now you see the parallel with the cults, do you not? The cults can do all that and they do. They can make people throw away pipes and pouches and give money and make sacrifices. They are doing it, hence their success. But my point is that this is not New Testament holiness, this is not New Testament sanctification.

What is New Testament holiness? What is sanctification? It is 'to be conformed to the image of his [God's] Son' (Romans 8:29). And it is because we forget this and concentrate on details that we can become such spiritual monstrosities. I have known people following the kind of negative teaching that I have described who have been very loud in their denunciation of Christians who still continue with certain practices such as smoking, which to them is horrible and terrible; but I have known the same people flagrantly guilty of wasting money.

We are dealing with details, so let us deal with details. I remember, it must be getting on for 25 or 30 years ago, a businessman who was attending services at our church. He had come under conviction and was aware that he had a soul and that he was a sinner. He asked me if I would tell him when I was going away to preach within 50 or 60 miles of his home. He said he wanted to know because he would like to come with me in order to 'keep under the sound of the gospel'. An occasion came when I had to preach away in the afternoon and evening, so I told him, and he kindly took me in his car. I was invited to tea there, and, of course, as my companion, he was invited with me.

I knew the people of the house well, but there was a visitor there, the sister of the lady of the house, who I did not know.

She had come up for these services and we were having tea together. We had just finished tea when this poor fellow with me, who was under conviction of sin, quite automatically, he did not think for a second, pulled out his cigarette case and lit a cigarette. The moment he did so, this sister of my hostess attacked him viciously for smoking. Now these were very good Christian people, yet she was attacking him. She did not know the truth about him, of course, and should not have interfered, she should have assumed that he was in my care. She was now undoing all that had been done over the weeks through the preaching under the power of the Spirit. But quite apart from this, she was concentrating on this one thing. The poor man was uncomfortable and unhappy and did not know what to do with himself, obviously feeling that he had let me down.

I had to decide what to do very quickly – I believe the decision was given me. The lady was waxing eloquent on the waste of money that was involved, saying that all this money that he was spending on cigarettes could be given to missionary funds and so on; you are familiar with the argument. Then when she had finished, I began, and I said, 'Now I do not want to be rude, but I would like to ask you one question: How much did you pay for that dress you are wearing?' And she blushed crimson. Of course she did. I said, 'Did you have to buy as expensive a dress as that? Could you not have had a cheaper dress that would look nice and neat and becoming in every respect? Then you would have been able to give probably half of what you paid for it to the missionary fund.' It had never occurred to her. But that is the sort of thing that happens if you start with yourself and with your actions and with particular sins. You throw away your pipe and pouch and think you have done everything. You do not smoke cigarettes but you are not aware of what you are doing in some other respect.

How do you deal with all this? Is there no way whereby we can cover all these possibilities and defects? There is: it is the way shown in the New Testament. You do not start with yourself, you do not start with particular actions, but you start with him and you say: 'I as a Christian am meant to be conformed to the image of God's Son.' If you have that in the centre of your thinking, the details will soon look after themselves. He will make certain things impossible, and they will not be only the ones that you happen to be very keen on avoiding and somebody else does not think about at all, but he will deal with everything. This is the only way. Holiness and sanctification are positive. It is not that I have got rid of certain things and then am a paragon of perfection. I am more likely to be a miserable, self-righteous Pharisee, criticizing others and setting myself up as a judge. Thank God, that is not New Testament holiness and sanctification.

No, New Testament holiness is positive. I see that God's Son, having given himself, having died for me, his body broken, his blood shed, has purchased me. I am not my own, I am bought with a price (see 1 Corinthians 6:19–20). What matters is what he thinks of me, my relationship to him, and when I am in this relationship with him, I will soon find what I am to do and what I am not to do. So you do not have to have these lists and techniques and categories – get rid of this or that and you are all right. No, no! 'Take time to be holy.' It cannot be done once and for ever on the side of a hill. 'Grow in grace, and in the knowledge of our Lord and Saviour Jesus Christ' (2 Peter 3:18). 'Work out your own salvation with fear and trembling. For it is God which worketh in you both to will and to do of his good pleasure' (Philippians 2:12–13).

My dear friends, these are the reasons why people know so little about conviction of sin and a sense of guilt. We are so self-centred, subjective and introspective; we start and end with ourselves, and the Holy Spirit becomes just some sort of agency to help us. No, no; sanctification is getting to know him. This woman of Samaria has met him, she has looked into his eyes, she has heard him. 'Come, see a man, which told me all things that ever I did.' George Müller said, 'Every sin that I had ever committed seemed to come back.' That is what our Lord does. Let him do it. He will through the Spirit. Do not quench the Spirit. Leave your over-anxieties with your methods and techniques and systems, and let the Holy Spirit do his own work.

# 44

# *This Is the Christ*

*The woman then left her waterpot, and went her way into the city, and saith to the men, Come, see a man which told me all things that ever I did: is not this the Christ? (John 4:28–29)*

We turn again to the first words that were uttered by the woman of Samaria to her fellow-townsmen when, having met the Lord Jesus Christ and come to some understanding of who he is, she rushes to tell them the news. It is the story of a great transformation that takes place in this woman's life, a woman who has been living in sin for years, and is undoubtedly notorious for her sinfulness in the city in which she lives. She has to go backwards and forwards several times a day to draw water from the well, and our Lord makes use of this to give her a great spiritual lesson. He says, 'Whosoever drinketh of this water [the water in the well] shall thirst again' – that is the world. The world cannot satisfy; it gives temporary relief, but it can never do more than that – 'but whosoever drinketh of the water that I shall give him shall never thirst; but the water that I shall give him shall be in him a well of water springing up into everlasting life.'

Now that is the message of the Christian faith, and that is what it offers to give us, that is what it offers to do for us. This is a message offering us a life that can give us complete satisfaction – 'shall never thirst' – whatever may happen. We are considering this great message because it seems to us that this is the most important question that can ever face any human being. I remember reading a book that started with these words: 'It is not life that matters, but the courage that you bring to it.' Well, the thesis of that book was wrong; not everybody has courage, and some have more than others. That book leaves it up to us to cope. But there is a sense in which there is something right in that statement. It is not life that matters. What really matters is whether or not we have the secret of the way of living that enables us to go through life triumphantly.

So I want to consider this great message given here by our blessed Lord to the woman of Samaria in the context of this particular day that is observed as Remembrance Sunday.[1] This passage shows us what the gospel does and what it really has to give, and it also shows us how false ideas with regard to Christianity are generally the greatest hindrance to men and women receiving this great and wonderful blessing. We have considered many such hindrances as we have gone through this story. This woman, like all of us, stumbles; she thinks she knows much more than she does. Our Lord has to deal with her and eventually he brings her to see the central truth, and that is what we are concerned about.

What does Remembrance Sunday mean to us? What have we ever derived from the observance of this day? What is the world

---

[1] Observed in Britain in November. Initially its purpose was to remember those who were killed in World Wars 1 and 2.

deriving from it this morning? At this very moment there are probably many thousands of people in religious services who only go this one day a year. What do they get out of it? What does it represent? Is that Christianity?

Now we know perfectly well that to many this Remembrance Day service is a formal, mechanical act, a kind of parade. There are those in the armed forces and in various movements and organizations who only go because it is the thing to do, and attendance may mean they can avoid other duties. I trust we are all clear that that has nothing whatsoever to do with true Christian living – nothing at all.

Then for large numbers of people in this country and many other countries, this service is purely national in its connotation. These people are concerned with their patriotic thoughts. This is an occasion for national pride and self-satisfaction. Clearly, again, it has nothing to do with the Christian faith.

Then to others this occasion is purely sentimental. It makes them think of death and suffering; it makes them think of loved ones who perhaps lost their lives in the last war or in the First World War. I am not saying that there is anything inherently wrong in this, but does it go beyond that? To many this day is wholly depressing because of thoughts of war and of loss and of bereavement and of sorrow. A certain type of music is always put on; there is an air of solemnity. I myself can clearly recall a time in my own experience when this day and similar days brought nothing but sheer depression, a sense of mystery, something pagan, thoughts of death and the fear of death. But is that Christianity? Is it not, rather, paganism?

A great characteristic of paganism, and of many of the religions that belong to the realm of paganism, is that they are all mournful and sad. Let us say this for them, they, at any rate, have sufficient understanding to see that you cannot dance your way through life. They see very clearly that life is real, life is earnest, full of problems and difficulties. But they have no relief and everything is finally completely hopeless. And a great deal that passes for Christianity is precisely that.

People often observe Remembrance Sunday because, in a sense, they are afraid not to, or they may think it is the right thing to do. But what is the effect that it has upon them? How does it leave them? Do they seek relief the moment the service has ended? Do they have to turn to alcohol to get over it? It is depressing and you try to forget it as soon as you can. Is that Christianity? No, Christianity is the exact opposite! People are hindered from really enjoying the blessings of the Christian faith because they imagine that something is the true faith when it is not.

And then, to finish this miserable list, there are those for whom Remembrance Sunday is merely an occasion to indulge in political talk. They use this day only to protest against war and against governments. It is an opportunity to talk vaguely of general uplift, and to try to get people to unite together to put an end to war. Now this will be done in abundance today, and people will think that Christianity is just some teaching about stopping conflicts in the world. And many have said that if that is Christianity, they are not interested in it, they can see through all that. So they have turned their backs upon God and upon the Christian faith. But I hope to make it perfectly clear that this, again, is not Christianity at all.

Then there are others – and I am much more concerned about them – who have been bitterly disappointed. They are searching for comfort: life has dealt blows to them, they have lost loved ones, their hearts are broken and they want help. So they come to the Christian church. And there is something soothing about it for the while. While they are there they feel eased and calmed by the solemnity and the ritual. But then they go out and where are they? Have they received anything that they did not have when they went in? Have they been given anything permanent? Are they able to look at life differently? And they find they are not. They just have to depend upon this Remembrance Day ritual as it comes round year by year, and they are sad and disappointed, and begin to wonder what this Christian faith is all about.

I want to show you, in the light of what we find here in John 4, how far removed all that is from the glorious blessed truth of the gospel. Here is the Christian message to the world, to this country, on a morning such as this. Let us look again at this woman of Samaria. If we would have this well of water springing up into everlasting life within us, if we would be in the position in which we shall never thirst again, if we would receive of this fullness, and grace upon grace, we must learn from our Lord's words to her. There are certain vital lessons here that are utter, absolute necessities, and if we do not accept them, if we quarrel with them, our entire lives will be spent in shallows and in miseries.

What are these lessons? Well, the first great lesson is that we must submit ourselves entirely to God and to his handling of our life. In many ways, this is the most difficult lesson of all. The trouble with all of us is that we tend to come with our own ideas and demands. We want certain things, so we approach Christ, we approach the Christian church, which represents him, and which has his message. What do we want? Well, we bring to him an almost endless variety of questions and problems and demands. Some are purely personal and subjective – we want comfort, perhaps; we want consolation; we want some medicament that can deal with the bruises of life. Or it may be that we want peace in the world and war to be banished; we are concerned about the state of the world and want to put things right. So we approach him and insist, as it were, on an answer to whatever problem has brought us to him.

And I do not hesitate to assert that as long as we are doing that, we will never get this well of water – never. That approach is entirely wrong and is the supreme hindrance to receiving the fullness of Christ. As long as we are coming with our demands and desires, almost insisting upon them and virtually telling God that if he does not give us what we want, we are not interested in him, and will turn our backs upon Christianity or denounce him, then we will continue as we are. That is the very reason why we are in trouble and in pain, in sorrow and in misunderstanding, knowing nothing about this blessed life that the Son of God came into the world to give.

Why is this? Well, one of the great fundamental principles of this faith is that the blessings of the Christian life are always only obtained as the result of something else. They can never be obtained directly. What a vital principle this is! We come, as I say, with particular desires, particular demands, and we believe we can get them directly. I have often used this illustration: we regard our Lord, we regard God, as some kind of slot machine. We come with our desires and make a request – we put our coin in the slot – this is what I want and I expect to get it. We are all doing that in some shape or form. But I do not get what I want and so I say, 'Well, Christianity doesn't do what it promised to do. I've done my best, I've prayed, I've asked, but I'm still unhappy. I haven't got the consolation I was looking for. I see the world in trouble still.' And the answer is, I repeat, that all the blessings of the Christian life are by-products. They cannot be obtained directly.

Now this is a teaching that comes out constantly in the New Testament. In the Gospel of John it is particularly evident.

This was the mistake that was made by Mary the mother of our Lord in the incident at the marriage feast in Cana of Galilee. We read there:

*And both Jesus was called, and his disciples, to the marriage. And when they wanted wine, the mother of Jesus saith unto him, They have no wine.*

What was she doing? She was telling him, in effect, 'Look here, the wine is finished – do something about it.' You remember the reply?

*Jesus saith unto her, Woman, what have I to do with thee? mine hour is not yet come. (John 2:2–4)*

Now that is a rebuke. He did deal with the situation but not at Mary's request, not in her time. He did it in his own way and in his own time. Even his own mother had to be rebuked because of this very attitude.

And then in the same chapter, we read:

*Then answered the Jews and said unto him, What sign shewest thou unto us, seeing that thou doest these things?*

They were saying, 'You're making a great claim for yourself, and we're ready to listen to you – just give us a sign and we'll believe in you.' And then we read:

*Jesus answered and said unto them, Destroy this temple, and in three days I will raise it up. (John 2:18–19)*

He answered them in a parable and they did not understand it. But that is the only way he does answer such people. At the very end of that chapter we read:

*Now when he was in Jerusalem at the Passover, in the feast day, many believed in his name, when they saw the miracles which he did.*

Exactly! People come to him wanting miracles, they want healing, or they want comfort or peace.

> *But Jesus did not commit himself unto them, because he knew all men, and needed not that any should testify of man: for he knew what was in man. (John 2:23–25)*

You see how fatal it is! You come with your demands and insist upon something, but you will not get it. Now this is clearly one of the fundamental facts that operates at the very beginning; our whole approach to God is involved here.

We find exactly the same misapprehension in the third chapter with regard to Nicodemus. He, again, thought that he was in a position to say, 'I've been watching you and I admire you. You're wonderful and must be a teacher sent from God, otherwise you couldn't do these things. Now then . . .' But our Lord stopped him: 'Verily, verily, I say unto thee, Except a man be born again, he cannot see the kingdom of God' (John 3:3). Stop! You must not come like this. The approach is wrong, and it inhibits the activity that leads to this great blessing.

Now in the case of the woman of Samaria, our Lord does exactly the same thing. He has to be almost brutal with her as he cuts across all her talk and says, 'Go, call thy husband, and come hither' – exposing to her that he knows all about the fact that she has had five husbands, and that the man she is living with now is not her husband at all, that she is living in adultery and in sin. This is essential; he takes charge; fullness of life has to come in his way.

Then take one other example, because it is so striking. In the sixth chapter, we find that after our Lord performed the miracle of feeding the five thousand, the people got very excited. We read in the fifteenth verse, 'When Jesus therefore perceived that they would come and take him by force, to make him a king, he departed again into a mountain himself alone.' They were actually going to lay hands on him. They had seen something of his tremendous power and said: This is the Deliverer, this is the one who is going to give us a great victory over our Roman conquerors. He will set himself up as king in Jerusalem and we Jews will be elevated to our old position. This is marvellous!

They were going to take him by force and, oh, how many are doing that this morning! They are trying to take him by force to make him a politician or a pacifist or a socialist or a conservative, I do not care what it is; they are all trying to use him for their own ends. And he will not have it. If you try to lay your hands upon him, he will depart from you; you will not get this blessing.

So you see, my dear friends, how vitally important this principle is. He has his own method, and blessings are only obtained as we submit ourselves utterly to him. I say once more that this Christian faith has no comfort, no consolation whatsoever, to offer to those who are not Christians. Now that sounds hard, does it not? But it is true, as every pastor, every minister, knows from his own unhappy experiences. There is nothing more difficult for a Christian pastor than to be confronted by a non-Christian who is desperately ill and may be dying, or to visit a non-Christian family who have lost a dear one – what comfort have you to give? To talk sentimentally is not Christian comfort. No, no; these blessings can only be given to those who have an understanding of the gospel. There must be something for you to build on.

For the Christian, there is glorious comfort and consolation. There is nothing like it; it makes us more than conquerors. But most Christian comfort is the result of a logical argument, it is a deduction, it is a by-product, and if certain fundamental postulates are not there, there is no comfort to give. Unless people are in a relationship with him, they cannot follow the argument. So the Christian church has no comfort whatsoever to give this morning to people who are not Christians. You cannot obtain the comforts and the blessings of the Christian life unless you first of all become a Christian.

Now all the confusion today in the church and in the world arises directly from the failure to understand this truth, which is so elementary, so primary, so fundamental in the whole of the teaching of the New Testament; and the church, of course, is mainly responsible. She has allowed herself to be put into the position of being just some great institution that gives people vague comfort and consolation. She is somebody or something that is called in on certain occasions – a birth or a marriage or a death – to do something vague and general. People think that is Christianity, but it is the very thing that is robbing them of the real blessings of the Christian faith. Now I could elaborate on that but I must not. There are people who are even seeking sanctification before they have justification. But it cannot be done. We cannot live holy lives until we are *made* holy, until we are regenerate, until there is in us the seed of the divine nature, until, indeed, we become, as Peter puts it, 'partakers of the divine nature' (2 Peter 1:4).

So I put this in the form of a general proposition: the first thing we must do is realize that we must put aside our demands and requests, and just submit to him. We come as we are and we allow him to deal with us and to handle us.

And then what will he do? This is again one of the primary, fundamental truths of Christianity. Do you know the first step the Lord Jesus Christ ever leads us to take? It is to ask the right questions; he makes us face the real problems, and these are very different from everything we have ever thought. The gospel is a complete contrast to all that we know by nature. That is why those who would represent Christianity as just one of the world philosophies or a movement for political change are the greatest of all deniers of the gospel. Our Lord never does what we expect him to do; he does the exact opposite. Even his own disciples, remember, were amazed that he was talking to this woman – any woman would have been bad enough, but talking to a Samaritan woman, and especially to a woman of this character, was astounding. But that is the sort of thing he does, and thank God for that! Thank God, he shocks us; if he has not shocked you, there is only one thing I can say to you, and that is that you have never met him, you do not know him. You get the biggest shock of your life when you meet Christ. He gets us to face the real, instead of the wrong, questions.

What do I mean? Well, as with this woman, he always starts by making us face ourselves. 'Come, see a man which told me all things that ever I did: is not this the Christ?' She has not been made to face herself before, we none of us have. As I say, we come with our questions, and our questions this morning are these, are they not: Why does God allow war? If God is a God of love, why does he allow this carnage to go on in Vietnam? That will probably be asked a thousand, a million times today. Why does God allow spastic children to be born?

You know the questions. We come, and we say, 'These are the questions I want answers to. Why is the world as it is? Why does the world deal with me as it does? Why have I known sorrow and bereavement? Why have I had trouble and unhappiness, other people haven't? So we come with all these problems – the problem of suffering, the problem of pain, the problem of war, the problem of misunderstanding, and we say that these are the great issues.

But, my dear friend, they are not. The first great question for every one of us is ourselves. It is astounding how blind we are to this; nobody thinks of it. I have been reading an article by an outstanding man who did brilliantly in Oxford and became a professor and a minister in a Christian church. But unfortunately, poor fellow, he gave way to drink and as a result lost his professorship and his position in the church. In the article he refers to another man, also a minister in the church, who, like him, had been unfrocked because of drunkenness. This second man was a poet and believed that a poet had licence to do more or less what he liked. The writer of the article says that he cannot understand why life has dealt so hardly with both of them. But, you notice, it is *life* that has done it. There is not a suspicion or a shadow of a suspicion in his article that he has done anything wrong at all. 'Some of us,' he says, 'do get dealt with very harshly by life in this world.' Self-pity!

And here in John 4 is a woman living in adultery. She probably feels that she is having a very hard time, that her great problem is not her adultery, but the way people look at her when she walks down the street, and when they nod to one another or wink at one another. That is her problem, she thinks, this society in which she is living. Perhaps she, like many today in this permissive society, says, 'Am I doing anything wrong at all? I'm as good as they are! What if their thoughts were revealed; who are they?' And she justifies herself. It does not matter how low people may fall, they can still justify themselves, it is innate: the world is at fault or other people or something. But our Lord, when he takes charge, immediately puts an end to all that. He makes us realize that the first question to be answered concerns ourselves, just as we are.

Our Lord so deals with us that we stop asking: Why does God allow war? Why do I suffer? Why am I sad? Why am I in pain? Instead, we ask: What do I really deserve? This is a very different question, is it not? Who am I? What have I a right to expect in this life, seeing I am what I am? These are the questions that he makes me face. I stop thinking of what the world does to me, what other people do to me, and just look at myself and say: What am I?

Then our Lord makes me think of my relationship to God. He makes me answer this question: You ask why God allows war, but how often do you actually think about God? What are your ideas about him? Where have you got them from? On what are they based? What right have you even to put that question? What right have you to sit in judgement on God? He makes me turn right in upon myself and face myself in this way. It is no longer something outside me, it is I myself.

And then I come with my question – war and the horror of war, and young men being killed in the very bloom and blossom of life – oh, what a terrible thing it is! And our Lord says, 'Yes, it is terrible, but, you know, the question for you is: Are you ready to die yourself? You have to. You are protesting, you are making your great statements and it is all outside you. Are you yourself ready to die? You do not know when it will be. This is your first problem – what is your total position?

And not only that, what happens, do you think, after you die? What lies beyond? Is it not tragic that the world does not look at the really big issues? There will be all this talk today, and preaching and so on, about the horror of war because it leads to death, yet people will not be made to face the fact that whether or not there is a war, they have got to die. It is not bombs that matter, it is not the way in which you die, it is the fact that you must die. There is no difference between being blown to nothing by a bomb and dying peacefully and quietly on a bed at home or in a hospital – essentially no difference at all. What is of the utmost importance is the fact of death, this great, startling thing, and whether we are ready to meet it.

All our questions are external, outside ourselves. Our Lord questions us personally, individually, directly: Where am I involved in all this? What right have I to ask my questions? What do I deserve in life? What right have I to expect blessings from God? What has been my relationship to him? Do I live to his glory? Do I keep his commandments? Do I worship him? Do I adore him? Who am I to ask for blessings? Who am I even to seek forgiveness?

Now these are the problems that our Lord makes us face. We do not like this, do we? The world does not like it. Our world is always living outside itself, and when we live in this way we manage pretty well with ourselves. But our Lord will not have this. If we are to know this well of water, then he must first clear out all that is inside us and make room for it. If you want the blessings, submit to him.

In contradistinction to our idea, based on the assumption that we are all right as we are, and that the problems are outside us, and that all we need is a better world in which to live, our Lord tells us: No, it was in Paradise that your first parents fell, and if you did banish war, life would still be what it is: it would still be a problem, it would still be pain and suffering and selfishness. All these horrible things are in the world because they are in us all. So you do not put yourself right by changing your circumstances. You are asking the wrong questions.

In other words, as we have seen, it is basic to the whole of the biblical teaching that the people who have received the greatest blessings of the Lord, and have known this well of water springing up within them, have always been those who have had the greatest realization of their sinfulness and their unworthiness. It is an absolute rule, an absolute law, that if you want to know what it is never to thirst but to have within you a well of water springing up into everlasting life, you must submit entirely to him, and allow him to turn you in on yourself, and show you the truth about yourself. 'Come, see a man, which told me all things that ever I did . . .'

That is the first step; there is a second, which is vital. Having made us face ourselves, our Lord makes us face him. 'Is not this the Christ?' That is what he did with this woman. Having shown her the truth about herself, he reveals himself to her. He makes us face himself as he is, and not merely his teaching. That is the travesty that takes place every year on this Sunday – the emphasis is on 'the teaching of Christ' – it is a misinterpretation, of course. Some people think that the Sermon on the Mount is nothing but a treatise on pacifism; others have different interpretations but all say that to solve its problems, all that the world needs to do is apply the teaching of Christ. But that is wrong! If you take the teaching of Christ and turn it into a philosophy, or an ideology or a political system, it will not work: he said so himself. It cannot work because we are left to put it into practice, and, as we are, we cannot.

No, no; what our Lord does is to bring us into a relationship with himself, he bring us to know him. That is what happened to this woman. She says, 'Is not this the Christ?' It is a rhetorical question – she is expecting the answer, 'It is!' She is not in any doubt at all. She is saying, 'Come and see him: this is the Christ.' It is rather a good way of putting it: 'Isn't this the Christ?' Of course he is! It is the person of Christ himself, and not his teaching that gives us hope and consolation.

So the great question we ask is not: 'Am I familiar with his teaching in a theoretical manner?' but: 'Do I know him?' And this is because, my dear friend, all blessings are in him. 'For it pleased the Father', says Paul, 'that in him should all fulness dwell'

(Colossians 1:19). Or listen to Paul putting it again: 'In whom are hid all the treasures of wisdom and knowledge' (Colossians 2:3). In Christ are 'unsearchable riches' (Ephesians 3:8). All God's blessings for us are in him, and in him alone. And we only obtain them as we get into contact with him, as we realize the truth about him. So we stop thinking about Vietnam and about bombs, and we think of Christ. The tragedy this morning, is it not, is that people are talking about everything else but Christ, the Messiah, the Saviour, the Deliverer.

And what does he make us see? He makes us see who he is: 'Is not this the Christ?' My dear friends, the only hope this morning for every one of us is that 'God so loved the world, that he gave his only begotten Son, that whosoever believeth in him should not perish, but have everlasting life' (John 3:16). This is the Son of God! I am not here to say you should not read history. Read it; history is most important. Read about births, marriages, deaths, wars, campaigns, victories, empires, but, in the name of God, do not stop at that. All that becomes nothing when put by the side of the fact that 'when the fulness of the time was come, God sent forth his Son, made of a woman, made under the law, to redeem them that were under the law' (Galatians 4:4–5). The birth of the babe of Bethlehem is the most staggering, amazing event that has ever taken place in history. He! Start with him. He has come into the world, he has taken our nature upon him. 'And the Word was made flesh, and dwelt among us' (John 1:14). 'I am he,' says he to this woman.

And then we consider what he has done: 'Is not this the Christ?' What does that mean? Well, the word 'Christ' is the Greek term for the Hebrew word 'Messiah', the promised Deliverer. The Samaritans were waiting for this Messiah, so were all the Jews. What was he coming to do? He was coming to 'save his people'. He was coming to rescue us from 'this present evil world', he was coming to 'reconcile us to God', he was coming to make us 'the children of God', and he has come! He wants us to realize that he has made it possible for us to have access into the presence of God. So we no longer talk about God and ask God pompous questions – Why do you allow this? If you are a God of love, if you are a God . . .

Oh, you stop all that and get to know God. You learn the way into the presence of God. You learn how your life can be linked to God. Messiah! Christ! The one who can save us from this horrible thing that we have become as the result of sin, and can make us new people even while we are still in this world. 'Is not this the Christ?'

He does that for us; and then he goes on to let us know what he can do for us having thus made us the children of God. What does he do? I shall only give you some headings. Go home and think about them and thank God for them. First, he will give you an entirely new understanding of life and of death and of eternity. 'This is the victory that overcometh the world, even our faith' (1 John 5:4). The moment you have faith in him, the moment he gives you this new life, you have new understanding, and do you know the first thing that it will do for you? It will enable you to see through the world, through all its illusions. I mean by that, you can see it for what it is. The pomp and the power and the glitter are nothing, nothing at all; it is children playing. He will enable you to see through all the sham and hollowness and vanity of the world and to see all that that leads to – the misery and the shame and all the problems.

At its best this is a land of sin and shame. So you will not pin your hopes to this world; you will realize that this is a temporary life only, and that you are just passing through. You belong to another realm now; your citizenship is in heaven. And so he will render you immune to, oh! all 'the slings and arrows of outrageous fortune'. You will come into the position of the apostle Paul:

> *Not that I speak in respect of want: for I have learned, in whatsoever state I am, therewith to be content.*

Is that true of you? This is true of anybody who has this well of water.

> *I know both how to be abased, and I know how to abound*

– I am not miserable when I have nothing; I do not lose my head when I have a lot –

> *every where and in all things I am instructed both to be full and to be hungry, both to abound and to suffer need. I can do all things through Christ which strengtheneth me [while I am left in this world].* (Philippians 4:11–13)

And then he will enable you to see death in a different way, and you will even see through that and beyond it.

> There is a land of pure delight,
> Where saints immortal reign.
> *Isaac Watts*

Death is just this little narrow sea that divides me from that 'land of pure delight'. You know the story, do you not, behind that hymn of Isaac Watts? He was born and brought up in Southampton, and it is said that he got the whole idea for the words of this hymn from looking across that narrow strip of sea to the Isle of Wight. That, he said, is death, nothing more. Look at it; look at the green fields, look at what is beyond the river, beyond the sea. He will enable you to see right into eternity, beyond time altogether. Christians have the 'blessed hope', they see the glory that is awaiting them. So they do not shiver on the brink! No, no; they see beyond it. They 'set [their] affection on things above, not on things on the earth' (Colossians 3:2) and even death loses its terrors and its horrors.

And while they are still left in this world of time, this blessed person, this Christ, is still with them. 'I can do all things through Christ which strengtheneth me' (Philippians 4:13). So that whatever may come to meet me, I shall not be moved. 'Whosoever drinketh of the water that I shall give him shall never thirst' – never, whatever happens – but the water that I shall give him shall be in him a well of water springing up into everlasting life.'

> All the way my Saviour leads me:
> What have I to ask beside?
> Can I doubt his tender mercy
> Who through life has been my Guide?
> *Frances J. Crosby*

No, no! This is the Christ, the Saviour of the world, my Saviour, my Lord.

> He knows the way he taketh
> And I will walk with him.
> *Anna L. Waring*

## 45

# *Captivated by Him*

*The woman left her waterpot, and went her way into the city, and saith to the men, Come, see a man, which told me all things that ever I did: is not this the Christ? (John 4:28–29)*

The Christian faith, as we have been seeing together, is a message that offers us a life in which we shall 'never thirst'. Christians never thirst because they have this 'life, and life more abundant' within them. As I have been emphasizing, it is most important for us to be certain that we have this life, and if we have not, to find out why not and to discover how we can obtain it. It is for this reason that the Scriptures have been given to us. The Lord, as we are told by Paul in Ephesians chapter 4, 'When he ascended up on high, he . . . gave gifts unto men . . . And he gave some, apostles; and some, prophets; and some, evangelists; and some, pastors and teachers' (Ephesians 4:8, 11). And he gave these gifts so that we might know the teaching given in the Scriptures. Though we are born again, we are not perfect; the world, the flesh and the devil are round and about us and are ever trying to rob us of the abundant life that our

Lord gives. So God has made this wonderful provision for us that we might examine ourselves in its light. We then discover what it is that stands between us and entering into this great possession.

We have been looking at the response of the woman of Samaria to our Lord, and have seen that the first essential to receiving the fullness of this life is conviction of sin. The woman was humbled and really saw herself for the first time. As a result, she submitted herself to him. And we have seen that if we resist him in any way, if we come with our demands, then we will not get anything. We must come to him realizing that we do not know what to ask for, and, therefore, leave ourselves in his hand, letting him speak to us and deal with us. He will do this: he has promised to. What he did for this woman, he will do for us. Thank God he will if we only allow him to.

But I would now like to call your attention to a further obstacle to receiving this fullness of life, and this is that our whole notion of the Christian life is defective. We may see our guilt clearly and we may see the folly of ever trying to justify ourselves by our works or our understanding. We may see clearly the need of justification by faith only, and of regeneration. We may see all this, and yet still have very inadequate views of the true nature of the Christian life.

I suppose that one of the main causes of our trouble is the instinct for safety and preservation. This instinct makes us realize acutely the need for forgiveness, but then we tend to stop at that; we are safe, and so we stay there. Notice how frequently in these New Testament Epistles the various writers – not only the apostle Paul but the others as well – reprimand the people to whom they were writing because they were remaining mere 'babes' in Christ. They were not progressing, they were not going on to perfection, they did not 'have their senses exercised' (Hebrews 5:14). So the writers had to keep on dealing with the first principles of the gospel of Christ while reminding their readers of the danger of staying there and of not realizing the tremendous and the glorious possibilities of this life into which he has brought us.

Here again we are helped by the woman of Samaria. We are told, 'The woman left her waterpot, and went her way into the city.' It is very important that we should understand exactly what she does and why she does it. One tends instinctively to imagine that she has been having a conversation with our Lord and he has just spoken to her about himself when the disciples suddenly appear, and seeing them, the woman gets excited and rushes back to the city, forgetting her waterpot.

But I think that is a complete misunderstanding. This is not a case of excitement or forgetfulness, as I think I can prove. She rushes to the men in the city and says, 'Come, see a man, which told me all things that ever I did: is not this the Christ?' Now she does not say, 'Go,' she says, 'Come'. In other words, she has not forgotten her waterpot. She has not just been carried away, as it were, and, not realizing what she is doing, has suddenly rushed back to the city. No, no; she quite deliberately leaves the waterpot at the well and goes to the city in order to invite these people and take them back with her. This is her whole intention.

So what does this teach us? Well, here we are led to two principles that I am anxious to enunciate. The first is that this woman has undergone a radical change. All her values have changed; she has become a different person. Hitherto her life was a life of sin and drudgery, of daily household chores, especially the tiring work of going back and forth to fetch water from the well. As we have seen, she goes to the well at midday, when the sun is directly overhead. She does not like to go when other people are about because she knows what they think of her and what they are saying about her. But now everything is changed, there is a revolution, and this comes out, it seems to me, in the fact that she deliberately leaves her waterpot and hurries back to the town to get the people.

This is a tremendous change and it leads us to see a number of facts that are always true about this Christian life of ours. It is important to examine ourselves in the light of all that we learn here. Let me begin with some negative points. The Christian life is not merely a slight modification, a slight change, in our existing lives, but is a complete change. The New Testament is full of this teaching. Our Lord has already put it to Nicodemus: 'Ye must be born again' (John 3:7). That is the essential truth about this Christian faith. Our Lord's conversation with the woman of Samaria demonstrates clearly that this is indeed a *life* – that is what he tells her; it is a 'well of water springing up into everlasting life'. Or let us put it like this – and this is where we are challenged and searched by this message – the life of the Christian is not like the life of everybody else with just the one difference that Christians have an extra interest added on. People should not look at Christians and come to the conclusion, 'Well, they're human beings like everybody else, with the same interests, the same pursuits as the rest of us. For six days of the week there is no difference, but they do this odd thing on the seventh day.'

Yet is this indictment not true of so many of us in this Christian life? You look at someone and you are rather surprised that he or she is a Christian. I remember a story told me by a man who had recently become a Christian. Shortly after his conversion, he fell ill, and for the sake of his health was advised to take a Mediterranean cruise. On their way down to breakfast on the first Sunday, he and his wife looked at the notice board and were delighted to see that at 11 o'clock the Captain would be holding a service in the lounge. They went to their table where there were a number of people whom they were getting to know, and immediately said how glad they were to notice that there was to be a service at 11 o'clock. Then to their utter astonishment, a lady sitting at the table also expressed her great delight and said how much she looked forward to it. Why were they shocked? Well, it had never occurred to them that she was a fellow Christian – never. Her conversation, her appearance, her demeanour, had given exactly the opposite impression.

That is an extreme example, perhaps, but is it not so often true that our Christian faith does not seem to be an essential, central part of our lives but an appendix, an addition? Or let me put it like this: far too often we give the impression that our Christianity is nothing but some sort of a brake upon our lives – I mean that mainly in a moral sense. There we are, doing what everybody else does, and then, suddenly, we will not do something and people are amazed. 'Why won't you do this?' they say. They had never thought that we were different and this holding back strikes them as an oddity. They are perplexed, but perplexed not so much that we do not do this particular thing as that this contradicts their estimate of our lives. Because there is not a wholeness about our lives and demeanour, we give people the impression that to be a Christian is to be an 'odd' person.

Or another way in which we can put this same point is this: far too often our Christianity seems to be something about which we have to remind ourselves. We have to pull ourselves up and remember that we are Christians. Or perhaps, indeed, we may be in such a state that other things have to pull us up. I have often been told by people, and I am sure this is true in the experience of all of us, that an illness or some disaster once pulled them up sharply and they were reminded of how they had been going on assuming their Christianity while, in a sense, forgetting it. If they had been questioned or examined, they would have been fundamentally all right, and would have given the right answers, but in their daily living, their faith had more or less not been there, and their life might have been the life of any non-Christian. But suddenly the illness reminded them.

Oh, how often this happens! The New Testament tells us that God himself has to chastise us at times because we are his children: 'For whom the Lord loveth he chasteneth' (Hebrews 12:6), and if we will not give a positive obedience, he will employ other methods in order to remind us of who we are and of our relationship to him. He reminds us that the whole glory of his gospel is in our hands, as it were, and that it is being tarnished. This is another way, therefore, in which we fail to demonstrate clearly the essential character of the Christian life.

Or another way in which I can put this first principle is this: Is our Christianity something that we take up as a duty? Ah, yes, there it is and it is a duty that we have, perhaps, to force ourselves to carry out. So often it is as if it is a sort of burden, a kind of weight that we are carrying. In other words, we have turned Christianity into a law, and we give the impression, very often, that it is against the grain and we just have to make ourselves obey God's instructions; and then we take credit to ourselves because we have done our duty.

But this is a kind of mechanical religion; we take it up and we put it down and we force ourselves to take it up again, and we feel we really have done very well because we have carried out certain duties – attendance at the house of God and so on. Now this is the opposite of what is illustrated in the story of the woman of Samaria and of the teaching throughout the New Testament.

And finally under this negative heading, let me put it like this: Is our Christianity merely a vague, general influence, something about which we are not clear and that we do not quite understand?

In other words, I am asking this one big question: What is the place and position of your Christian faith in your life? I have subdivided this first principle in order to make it more obvious, but it really all comes to that: Where exactly does the Christian faith come in my life? Is it only the appendix, or is it right through the whole book? And this is what I see so clearly in the case of this woman. She is an illustration of our Lord's teaching about the rebirth, about being born again. Here is a woman who has been changed entirely.

Of course – and this is the second principle – we must go on to point out that this change is entirely due to the fact that the woman's life is now dominated by our Lord. Until this point, she herself has been in control of her life – I mean, in the sense of what she did. She had to do her work, she thought about it, and carried it out. She had gone from home with the intention of filling that waterpot again and taking it back and going on with the work in the house. Then she had her pleasure and her unworthy lifestyle. But she had her programme, and she lived according to it.

But suddenly that programme is upset. She leaves her waterpot and does something else; she has got time. Why? Well, a revolution has taken place; her outlook upon waterpots and everything else has changed completely. What has caused the change? The Lord Jesus Christ himself. This is the great central theme of the New Testament. When we really are in this position to which he would have us come, he determines our lives, he controls them and dominates them in every respect. And this, once more, is the difference between religion and Christianity.

Now in the days of his flesh, our Lord was always making this kind of demand. He would constantly look at a man and say to him, 'Follow me' – and he meant by that that the man had to leave what he was doing. He said, 'Follow me' to Peter and Andrew, and James and John, these fishermen. James and John were with their father, Zebedee, mending their nets, Simon and Andrew were fishing, when suddenly our Lord came and said, 'Follow me.' They left Zebedee and the boats and the nets and everything else, and went after him (Mark 1:16–20). Matthew was 'sitting at the receipt of custom', that was his job, he was earning his living, when again our Lord said, 'Follow me.' And Matthew got up and left it all (Matthew 9:9).

Now this was our Lord's demand, it was always a totalitarian demand. The point I am emphasizing is that following him is not merely a question of taking up his teaching and trying to implement it. He goes beyond that. You and I can take up teachings, and the grave danger is that we may take up the Christian faith in that way, taking it up, and then putting it down again, living lives that are exactly the same as everybody else's, as we have seen. That is not what he wants, that is not what he will have. 'Follow me!' 'If any man will come after me, let him deny himself, and take up his cross daily, and follow me' (Luke 9:23). He is the leader, he is the director, he is 'the author and finisher of our faith' (Hebrews 12:2), and we follow him. He controls the life, he dominates the life. It is obvious that the Samaritan woman's life has now been changed entirely. Waterpots! What are waterpots? It is, 'Come, see this man.' There will be time for the waterpot; it will find its own place.

There are many illustrations of this principle. We see it perfectly in two other women and the contrast between them – Martha and Mary (Luke 10:38–42). There is Martha, busy with many tasks: coming and going, making food; there is Mary, sitting at the feet of the Master. Of course, it is important to be hospitable and to prepare food and to be kind and so on, but when he has arrived, there is something more important: you sit at his feet instead of fussing and bothering. 'One thing is needful: and Mary hath chosen that good part.'

We find the same teaching in the epistles of the great apostle Paul. Look at how he puts it in writing to the Galatians:

*I am crucified with Christ: nevertheless I live; yet not I, but Christ liveth in me: and the life which I now live in the flesh I live by the faith of the Son of God, who loved me, and gave himself for me'* (Galatians 2:20)

And, again, we read the great statement in the first chapter of the Epistle to the Philippians: 'To me to live is Christ' (Philippians 1:21). Paul said: This is life, this is the essence of life. Christ is not somebody I remember now and again; he is not somebody whose teaching I am trying painfully to put into practice. He is my life; he dominates my life.

Someone once said that Paul was a Christ-intoxicated man. It is a very good expression. Christ-intoxicated! But the apostle himself has a better way of putting it. He likes to call himself 'the bond-slave of Jesus Christ' (Romans 1:1) – the Authorized Version has 'the servant', but the Greek word means not only 'slave' but 'bond-slave'. I am not my own, Paul says. He belongs to his Master. In other words, though Paul was a genius, and though as a natural man he was very self-willed, as he makes plain in that bit of autobiography that we read in Philippians 3, the astounding thing that happened to him was that this determined, self-righteous, brilliant man became as a little child, and his whole life was dominated by the Lord Jesus Christ.

Ask yourself for a moment: What governs my life? What is it that determines how I will live this next week? And as we answer those questions, we will soon discover, I think, that we have become the victims, the slaves, of habits and customs and of duties. Now do not misunderstand this. The woman of Samaria did not leave her waterpot by the well permanently. No, no; life has to go on, and we must live, we have our duties to carry out. All I am saying is that the relative position changes, the waterpot no longer dominates, it does not determine her life, but, rather, she does, and she because of him.

I am trying to show that the central control of life changes – that Christianity is not something added on, it is not the cloak we put on, it is not a bag that we take up or something that comes and goes spasmodically, but is a well of water within you springing up into everlasting life and fructifying everything, making a difference to everything that it controls.

How, then, does this change of control within us show itself? The first way is this: there is a change in our mind and in our outlook and in our thinking. In 1 Corinthians 2:16, the apostle Paul says one of the most amazing things he ever said: 'We have the mind of Christ.' These words are a climax to the chapter. In verse 15, Paul says, 'He that is spiritual judgeth [understands] all things, yet he himself is judged of no man.' He has become a problem and an enigma, he is a changed person, and he has an understanding of spiritual things. The natural man has not, Paul has just been saying that (verse 14), but the spiritual man has – 'Who hath known the mind of the Lord, that he may instruct him? But we have the mind of Christ.' Now Paul means that the Lord Jesus Christ dominates our thinking and we no longer think as we used to think or as others do.

First and foremost, of course, this applies to our way of looking at things. You remember how in the Epistle to the Romans, the apostle Paul contrasts 'they that are after the flesh' and 'they that are after the Spirit'. This is the fundamental difference. By nature we are all 'of the flesh' and we think 'according to the flesh'. Let Paul say it:

*They that are after the flesh do mind [think of] the things of the flesh*

– not only that, they think in a fleshly way –

*but they that are after the Spirit the things of the Spirit. For to be carnally minded is death; but to be spiritually minded is life and peace. Because the carnal mind is enmity against God: for it is not subject to the law of God, neither indeed can be. (Romans 8:5–7)*

One of the first things that happens when you become a Christian is a complete change of mind. Yes, says Paul again, you are 'renewed in the spirit of your mind' (Ephesians 4:23). Now this is a tremendous fact, and it is because of this that the whole life is changed. So we ask ourselves this simple question: Do I see everything in a different way from the people in the world? If I am a Christian, I should. Again, we see this in the change that took place in the apostle Paul: 'What things were gain to me,' he says, 'those I counted loss for Christ' (Philippians 3:7).

Now you cannot argue with this; it is something that happens. You do not have to force yourself, you do not suddenly put down one lot of spectacles, as it were, and put on another. No, no; it is there within you and it comes out. By nature, we are all out for the world, and the world appeals to us. What the world has got is so wonderful, it is so marvellous – look at the way people get excited about it all. But Christians find that now they are no longer interested. They see the world in a different way, as the apostle James puts it, they see that 'whosoever therefore will be a friend of the world is the enemy of God' (James 4:4), and as John in his first epistle says, they know that: 'For all that is in the world, the lust of the flesh, and the lust of the eyes, and the pride of life, is not of the

Father, but is of the world' (1 John 2:16). And they are amazed to find themselves looking at everything in this new way.

But I am anxious to put it in this form also: this change is not merely a different way of looking at things, but is also a considering of all things in terms of the Lord Jesus Christ. Now we sometimes use the word 'Christian' in a very loose way, with people talking about 'Christendom', 'Christian culture' and so on. I know that in a sense they are right, and there is a kind of Christian philosophy, but using these terms can be a very great danger because what you find in the New Testament is not a Christian philosophy, but a mind and an outlook dominated by the Lord himself. And that, in turn, means that we view all things in the light of the fact of the Lord's coming, and of what he has done and where he is, and what he is yet going to do; this dominates the whole of our lives and all our thinking. In the life of the woman of Samaria, it shows itself in a big detail – the waterpot, and the place of the waterpot in her life, as we have seen – but this is only one illustration.

And so we examine ourselves. Do we view all things in the light of the facts that we believe concerning our blessed Lord? How do we react to things that happen? It is a very good test. Christians 'set [their] affections on things above, not on things on the earth' (Colossians 3:2). And it is because of that, that they develop a relative immunity to the things that happen round about them. 'His heart is fixed, trusting in the LORD' (Psalm 112:7). They do not become panicky; there is a stability about them. The Lord has opened their eyes, they see through the world, they see it for what it is, they see beyond it. They do not expect too much in this world, and, therefore, they are not so disappointed.

It is only in Christ that we know the truth about this world and all its attendant circumstances. The apostles are constantly pressing this point. In all their writings, they begin by laying down the great doctrine and then they apply it. We see it in Romans 12:1–2, where Paul goes on to say:

> *I beseech you, therefore, brethren, by the mercies of God, that ye present your bodies a living sacrifice, holy acceptable unto God, which is your reasonable service. And be not conformed to this world*

– now that is first, remember, in your thinking –

> *but be ye transformed by the renewing of your mind, that ye may prove what is that good, and acceptable, and perfect, will of God.*

This is it, this transformation: the Christian is no longer 'conformed to this world'.

Now when Paul says 'present your *bodies* a living sacrifice', he does not only refer to the body and what we put on it and what we put in it and what we do with it. Paul's words do include those details, but also refer to the whole of our thinking. We are not to be conformed to the world in our political thinking, for instance. We do not get excited about politics if we are Christians. Now I am not denouncing politics; politics is essential, government is essential. Whether we live in a monarchy or a republic, a democracy or under some other form of government, it does not matter. '. . . the powers that be are ordained of God' (Romans 13:1). What I am saying is this: Christians do not pin their faith to it, and they are not disappointed when things go wrong. They know that this is a world of sin. They understand the problems of this country today as nobody else does. It is not a question of a quarrel between the Labour Party and the Conservative Party, both parties have the same problem, which is that nobody believes in work, everybody is out for pleasure, whether employer or employee. They have other interests, and money is just a means for them to get their pleasure. Nobody wants to work, but each, of course, blames the other for not working.

Now Christians see through both sides of the argument, and they know that all our fundamental problems are due to the fact that men and women are selfish in sin, that they are lawless, that they are disobedient. Ah, yes, you can get excited, perhaps, if you hold a certain set of views about the lawlessness of the trade unions, but what about the lawlessness of the whole of humanity before God? It is the same type of sin but to an infinitely worse degree; that is the only difference. How easily we condemn others! Christians see life in its totality, they see everything in the light of this blessed Lord who has come into the world. And he came because the world was in such a rotten condition, such a desperate plight, that nothing else and no one else could possibly save it. He came 'to seek and to save that which was lost' (Luke 19:10).

Christians see all that, they are not 'conformed' to the world in any sense whatsoever. As Paul puts it in Ephesians 4: 'Ye henceforth walk not as other Gentiles walk, in the vanity of their mind, having the understanding darkened . . .' (verses 17–18). They used to be like that, but they are no longer: 'Ye have not so learned Christ; if so be that you have heard him' (verses 20–21). He says, in effect, 'I am beginning to be doubtful about you; the way you think, the way you speak, the way you live: Have you really heard Christ? Have you really learned from him?' This is a complete change in the mind.

But I want to show you also how there is also a complete change in our interests. This is very clear in the case of this woman, is it not? What a change! Waterpot, family, all that she had to do, the drudgery of domestic duties, had dominated her life and her sinful manner of living, but now she leaves her waterpot, she goes to the city and brings the men back with her. Why? Well, her interest now is in him, he is what matters. The rest can wait. A modern phrase puts it so well, does it not: 'What are your priorities?' Is he always first? Does he dominate everything else? To the Christian he is the main interest in life: the main interest!

Now this shows itself in many ways. Look at what we are told about the very first converts in Jerusalem on the Day of Pentecost. Here are people who have known many a previous Day of Pentecost, and here comes another – of course, an important festival. But they have no idea what is going to happen to them. They are a part of the mob, the crowd that had cried a few weeks before concerning our blessed Lord, 'Away with him! Crucify him!' But now they suddenly hear a great commotion; something has happened to the men who used to follow that Jesus. There they are standing up and one of them is preaching. The people begin to listen, and as they listen they are convicted, for the speaker tells them that they have crucified the Son of God, that they, by wicked hands and through wicked men, have crucified the Lord of glory and that they and their rulers are guilty of the most terrible crime, the greatest enormity ever committed by humanity. And suddenly they are convicted of this and they see it, and they cry out, 'Men and brethren, what shall we do?' They are given the answer, and they are entirely changed. Three thousand of them!

And what do they do? Well, immediately they do the very thing that this woman did; they give evidence that their whole life has been changed. There is a new evaluation of everything, there is a new orientation, there is a difference in the centre. So we are told:

> *They continued stedfastly in the apostles' doctrine and fellowship, and in breaking of bread, and in prayers . . . And they, continuing daily, with one accord in the temple and breaking bread from house to house, did eat their meat with gladness and singleness of heart. (Acts 2:42, 46)*

This was the big thing in their lives. They did not think they had done wonderfully if they went to church once on a Sunday, or perhaps once a month, they did not have to be driven and cajoled. No, no; nothing could keep them away, it was the one dominating interest and it governed everything. This is Christianity.

And, again, go back and look at the great apostle Paul – what a revolution! The old things had become 'dung' (Philippians 3:8), and what was his desire? 'That I may know him, and the power of his resurrection, and the fellowship of his sufferings' (Philippians 3:10). Paul was a very busy man, remember – travelling, preaching, organizing churches, working with his own hands as a tentmaker, never did a man work harder. But there he was, this was the dominating desire: 'That I may know him.' This is the Christian's saving interest. Or, to put it negatively, the Christian is unlike Demas, who 'loved this present world' more than the Lord and all who belonged to him and his kingdom (2 Timothy 4:10).

And then in exactly the same way, there is also a change in the realm of the will. The will is dominated by our Lord. Your relationship with him is such that the will is won over. You do not have to force yourself to live the Christian life, it is what you desire to do and enjoy doing. Again, look at the apostle Paul in his very conversion on the road to Damascus. One of the first things he says is, 'Lord, what wilt thou have me to do?' (Acts 9:6). Until then he had made the decisions. 'I verily thought with myself, that I ought to do many things contrary to the name of Jesus of Nazareth' (Acts 26:9). It was he who decided to go down from Jerusalem to Damascus. He was in control, he ruled his own will. But then, 'Lord, what wilt thou have me to do?' He was almost afraid to do anything, he had made such tragic mistakes; he wanted to know his Lord's will.

Thy way, not mine, O Lord,
However dark it be!
     *Horatius Bonar*

And, finally, there is a complete revolution also in the realm of the heart and of the feelings. Do you not see it in the case of this woman? See her rushing off to the city. That is not performing a duty, is it? That is not mechanically saying that you are a Christian. No, no; quite the opposite. Can you not picture her? Can you not see the animation in her face? Can you not hear the excitement in her voice? I do not see how anyone can be a Christian without being thrilled. There is a passion, there is feeling. You cannot really believe in the Lord Jesus Christ without any movement of your heart.

If our hearts are not moved, my dear friends, are we Christians at all? This idea that our Christianity is a duty, this being rather pleased with ourselves when we have not done some things and when we have done others, is almost a contradiction of Christianity. If you are not moved and thrilled, if knowing him and belonging to him is not to you the most wonderful thing on earth, and the most wonderful thing in heaven, you had better examine yourself again. I have often quoted that statement of Count Zinzendorf: 'I have one passion! It is he! and he alone!'

May God give us such a knowledge of him that we shall be able to say the same thing honestly. The mind, the interest, the understanding and the will, the heart, the passion, all are captivated by him.

O Jesus Christ, grow thou in me,
And all things else recede.
     *Johann C. Lavater (trans E. L. Smith)*

46

# *A Living Communion*

*The woman then left her waterpot, and went her way into the city, and saith to the men, Come, see a man, which told me all things that ever I did: is not this the Christ? (John 4:28–29)*

The true Christian, we have seen, is 'the bond-slave of Jesus Christ'. We have looked at this in general and have shown that he dominates us in mind and heart and will. But now we must take this a step further because over and above this general influence that he exerts, is the fact of our Lord himself, the realization of his presence and of his nearness and of his companionship. In other words, I am anxious to show that the relationship between Christian believers and their Lord is not confined to a general influence but goes beyond that. There is, indeed, a personal relationship, and the life of the Christian is a life that is lived in his presence, a life of companionship and of fellowship with him.

Now this is very obvious in the case of the woman of Samaria. Christians are not merely those who believe a number of correct things about this person who lived two thousand years ago and now belongs to history. Christians do not merely believe in the truths that are derived from the account of what that person said and did. They do, of course, believe in the historical person of Jesus of Nazareth, whom they believe to be the Son of God. There he is, he belongs to history. But Christians do not merely believe in him as someone who once acted in this world, but who has ceased to do so except that there is some kind of general influence remaining through the activity of the Spirit.

Far too often people's idea of Christianity is that you take this body of truth, these propositions, concerning the Lord Jesus Christ and accept that and now do your utmost to live according to them, praying to God for strength and help. But now I want to show you that this is a quite inadequate idea of the Christian life, indeed, it can even be false because the very essence of the Christian position is that it is a life that is lived with him, in the consciousness of his presence.

Let us approach this whole matter by asking: Is what I have just said really possible at the present time? In other words, is it in your mind to say something like this: 'Well, now, of course I can understand the case of the woman of Samaria. Here was our Lord actually in the world, she was in direct personal contact with him. She could look into his face, she could hear his actual words, his accents. But that is no longer possible, he is no longer in this world.' Have you ever thought that? Have you not sometimes had this kind of feeling and wished you had been alive at that time? You have said to yourself, 'If only I could see him, if only I could literally meet him, then, of course, all my problems would disappear immediately, there would be no difficulties left. If only! But we don't see him, he's no longer here.' And therefore one has a feeling that then was the glorious time, and somehow we are now at a disadvantage.

Now this is a very common attitude and it is a most serious cause of trouble in the Christian church at the present time; and when I say 'Christian' church I am referring particularly to those who do still believe the truth. There are those who do not believe in the deity of Christ – I am not concerned about them, they are not Christians. They call themselves Christians, many of them, and they may be members of a church, but that does not make them Christians. No, I am talking about people who really do believe the correct truths concerning the Son of God. I am talking about those who believe the Bible as the word of God and who are orthodox in every possible respect. Often, the most serious cause of trouble for such people is just this very tendency to say that the experiences people had of our Lord in the New Testament were only for the people who lived then. Or they may go further and include the period of the apostles, but since that time is now over, and since we have the written word of God, then the position is now quite different.

Here is obviously a very serious matter. You are familiar, I am sure, with this very common position. That is what I would call turning Christianity into religion; it is something that excludes the subjective element, something that, in a way, excludes the heart and the feelings and the emotion. I was recently reading an article by a well-known evangelical writer, who quite deliberately said that assurance of salvation has nothing to do with feelings. Assurance of salvation, he said, consists entirely of 'believing the statements of the Scriptures'. Not a matter of emotion, not a matter of the sensibilities, it is simply believing the Scriptures. Today, this is the commonly held view of assurance of salvation. If you go to people who hold this view and say, 'I'm not quite happy about my salvation,' they will say, 'Well, it's quite simple; listen . . .' Then they will take you to a chapter such as the third chapter of the Gospel according to St John, and read:

*God so loved the world, that he gave his only begotten Son, that whosoever believeth in him should not perish, but have everlasting life. For God sent not his Son into the world to condemn the world; but that the world through him might be saved. He that believeth on him is not condemned: but he that believeth not is condemned already. (John 3:16–18)*

Then they say, 'Do you believe in him?'

You reply, 'Yes, I do believe.'

'Very well,' they say, 'here it is. Don't worry about your feelings, just believe in him. We're told here that "he that believeth on him is not condemned", what more do you want?'

And that, they say, is the totality of assurance. I agree, of course, that accepting the statement of the Scripture is the beginning of assurance, but I am here to suggest as strongly as I can, by the aid of the Spirit and under the power of the Spirit, that that is the lowest level of assurance, and that there is a higher form, which includes the sensibilities and the feelings and which is direct and immediate.

I use that simply as an illustration of the whole modern tendency. The position I am depicting is the commonly held view that there is no consciousness of the Lord himself, that there are no direct dealings with him, that he does not deal with us intimately and directly as he did with the woman of Samaria and others in the Scriptures – since he is no longer in the world, all that has finished.

Now I say again that this is obviously a very serious matter, and to me it involves, in many ways, the very essence of the Christian faith. I am certain that the main trouble with the Christian church today is that it tends to be dominated by that kind of thinking, and that is why we do not experience revival, that is why the church counts for so little in the modern world, and that is why the position today is such a contrast to the New Testament itself, and to what has invariably been the case in all periods of reformation and of revival. We really must examine this, therefore, because if we are bypassing what the Scriptures teach on this subject, we obviously will continue exactly as we are, and we shall never know much about this 'well of water springing up into everlasting life'.

But why do I say that this kind of attitude is so entirely wrong? There are a number of reasons. First of all, I would suggest that it involves a misunderstanding of salvation itself. What is salvation? My answer would be that salvation is not merely accepting a number of propositions, however right and true they may be. Salvation does not consist in accepting teaching. I realize that everything I am saying is liable to misunderstanding. Obviously, salvation includes believing these propositions, but what I am asserting is that that is not salvation. The essence of salvation is a relationship to God through our Lord Jesus Christ, and coming to know him as our Father. Man was originally made, as you know, in the image and likeness of God and he had companionship with God, he had fellowship with him. But what sin did was break that fellowship. Salvation, therefore, obviously, by definition, is that which restores the fellowship.

Now fellowship does not just mean believing that God is, and that certain other things are true about him. Fellowship means communion, it means communication, it means entering into a personal relationship. So the terrible possibility is that you can subscribe to a number of perfectly orthodox propositions but, because you have not entered into this fellowship, nevertheless not be a true Christian.

So often evangelism itself causes this misunderstanding, does it not? You are presented with a number of propositions: Do you believe this? Do you accept that?

You say, 'Yes!'

All right!

But is it all right? There is the great question. It seems to me that at this point we are tending to forget the whole doctrine of regeneration and the new birth. You have to believe the truth, you have to believe the propositions, but I say again that that is not salvation.

Or let me put it like this: What is the real purpose of the Scriptures? I think this will bring us to the heart of the matter. The answer is that the Scriptures in and of themselves are not salvation. What saves us is not so much that we believe the Scriptures, as that we believe what the Scriptures say concerning him. You see the distinction? It is possible for us to be interested in the Scriptures, it is possible for us even to defend them, it is possible for us to defend the particular propositions of the Scriptures, while remaining purely intellectual. We can study the Scriptures exactly as we take up any other subject – geometry, science. We can take hold of the biblical principles and believe them and accept them but if we stop at that, it is not true Christianity, and, indeed, we are misusing the Scriptures. We must not stop with the Scriptures. They are the means of bringing us to him.

Now let me prove this to you; I can do so quite simply. Take this modern teaching that we have just considered that tells us that we must not consider our feelings when looking for assurance but simply accept what we find in the word of God. Well, then, all I ask is this: How did the early Christians have assurance of salvation since they did not have the Scriptures? Jews had the Old Testament, but Gentiles did not even have that. There were no Gospels, no book of Acts, none of the Epistles. How did the first believers have assurance of salvation if assurance of salvation is simply taking the word and accepting what it says without feeling anything at all? It was not possible – and yet they had a great and glorious assurance. So you see the contradiction in the position.

Someone may think that I am now setting the Scriptures aside. They may say: 'You are maintaining that the first Christians did not have the Scriptures but had these marvellous experiences. Are you not suggesting, therefore, that we do not need the Scriptures at all but should try to recapture what the early Christians had?' Now that, of course, is a very serious error. Again, it is the error into which the Quakers fell, and into which many of the mystics have fallen. But I am not saying that. The Scriptures have a very definite and a very real function and purpose.

There are two extremes here: those who are bound only to the Scriptures and who simply accept scriptural statements without their feelings being involved, and those who say we do not need the Scriptures at all. Both are wrong. The true position is to say, Yes, the word is essential, that is why it has been given. The Scriptures are essential because their purpose, finally, is to strengthen our faith. In the early church, there were false teachers who were querying and questioning many aspects of the truth, such as the truth about our Lord's deity and the truth of the incarnation. So one of the reasons for the Gospels was – as John tells us in this very Gospel – to let us know 'that Jesus is the Christ, the Son of God' (John 20:31). That is to strengthen faith: that is one of the functions of the Scriptures. Another function, of course, is to instruct us and to lead us on. The apostles did that while they were alive, and wrote their teaching down under divine inspiration in order to give us greater knowledge. Not only that, the Scriptures are given to us in order that we may check our experiences, in order that we may be safeguarded against heresy and against various forms of false teaching that can lead us into grievous error and trouble.

Now that is the main function of the Scriptures; they have been given to establish us, to teach us, to lead us on, to safeguard us, to give us checks, helps and aids, and so to make us perfect and complete. But salvation is possible without the Scriptures – as we see in the case of the first Christians. So we must not say that it is all in the Scriptures exclusively and entirely. We must not exalt the Scriptures into the supreme position. We must never say that the truth about Christian people is that they believe the Scriptures. You do not stop at that. They believe the Scriptures only in the sense that they help them to come to a belief in the Lord of the Scriptures, in the Lord Jesus Christ himself. The Scriptures per se do not save us, but they tell us of the one who does save us.

Another argument, therefore, that I can adduce, is that if the Scriptures are really only describing the Christian life as it could be lived in the first century, then they are very misleading. Here they are, they are all I have, but if I am told, 'Ah, but you must not expect that now, that was only true while he was here, or while the apostles were still alive,' then I ask: What is the value of the New Testament to me as a whole? What is the value of an incident such as our Lord's meeting with the woman of Samaria? What is the value of the history of the book of the Acts of the Apostles? What is the value of the teaching of the Epistles? If I am to be told that I must not expect it all to be true for me now, then it means that the New Testament is always exhorting us to a level of life that we cannot attain unto, and that surely is to discourage us and to be utterly unfair to us.

Or, finally, if this attitude towards salvation and towards the Scriptures is true, then it seems to me that we must say that the people in the Old Testament dispensation were in a superior position to us, because in the Old Testament God dealt directly with men and women and spoke to them, as we see in the experiences of the psalmists and of David and others. And, of course, many Christians are honest enough to admit that. There are many who are ready to confess that they are on a lower level than the psalmists. They have not had the experience of the psalmists, who could say, 'When my father and my mother forsake me, then the LORD will take me up' (Psalm 27:10). They have to confess that they do not know much about that.

Now that is quite inevitable according to this teaching that I am criticizing, but it is hopelessly and entirely wrong. The Christian is in a superior position to all the saints of the Old Testament. It was our Lord himself who said concerning John the Baptist, who was the last of those great prophetic figures of the Old Testament dispensation, that while it was true to say that 'among them that are born of women there hath not risen a greater than John the Baptist: notwithstanding he that is least in the kingdom of heaven is greater than he' (Matthew 11:11). Any teaching that makes you feel that the Old Testament saints were in a superior position to you, or had an advantage over you, is of necessity a false teaching.

There, then, are some general considerations to show you the fallacy of this modern teaching that tends to represent the Christian as someone who simply accepts New Testament statements and propositions without of necessity feeling anything at all. But I want to go further; it is a blank contradiction of our Lord's own teaching, and this is what we are particularly concerned about as we study John chapter 4. Let us never forget that our Lord said that he had come 'to give us life'. Life! He did not merely come to give us a teaching that would satisfy us in certain respects, but he came that we might have life, and that we might have it 'more abundantly' (John 10:10).

Now life, as we have been seeing, includes every part of us. Life does not merely satisfy the intellect and make us live solely in terms of our understanding. No, no; it takes up the entire person, the totality of our being. This is of necessity true, by definition. But take some of the specific statements that are found in John chapter 14. 'Let not your heart be troubled' (verse 1). Why did our Lord say that? He said it because he had just told the disciples that he was about to leave them:

> *Now is the Son of man glorified, and God is glorified in him . . . Little children, yet a little while I am with you. Ye shall seek me: and as I said unto the Jews, Whither I go, ye cannot come; so now I say to you . . . (John 13:31, 33)*

Peter as usual acted as spokesman:

> *Simon Peter said unto him, Lord, whither goest thou? Jesus answered him, Whither I go, thou canst not follow me now; but thou shalt follow me afterwards. (John 13:36)*

That was why they were utterly cast down – it was because their Lord was telling them that he was on the verge of leaving them. But this was his response: 'Let not your heart be troubled: ye believe in God, believe also in me. In my Father's house are many mansions . . .'

The whole of chapter 14 is devoted to this theme. This is what our Lord keeps saying.

> *I will not leave you comfortless: I will come to you.*

Now here is one who has just said that he is going to leave them:

> *Yet a little while, and the world seeth me no more; but ye see me: because I live, ye shall live also. (verses 18–19)*

Now these words of our Lord do not only refer to the resurrection; that is included, but they go beyond that. Later in this chapter, our Lord puts it quite plainly:

*He that hath my commandments, and keepeth them, he it is that loveth me: and he that loveth me shall be loved of my Father, and I will love him, and will manifest myself to him. (John 14:21)*

Now this does not simply refer to the mere forty days of our Lord's resurrection appearances – this is permanent, this is the Christian life as it is going to be lived; and the great emphasis is: 'I will not leave you comfortless: I will come to you.' Our Lord is going to manifest himself, of course, in a different way, but the point that he constantly emphasizes is that they have nothing to be downcast about. This is not the end of that marvellous period when he was with them. But that is the tendency of this teaching that is so popular. 'If only we had been alive then!' No, no; our Lord says: Do not be comfortless.

And, of course, in the sixteenth chapter, he goes even further:

*But these things have I told you, that when the time shall come, ye may remember that I told you of them. And these things I said not unto you at the beginning, because I was with you. But now I go my way to him that sent me; and none of you asketh me, Whither goest thou? But because I have said these things unto you, sorrow hath filled your heart. Nevertheless I tell you the truth; It is expedient for you that I go away*

– could anything be clearer? It is a good thing for you; it is to your advantage; it is 'expedient' for you that I go away –

*for if I go not away, the Comforter will not come unto you; but if I depart, I will send him unto you. (John 16:4–7)*

And, indeed, our Lord goes further and tells his disciples that far from weeping, they ought to be rejoicing in this:

*Ye have heard how I said unto you, I go away, and come again unto you. If ye loved me, ye would rejoice, because I said, I go unto the Father: for my Father is greater than I. (John 14:28)*

Now all this teaching fits in together, and what it really means is this: our Lord is saying to these men, in effect, 'Now I have been with you for these three years, and during this time I have shown you what is possible for you. But you are going to experience very much greater and bigger things.' This is astounding! He looks forward to the future after he has gone, and after he has sent the Holy Spirit. That is what he is dealing with in John 14, 15 and 16. He is saying, in effect, 'Do not go and be mournful, you ought to rejoice, because it means I am going to my Father, and he will give me the gift of the Spirit, and I will send him upon you. What has been happening now while I am here is nothing in comparison with what will happen then.' He even says that they ought to believe him because of his very works:

*Believe me that I am in the Father, and the Father in me: or else believe me for the very works' sake. Verily, verily, I say unto you, he that believeth on me, the works that I do shall he do also; and greater works than these shall he do; because I go unto my Father. (John 14:11–12)*

In other words, in the Gospels we are given but illustrations in a very human, practical form, of something much greater that will happen after Christ has returned to the glory. So what he is able to give to the woman of Samaria in the days of his flesh, he is able to give us, but in a greater manner. Let me give you another statement of his on this same theme of the Holy Spirit:

*In the last day, that great day of the feast, Jesus stood and cried, saying, If any man thirst, let him come unto me, and drink. He that believeth on me, as the scripture hath said, out of his belly shall flow rivers of living water.*

And then John explains:

*(But this spake he of the Spirit, which they that believe on him should receive: for the Holy Ghost was not yet given; because that Jesus was not yet glorified.) (John 7:37–38)*

The teaching is exactly the same both here and in the fourteenth, fifteenth and sixteenth chapters of John. Our Lord says, 'It is expedient for you that I go away.' It is better for Christians that he should not be here in the flesh, but that he should be dealing with us as he now deals with us. Not only is our position not inferior to those who were alive in the days of his flesh, it is superior.

And then go on to the seventeenth chapter of John: 'This is life eternal, that they might know thee the only true God, and Jesus Christ, whom thou hast sent' (John 17:3). What a statement! But to 'know the only true God, and Jesus Christ', does not mean 'accept the propositions concerning him'. He does not say that life eternal consists in knowing *about* God. There many people who know about God who are not Christians. The Jews know about God. You can know about God as Creator, you can know the teaching of the Scriptures about God. You can accept all the theology, all the propositions, but that is not what our Lord is talking about. Adam knew him, but Adam sinned and lost that knowledge, and man has lost the knowledge ever since. No, the restoration that salvation brings is not a mere knowledge about God – 'The devils also believe, and tremble,' as James tells us (James 2:19) – but it is 'to know God'. The knowledge we have lost is restored, and it is a knowledge of communion and of fellowship. There is an intimacy, there is a personal quality; we must never detract from this.

And then, to clinch the whole thing, as it were, we have those famous words that our Lord uttered to doubting Thomas, Thomas who could not believe the testimony of his fellow apostles that the Lord really had risen. Our Lord had appeared to them when they were gathered together, but Thomas had not been there. And Thomas had said very stubbornly, 'Except I shall see in his hands the print of the nails, and put my finger into the print of the nails, and thrust my hand into his side, I will not believe.' This is how John's Gospel continues:

> *And after eight days again his disciples were within, and Thomas with them: then came Jesus, the doors being shut, and stood in the midst, and said, Peace be unto you. Then saith he to Thomas, Reach hither thy finger, and behold my hands; and reach hither thy hand, and thrust it into my side: and be not faithless, but believing. And Thomas answered and said unto him, My Lord and my God. Jesus saith unto him, Thomas, because thou hast seen me, thou hast believed: blessed are they that have not seen, and yet have believed. (John 20:25–29)*

Now that is a rebuke, and I feel it is a rebuke that comes to many of us who tend to say the same sort of thing, but we put it like this: 'If only I had been alive then. If only I could have seen him.' As if the manifestations of the Son of God were confined solely to his days on earth.

So there it is in the plain teaching of our Lord himself. So to say that the Christian simply lives on believing and accepting intellectually the statements and the propositions of the Scriptures is a denial of our Lord's own teaching. To exclude the feelings, the emotion, the whole person, the sense of personal relationship, is to deny his own teaching.

And it also denies the teaching of the book of the Acts of the Apostles. Do you not see, as you read through that book, that those people were living a life in conscious communion with the Lord? They were not living on memories, they were not living simply on what he had taught them. In the fourth chapter, we read that they are in trouble, and we find them praying. They pray to God directly, and God answers them directly: 'When they had prayed, the place was shaken.' These people were not holding on to propositions only. Many were doing that, of course, but they wanted more than that, they wanted some demonstration, they asked for it and they got it:

> And when they had prayed, the place was shaken where they were assembled together; and they were all filled with the Holy Ghost, and they spake the word of God with boldness . . . And with great power gave the apostles witness of the resurrection of the Lord Jesus: and great grace was upon them all. (Acts 4:31, 33)

Now the apostles, you see, did not merely make an intellectual statement, putting forward the propositions concerning Jesus Christ and what they had heard him say, and how they had seen him crucified, and how he had been buried, and how they had seen him rise again. They did that but what is emphasized is the power, the authority, the afflatus, the whole might of the Spirit upon them. The certainty, the absoluteness – this is what is stressed. And this, of course, is what we find running right through the whole of this book of Acts. Take, for instance, the story of that man Stephen, who became the first martyr. This is the description we are given when he was brought before the court: 'And all that sat in the council, looking stedfastly on him, saw his face as it had been the face of an angel' (Acts 6:15).

This had happened to Moses after he had spent forty days with God on Mount Sinai. He had been in a living, vital communion with God and his face was shining when he came down. Stephen, too, was in the realm of the Spirit, and his face was shining like that of an angel. But you remember the end of the story? At the end of Acts chapter 7, where we read about the martyrdom of Stephen, we are told:

> *But he, being full of the Holy Ghost, looked up stedfastly into heaven, and saw the glory of God, and Jesus standing on the right hand of God, and said, Behold, I see the heavens opened, and the Son of man standing on the right hand of God. (Acts 7:55–56)*

Now Stephen was not merely bearing witness to a number of propositions that he had believed. He was seeing the risen Lord in some manner or other. This happened after our Lord had gone back to heaven; it was real, it was living, and it was vital. So he was able to die 'calling upon God, and saying, Lord Jesus, receive my spirit'.

Now I am simply quoting these passages to you to show you that these people expected that kind of thing. I shall deal with this later, God willing, lest anyone misunderstand what I am saying. For now, I am simply giving you the evidence, I am simply breaking down this notion that all we can do today is live by faith in propositions, that we are left to that, and cannot expect a living communion such as the woman of Samaria had; I am simply breaking down that erroneous, crippling teaching by giving you scriptural evidence.

No, as these people go on, they do not live on propositions – there is a living communion. Listen to the beginning of the thirteenth chapter of Acts: 'As they ministered to the Lord, and fasted, the Holy Ghost said, Separate unto me Barnabas and Saul for the work whereunto I have called them' (verse 2). How did he say that? They did not have these Scriptures. He spoke directly. The Holy Spirit does speak directly. He deals with us. Christians are not merely trying to live on and implement the propositions that they have believed concerning the Lord Jesus Christ. No, no; I say again, there is a living communion with the Holy Spirit – 'the communion of the Holy Spirit', and the communion with the Son, and the communion with the Father.

We see this again in Acts 15; the council of Christians at Jerusalem sent a letter to the churches, and this is how they put it: 'It seemed good to the Holy Ghost, and to us' (Acts 15:28). They knew that it seemed good to the Holy Ghost because he had told them so. This is a living relationship. In Acts 16, too, it is the same:

*Now when they had gone throughout Phrygia and the region of Galatia, and were forbidden of the Holy Ghost to preach the word in Asia, after they were come to Mysia, they assayed to go into Bithynia: but the Spirit suffered them not. (Acts 16:6–7)*

This is the direct, immediate guidance of the Spirit, and if you are denying this, you are robbing yourself of a living fellowship with the blessed Persons in the Holy Trinity, you are robbing yourself of this 'well of water springing up into everlasting life'. Listen to this again in Acts chapter 18. Paul is in trouble at Corinth and has great opposition, but I read in the ninth verse, 'Then spake the Lord to Paul in the night by a vision, be not afraid, but speak, and hold not thy peace.'

My friends, this is direct dealing with human beings by the living, risen Lord. He has not ceased to do this. Another example – to complete this evidence for you – is in Acts 22. Paul is giving his defence and he says:

*And it came to pass, that, when I was come again to Jerusalem, even while I prayed in the temple, I was in a trance; and saw him saying*

– this blessed Lord, Paul saw him saying to him –

*Make haste, and get thee quickly out of Jerusalem: for they will not receive thy testimony concerning me. (Acts 22:17–18)*

And, again in Acts 23:

*The night following the Lord stood by him, and said, Be of good cheer, Paul: for as thou hast testified of me in Jerusalem, so must thou bear witness unto me at Rome. (Acts 23:11)*

And so as our Lord ministered to the woman of Samaria in the days of his flesh, so he does still, and we must not rob ourselves of the glorious benefits and blessing and privilege of his ministrations. 'A well of water springing up into everlasting life'; yes, and it is through that life that we have fellowship and communion with him.

47

# *Joy beyond Words*

*The woman then left her waterpot, and went her way into the city, and saith to the men, Come, see a man, which told me all things that ever I did: is not this the Christ? (John 4:28–29)*

The Christian, as we have seen, is not only someone who believes in the Lord Jesus Christ as a man who lived nearly two thousand years ago, who gave incomparable teaching, who died and rose again and who outlined a way of life for us. Christians believe that but they do not stop there. They believe that their salvation is the result of the death of the Lord Jesus Christ, and, over and above that, they believe that they are meant to enjoy fellowship, communion, with him – they believe they meet with him.

We have been dealing with this tremendously important matter. There are many people who shut out a living, real experience of our Lord and try to argue that obviously this cannot happen now, but belongs to the days of his flesh. Many are afraid of enthusiasm, they are afraid of ecstasy, they are afraid of excesses;

and they are so afraid of these things that they have reduced the Christian faith and the Christian experience merely to an intellectual acceptance of a number of propositions. We have seen that this view is utterly wrong and contradicts the plain teaching of the Scripture itself. I have adduced words from our Lord's own lips to prove this and have quoted from the book of the Acts of the Apostles to show how, after our Lord's death and resurrection and ascension, he still continued to manifest himself to people, as he had said he would.

It is tremendously important that we should realize what the Scriptures really do teach us, so I would now like to show you further evidence from the Epistles. We have many examples of this teaching – I am simply picking out one or two that show it very clearly. Take, for instance, the apostle Paul's words about himself in 2 Corinthians chapter 12:

> *It is not expedient for me doubtless to glory. I will come to visions and revelations of the Lord. I knew a man in Christ above fourteen years ago, (whether in the body, I cannot tell; or whether out of the body, I cannot tell: God knoweth;) such an one caught up to the third heaven. And I knew such a man, (whether in the body, or out of the body, I cannot tell: God knoweth;) How that he was caught up into paradise, and heard unspeakable words, which it is not lawful for a man to utter. Of such an one will I glory: yet of myself I will not glory, but in mine infirmities. (2 Corinthians 12:1–5)*

The apostle is there relating an experience that happened to him 14 years earlier. He confesses he does not quite understand it, 'whether in the body, or out of the body', but what he does know is the reality of the experience. It was a manifestation of the Son of God; he calls it 'revelations of the Lord' and he was lifted up into the third heaven. That was an experience given to the apostle long after the ascension of our blessed Lord and Saviour, and it is in line with his experiences that are recorded in the book of Acts. He puts this in a more didactic form in the Epistle to the Philippians, where he describes his supreme ambition: 'That I may know him, and the power of his resurrection, and the fellowship of his sufferings, being made conformable unto his death' (Philippians 3:10).

Now the important expression there is, 'that I may know him' and that clearly does not mean to know about him, because the apostle already had that knowledge in great fullness and was a teacher and an apostle. No, all the authorities are agreed that it cannot be reduced to anything less than personal knowledge, intimate knowledge, direct communion. The apostle is there expressing his desire that over and above all the direct and immediate knowledge that he had, he might have yet more. That was his greatest desire, the greatest longing of his heart. He had had these experiences, and because of that he desired to have more. And so you find him saying in his very last letter, the Second Epistle to Timothy, where he is giving an account of what had happened to him in his trial: 'At my first answer no man stood with me, but all men forsook me: I pray God that it may not be laid to their charge. Notwithstanding the Lord stood with me, and strengthened me' (2 Timothy 4:16–17).

Now Paul was conscious of the Lord's presence. He is not making a general statement that he was given strength and power, but goes beyond that: 'The Lord stood with me.' At this trial no men had stood with him; as far as his accusers were concerned, Paul was standing alone. But he was aware in the dock that the Lord was standing by him; it was real to him, it was living. There are other examples, I am only selecting a few out of the writings of the apostle Paul.

And it is the same with all the other apostles. The apostle Peter has exactly the same teaching. I have often quoted the next verse from this pulpit because I have always regarded it as the greatest challenge to all Christian people. This is Christianity. Peter is writing to a number of people whom he has never seen and does not know. He can only address them as 'strangers scattered throughout Pontus, Galatia, Cappadocia, Asia, and Bithynia' (1 Peter 1:1) But what he does know is that they are passing through a great trial. He says:

> *Wherein ye greatly rejoice, though now for a season, if need be, ye are in heaviness through manifold temptations: that the trial of your faith, being much more precious than of gold that perisheth, though it be tried with fire, might be found unto praise and honour and glory at the appearing of Jesus Christ: whom having not seen, ye love; in whom, though now ye see him not, yet believing, ye rejoice with joy unspeakable and full of glory. (1 Peter 1:6–8)*

Now Peter is not writing, let me remind you, to apostles, but to people we may term 'ordinary Christians'. You know what I mean by that – no Christian is ordinary, but there are differences between Christians. These people are not officers, they are not apostles or leaders in the church, and he says that they rejoice in him with a joy that is 'unspeakable', and even more, this joy of theirs has something of the glory of heaven itself – 'full of glory'.

That is Christianity. It is not merely that you deduce from the Scriptures that you are saved – 'Whosoever believeth is not condemned': I believe and therefore I am not condemned – an intellectual acknowledgment and that is it. No, no! It is that you know a joy that is – well, it is beyond words, it cannot be expressed. As the apostle Paul said of the words he heard in his vision, as we have just seen (2 Corinthians 12:4). Though the Christians to whom Paul is writing are passing through 'manifold trials', they have a joy that is 'unspeakable and full of glory'. This same joy is meant for us and is possible for us. That is the teaching. And you and I have no business to be content with anything less. It is another way of putting the statements in John about never thirsting again, and the 'well of water springing up into everlasting life'.

Or take it as the apostle John expresses it: 'These things write we unto you, that your joy may be full' (1 John 1:4). What are 'these things'? They are 'that which we have seen and heard'. John says that these 'declare we unto you' – what for? – 'that ye also may have fellowship with us: and truly our fellowship is with the Father, and with his Son Jesus Christ' (verse 3). Now the words that are really important there are, 'that ye also may *have fellowship* with us'. The expression 'have fellowship' is most important. Have you ever realized what it means? One of the grammarians, the people who are interested in the Scripture from the standpoint of words and exact meanings, says that it is an extremely strong expression, and denotes enjoyment and the realization of fellowship as compared with the mere fact of fellowship. In other words, John is not merely concerned to let his readers know that because they are believers, they have fellowship with the apostles, and in turn, therefore, with the Father and the Son. No, he says: I am writing in order that you may have the enjoyment and the realization of this fellowship that is with the Father and with his Son Jesus Christ.

Now there again there is something that I must emphasize. John does not say, 'and truly our fellowship is with the Father, and Jesus Christ his Son'. No; he goes out of his way to say, 'our fellowship is with the Father, and with his Son Jesus Christ'. They have fellowship with the Father, they have fellowship with the Son, they have fellowship with the Holy Spirit – distinct and separate. This is not merely something of which you say, 'Oh, of course, this must be true of us because we are Christians.' I am emphasizing this because I know how glib we are in our thinking and in our speaking. We slide over these momentous, profound statements and miss the glory and the experience of them. John would not have written this letter merely to tell his readers that because they are Christians, they have fellowship; with the Father and with the Son. He is saying: 'I am writing that you may have the enjoyment and the realization of this.' Not the fact, but beyond it. So he adds: 'These things write we unto you, that your joy may be full' (verse 4). This is the plain teaching, you see, of the First Epistle of John, and the whole object of the entire epistle is really just to bring out that teaching.

And then we turn to the last book of the Bible, the book of Revelation, and we know its message from its very title, do we not? It is a book of 'revelations' – not mere teaching but beyond teaching, revelations given to John. Read that book again for yourselves and be especially careful about reading the introduction where John is quite plain and clear about what has happened to him: 'The Revelation of Jesus Christ, which God gave unto him, to shew unto his servants things which must shortly come to pass', and so on. And then John goes on to say how this revelation, this manifestation of the Son of God, came to him:

> *I John, who also am your brother, and companion in tribulation, and in the kingdom and patience of Jesus Christ, was in the isle that is called Patmos, for the word of God, and for the testimony of Jesus Christ. I was in the Spirit on the Lord's day*

– that is the way to get this intimate knowledge: 'in the Spirit'. John does not mean that every Christian is 'in the Spirit'. That is the teaching today. It is said, 'We are all in the Spirit because we are Christians.' No, no! He says that over and above what is normally true of him, on this great and special occasion he was 'in the Spirit' in an unusual manner –

> *and heard behind me a great voice, as of a trumpet, saying, I am Alpha and Omega, the first and the last: and, What thou seest, write in a book . . . And I turned to see the voice that spake with me. (Revelation 1:9–12)*

And John goes on to give an account of the vision. But I want to emphasize in particular verse 20 of chapter 3 of Revelation: 'Behold, I stand at the door and knock: if any man hear my voice, and open the door, I will come in to him, and will sup with him, and he with me.' Do not forget that this was written to church members, to Christian believers, and our Lord is saying that over and above the fact that they are Christians, he is prepared to enter in, to sup with them and have this intimate fellowship and communion.

There, then, is the evidence of the Scriptures: but what people say in reply is this: 'Yes, that's quite true. But all that came to an end with the death of the apostles. That is how God dealt with his people till the Scriptures were written, but after the Scriptures had been given, that sort of thing was not needed any longer. As Christians, we are to live on the Scriptures.' This means that all the passages that I have been reading and referring to are not for us, and we should not expect the experiences they describe, indeed, it is wrong for us to expect them. We are facing the great danger of becoming enthusiasts if we look for these experiences.

Now this is a very serious tendency in the Christian church at the present time. But it seems to me to be a tragic misuse of the Scriptures. What is the object of the Scriptures? When I read of the early Christians rejoicing with a joy unspeakable and full of glory, do I say, 'Well, of course, that is not meant for me, I am not near enough to the Lord; the apostles are not still alive and therefore I cannot expect to rejoice with that joy. That was only for the first century.' If so, why are the Scriptures preserved? Why was the church guided in the arrangement of the canon? What is the value of the Scriptures at all if that is what I think about them? Yet that is the common argument in evangelical circles at this present time, and it seems to me that it accounts for the poverty of the life of the church and her ineffectiveness and, therefore, the condition of the world.

The Bible tells us that God reveals and manifests himself. Let me put it to you like this: If this modern attitude is right and we as Christians must never expect anything beyond reading and understanding the Scriptures, at times feeling a sense of joy and of happiness as we do so, but nothing beyond that, then I stress again that in that case the Christian today is in an inferior position to the Old Testament saints. God made himself known to the boy Samuel, did he not? He spoke to him. Samuel did not understand it; nor did Eli at first. But subsequently he did. Look at all those instances in the Old Testament: I am not thinking only of the theophanies, the appearances of God in human form, for example, to Abraham on more than one occasion, I am thinking also of occasions such as the call of Gideon in the time of the Judges. Gideon again had one of these manifestations, one of these revelations, quite unexpectedly; he was called to perform his great task in that way (Judges 6).

The Old Testament saints had direct dealings with God, and are we not to have direct dealings also? The author of the Epistle to the Hebrews put this in a very striking way, which denies all this modern teaching completely. In the eleventh chapter he gives a great list of Old Testament heroes of the faith, and then, having told us of some of the astounding experiences that they had, he says, 'And these all, having obtained a good report through faith, received not the promise: God having provided some better thing for us, that they without us should not be made perfect' (Hebrews 11:39–40). This teaches that not only do we have something more than they had, which is the teaching of the New Testament everywhere – indeed, of the Old as well because the Old is always pointing forward to the new – but also that still greater things are coming. The great prophetic message is that the Spirit will be poured forth in great profusion in that future time: not occasionally as in the Old Testament dispensation. But this modern teaching denies that completely.

And that is why, as I have said, it so often comes to pass that many a modern Christian reading the psalms feels that he does not know God as well as the psalmists did – and that is a terrible thing to say. You and I are in a better position than the psalmists – even, as we have seen, in a better position than John the Baptist. Why did our Lord come into this world? Peter tells us: He came 'that he might bring us to God' (1 Peter 3:18). Not theoretically, but in a living, experiential, vital manner, so that we might *know* God. This is what we are meant to enjoy. This is the glory that the New Testament constantly speaks about. Therefore to deny that this is possible for us is to deny the Scriptures themselves and, indeed, to make them very misleading. They have no function at all if I am to explain away all their greatest statements as belonging only to the first century.

But I have a stronger argument still to put to you. It is that the subsequent experience of God's people throughout the centuries shows how utterly false the notion is that it is not possible today to have direct and immediate experiences of God. Long after the end of the time of the apostles of the first century, long after the canon of Scripture had been fixed, people continued to have living and direct communion with the Lord. What is a revival? We read of the great revivals in the church. Well, as has often been pointed out, a revival is nothing but a repetition of the book of

Acts. The whole story of revivals is of God manifesting himself in an unmistakable manner. In a revival, a large number of people at the same time are aware of God. I was reading again a manuscript on the history of the last revival in Wales in 1904–5, and that is what stands out so directly and amazingly.

I remember the story of one man in a meeting; for years he had been going to Christian meetings, he was a good Christian man, but when he was in this meeting, he said, 'God is in this place.' And God was in that place and making himself known. His power was there. They were conscious of his very presence. This happens in revivals, and what I am trying to emphasize is that it should happen to every Christian, and every Christian should be seeking this experience of God.

Now, I repeat, this does not apply only to exceptional people. This is another favourite way of getting out of all this, is it not? People say, Ah, yes, you've been quoting Paul, you've been quoting John – apostles; you've been quoting Samuel – a mighty prophet; you've been quoting Gideon – a great judge. Of course, they say, we expect these exceptional people to have such experiences. The answer to that is in Peter's words in 1 Peter 1, and they are enough: 'strangers scattered abroad'. The Bible never says that this is limited only to the exceptional: 'For the promise is unto you, and to your children, and to all that are afar off' (Acts 2:39). It is all-inclusive! To deny that is to be guilty of introducing distinctions that are never found in the Scriptures or, as I have said, in the subsequent history of the church.

Now in order to establish this point, I want to read to you some experiences of Christian people so that you may know the kind of thing about which I am speaking. Let me tell you about A. B. Earl, a man who was greatly used in America in the last century. He was born in 1812 and began preaching in 1830 after his conversion at the age of 18. He was a good preacher and for the next 33 years had a successful ministry. But in 1863 he began to feel that there was something lacking, that he was just an advocate instead of being a witness; and what a different there is between the two! The advocate talks about what has been happening to others, he has his brief, but he is outside it. The witness, on the other hand, tells us what has happened to him, he is giving his testimony. Now this is what A. B. Earl says:

> I felt that I must have in my heart something that I did not then possess. Before I could be filled with the fullness of Christ's love I must be emptied of self. Oh, the longing of my heart for what I then believed, and now believe, to be sweet and constant rest in Jesus. I believed I should receive and thought it was near.

He was right, of course, for Jesus it was who had said to the woman of Samaria: 'Whosoever drinketh of the water that I shall give him shall never thirst' – 'sweet and constant rest'; 'never thirst'. Then he says:

> I soon found it was easier to resist temptation. I began to trust Christ and his promise more fully. With this mingling of faith, desire and expectation I commenced meeting on Cape Cod. After rededicating myself, in company with others, anew to God, I was in my room alone pleading for the fullness of Christ's love, when all at once a sweet, heavenly peace filled all the vacuum in my soul, leaving no longing, no unrest, no dissatisfied feeling in my bosom. I felt I knew that I was accepted fully in Jesus. A calm, simple, childlike trust took possession of my whole being, then for the first time in my life

– and he was 51 then, remember –

> I had the rest which is more than peace. I had felt peace before but feared I should not retain it. Now I had peace without fear and which

really became rest. This change occurred about five o'clock on the evening of the second day of November 1863, and although I never felt so weak and small yet Jesus has been my all since then. There has not been an hour of conscious doubt or darkness since that time. A heaven of peace and rest fills my soul. Day and night the Saviour seems by me. My success in leading souls to Jesus has been much greater than before. Temptation is presented but the power of it is broken. I seem to have a present Saviour in every kind of need, so that for several years I have done the trusting and Jesus the keeping.

Now that is Christianity, and there is a man in the nineteenth century.

'Ah,' you say, 'but there again is a preacher, an evangelist, a man whom God was using in a signal manner.'

Well, now, let me read to you an experience of a woman, certainly a woman who became a minister's wife, a very able woman who had been born into a wealthy family, brought under conviction and converted, as a result of which she suffered a lot, even at the hands of her own mother. But though she was a true Christian, she was still not satisfied. She describes how she was listening to a sermon on Trinity Sunday in June 1776 and tells how the preacher had been preaching about the Holy Spirit. She writes:

He spoke also much of the near union and communion with God which believers might enjoy, especially those perfected in love. My soul was led into depths unspeakable and saw such a fullness of God ready for me to plunge into that what I now felt seemed only as a drop compared with the ocean. As I came into the chapel yard I felt peculiar communion with the adorable Jesus in all his offices of redeeming love, and that verse of a hymn was so powerfully sweet as I had never felt it before:

The opening heavens around me shine
With beams of sacred bliss,

While Jesus shows his mercy mine
And whispers, I am his.

I was deeply penetrated with his presence and stood as if unable to move, and was insensible to all around me. While thus lost in communion with my Saviour, he spake these words to my heart: 'All that I have is thine. I am Jesus in whom dwells all the fullness of the Godhead bodily. I am thine. My Spirit is thine, my Father is thine, they love thee as I love thee; the whole Deity is thine. All God is and all he has is thine, he even now overshadows thee, he now covers thee with a cloud of his presence.' All this was so realized to my soul in a manner I cannot explain, that I sank down motionless being unable to sustain the weight of his glorious presence and fullness of love.

At the altar this was renewed to me but not in so large a measure. I believe indeed if this had continued as I felt it before but for one hour, mortality must have been dissolved and the soul dislodged from its tenement of clay . . .

I grew through boundless mercy and free grace an increasing intercourse and communion with my God every day. I live and move in him alone. Wherever I go, whatever I do, I feel the presence of the great Three in One. Yea, he dwelleth with me and shall be in me. This is his promise to my soul. I feel I am under his loving eye and the continual guidance of his Spirit. I do indeed dwell in God, and God in me. O love unsearchable to such a worm! I loathe myself when God I see, and into nothing I fall.

*Hester Ann Rodgers*

Here is a final quotation from that life. She describes how her husband was suddenly stricken by illness. He had fallen down as suddenly as if he had been shot, and still continued very unwell.

Yet in secret prayer the Lord assured me that he should not die at this time but live. Oh, what should I do at a time like this if I had not a constant intercourse with God. But blessed be his dear name, I have access to him. He is indeed my refuge and strength, a very present help in trouble, and fills my soul with strong consolation.

Well, my dear people, these are but two illustrations out of a large number, a great host, that I could have given you. I have quoted to you in past times the experience of some of the Puritans. The Puritan John Flavel said that in one moment, as it were, of this realization of the manifestation of the Son of God, he had learned more than he had learned from all his books and all his own preaching and teaching over 50 years. The same is true of John Howe. How often have I quoted from Whitefield's journals! How often have I reminded you of what happened to D. L. Moody and Charles Haddon Spurgeon. Now these are men and women of different types, of great abilities and ordinary abilities. In revival, as I say, some of the most ordinary people have had some of the most amazing experiences of the direct and immediate presence of the Lord.

You say, 'Is this enthusiasm?'

Well, all I can say is that if it is, God grant we all may become enthusiasts. These are sane, balanced people – people of intellect, people of knowledge, people of understanding, many of them people with great training, people who have been benefactors to the church, to their own families and to the community at large. These – what are they? I say, they are nothing but people who through the running centuries are verifying in their experience precisely what we are told in the New Testament is possible to every Christian. These examples I have just read are but examples and illustrations of people in the eighteenth and nineteenth centuries rejoicing in him 'with a joy unspeakable and full of glory', so conscious of him, and of his nearness and of his presence, his love and his glory and his power, that it was almost more than their physical frames could stand.

God in his infinite kindness and grace has seen to it that the story of the meeting of the woman of Samaria with the Lord Jesus Christ should have been recorded and should be here available for us in order that you and I might know this, that as she met him by the well, so you and I can meet with him. Remember the words I quoted last time – our Lord said to his disciples, 'It is expedient for you that I go away' (John 16:7). You will be in a better position, he said, when I go away.

So you need not say, and you must never say again, 'Oh, that I were there with the woman of Samaria! Oh, that I were one of those Samaritans who she called out to see him! Oh, I can imagine what I would have felt!' If you say that, you are denying the teaching of the Scriptures, you are denying his own words. This incident at the well is only an illustration to show us that we can enjoy that same fellowship, the same communion in a much greater, in a much more real, manner than the woman of Samaria did at that particular time in the history of the world.

We shall go on with this; we shall have to go on to consider how it is he manifests himself. All I have been concerned to do so far is to establish the fact that he does, and that unless we know something about this, we are robbing ourselves, and at the same time putting a limit upon the greatness and the glory of this salvation that he came into the world to give us. May God open our eyes and deliver us from reducing the Scriptures to the level of our own poor experiences; may he open our eyes to the full message of the Son of God and his so great salvation.

48

# Experiences of the Lord's Presence

*The woman then left her waterpot, and went her way into the city, and saith to the men, Come, see a man, which told me all things that ever I did: is not this the Christ? (John 4:28–29)*

We have been seeing that according to the Scriptures, it is as possible for us to realize the presence of our Lord today as it was for the woman of Samaria. Having established that, we must now go on to consider a question that people are always, and very rightly, very ready to ask: How, then, does our Lord manifest himself now to Christian people? He has promised to do so. He has said, 'I will love him, and manifest myself to him' (John 14:21). But how does he?

Here is a question that has perplexed many people, and in many ways it is a subject that is surrounded by certain dangers. There is nothing in this Christian life or teaching but that is surrounded by dangers. That is because of the devil, and because of the effect of sin and the Fall upon us – every one of us. People sometimes go off at a tangent, many have done so and have sought visions and have imagined things and confused the psychological and psychic with the spiritual. Yes, but that does not mean that we are to avoid the subject altogether: quite the reverse. That should urge us to examine it scripturally, carefully, in the light of the help that we are given by the saints throughout the centuries.

Because of certain possible dangers, there is a fatal tendency at the present time to have nothing to do with the subject. There are people who are so afraid of excesses that there has really never been much evidence of life in them. As I have often pointed out, it is not difficult to keep order in a cemetery, but when you have a houseful of children, you have a problem, and I prefer the problem of a houseful of children to the dead, legalistic orderliness of people who are afraid of excesses and afraid of enthusiasm and of ecstasy. Do not be troubled by that. But I say this because it is important that we should have some clear idea in our minds as to what we can legitimately expect, and, indeed, what we can legitimately seek.

So, then, how does our Lord manifest himself? The answer is, of course, that it is a spiritual manifestation. The woman of Samaria is in our Lord's physical presence. We do not seek that. We seek *spiritual* manifestations. And what are they like? Let me quote you the saintly John Fletcher of Madeley who knew so much about this. He says: 'The tongues of men and angels want proper words to express the sweetness and the glory with which the Son of God visits the soul that cannot rest without him.' Now that last phrase, 'cannot rest without him', is one that I shall have to open out later on. It is to the people who cannot rest without him that our Lord manifests himself. But what Fletcher is emphasizing here is that the manifestations are such that words are inadequate. So he goes on to say, 'It is not to be described but to be enjoyed.' This is something, of course, that transcends all human ability to describe. It is comparable to what we saw when we were looking at the experience that Paul described in 2 Corinthians 12.

We must expect this. It is fatal to try to confine what is possible to us in the Christian life to our understanding and our terminology. Let me use an illustration to show what I am referring to. People often ask questions about heaven. They want to know what it is like and what will happen there and so on. I suppose that such questions are among those I am most frequently asked. Many people are a bit troubled by the fact that we are not told very much about heaven in the Scriptures. But you should not be surprised by that; the explanation is perfectly simple. The glory of heaven is such that our highest and best language is inadequate to describe it and is inevitably bound to detract from it.

There is a similar difficulty with the word 'love'. However noble your conception of love, it falls, oh, how almost infinitely short of what love really is, for God is love. You and I cannot use the word 'love' without, of necessity, its carrying certain human, carnal, even sinful implications. And I believe that this failure of language is why, in the kindness and the goodness of God, we are not told more than we are about heaven. We are told enough to make us realize that it is infinite in its glory, in its perfection and joy. We are told that, but we cannot be given detailed descriptions. The nearest the Scriptures come to it is to say that 'the street of the city was pure gold' (Revelation 21:21). Now that is imagery. It is not a literal description. The book of Revelation is a book of imagery and of symbols, and this is just an attempt at a description by taking human categories. Gold is regarded as wonderful, there is nothing beyond it. Yet to say that the streets are paved with gold is totally inadequate, it simply gives us some vague notion.

And that is precisely what John Fletcher of Madeley is saying in those words that he uses. It follows from this that you find certain symbolic terms and metaphors employed in the Scriptures. Take, for example, the expression used in the letter to the church in Pergamum: 'I will give to eat of the hidden manna' (Revelation 2:17). Now that term indicates the kind of experience that this is. Manna was given to the Children of Israel. It was miraculous food from heaven, something nobody could explain, but it satisfied the people in the wilderness when they had no food to eat. But this is '*hidden* manna', which means that there is an element of mystery about it. It is something strange and unusual. Our Lord, as we have seen in connection with the woman of Samaria, tells the disciples, 'I have meat to eat that ye know not of.' This is the hidden manna. Another expression with a similar connotation is found in the letter to the church in Philadelphia: 'I will write upon him my new name' (Revelation 3:12). It is a name that nobody knows about.

These terms suggest that there is an element of mystery, in the New Testament sense, and that the experience of our Lord's presence so transcends our ordinary experience and even our thinking and all our categories that symbolism has to be used in order to give some impression of it. What we are talking about is, by definition, something that is completely meaningless to people in the world. They cannot begin to understand it. They do not understand the gospel in its most open and explicit form, they do not understand the way of salvation – even that is rubbish to them. So if they do not understand that, how can they understand this? And that is why the world has always tended to regard Christians who know something about these experiences as being almost insane. This, of course, is a very good test of those of us who are members of the Christian church. People in the church who have known this experience have generally been regarded as oddities by the majority of church members. They even ask: Are they Christians at all? The manna is 'hidden manna', and only those who have tasted it know about it. And this 'new name' is a secret between the Lord and the believer.

> The love of Jesus, what it is,
> None but his loved ones know.
> *Bernard of Clairvaux*

It is not to the world that our Lord says he will manifest himself (John 14:19, 22). And he says of the Holy Spirit, 'whom the world cannot receive, because it seeth him not, neither knoweth him: but ye know him' (John 14:17).

All this is one of the most remarkable and glorious aspects of the Christian life. That is why Paul says about the Christian, 'He that is spiritual judgeth all things, yet he himself is judged of no man' (1 Corinthians 2:15) – which simply means this: 'He that is spiritual' has an insight into these things and a knowledge of them, and the non-Christian does not understand him at all and thinks there is something peculiar about him. He can see that the Christian is being ravished by something that is real to him, but he himself knows nothing at all about it. This is something that is difficult to describe because it belongs to a realm, and to an order, that is so essentially different from everything to which we are accustomed.

It also follows that the experience is not only very wonderful but also sacred. That is why you will find that the people who have known most about it have generally been reluctant to say very much. For instance, even D. L. Moody, who was by nature an extrovert, very rarely spoke of that great experience that he had in New York City, that experience that changed the whole of his life.

And the reason is that it is wonderful, it is spiritual, it is mysterious and it has an element of intimacy with the Lord. There are certain things in natural, ordinary life that you do not broadcast. You do not share your most wonderful experiences with many people and you do not make known to the public the most intimate parts of your life's story.

This is a very good way of testing a spiritual experience and where you are helped when you are concerned to avoid the psychological or even the psychic. People who have had some psychological or psychic experience are always very ready to talk about it. Those who are always getting visions are always talking about them. That is how they betray themselves. But the very characteristic of this experience of which we are talking is that there is, I repeat, something sacred about it, and therefore one is afraid, as it were, of betraying a confidence. There is a secret between you and the Lover of your soul, and you do not broadcast that. In order to help others, you may mention it, you want them to know something about it, and thank God that people have done so, but almost without exception there is a reluctance or hesitation. There is a fear lest you detract from it, or boast of it 'in the flesh'. But you cannot boast in this realm, it is too sacred, it is too pure, it is too wonderful. So it follows that all who know something about this are careful and hesitant and do not parade it. The whole trouble with the church in Corinth was that it was 'parading' the gifts. Bear that in mind, it is one of the best and most delicate tests when you are sifting between the true spiritual experience and the psychological or psychic.

A further general remark is that there is also a great variation in spiritual manifestations. Sometimes such an experience will come instantaneously, without people seeking it, without their having known much about it. For other people, it may be very gradual.

You read of some who have sought this, and sought it diligently and long and have almost come to the point of despair before entering into it. You cannot stereotype these things. Again, this is a useful and a valuable discriminating test. Any experience that you can produce at will – I do not care what it is, speaking in tongues or anything else – is, by definition, not a spiritual experience. If a man tells me he can speak in tongues whenever he likes, I am doubtful as to the character and the nature of his speaking in tongues. We do not control these things; there are no absolute rules we can apply to bring them about, there is no legalistic element, as it were.

These spiritual manifestations lie entirely in our Lord's sovereign power – that is the reason for their great variety. You cannot find him whenever you like. You can seek him, but you cannot guarantee that you will find him. We ought to be able to see this quite clearly from human analogies. If delicate human relationships and associations cannot be commanded, how much less can these spiritual manifestations of the Son of God.

Not only the timing, but the type of experience, also, varies greatly from person to person. It is very difficult to know why. The only explanation that I would have is that, again in a sense, you would expect it, because, using once more the human analogy, you do not treat all the people you know in exactly the same way. This applies even to people who, as far as you can tell, you like and love to the same extent. This is because, if you are a person with any sensitivity at all, you are so concerned to help others and to be pleasing to them that unconsciously your conduct changes as they call out different things in you; not only that, you consciously change as you feel that they need different things from you. And so, looked at in general, though you may take the same view of persons, there is always a subtle difference in your treatment of them.

You do not deal with two, or three, or four, or five children in a family in exactly the same way. If you are a good parent, you do not have favourites and fundamentally you treat them all in the same manner, yet you are aware that there are differences in these children, and you deal with them according to your knowledge of these differences. One child, for instance, is born demonstrative, while another is almost offended by displays of feeling. So though you love both equally, you do not show your love to them in exactly the same way. I believe that this is true in the spiritual realm, and thank God for it. We are not machines, we are persons, we are human beings, and God our Father and the Lord Jesus Christ know us; and they know us so intimately that one person gets this kind of manifestation, while the other gets that.

Now I say this because there is always a tendency for people to stereotype these things. This is where the influence of the cults and psychological and psychic methods tend to come in. The same thing is always done in the same way. That to me is abhorrent. Forgive the expression – but there is a kind of 'sausage-machine' mechanism in which people are treated almost as if they are all identical. Now that approach is mechanical, it is not spiritual. With the Holy Spirit there is always a wonderful variation, showing the marvellous fatherly love of God to us.

But we can go even beyond that and assert that there are variations in the same person, and this, too, is most important. How often have the saints got into trouble over this! How often have we got into trouble ourselves because, having had one experience, we set that up as a norm and a standard, and are so intent upon getting a repetition of that, that we do not recognize other manifestations. You see the danger? God our Father, gives us other things, but we are not looking for them. We are looking there and we do not realize what is happening here.

It is so sad that we should so often rob ourselves because we do not realize that God varies the experience even from person to person. There are some people who have an extraordinary experience at the beginning of their Christian life, which they can never get again, but they receive many others and they should not be sad. With others it is the other way round; they seem to spend many years in 'shallows and miseries'. They spend a long time under clouds, but suddenly the clouds break and the sun shines upon them, some even on their deathbed. It is of great importance that we should understand these factors as they help us to sift the true from the spurious.

And then another general point that I must make is that generally these experiences come to us through the medium of the Scriptures – generally, I say. But I must be careful to point out that they are not confined to that, that though they are normally mediated to us through the Scriptures, they may come directly. Again, thank God for this. And this is where we must be so careful: we must watch that we do not exclude certain elements of our Lord's dealing with us. Again, it is the spirit of fear that makes people do this. They are so afraid of anything that happens to us apart from reading the Scriptures that they shut it all out and thereby rob themselves in a most grievous manner, because as we have been seeing, the fact is that our Lord comes to us not only in the mediate, but the immediate, not only in the indirect, but the direct. It is for him to decide. He cannot be limited. As he appeared to men and women in the Old Testament and in the New so he can still. But normally – and you would expect this – he comes to us as we are reading the Scriptures, or by bringing into our minds a verse of Scripture; but I repeat that we must not lay down rigid rules.

And then my last general point is that most frequently our Lord comes to us through our internal senses; but, once more, we must not make this absolute. He may, and sometimes he does, appear to the external senses. Now what do I mean by that distinction? When I refer to the 'external senses' I mean seeing with the literal, physical eye, hearing with the external ear, feeling and touching. John in his first epistle puts it in terms of the external senses: 'That which was from the beginning, which we have heard, which we have seen with our eyes, which we have looked upon, and our hands have handled, of the Word of life' (1 John 1:1). That is what I mean by the external senses.

But in addition to our external senses, we have internal senses. The apostle Paul, for instance, in writing to the Ephesians says in his prayer for them, 'The eyes of your understanding being enlightened . . .' (Ephesians 1:18). Now there he does not mean the physical eyes. There is a spiritual eye, a spiritual way of perceiving. Similarly, there are spiritual ears: you can hear without hearing an audible voice; you are hearing by the internal senses. And it is the same with all the other senses. And, generally speaking, the intimations and manifestations that come to us from God are given to the internal senses.

Let me give you some illustrations of what I mean when I talk of the spiritual eye being opened. The practical outworking of what Paul was praying for those Ephesians may be experienced in this way – have you known this? You are reading scriptures, which you may have read many, many times before, scriptures concerning him, the Son of God, and suddenly they are illuminated and you are conscious that you are meeting with him, that he is there. You do not see him but you see him in the Scripture. He becomes alive to you. You see the person of our Lord, his person is made real to you and you realize you are not merely reading about some historical figure. You not only see the truth about him but you realize the glory of his person in a way that you have never done before.

And in addition to that, you realize the truth concerning him as it is revealed in the Scripture. You realize in a new and living and more vital way, the great truth concerning what he has done for us and for our salvation. Now you knew this before, you knew this with your brain, you knew it with your intellect, you knew it with your understanding in the way that anyone can perceive certain truths. But there is all the difference in the world between seeing that with your mind and suddenly seeing it in a living, internal, spiritual manner. You knew it, you were aware of the statements, you were aware of the facts, you could have given the correct answers, but suddenly it all becomes alive to you.

I am using terms that we tend to use, do we not, even in a natural and secular sense. You may, for example, be listening to a piece of music that you have always enjoyed, when suddenly it gets to you, becomes alive to you. This can happen with a poem also, or with something you are studying. You struggle along and you are taking in the facts and you know them, but suddenly they are all fused together and you have it in a way you did not have it before. I am only using illustrations, but the spiritual experience I am describing is comparable to that. And so it is possible for us to see and to know something of the glory of his person and the glory of what he has done for us, and, indeed, of the glory that he is preparing for us, even while we are here in this world of time.

> The men of grace have found
> Glory begun below;
> Celestial fruits on earthly ground
> From faith and hope can grow.
> *Isaac Watts*

Your spiritual eyes are open and he manifests himself to your spiritual eyes.

And, similarly, we may hear him with the spiritual ear and this is a marvellous aspect of this spiritual experience. We find it in the testimonies I quoted to you last time. I read to you the account given by Mrs Hester Ann Rodgers in which she said that she heard the Lord speaking. This was not with the external ear but it was as definite as if it had been. There is a hearing that is not physical. It is a realm of mystery. Take what we are told about the conversion of Saul of Tarsus on the road to Damascus. He had a number of people with him and when he was suddenly addressed by the voice from heaven, these other people, we are told, heard a sound but could not make out what it was (Acts 9:7).

Can you explain that sort of thing? I cannot. I remember a man once trying to explain it; he said that it is a matter of this new electronics, wavelengths and so on. All right; if your natural, material explanations help you to go a certain way along this line, all well and good. All I can say is that if it is true in that realm, how infinitely more true it is in the other realm. There are spiritual wavelengths that enable you to hear without hearing an audible voice; and this internal 'hearing' is much more wonderful than the external hearing. Our Lord can tell you in an unmistakable manner certain things that will give you a clear and a full assurance. He can say to you, 'Thou art mine, and I am thine.' He can say, as I quoted last time, 'Thy sins are forgiven.' That is what happened to John Wesley at that meeting in Aldersgate Street about which he wrote in his journal. He said he knew that 'my sins, even mine' were taken away. The Son of God may say to you, 'I died for thee.' He may speak through the Scriptures. He may say, 'Now what you are reading is true of you', or he may speak directly, when you are not reading the Scriptures.

This is what I mean when I refer to this 'hearing with the spiritual, with the internal, ear'. No voice is heard, but it is not only as definite, it is more definite than hearing a voice; there is absolute certainty. This is why many of the saints, especially the hymn writers desire this. They are asking for something that they know can happen:

> Tell me thou art mine, O Saviour,
> Grant me an assurance clear.
> Speak, I pray thee, gentle Jesus,
> Oh, how passing sweet thy words.
> > *William Williams*

Or he may communicate directly to the feelings and to the emotions. You may have been under a spirit of heaviness or of dullness or of bondage, and you may have been like that for months. You may have been doing everything you can to be free of this – reading your Scriptures, praying, attending public worship – but still there is a sort of heaviness that you cannot get rid of. Then suddenly you find it has gone. The cloud breaks, the sun shines and so darts a beam upon your soul. You cannot explain it, you cannot understand it, but you have a sense of peace and of joy. Again, the hymn writer expresses this:

> Sometimes a light surprises
> The Christian while he sings;
> It is the Lord who rises
> With healing in his wings.
> > *William Cowper*

It is surprising, but the Lord does it, and you cannot explain it. Suddenly your whole mood, as it were, has been changed, you are transformed, the heaviness has gone and you are free, and you cannot believe that you had ever known a spirit of heaviness.

In the same way, you can have a sense of his presence and of his glory. You do not see him with your physical, external eye, but you know he is there. There is nothing more wonderful than just to feel that the Lord is with you in the room – the glory of God, the glory of the Son. Without your doing anything, he suddenly gives you this manifestation in his love and in his mercy and in his compassion. Now once a man or woman has known something about that, they will never be the same again, and they will never be really satisfied until they know this more and more. Take the words of another hymn:

> Oh that I could ever sit
> Like Mary at the Master's feet,
> Be this my happy choice;
> My only care, delight and bliss,
> My joy, my heaven on earth, be this,
> To hear the Master's voice.
>
> *Charles Wesley*

That is the prayer and the longing of anyone who knows anything about these manifestations of the Son of God to the internal senses.

Then, finally, sometimes he manifests himself to the external senses. This is, of course, most mysterious, but you find it in both the Old Testament and the New. In the Old Testament there are what are called 'theophanies', when suddenly the Angel of the Covenant appears in a human form. The authorities are agreed, and it seems to me to be beyond any doubt, that these were always appearances of the Lord Jesus Christ himself. The people saw him and then he would suddenly disappear.

It is the same in the New Testament and in the history of the church. Now this is the point at which, of course, we have to be most careful, and I will give you just one example and illustration.

There is a book with the title *Remarkable Passages in the Life of Colonel Gardiner*. This was written by the famous Philip Doddridge, the hymn writer, a preacher of 200 years ago, a man who ministered at Northampton and kept an academy there to train young preachers. I am saying all this to tell you that by nature, Philip Doddridge was one of the most careful and judicious of men. Not a hothead, not an excitable person, but a calm and cool and highly rational person. He wrote this account of his friend Colonel Gardiner, and Colonel Gardiner, again, was a man who was famous for, and characterized by, his judicious spirit, not only in his military career, but in every respect. He had no psychic interests, quite the reverse.

With some reluctance, Colonel Gardiner told this story, emphasizing that he only told it to the glory of God. He was a man who had got on well in his profession, but he was living an utterly godless life, until one night, when a great experience came to him. He had spent the evening drinking and talking, not to excess, but amusing and entertaining himself. Then he had gone back to his room to wait until midnight, when he had an assignation with another man's wife. So there he was, not knowing quite what to do while he waited. He casually picked up a book, a religious book, which his good mother or aunt had slipped into his portmanteau without his knowledge. The title of the book was *The Christian Soldier, or Heaven Taken by Storm* and it was written by Mr Thomas Watson. As Colonel Gardiner was holding this book, and glancing through it, an impression was made upon his mind which drew after it a train of the most important and happy consequences.

What happened? Well, this is what he describes. He repeated it more than once to Philip Doddridge, and he also repeated it to another divine. Philip Doddridge writes:

He thought he saw an unusual blaze of light fall on the book while he was reading, which at first he imagined might happen by some accident in the candle. But lifting up his eyes he apprehended to his extreme amazement that there was before him, as it were, suspended in the air, a visible representation of the Lord Jesus Christ upon the cross, surrounded on all sides with a glory, and was impressed as if a voice or something equivalent to a voice had come to him to this effect (for he was not confident as to the very words), but the voice said, 'O sinner, did I suffer this for thee, and are these the return?' But whether this were an audible voice, or only a strong impression on his mind, equally striking, he did not seem very confident, though to the best of my remembrance he rather judged it to be the former.

Struck with so amazing a phenomenon as this, there remained hardly any life in him, so that he sank down in the armchair in which he sat and continued he knew not how long insensible. But however that were, he quickly after opened his eyes and saw nothing more than usual. But, of course, from that point on he was a new man, a complete change in his life, he became a great saint.

Now, like Philip Doddridge, I quote this to you for one reason only, and that is to warn you not to put limits upon what the everlasting God may do. We must not deny these things, we must not dismiss them as belonging to the realm of fancy, disordered brain, enthusiasm or dangerous ecstasy. We do not seek them, we seek the spiritual manifestation, but we must not deny that in his own time and according to his own sovereign will, God may choose to do to some what he did to Colonel Gardiner on that amazing occasion.

My dear friends, heaven is round and about us. The supernatural is ever with us. There are myriads of angels. Do you believe in angels? The spiritual realm is round and about if we but realized it. And, as I say, these are some of the ways in which the Son of God may manifest himself to his children. You realize, therefore, how careful all those who know anything about this kind of experience have always been and how reluctantly they have spoken about it, and yet, my dear friends, we must speak because this is the salvation that is offered us. Not a mere intellectual belief that you are always having to manipulate and persuade yourself about. No, no; our Lord died to bring us to God, to restore to the fallen race of Adam the knowledge of God that he lost in the original form.

> Talk with us, Lord, thyself reveal,
> While here o'er earth we rove;
> Speak to our hearts, and let us feel
> The kindling of thy love.
> *Charles Wesley*

# 49

# *Finding the Lord's Presence*

*The woman then left her waterpot, and went her way into the city, and saith to the men, Come, see a man, which told me all things that ever I did: is not this the Christ? (John 4:28–29)*

We have realized that the whole purpose of our Lord's meeting with the woman of Samaria is to bring us to that place where we shall see that it is possible for us to have communion and fellowship with the Lord, even as these people did in the days of his flesh, and we have been dealing with the ways in which this becomes possible. We have seen that we must not put limits upon what God does, but recognize that there is a great variety in the ways in which our Lord manifests himself to his people in a spiritual sense. We ended by saying that while we normally know our Lord's presence by means of our internal senses, he does sometimes manifest himself even to our external senses, and I quoted to you the famous case of Colonel Gardiner, who lived in the eighteenth century.

This, then, is the point at which we have arrived. Our position as Christians is not simply that we believe certain things about someone who once lived, and now we live on the teaching that we have concerning him in the Bible. Over and above that, the Scriptures clearly teach that we can have a spiritual fellowship with him, a communion with him, the kind of experience that the apostle Paul has in mind when he says in Philippians 3:10: 'That I may know him, and the power of his resurrection, and the fellowship of his sufferings.' And when Paul goes on to say, 'Not as though I had already attained', he does not mean that he is uncertain about his salvation – he is absolutely certain about that – but that what he longs to have is more and more of this personal, intimate, immediate knowledge of the Lord himself. That is what Paul is striving after, the mark he is pressing towards (Philippians 3:14). He knows that this personal communion and knowledge will only be perfect, of course, at that great day when the Son of God will come again from heaven, and manifest himself in all his glory. That is the day when we shall be changed, and see him as he is. But, in the meantime, Paul's greatest desire is to know Christ.

So the question therefore that remains for us is this: If this knowledge of our Lord is possible for us all, how do we attain it? This is a very practical matter, and unless we can deal with it, we will fall far short of our Lord's purpose for us. But, thank God, there is sufficient instruction given to us in various parts of the Scriptures to enable us to answer this question.

The first essential is that we believe in its possibility. I do not want to stay with this because, in a sense, all I have been saying so far has been dealing with this aspect of the question. Undoubtedly the greatest difficulty, however, is that people do not believe in the very possibility of this personal communion. We have become so accustomed to something purely objective that we tend to forget the subjective. It is interesting to notice that throughout the history of the church there has been a kind of oscillation from one to the other. We also find these different emphases in different types of people. Some are purely objective, some are purely subjective – and both extremes are wrong. The glory of the gospel is that it takes up the whole person. It is not merely for the intellect, it is also for the sensibilities and for the feelings. Some people are afraid of excesses and others are afraid that they are entering into the realm of the mystical. But we find a constant warning in the New Testament not to 'quench the Spirit' (2 Thessalonians 5:19), not to put our carnal, human limits upon what is made possible for us by this great and wonderful gospel in which we partake together. So we must get rid of all negative ideas.

And then we must get rid of the notion that this experience is only for very outstanding people. That is a very common ruse of the devil. He says that it is all right for apostles, that it is all right for saints. You know how, under Roman Catholicism, there is a very wrong and unscriptural division, not only between clergy and the laity, which in itself is not a New Testament distinction, but also even beyond that into extra-ordinary and ordinary Christians, saints and those who are not saints. But the New Testament says that we are all 'called to be saints' (Romans 1:7), and that therefore all these experiences are possible to all of us. There is no need to become a monk or a nun and to go out of everyday life in order to cultivate this religious life, and then receive great and marvellous experiences. That is one of the most erroneous teachings that has ever been introduced into the church; yet the tendency to think in this way has percolated into even Reformed and Protestant circles, so that we say, 'Ah, yes, that's all right for people who don't have to go to work every day, or who aren't engaged in business or aren't housewives with a lot of work. If only, of course, I had nothing else to do but cultivate my soul, then I could expect this kind of experience.'

And the simple answer to that, I repeat, is that people of all types and kinds have known this experience. I have read examples and illustrations to you already to show you what I mean and how this is possible. If you are not clear about its possibility, then you cannot proceed any further. If in some way or another you are saying, 'This isn't for me'; if you begin to bring in psychological terms and say there are certain people who by nature seem to be 'given' to this kind of mystical experience, then, again, you are making the whole thing impossible as far as you are concerned. There are no such distinctions in the New Testament, none whatsoever. 'For the promise is unto you, and to your children, and to all that are afar off' (Acts 2:39). We must be clear about that.

Then, secondly, we must seek this diligently. Now I put my emphasis upon the word 'diligently', but I must also stress the seeking. There is great variation in how this kind of experience comes to people, as we have seen. Sometimes it is given without any seeking at all, as with Colonel Gardiner [see the last chapter]. But that is not the common rule. The usual experience is that men and women, having realized the possibility of this communion with our Lord, have started to seek. How do you do this? Well, the first way is to seek him in the Scriptures.

Let me give you an example. It is shown perfectly in Luke 24, in the famous story of the two men on the road to Emmaus after the resurrection. Her are two men, cast down and dejected. When the Lord joins them, they do not know him. What does he do with them? He takes them through the Scriptures. That is his antidote to their depression. He says, 'O fools, and slow of heart to believe all that the prophets have spoken: ought not Christ to have suffered these things, and to enter into his glory?' And so he takes them right away back, as we are told, 'Beginning at Moses and all the prophets, he expounded unto them in all the scriptures the things concerning himself' (verses 25–27). Now that is the perfect example.

And later on in the same final chapter of Luke's Gospel, we find the same method. Our Lord says:

> *These are the words which I spake unto you, while I was yet with you, that all things must be fulfilled, which were written in the law of Moses, and in the prophets, and in the psalms, concerning me. Then opened he their understanding, that they might understand the scriptures. (Luke 24:44–45)*

If you want to find him, therefore, the first place to look for him is in the Scriptures. So you just read your Scriptures, not in a mechanical, thoughtless manner, not simply that you may read your portion of Scripture; no, you deliberately read your Scriptures to look for him, and suddenly you find him. You will find him in unexpected places in the Old Testament, in the prophecies, in the psalms, and even in the five books of Moses, as he said himself. And he comes to you and he speaks to you through the Scriptures. He says: That is about me.

Then you come to the New Testament and you do not just read your four Gospels as ancient history. They are that, but you say to yourself: Now as he appeared to these people when he was here in the days of his flesh, so he still appears to his people. Here I read of somebody meeting him. I can meet him! Here's a woman who met him by the side of a well, and he's still the same person, he's still real. I don't see him with the naked eye, but he's exactly the same person and is as real as he was when he met with that woman. I, too, can meet with him. And as you read in this living way, you will often find that you meet with him and he becomes real and manifests himself to you.

Then you go on; you read the book of Acts and find how he appears to people; you read the Epistles, you read the book of Revelation, and all along what you are being told is that he is present, he is everywhere and he is always ready and willing to meet with his people. That is the commonest way of all, and that is the way that God has most blessed his people throughout the running centuries. You deliberately seek him in the Scriptures. It is as you do so that he will come to you.

And then you do exactly the same thing in the sacraments. That is one of the objects of the sacraments – not so much what they do to us as what they tell us about him. So often people have met with him in obedience to his command when they have partaken of the sacraments, the Lord's Supper in particular, which is just, in the first instance, a reminder of the Last Supper. Our Lord said to his disciples, 'This do ye, as oft as ye drink it, in remembrance of me' (1 Corinthians 11:25), and one of the objects of meeting together at the Lord's Table is to remind ourselves of him. He said that he would meet with his people in that special way.

Now, again, the devil has obviously been very busy at this point, and that is where the whole notion of transubstantiation has come in. Transubstantiation, which is the idea that the bread changes into our Lord's very body, is an attempt to make his presence real, 'the real presence', as it is called. But it is not a real presence at all, it is a mere figment. But the idea behind that was right, in a sense, and that was that people should realize that they were not only eating bread, they were not doing something in a mechanical manner in connection with someone who now belonged to the past. The idea was to realize his presence. But the way we understand that is to say that he is present spiritually. This has been the great Reformation declaration on the Lord's Supper: the spiritual presence of the Son of God.

You say, 'But is he in the bread?'

No, no; he is not, and he is not with the bread, as Luther taught. He himself has said, in effect, 'As you do this in remembrance of me, in accordance with my command to you, I will be with you, I will manifest myself to you.'

And thus, as you read the long history of the church, you will find that there have been glorious manifestations of the Son of God at various Communion seasons. I have often referred to that famous occasion at Cambuslang, now part of Glasgow, in the eighteenth century; that famous Communion season when George Whitefield was present and was preaching. It is perhaps one of the most astounding manifestations of the Son of God among his people ever recorded by history. It was a great revival, a great outpouring of the Spirit of God, and came about through the medium of the Communion service. As the Lord's death was declared and remembered till he come, suddenly he appeared among his people. So that is one of the reasons for partaking of this sacrament.

And then, of course, another way of finding the Lord is prayer – prayer that concentrates on this very thing; you are not merely praying in general, you are not only worshipping God, you are not only making known your petitions and desires, you are going beyond that and are deliberately seeking, deliberately making this effort and asking him to manifest himself to you. You start with the desire – 'Oh, that I knew where I might find him!' and then you go after him, as it were, and you plead with him to manifest himself to you. This is something that the saints have done. The words of one of our hymns are a perfect illustration of this cry that you make to him:

Speak, I pray Thee, gentle Jesus,
Oh, how passing sweet thy words,

> Breathing o'er my troubled spirit
> Peace which never earth affords.
>                 *William Williams*

This is something that we have to do deliberately, volitionally, realizing that there is a possibility. You go out, as it were, in prayer, and you try to lay hold upon him, and you cry unto him to be pleased to look upon you and to manifest himself to you.

Then the third very practical step is the one I have already been illustrating to you: you read the lives of the saints, you deliberately study the biographies and the histories of men and women who have had great and notable experiences of this very experience to which I am referring.

Let me give you one further example to stimulate you yet more – a practical example of what I mean. I shall read something written by a most remarkable man of 300 years ago, a man by the name of John Lilburne. He is a man of interest, quite apart from his Christian experience. He was the real founder of the people who became known as the 'Levellers', and in many ways he is the father of democracy in this country. Here is a man who, 300 years ago, agitated for certain things that have only come to pass in this present century. But he was first and foremost a highly spiritual man and he had amazing experiences:

> I assuredly know that all the power in earth, yea and the gates of hell itself shall never be able to move me or prevail against me, for the Lord, who is the worker of all my works in me and for me, hath founded and built me upon that sure and unmovable foundation, the Lord Jesus Christ . . . for which with courage and rejoicing I now bear witness to and am close prisoner in bonds [he was in prison when he was writing this], lying day and night in fetters of iron, both hands and legs. If even worse things should be inflicted upon me, I should

sing, rejoice and triumph in them all, for my God makes me glory in my tribulation, and my soul is filled so full of that sweetness and joy that it finds in my God alone, that my tongue and pen is never able to the full to express and utter it . . .

He hath crucified the world and all things here below unto me, and hath enabled me to account and esteem all things beside himself as dung and dirt, not being worth of casting any affectionate eye upon them. I am as merry, yea, more cheerful than ever I was in any condition in my life, and can sleep as soundly in my boots and irons as Peter did between the two soldiers when he was in prison.

Now there is a man enduring in the Fleet Prison here in London the most cruel imprisonment, yet who is able to say that he is having the full experience of the apostles. He does not hesitate to claim that he has as much joy and peace and happiness as Peter when he was asleep that night before he was due to die, lying between two soldiers and bound with chains (Acts 12). Here is a man, a man like ourselves, a man of ability and understanding, not this strange, ascetic kind of person that the psychologists would speak of, but a man who was intensely practical, even political in his outlook. Here he is, having such experiences that he is able to say, 'If even worse things should be afflicted upon me, I should sing, rejoice and triumph.' He has reached a place in which he is so certain of the Lord, and of God the Father, God the Son, and God the Holy Spirit, that he is quite immune to anything that man in his malignity might do to him.

So this is the way to seek this experience; you read an account like that and you say to yourself, 'If that was possible to John Lilburne, why is it not possible to me?' And he is only one of many, many, in that century in particular. Read the stories of some of the early Quakers – it is just the same.

I know something about the danger of reading the Scripture in a very mechanical manner. You can, as I say, read your daily portion and perhaps a little commentary on it, and you think you have done well. But the question is: Have you really got the message of the Scriptures? Have you got a living message? Do you just stop at having done your duty, as it were, or does this urge you to seek for the fullness that is in Christ Jesus? So I am a great advocate of reading about the actual lives of men and women like ourselves, people living in this world, people who are suffering, not monks, not anchorites, not hermits, but people in the midst of life, with all its difficulties and trials and problems. This is how they were able to find the Lord in their need, and to rejoice in him 'with a joy unspeakable and full of glory'. So, my dear friends, use the biographies of the saints as commentaries upon your commentaries, use them as commentaries on the Scriptures. Here are people who have applied the Scriptures, and if they were able to do it, you and I should be able to do it also.

Then, fourthly, I come to another very practical matter – we must always be obedient to him. We must never lose sight of the fact that we are dealing with a personal relationship, and with an experience of a person. I am not talking merely about feelings and sensations; I am referring to what the apostle Paul talks of in Philippians 3:10: 'That I may know him.' You are seeking knowledge of a person, you are seeking experiences of communion and fellowship with this blessed person. So there is nothing more important than that we should be obedient to him. In what way? Well, in this way: you must learn to be responsive to his 'drawings'. Now that expression, 'his drawings', was used by the Puritans and has always been used by the great Christian mystics. This is a scriptural term: 'I drew them with cords of a man, with bands of love' (Hosea 11:4). Or, as Philip Doddridge puts it:

He drew me, and I followed on,
Charmed to confess [and to follow] the voice divine.

Here is something that is most wonderful in the Christian life and experience. It is, of course, indicated clearly in the Scriptures. The greatest possible encouragement we can have is that he approaches us through the Spirit. He does not leave it entirely to us. He gives us encouragements; and there is nothing more important in the Christian life than to be sensitive to his approaches, to the times when he draws near and gives us a kind of manifestation of himself. You know the sort of thing to which I am referring, it is generally a surprise to you, sometimes coming when you least expect it. It is put in that hymn to which I have already referred:

Sometimes a light surprises
The Christian while he sings.
*William Cowper*

You are aware of a kind of softening of experience, a tenderness in your spirit. That is undoubtedly one of his 'drawings'. So Isaiah, in a prophetic manner, says: 'Seek ye the Lord while he may be found' – that is it – 'call ye upon him while he is near' (Isaiah 55:6). Is this not something you know in experience? There is this variation; sometimes he is near, sometimes he seems to be far off, distant, remote. And the essence of wisdom in this matter is that if ever you have the feeling that he is near, that he is drawing you and that he is speaking to you, respond immediately.

I could show you this in many different ways. I will put it in the negative, which is perhaps the most helpful of all: we must be the exact opposite of the spouse, the bride, who is depicted in the Song of Solomon:

*I am come into my garden, my sister, my spouse: I have gathered my myrrh with my spice; I have eaten my honeycomb with my honey; I have drunk my wine with my milk: eat, O friends; drink, yea, drink abundantly, O beloved.*

Then:

*I sleep, but my heart waketh: it is the voice of my beloved that knocketh, saying, Open to me, my sister, my love, my dove, my undefiled: for my head is filled with dew, and my locks with the drops of the night.*

Then she replies:

*I have put off my coat; how shall I put it on? I have washed my feet; how shall I defile them? My beloved put in his hand by the hole of the door, and my bowels were moved for him. I rose up to open to my beloved; and my hands dropped with myrrh, and my fingers with sweet smelling myrrh, upon the handles of the lock. I opened to my beloved; but my beloved had withdrawn himself, and was gone: my soul failed when he spake: I sought him, but I could not find him; I called him, but he gave me no answer. (Song of Solomon 5:1–6)*

He approaches her, he draws nigh. This is one of the 'drawings'. He asks her to open the door to admit him into this fellowship, but she cannot be bothered, cannot put on her cloak again, she cannot defile her feet, they would need washing again, and so she resists him. And then he gives a further manifestation and now her heart is ravished and she rushes to open the door; but he has gone. Why? Well, she did not respond to the first approach! And this is so true in this spiritual life. Apart from anything else, there is nothing that is so foolish as to put him on one side because you are too busy.

If I may give a word from my own experience, there is nothing that I have had to learn more – and I thank God that I have at last learned the lesson, but it took me time to learn it. It does not matter what you are doing, if he draws near to you, put everything else down. Even if what you are doing is reading your Bible, stop for the time being and talk to him directly. Whatever your occupation, clutch at every approach, take advantage of every 'drawing'; give him this implicit obedience; leave yourself in his hands.

But we must obey our Lord not only in his 'drawings', it is equally important that we should obey him in his rebuking, because he will rebuke us; he is concerned about our sanctification. He came into the world, he died, he rose again and he is at the right hand of God, in order that we might come to a final, full redemption and glorification. But he knows us in a way that we do not know ourselves. That is the meaning of those great words in Hebrews 12:6: 'For whom the Lord loveth he chasteneth, and scourgeth every son whom he receiveth' – whom he is calling unto righteousness. In other words, in order to bring us into this intimate fellowship and communion with himself, he will point out to us the hindrances, the obstacles. The effect of sin upon us and the effect of the devil is to make us think, 'Ah, yes, I would like this wonderful experience,' but we rather want to have that and to have something else at the same time. But the two are incompatible, and he will tell us so in various ways. He says, 'I cannot come to you while that is true of you.'

Go back to the letter that he wrote to the church of the Laodiceans and there you find it all. Before our Lord says, 'Behold, I stand at the door, and knock,' he tells them exactly what they must give up and what they must take on (Revelation 3:14–20). There are certain rooms into which he will not come, there are certain things that must be put out, before he will enter. He will point this out to us, and he will chide us and rebuke us.

He speaks within us in the Spirit, and, again, this often happens when we are not even thinking about these things. Something will be put before us and we will try to explain it away. But if we go on trying to explain it away, we need not expect to have any knowledge of these spiritual manifestations of the Son of God. No, no! He will rebuke, he will chastise, he will indicate, and he will make it quite clear to us that they must be got rid of, and then – and only then – will he manifest himself to us. So we must be entirely obedient to him. I add to that: we must resign ourselves to him completely and entirely. The lesson here is just this: he is not at our command; we are to be entirely at his command.

Shall I give you a simple illustration that will put it quite plainly? Take the condition or the relationship of any one of us to a royal personage. You do not make demands of the Queen, but you respond to what she says, what she does. You do not bombard such a person; because of the dignity of the person and the office, because of all that is so true of such a person, your attitude is one of resignation. You do not send in a request demanding an appointment; you do not lay down the terms and conditions. You do not say, 'I'm very busy all day but at six o'clock it is possible for me to see you.' Well, multiply that by infinity, and there is your relationship and mine to our blessed Lord. It is he who determines the time, not us. We have a tendency to say, 'When I have done other things, then . . .' It is no good, my friend. We must be at his disposal.

And our Lord not only determines the time, he determines the manner in which he will manifest himself to us or grant us an audience or admit us into his presence. It is entirely his royal prerogative and he will never surrender it. And you find this not only in the Scriptures, but also everywhere in the subsequent testimony of God's people. They have been most careful and punctilious to stipulate that they do not demand, they do not insist, they do not become impatient and show their annoyance; they leave themselves entirely in his hands; the time, the way, the manner, the particular form – all are left to him.

So you do not go on demanding an experience exactly like that of somebody you have read about or somebody you know. You say, 'All I am anxious for is to know him and to love him and to serve him. I don't care how he manifests himself as long as he does. What I want is to know him – as the apostle Paul says, "That I may know him, and the power of his resurrection, and the fellowship of his sufferings, being made conformable unto his death" ' (Philippians 3:10). But, remember, to say that is to say a very big thing. Sarah Adam's hymn puts this in an extreme form:

Nearer, my God, to thee,
Nearer to thee!
E'en though it be a cross
That raiseth me.

That is the question. Here are people at the topmost height of their experience and they know that nothing matters as far as they are concerned except that they have this experience. They do not care what it is as long as it brings them 'nearer to thee'. And, remember, what I feel should always be a footnote to that. You do not offer that prayer in that hymn only when your ship *Titanic* has struck the iceberg and you are sinking; you always offer that prayer, you are always in that condition, it is a desperate cry. You do not get the answer very often and you are not entitled to expect one. No, no; this is the prayer of someone who realizes what is possible and says, 'I don't care how as long as I know thee.' 'Though he slay me,' says Job, 'yet will I trust in him' (Job 13:15). That is the final resignation that is so essential in these matters.

And that brings me to my last point, which is obvious: it is the element of persistence. 'Take time to be holy,' says a hymn, and how true that is. This is the whole trouble with the modern world, is it not? We all say we are so busy. But that, of course, is ridiculous. Why should we find the problem of time so difficult? We have more leisure than people have ever had. Our whole outlook upon life is wrong if we, as Christians, say, 'I haven't got the time.' You have to 'take time', you have to 'make time', you have to get your priorities right, as the phrase puts it.

You must draw up a programme, you must realize that you have to fight for these things. The world does not want you to; 'the world is too much with us'; that is our whole trouble. The world determines our programmes and we are manipulated by other forces and factors. You must take charge of yourself and say, 'I don't care what happens, this is the most important thing of all.' Persistence! Not fits and starts. Not a great spasm and cooling off and forgetting, and then returning. That is our story, is it not?

You must discipline yourself – it demands great discipline. The saints have always been characterized by their stern self-discipline, and it is absolutely essential. We fritter away our days and then we excuse ourselves with the words, 'Of course, I'm not an apostle. I'm not a saint. I'm not living in the first century. These experiences are not meant for us now. Other people don't read the Bible at all, so if I read a few verses, I'm very spiritual.' Spiritual? You are a very, very little babe; you are the merest infant. No, no; this is the way, and it is a way of persistence, a way of discipline. You take the steps that our Lord has indicated: Ask; seek; knock (Matthew 7:7). It is a rising gradation. You ask, but you do not seem to get an answer; then you begin to seek, like the bride in the Song of Solomon, and you look for him everywhere and you ask people, 'Where is he?' Like Job, you say, 'Oh that I knew where I might find him!' (Job 23:3). You have gone beyond asking, you are seeking, and now you have become desperate and you are knocking. 'Ask . . . seek . . . knock.' Those are our Lord's own words.

Or let me put it to you in the words of Jacob: 'I will not let thee go, except thou bless me' (Genesis 32:26). Our Lord likes that kind of 'holy boldness'. Let there be an urgency, let there be this spirit of seeking, let us know something of the holy ambition of the apostle Paul: 'I press toward the mark' (Philippians 3:14). I am always on stretch fully, I am after him, I am seeking him. I have known so much of him that I want more of him. 'For to me to live is Christ, and to die is gain' (Philippians 1:21). So you seek him in these various ways. I quote those words that were so vital to Hudson Taylor:

> Lord Jesus, make thyself to me
> A living, bright reality,
> More present to faith's vision keen
> Than any outward object seen;
> More dear, more intimately nigh
> Than e'en the sweetest earthly tie.
> *Charlotte Elliott*

That was Hudson Taylor's prayer. It has been the prayer of every saint in some shape or form. It should be our prayer. There you have the possibility and the persistence. Refuse to be discouraged; do not give in; go on. 'Watch and pray' (Matthew 26:41). Seek him! Be sensitive to him. He will lead you on. There are some things about which we are not certain, but of this we can be certain: it is his desire that we should know him. He is standing at the door and knocking. Have you heard him? Take time to listen to him. Always be ready. Whatever you are doing, have your ears open. Whatever you are concentrating on, always be sure that you can hear him. He will knock at the door, and the moment you hear that knock, put everything down, open the door, and he will enter in and have fellowship with you, and he will sup with you, and your heart will be ravished.

Now it is an extraordinary fact, and it is a terrible condemnation of us as human beings, but it does seem to me to be the case, as I judge from my reading in these matters, that the people who have had most experience of what we are talking about have tended to be people who have been enduring some cruel persecution. I have read to you from John Lilburne. John Lilburne had his greatest experiences when he was in the prison, and so did John Bunyan. What a terrible condemnation of us that it takes a prison, or something like that, to cut us off from the things that stand between us and him. But we should learn a lesson from that. Let us put ourselves into a kind of prison by cutting off these things in order that we may have time for him.

There can also be no doubt of the fact that our Lord has often given manifestations of his presence to people before they have had prison experiences, to prepare them for it. You will often find that revivals come to countries that have some great trial to pass through. It happened in the Congo, it has happened in Korea, among many other countries. So this experience may happen before a trial, or you may be put through the trial in order that you may meet with God. But both come down to the same thing and that is that we have to concentrate on him. It is when we are cut off from everything else that so many of us begin to get the sense to seek for him, and to seek for this intimate knowledge. Many people have left it even to their deathbed, but thank God he has not refused them even there. Even there he has granted them the manifestation of his presence and looking back on their life, they say, 'What a fool I've been!' I might have enjoyed this throughout the years, but I was so busy here and there, and coming and going . . . oh, what a fool!' They have left a dying testimony and statement.

So let us learn from them, and let us realize that our Lord is as ready to speak to us today as he was to that woman by the side of the well. He is ready to give us assurances of his love and to make himself known to us.

50

# 'Is not this the Christ?'

*The woman then left her waterpot and went her way into the city, and saith to the men, Come, see a man, which told me all things that ever I did: is not this the Christ? (John 4:28–29)*

I now want to consider with you this great question that was put by the woman of Samaria after her encounter with our Lord and Saviour at the well, the question that she put to her fellow townsmen: 'Is not this the Christ?'

Now she puts this question in a form in which she makes it quite clear that she is in no doubt whatsoever with regard to the answer. It is not a question asking for information, it is an assertion. She does not ask, 'Is this the Christ?' but, 'Is not this the Christ?' by which she means, obviously, that he is, he must be. It is important that we should realize that she puts the question expecting a positive answer.

So here we are face to face with the most important question that can ever be asked. There are many serious questions facing the countries of the world at the present time, but, as Christians, we say that this is the greatest of all. Who is he, this babe who was born in Bethlehem nearly two thousand years ago?[1] Is he or is he not the Christ?

Now let me start by putting a question to you: Have you ever asked this question and have you been so certain of the answer that you have put the question to others as this woman of Samaria did? She is now on an evangelistic errand; it is because she is so certain that he is the Christ that she wants these people to come to meet him and to hear from his own lips the kind of thing that she has already been hearing. This is what makes us Christians and this is what proves that we are Christians – that we have come to see that Jesus of Nazareth is the Christ, the Messiah, the Deliverer, the Saviour of the world, and are anxious for others, too, to know this.

But that immediately raises in our minds this question: On what grounds are we satisfied that he is the Christ? The word 'Christ' is the Greek form of the Hebrew term 'Messiah', the Deliverer who was to come. Here is a woman who is quite sure of it, and gives us her main reason: 'Come, see a man, which told me all things that ever I did.' We have been seeing that this statement is a vital part of the evidence, but it is not the only evidence. If we are satisfied that he is the Christ, on what grounds are we so satisfied? It seems to me that the only object and purpose of our observing this particular season of Christmas is that we may put questions like this to ourselves. There are sections of the Christian church, as you know, who do not believe in observing Christmas. I think they are wrong. I understand their point of view, I know that it is a reaction against the errors and the paganism that has been introduced, mainly by the Roman Catholic Church, into this season but, nevertheless, I think it is an error because it is

---

[1] This sermon was preached on Christmas Eve, 1967.

good for us from time to time to face the facts and to look at our whole position, lest we assume certain things without being clear in our minds about them.

On what grounds do we believe that Jesus of Nazareth is the Christ? Now fortunately this claim can be tested objectively and the point that I really want to establish this morning is that our faith is not based on some subjective experience. There is a subjective experience in the Christian life, as we have been seeing, otherwise we are not Christians at all; but our position is not based upon anything we may feel. So our approach as Christians to this season is not the sentimental one with which the world approaches it; rather, we approach it historically, and we do so because the very glory of our position as Christians is that our faith is based upon a very solid foundation, upon facts. We are not worshipping a beautiful theory, we have not just got an idea.

There are many today who are trying to persuade us to think not so much of the Lord Jesus Christ as of love as a principle. The great message of Christmas, they say, is the message of love. I think that is quite wrong. The great message of Christmas is not the message of love – though it is incidentally and indirectly a message of love – but of these great historical events that have taken place. So we do not consider love primarily, we consider the person, the Lord Jesus Christ, as this woman does. She does not go to the city to tell men to consider some teaching, she says, 'Come, see a man . . . is not this the Christ?' – this Deliverer.

So we can ask ourselves this question: Are we satisfied that Jesus is the Christ? If so, why are we? What are our criteria? It is not enough just to say, 'I believe this is the Christ'; somebody may say to us, 'What are your reasons?' There are all sorts of myths and stories in literature and in history; how do we substantiate our claim that this baby is the Christ? What are the tests that we apply?

Now I suggest that the following tests must be applied, and as we do this, they should strengthen our faith and give us a great certainty and assurance concerning our whole position. Look at him. How do I know that he is the Christ? What do I insist upon before I come to this conclusion? Well, the first answer is this: he must fulfil the prophecies of the Old Testament. I put that as my first test because that is what is done in the New Testament itself. In practically every book of the New Testament this point is made strongly. The apostle Paul, for instance, in a very typical manner, puts it like this in the Second Epistle to the Corinthians: 'For all the promises of God in him are yea, and in him Amen, unto the glory of God by us' (2 Corinthians 1:20).

Peter makes the same point: 'We have not followed cunningly devised fables,' he says, and goes on to give the evidence of what happened on the Mount of Transfiguration, but then he hastens to say: 'We have also a more sure word of prophecy; whereunto ye do well that ye take heed, as unto a light that shineth in a dark place, until the day dawn, and the day star arise in your hearts' (2 Peter 1:16, 19). The fulfilment of prophecy is the first great proof, therefore.

So, then, let us apply this test to Christ. What have the prophecies of the Old Testament told us concerning the Messiah who was to come? They are there in great profusion. First, there are certain general statements. The first of these is found away back in the third chapter of Genesis: 'Her [the woman's] seed shall bruise thy [the serpent's] head' (Genesis 3:15). Those are the words of God himself immediately after the Fall. The enemy has conquered, the serpent has prevailed, and mankind has fallen and is in a state of sin and bondage; and God goes on to say that there will be a great enmity between the seed of the woman and the seed of the serpent. But here is the great promise – the first great promise – of the coming of the Messiah, the Christ.

Now that expression 'the seed of the woman' is very significant. No father is mentioned; the suggestion is immediately conveyed that the Deliverer will arrive in this world from a woman, and from a woman only. And so it is not surprising to find the prophetic statement in the book of the prophet Isaiah: 'Behold, a virgin shall conceive, and bear a son' (Isaiah 7:14). Now do not be misled by much of the popular talk on this subject. The best scholarship still says that this word means 'virgin', as it has always been taken to mean throughout the centuries. So there we have Old Testament prophecies with the strong suggestion that the Christ, the Messiah, when he comes will come of a woman and specifically of a virgin.

And so when we come to the New Testament, it is not surprising to find an emphasis upon this very prophecy. Matthew's Gospel states explicitly that our Lord had no human father, that he was born of a virgin. You find exactly the same statement in the announcement to Mary, his mother, by the angel Gabriel: 'The Holy Ghost shall come upon thee . . . therefore also that holy thing which shall be born of thee shall be called the Son of God' (Luke 1:35). And the apostle Paul, looking back, describes him as having been 'made of a woman, made under the law' (Galatians 4:4). So here is our first test and it is more than fully satisfied. It had been said in the Old Testament that when the Messiah did come, he would come in this way, in a strange, a miraculous, in a marvellous manner, without a human father – the miracle of the virgin birth. This is one of our greatest proofs and it is one of the strongest reasons for believing in the virgin birth. It is not something that you can sacrifice lightly; it is one of the most striking fulfilments of prophecy that we have.

I am trying to give you a list of points to strengthen your faith. What else are we told about him? Well, according to the prophecies, he must also be 'of the seed of Abraham'. When God called Abraham out of Ur of the Chaldees, he told him immediately that in him all the nations of the world would be blessed (Genesis 12:1–3), and he promised him a seed (Genesis 13:16). This is the great line that runs right through the Old Testament from that twelfth chapter of Genesis onwards, and all along there is an emphasis upon the fact that the Christ, the Messiah, would be 'of the seed of Abraham'. And this promise was repeated both to Isaac and to Jacob.

Then comes a most interesting and important point. Jacob had twelve sons, and one of these sons, Levi, was the one from whom the priesthood came. Now one would have naturally expected that the Deliverer would belong to this particular tribe; but the promise was not given with respect to Levi; it was given to the tribe of Judah. You will find that in the forty-ninth chapter of Genesis. The promise is being narrowed down. It is now specifically this child out of the tribe of Judah. Of course, Judah had many children, and they had children, and they had children and so on, but the promise is narrowed down further by the prophecies to a particular descendant of Judah, and his name was David – King David. This Deliverer would be of the seed of David (2 Samuel 7:16; Psalm 8:3–4). You cannot read the Old Testament without being impressed by the fact that this promise has been coming down and narrowing down like this, so that the Messiah when he comes must be 'of the seed of Abraham, the seed of Jacob, the tribe of Judah' and in particular 'of the house and lineage of David' (Luke 2:4). This is one of those prophecies, therefore, that must be satisfied and fulfilled.

And so when we come to the New Testament, we see how punctilious the writers are to give absolute proof of the fact that our Lord has indeed come from this particular line. Take, for instance, the way Matthew opens his Gospel 'The book of the generation of Jesus Christ, the son of David, the son of Abraham.' There it is in summary form. Paul, years afterwards, wrote to Timothy: 'Remember that Jesus Christ of the seed of David was raised from the dead according to my gospel' (2 Timothy 2:8). Remember, too, the blind men shouting out to our Lord: 'Thou Son of David, have mercy on us' (Matthew 9:27). So, again, this criterion is more than fully satisfied.

Then, in addition, something else is said that is of great importance. The Old Testament is very careful to point out to us that while the Messiah will obviously be a man, 'born of a woman', of a specified line and lineage, there will also be a mystery about him, something strange, something inexplicable, something that suggests that he is more than a man. Take Psalm 110, where David writes, 'The LORD said unto my Lord, Sit thou at my right hand, until I make thine enemies thy footstool' (Psalm 110:1). Now here is a suggestion of someone greater. Our Lord himself made use of that argument later on. When he was being questioned and cross-examined by the Pharisees and others, he asked them to explain David's words in Psalm 110. These words cannot refer to David's son because David says, 'The LORD said unto my Lord.' There is someone above and beyond David (Matthew 22:41–45).

And as we read a great passage like Isaiah chapter 40, we get the same impression of a great personage who is going to come. He is such a mighty personage that a great highway must be prepared for him: 'Every valley shall be exalted, and every mountain and hill shall be made low' (Isaiah 40:4). So these two elements are here for us in the prophecies of the Old Testament. And when we come to the New Testament, of course, we see both so clearly every time we look at him.

Something else that is stated in the prophecies is the particular time of his coming – and this is most astounding. There are many suggestions about the timing, but in the ninth chapter of the book of the prophet Daniel the very period is narrowed down in a most explicit manner. It was not that he might come some time or other in some vague distant future. No, no; it is narrowed down, and when the experts came to look up the records, they were able to verify this. So he even fulfils this particular test of the time when he would appear in this world. But, of course, the Jews had become neglectful of this teaching, and so when the Messiah did come, they were not expecting him. That was due to their lack of diligence and to their failure to understand the character of their own prophecies.

Even the place of Christ's birth is prophesied – by the prophet Micah, who said that the Messiah would be born in Bethlehem (Micah 5:2; Matthew 2:5–6). Here, again, is something that is astonishing. It is unexpected, yet nevertheless it is true. Reading the Old Testament prophecies, I see that when the Christ comes he must be born in Bethlehem – and he was born in Bethlehem. Not only that, I find according to these prophecies that he must have lived for some time in a place called Nazareth. And so when Matthew comes to write his Gospel, he says in the last verse of the second chapter that Joseph and Mary took the child and 'came and dwelt in a city called Nazareth: that it might be fulfilled which was spoken by the prophets, He shall be called a Nazarene' (Matthew 2:23). And he was called a Nazarene – he was known as Jesus of Nazareth – that was actually foretold in the Old Testament prophecies.

And the final fact that I adduce under this general heading is that it was even prophesied that he should be taken down to Egypt. In that second chapter of Matthew's Gospel, we are told that because of the malice and malignity of King Herod, who was trying to put him to death, Joseph took Mary and the child down into Egypt. We read: 'And was there until the death of Herod: that it might be fulfilled which was spoken of the Lord by the prophet, saying, Out of Egypt have I called my son' (Hosea 11:1; Matthew 2:15).

Now here is most striking evidence. 'Is not this the Christ?' Certain desiderata are put forward by the Old Testament prophets, and whatever the effect he has upon me, he is not truly the Christ unless he satisfies these criteria. But he does satisfy them, he satisfies every one, and this is a part of the basis on which our faith rests.

But wait a minute; let us go on and consider, in the second place, his character. The prophecies emphasize the Messiah's greatness, his majesty, his dignity. I have quoted to you from the fortieth chapter of Isaiah – everything there suggests that he will be someone quite unusual. In verse 5, Isaiah writes, 'And the glory of the LORD shall be revealed, and all flesh shall see it together.' There would be a glory about the Messiah, and the moment we come to the New Testament we find that prominence is given to this glory – look at the announcement to the shepherds. This is not an ordinary birth, this is something unusual. The angelic hosts are singing, an announcement is made to the shepherds, and they go and they see. And ancient Simeon is filled with a sense of marvel, Anna the prophetess also, and the wise men from the east. Why? Because this child, this babe, is a great King, the King of kings, the Lord of lords. There is a majesty and a glory about him. All this is adumbrated and suggested and prophesied in the Old Testament Scriptures.

Yet here we come to something remarkable, because alongside these prophecies of glory, the Old Testament makes it quite clear that the Messiah will be exceptionally meek and pacific. Isaiah, for instance, compares him to a lamb led to the slaughter (Isaiah 53:7). This is the paradox of the person. One very striking prophecy is quoted in Matthew's Gospel. In Matthew chapter 12, we read:

*Then the Pharisees went out, and held a council against him, how they might destroy him. But when Jesus knew it, he withdrew himself from thence: and great multitudes followed him, and he healed them all; and charged them that they should not make him known.*

Why did he do this?

*That it might be fulfilled which was spoken by Esaias the prophet, saying, Behold my servant, whom I have chosen; my beloved, in whom my soul is well pleased: I will put my spirit upon him, and he shall shew judgment to the Gentiles. He shall not strive, nor cry; neither shall any man hear his voice in the streets. A bruised reed shall he not break, and smoking flax shall he not quench, till he send forth judgment unto victory. And in his name shall the Gentiles trust. (Matthew 12: 14–21; Isaiah 42:1–4)*

And when we look at him, is that not what we find – this mighty King, this King of kings, and Lord of lords, yet how humble, how gentle; tax collectors and sinners draw nigh unto him, the poor draw nigh unto him, the people who were condemned as outcasts by the Pharisees – he was prepared to touch them and to help them. This is the great characteristic that we find in him. And so, again, as we look at his character, we see that he fulfils the two elements that are most emphasized about him in the Old Testament Scriptures.

And then we come to our Lord's works – his miracles. In many places in the Old Testament there are prophecies that the Messiah will work miracles. In Isaiah 35, and in many other places, it is forecast that the blind will see, the deaf hear, the lame man leap as the hart and the dumb sing (verses 5–6). It is to be expected, of course, there will be something unusual about him because if the Son of God is going to come into the world, then he will attest his person, he will give evidence of being someone entirely above ordinary humanity. And when our Lord came, this is precisely what he did. He himself made use of this very argument on a very interesting and important occasion connected with poor John the Baptist.

John was the forerunner; he had the great privilege of 'preparing the way' for the Lord, and yet John was arrested and thrown into prison. There in prison, he is obviously ill. Doubts begin to assail him, so much so that when he hears about the works of Christ, he sends two of his disciples with the question, 'Art thou he that should come, or do we look for another?' (Matthew 11:3). Now you see the difference between John's question and the question of the woman of Samaria? The woman of Samaria rushes to the men and says, 'Is not this the Christ? Come!' John the Baptist asks whether they should look for another. Having thought that our Lord was the Christ, he is now beginning to doubt whether he is the Christ.

Why is this?

It is because John is surprised that our Lord has not gone up to Jerusalem and set himself up as a King and gathered an army together. John, a typical Jew, has, in a measure, a false notion concerning the Messiah. Poor John, there he is languishing in prison. He is the one who foretold the coming of the Messiah; surely, if our Lord is the Messiah, he will set John free. But he is not doing that. 'Is this the Christ?' And this is our Lord's reply to John's disciples:

*Go and shew John again those things which ye do hear and see.*

What are they?

*The blind receive their sight, and the lame walk, the lepers are cleansed, and the deaf hear, the dead are raised up, and the poor have the gospel preached to them. (Matthew 11:4–5)*

What is our Lord doing there when he replies like that? In effect, he is saying, 'Go back and tell John to read his prophecies again, tell him to read the prophets, and there he will find that they have said that the sign of the Messiah when he comes will be just this that you have seen and heard. Go and tell him.' It was predicted that the Messiah would work miracles and if he had not done so, he would not have been the Christ. But he did work miracles, and therefore we say with the woman of Samaria, 'Is not this the Christ?'

Or take another example. Here he is working some of his mighty miracles, and Matthew reports it like this:

*When the even was come, they brought unto him many that were possessed with devils; and he cast out the spirits with his word, and healed all that were sick: that it might be fulfilled which was spoken by Esaias the prophet, saying, Himself took our infirmities, and bare our sicknesses. (Matthew 8:16–17)*

The miracles are a fulfilment of the prophecies. Our Lord himself again makes use of the same argument when he turns to those doubting disciples of his and says: If you do not believe me when I speak to you, 'Believe me for the very works' sake' (John 14:11). The works that I do prove to you that I am indeed the Christ, the Son of God, the Saviour of the world.

Further proof that he is the Christ is seen in our Lord's death and his resurrection, because these, again, were prophesied and predicted in the Old Testament. This is a most valuable part of our proof and a substantiating of our belief. Even our Lord's disciples were too blind to see this. They had become so ignorant of their Scriptures and so misled by the wrong teaching of the Pharisees, that when he was put to death, they were dumbfounded and cast down, and really came to the conclusion that the one whom they had thought was the Christ was actually not the Christ at all. You find this typified perfectly in the story of the two dejected men on the road to Emmaus on the evening of the day our Lord rose from the dead. Our Lord joins them, and at last, when they give him a chance, he speaks to them and this is what he says:

> *O fools, and slow of heart to believe all that the prophets have spoken: Ought not the Christ to have suffered these things, and to enter into his glory? And beginning at Moses and all the prophets, he expounded unto them in all the Scriptures the things concerning himself. (Luke 24:25–27)*

Now this is a most vital bit of proof for us. There are people today who are troubled by our Lord's death and resurrection – they do not understand them. They do not understand them in terms of the biblical teaching, and depict him dying as a pacifist. They do not believe in the resurrection of the body, and thereby, of course, they show their utter disbelief. I put it as strongly as this: if our Lord had not been crucified, if he had not risen again in the body out of the tomb, I would say, 'He is not the Christ.' But because he was crucified, and fulfilled Psalm 22 as he was hanging there on the tree, and because he literally came in the body out of the grave, I say, 'Is not this the Christ?' He is!' He has fulfilled the prophecies concerning his death on the cross and his resurrection in the body.

What else? The next bit of fulfilled prophecy is in the sending of the Holy Spirit on the Day of Pentecost. Go back to the Old Testament and you will find prophecies that will tell you that this Messiah, when he comes, will send the Holy Spirit in mighty profusion upon his people. You find it in Ezekiel 36 and in many other places. And so the Holy Spirit is called 'the promise of the Father' (Acts 1:4). You remember the prophecies of Joel in Joel 2:28–32: 'It shall come to pass afterward, that I will pour out my spirit upon all flesh' – this great outpouring of the Spirit of God. And so as I look at him I ask myself: 'Is this the Christ?' I say, 'Has he shed forth the Holy Spirit?' And I go to Acts 2 and I find that he has, and I say with the woman of Samaria, 'Is not this the Christ?' And if he has not shed forth the Holy Spirit on the Day of Pentecost in Jerusalem, he would not be the Christ. This was prophesied and he has carried it out.

And the last bit of evidence concerning the prophets is that though he himself is a Jew, he will have a message for the Gentiles. Search in the Old Testament and you will find this prophesied; come to the New Testament, and you will see that this is the very thing that happened. He prophesied himself that his message should go out not only to Jerusalem but to the whole of Judea, to Samaria, and to the uttermost part of the earth (Acts 1:8), and that 'this gospel of the kingdom shall be preached in all the world for a witness unto all nations; and then shall the end come' (Matthew 24:14). So you see this abundant and amazing and astonishing evidence that we have concerning this person.

'Is this the Christ?'

'Of course he is!' He fulfils all these prophecies. 'For all the promises of God in him are yea, and in him Amen, unto the glory of God by us' (2 Corinthians 1:20).

But I have still other tests that I must apply. We have already referred to the prophecy in Genesis 3:15 that the seed of the woman shall bruise the serpent's head. The Messiah, the Christ, when he comes, must be one who can conquer the devil and destroy all his works. Here is a promise, plain and clear. This is what the Christ is going to do. As the result of his listening to the devil, man has become the slave, the bond-slave, of the devil and needs to be set at liberty. So the Christ must deliver us from the devil and all his power and all his might. Let us apply this test to him. What do we see? In his life our Lord conquered the devil completely; he repulsed his every attack. For forty days and forty nights the devil tempted him in the wilderness and was routed. In his life, our Lord cast out devils; no devil could withstand him. He is Master over the realm of evil and all its forces.

But, still more strikingly, he finally routed the devil in his death on the cross. He said so himself just before he died: 'Now shall the prince of this world be cast out' (John 12:31). As Paul puts it to the Colossians, in the cross he triumphed over all the principalities and powers and 'made a shew of them openly, triumphing over them in it' (Colossians 2:15).

And this defeat is seen even more clearly in the resurrection: 'The last enemy that shall be destroyed is death' (1 Corinthians 15:26). By the resurrection our Lord has conquered the devil, who is the one who has the 'power' of death. He has destroyed the devil himself, all his emissaries and powers and works, and our Lord has set free all those who believe in him.

Having, then, looked at the objective criteria for believing that our Lord is the Christ, let me in a few words also suggest a few subjective criteria. You notice the order in which I have put them before you – always start with the objective. Here you have evidence that is irrefutable; it can never be turned back. You have got the Old Testament prophecies written before he ever came, you have got the fulfilment in the New, and they fit perfectly. That is the evidence, there is the basis.

But, then, we are all in the flesh and we are subjective and we have our subjective tests. There are certain things that I, as a human being, ask of the Messiah, of the Christ. There are certain things that I need. What are they? What do I mean? First, I need wisdom, I need knowledge. How little we know, how dark our understandings. We do not understand life, we do not understand ourselves, we do not know God. We know nothing about death, we know nothing about what lies beyond it. We are ignorant. We need light and we need instruction. I am faced with these ultimate questions, and no man can give me the information I need.

Here is the only one who can help me. God gives 'the light of the knowledge of the glory of God in the face of Jesus Christ' (2 Corinthians 4:6). I do not want human speculation about God; I can speculate as well as anybody else, but it is only speculation. I want someone who can speak with authority and here is the one who does. 'We speak', he says, 'that we do know, and testify that we have seen' (John 3:11). 'No man hath seen God at any time; the only begotten Son, which is in the bosom of the Father, he hath declared him' (John 1:18).

Here is the only knowledge of God. He gives me knowledge of myself, he shows me my sin. I say with the woman of Samaria: 'Come, see a man, which told me all things that ever I did.' It is in him I see my sin, my lost condition. He condemns me utterly. He alone reveals to me the condemnation of the Law. He does it in his teaching, in his perfect life, as he dies upon the cross.

What else do I need? Well, I need righteousness. I know that I am guilty before God. I need to be forgiven, I need to be reconciled with God. I want to get rid of the fear of God that is in me instinctively. I want to feel that I can approach God. Who can help me? The Christ when he comes must do this. And as I look at this babe of Bethlehem, I find the only one who does: 'Who his own self bare our sins in his own body on the tree, that we, being dead to sins, should live unto righteousness' (1 Peter 2:24). 'God was in

Christ, reconciling the world unto himself' (2 Corinthians 5:19). My sins are forgiven, I am reconciled to God by this person and by him alone. He satisfies that need.

But I want more. I want a nature that corresponds with the nature of God, I want to commune with God, I want to have fellowship with him, and 'what communion hath light with darkness?' (2 Corinthians 6:14). I want eventually to stand in the presence of God and to spend my eternity with him – so I must be like God. How can I be? I cannot change myself, no man or woman can change me. I need a new nature – and that is precisely what he gives me. He said, 'Verily, verily, I say unto thee, Except a man be born again, he cannot see the kingdom of God . . . Marvel not that I said unto thee, Ye must be born again' (John 3:3, 7). I can be born again. I am born again. He has given me new life and it is his own life, a holy life. He has put his Spirit within me, and the Spirit does his progressive work of delivering me from the pollution as well as the power of sin in order that eventually I might stand before God – and that is the ultimate thing that I need.

I have told you that he has already conquered my last enemy, which is death, but what of the realm that lies beyond? And there he still satisfies me. 'Christ Jesus, who of God is made unto us wisdom, and righteousness, and sanctification, and redemption' (1 Corinthians 1:30) – and 'redemption' there means glorification – my very body delivered, free from infirmities, free from sin, free from all weakness, free from disease, free from everything that gets me down. He guarantees my eternal future. 'Beloved, now we are the sons of God, and it doth not yet appear what we shall be: but we know that, when he shall appear, we shall be like him; for we shall see him as he is' (1 John 3:2).

So we have looked at him together. There he is, the babe of Bethlehem. Watch him growing as a boy, through to manhood, see him setting out at the age of 30 to preach, to teach, to work miracles; see him dying on the cross, see him laid in a tomb, see his rising, see him ascended, watch him sending the Holy Spirit, think of him seated at the right hand of God. . . 'Is this the Christ?' We have examined him in the light of the evidence that God himself has given us in all the teaching of the prophecies of the Old Testament. There is the picture of what he will be like. Look at him in the days of his flesh – what do you see? A fulfilment in every detail, in every jot and tittle. He satisfies every prophecy, and he satisfies my every need.

There is only one thing that we can say, having looked at him together again, and this is what we must say to everybody whom we know, and everybody in the world, as we are given opportunity to do so. We must rush to them and say, 'Come, see a man, which told me all things that ever I did: is not this the Christ?' Come and see him, test him, and see with us that this is indeed the Christ of God, the Saviour of the world.

51

# Facing a New Year

*The woman then left her waterpot, and went her way into the city, and saith to the men, Come, see a man, which told me all things that ever I did: is not this the Christ? (John 4:28–29)*

We are interested in this extraordinary act on the part of this woman of Samaria because by doing what she did and saying what she said, she gave what we must regard as the typical response to the Lord Jesus Christ of all who believe in him.

Here we are, on the first Sunday morning of a new year, not that that matters in and of itself; we know that these divisions that the world recognizes with respect to time are more or less irrelevant, and yet there is value in them and it is good that we should observe them. As Christians, we have a new view of time; time, for us, is divided up entirely in terms of the Lord Jesus Christ. We think of time as time before he came, when he came, after he came and when he will come again. But as the world to which we belong does recognize these other distinctions and divisions, and this is the first time we are meeting together on a

Sunday morning in 1968, it is good that we should examine ourselves and our whole relationship to time and to life in this world.

Now how do we examine ourselves? Well, the one thing that
matters above everything else is that we should do so in terms of
our relationship to the person of the Lord Jesus Christ. Here is a
woman who, having met him and heard him, realizes that he
matters above everything else and that her relationship to him is
the most important thing in the world; that is why she rushes back
to the city to invite her fellow townsmen to come out to see him.
So let us examine ourselves in the light of what we are told here
about this woman.

There are many reasons why this process of self-examination is
very necessary. One is that Scripture itself frequently commands
and exhorts it. Perhaps one of the most striking examples is in the
Second Epistle to the Corinthians: 'Examine yourselves, whether ye
be in the faith; prove your own selves. Know ye not your own selves,
how that Jesus Christ is in you, except ye be reprobates?' (2
Corinthians 13:5). Now the apostle says that because of certain
things that were happening in the church at Corinth. This church,
though it was a Christian church, was in a very unsatisfactory condition, both in general and in the lives of many individual members.
In the light of this, Paul tells them that he can do nothing but exhort
them to examine themselves. Are they truly Christian? Are they in
the faith? Is Christ Jesus in them? The New Testament, with its
characteristic honesty, makes it quite clear to us that it is possible for
us to be members of the church without being Christians.

John reminds us that there were some who had joined the
church and yet, he says, in effect, 'They have gone out from us
because, though they were among us, they never really belonged to
us' (see 1 John 2:19). And we have been seeing on Sunday nights,
some of us, how that man Simon Magus in the city of Samaria had

been accepted into the church and had been baptized, but clearly was never a Christian at all (Acts 8:9–24).[1] The Scriptures exhort us to examine ourselves lest we assume that we are Christians when we are not. We are all open to this delusion, we are all liable to it. Many of us have been brought up in Christian homes and taken to a Christian church, and have assumed, therefore, that we are Christians. But that does not make us Christian.

But even if we know and have had a very definite Christian experience, it is very necessary, is it not, indeed, it is essential, that we should periodically examine ourselves and really make sure that we are in the faith because, again, the New Testament shows us the danger of drifting. 'Therefore we ought to give the more earnest heed to the things which we have heard,' says the author of the Epistle to the Hebrews, 'lest at any time we should let them slip' (Hebrews 2:1). There is a danger of drifting – drifting away from the foundations, drifting away from the moorings, drifting away from everything that should hold us to the truth.

Now the experience of the church throughout the centuries confirms this danger. The graph of the history of the church, as I have often pointed out, is never a steady one, certainly there is not a general ascent. It is a history of ups and down, great periods of revival followed by periods of lethargy, of deadness and failure, and of formality. That, again, should urge us to examine ourselves. You can be a Christian and yet you can become slack, you can become indolent, you can drop to a lower level and fail to maintain an experience you once had.

---

[1] These sermons have been published in D. Martyn Lloyd-Jones, *Authentic Christianity: Sermons on the Acts of the Apostles: Volume 6*, The Banner of Truth Trust, 2006, and in the USA by Crossway Books under the title *Compelling Christianity*.

But how do we examine ourselves? It seems to me that there is only one big question to ask, and it is the very question suggested by this story of the woman of Samaria. In the end, it all comes down to this: What does our Lord himself mean to us? That is the great question. 'Come, see a man, which told me all things that ever I did: is not this the Christ?' This person. This woman is now dominated by him. He is everything to her.

But even here we need help and instruction. I ask what our Lord means to us, but how do we decide that? Do we find out in a purely subjective manner? No! We must have certain objective standards and tests in order to make sure that our subjective reactions and responses are really true. What is the true response that is required of us? There is abundant material in the Scriptures to help us. To find out what he means to us, we must go back to these Gospels and see how men and women responded to him in the days of his flesh. The Gospels were written partly in order to bring this out and to help us. We see people amazed at him, astonished at him, loving him, falling at his feet. And when we look at those who were given the great privilege of seeing him after his return to heaven, we see that what always impressed them was that he was the same person. Though glorified, he is still 'the Lamb that was slain' (Revelation 5:12).

But then we go on to the Acts of the Apostles. Now our Lord has gone back to heaven and here are his people left in the world with persecutions and trials and troubles and tribulations; what was their relationship to him? What did they think of him? What part did he play in their lives? And I would remind you again that the book of Acts is meant to be a norm. Of course, in Acts there is an unusual intensity, but we must not isolate this book and segregate it, as it were, and say that it has nothing to teach us. We see there how Christian people are meant to live – so there we have another test.

And then we go on to the teaching of the Epistles, and constantly, as I have shown you, the apostles are asking their questions. They remind the readers of their true relationship with Christ: 'Ye have not so learned Christ' (Ephesians 4:20). And they put questions: Is he that to you? 'Examine yourselves, whether ye be in the faith; prove your own selves' (2 Corinthians 13:5) and so on. And we end with the book of Revelation, where he again dominates the whole scene, and where the concluding cry is: 'Even so, come, Lord Jesus.' His followers are still in this intimate communion with him. So there we have abundant evidence whereby we can test our relationship to the Lord.

But we can supplement even that, and it is most important that we should. I have already emphasized that a great danger in the Christian church at the present time is the danger of putting a wedge, as it were, between the New Testament and ourselves, and saying that all we read there only belongs to that time and is impossible now, and we should not even seek it. There is a fatal assumption that the whole of the New Testament describes some ideal position that never is to be repeated. To me, this is the greatest fallacy of all; nothing is so responsible for the quenching of the Spirit as just that attitude.

Now the best way to correct that wrong view is to turn to the whole history of the church subsequent to the first century. We can do that in many ways. We can read church history itself and see the great tides, the great movements, of the Spirit of God when the church and her people were lifted back up again to the position of the book of Acts. Then we can take the biographies of individuals – sometimes, even in a time of drought and aridity, some saints were given experiences that were exactly like those that we read of in the New Testament, thus giving the lie direct to the false teaching that would discourage us from seeking the New

Testament kind of experience. And then we can always turn to our hymn books, and especially the great hymns of the great centuries, the eighteenth century in particular – that was the great century. Go back to these hymns and there you will find accounts in verse of experiences of the relationship between these people and our blessed Lord and Saviour. So let us make use of all this, and as we do so, we get a clear picture: it is the picture we are given here of this woman of Samaria. He means everything to her: 'Come, see a man . . .' The picture is always the same.

In the light of all this, let us examine ourselves on this first Sunday morning of a new year. I again put my question to you – it is the one thing that matters – What does he mean to you? Let us consider this question in two main ways: first, by looking back at the past. Here we are, changing from one year to another, and as we start a new year, it is good to look back. The Bible is always doing this. Take the psalmists, they are constantly reviewing their own personal histories and the history of the nation of Israel. They look back at the history, they start from the beginning and see the various vicissitudes that occurred. It is excellent to do this. Let us do the same.

As we look back, I think these are the questions we should face. First, can we say quite honestly that our coming to know him is the greatest thing that has ever happened to us? Now that was true of this woman. She had her past history, but here she is asseverating that meeting this person is the biggest event of her life; at last she has discovered reality. As we look back across our lives, can we say that without any question that is also true of us? Many things have happened that have given us much pleasure – we have had successes, joys, happiness – but here is the question: Are we perfectly clear that greater than all else is our relationship to him?

Many things have controlled our lives, many factors have been bearing upon us – family, home, upbringing, associations, school, university, perhaps, business, whatever it is, it does not matter. Many things and many people have influenced us. But here is the second major question: What has been the biggest influence in our lives? What has been the dominating influence? It is no use saying, 'Yes, I'm a Christian, and I'm applying certain Christian principles in my living.' All right, I accept that that is important – but it is not quite enough. Here is the question of questions: Is he the biggest factor in your life? Has he been controlling your life? Can you say as you look back, 'I've made many mistakes, I've fallen into sin, yet I know that the controlling influence in my life has been the Lord Jesus Christ'?

Or, thirdly, let me put it like this: Are we more proud of our association with him than of anything else? I like to think of it like that. We are proud of many things in our lives, proud of many associations – there is nothing wrong in that. The Bible does not condemn them as long as they do not become 'inordinate'. We must not love the world, but it is right and legitimate to take pride in certain things that have happened to us in this world and of certain associations that we have. But this third question is always the test of tests. If called upon to do so, would we always have been ready to sacrifice every other association for his sake?

These first Christians were called upon to take such a decision; this was the great problem for every Christian in the Roman Empire: Were they prepared to go on saying, 'Jesus is Lord,' or would they say, 'No, Caesar is Lord'? They were pressed to make this decision, and they were told that unless they said, 'Caesar is Lord,' they would be put to death. And this was the test that they passed so gloriously. They would not deny him for the sake of Caesar, for the sake of saving their lives. No, no! They preferred to be martyred, crucified, torn limb from limb by the lions in the arena – anything. 'Jesus is the Lord!' Their boast was in him.

Has our boast been of him, or have we denied him for the sake of popularity or applause from human beings? Have we denied him in order to gain something for ourselves? This is the question. This woman, because of her evil life, because she knows exactly what everybody thinks about her, avoided people, as we have seen. But all that has gone now. She does not care what they think of her; what matters is what they think of him. And so we can test ourselves in that way.

Then, fourthly, a very good way of examining ourselves is to ask: What has he done for me? You have rejoiced, you have known happiness, but is the great source of your joy and rejoicing your knowledge of what he has done for you? This woman says, 'Come, see a man, which told me all things that ever I did.' He has done that for her. She knows he has done other things for her, too: she is aware of a change within herself. And that is the question I am asking: Do you know that your sins are forgiven? These are the questions by which we examine ourselves and decide whether or not we are Christians. We are paying heed to the apostle's exhortation: 'Examine yourselves, whether ye be in the faith; prove your own selves.'

Are you still troubled about your past sins? Are you still doubting whether you are forgiven? Well, if you are, my friend, I take leave to ask you to be sure again that you are a Christian at all, for Christians are people who know that their sins have been forgiven; they know that among the other sins that God the Father laid upon our Lord were their sins; they know that their sins have received their punishment, that Christ has borne them and they have been blotted out of God's book. And as the result of that, they have peace with God: 'Being justified by faith, we have peace with God through our Lord Jesus Christ' (Romans 5:1). Have you found heart and conscience at peace? Peace in your mind, peace in your conscience, peace between you and God.

Oh, let us examine ourselves! Are you still trying to make yourself a Christian? Are you still trying to find a way of delivery and of salvation? Are you waiting for some book to appear that will give you some new insight? Are you dependent upon the researches of modern scientists – is that your position? Are you still in uncertainty and looking and searching and hoping to arrive at some truth? Or do you know that he is 'the way, the truth, and the life' (John 14:6), and that you have come to the Father by him? Is your mind at rest? Has the weary searching and straining and travailing of looking come to an end, and do you know him who is the light of the world, and can you say with the apostle Paul, 'God, who commanded the light to shine out of darkness, hath shined in our hearts, to give the light of the knowledge of the glory of God in the face of Jesus Christ' (2 Corinthians 4:6)? Do you know that all is well with your soul, and well between you and him?

Or let me put it like this to you: Do you have peace with God through Jesus Christ – is this what matters to you above everything else? If it is, you are a Christian, however unworthy, however much you fail. If it is not, I take leave to suggest that you are not a Christian. And have you got, in addition to that, a sense of sonship, a sense of belonging to God as his child? Paul says, 'As many as are led by the Spirit of God, they are the sons of God' (Romans 8:14). He continues: 'For ye have not received the spirit of bondage again to fear' – are you living in fear, the fear of God, the fear of judgement, the fear of death, the fear of hell? Are you still in a spirit of heaviness and bondage? That is not the spirit of the child of God. No, no! – 'but ye have received the Spirit of adoption, whereby we cry, Abba, Father' (verse 15). Tell me, has that cry arisen from your heart as you look back? I say again, however unworthy and failing, you still know and you say with Peter, 'Thou knowest that I love thee' (John 21:17).

And are we aware, as we look back, that we have had a sense of his nearness and of his help? This is real, it is not theoretical. 'He hath said, I will never leave thee, nor forsake thee' (Hebrews 13:5). Have you found him 'a very present help in trouble' (Psalm 46:1)? Has he made all the difference to you at certain points of crisis? This is the test. It is comparatively easy for a man like me to preach and for you to come and listen and worship God, but the real tests of life and of our faith and of our relationship to him come when we are in trouble. What are we like in temptation and trial? Look back across you life, has he made all the difference to you? He always does when you really know him. You see, it is not enough to say, 'Yes, I believe, I have subscribed to the truth,' you can do that intellectually. No, here is a profound test: In the moment of agony has he suddenly appeared, and then has everything been different? I must quote that hymn again:

> Sometimes a light surprises
> The Christian while he sings;
> It is the Lord who rises
> With healing in his wings.
>                     *William Cowper*

Have you known that? It has been the universal experience of the saints throughout the centuries.

And, lastly, as you look back, have you been conscious of his working in you? Have you been conscious of the fact that he will not leave you alone? Oh, that is a wonderful test! It can be a very painful one, but it is a very delicate test. He will not allow you to go away. 'O love that wilt not let me go' – have you known that? Have you known that the pressure of his hand is upon you, that he is dealing with you, manipulating your life? For he does. This is the whole teaching of the Scripture. Again, this is the universal testimony of his saints at all times. As you look back, are you staggered as you see the way that he has led you and brought you, anticipated you, manipulated circumstances – how all along he has been there? Are you conscious that he has been working in you 'both to will and to do of his good pleasure' (Philippians 2:13)? These are infallible signs of our being in the true and right relationship to him.

And I want to supplement all this with yet another question before I leave the past: Has your knowledge of him increased during the last year? It should have done. This notion that you get your really big experience when you take your decision for Christ and for the rest of your life you try to maintain that and probably fail rather than succeed, is an utter travesty of the New Testament teaching. He is a person and he is endless: the apostle Paul, in praying for the Ephesians, asks that they 'may be able to comprehend with all saints what is the breadth, and length, and depth, and height; and to know the love of Christ, which passeth knowledge' (Ephesians 3:18–19).

Do you know him better than you did twelve months ago? Is he more real to you, more vital? Are these assurances that come from him more and more precious to you? Tell me, my dear friends, are you more amazed at him than you have ever been? Are you amazed at the Scriptures? Are you enjoying them more than you did? Are you ravished by them? Are you thrilled by them? Does this knowledge seem to you more and more precious? Your personal knowledge of him, your awareness of his presence, your confidence in him, your understanding of the way of salvation – has all this been increasing? These are the ways whereby we discover our true relationship to him. These are what ultimately count.

So, then, we have been looking at the past; now let us turn and look at the future. That is what you do at the beginning of a year, is it not – inevitably. And it is important that we should do this. Here we are, we are starting a new year, how do we contemplate it? Again, I would say that the vital test is this: Are we all of us facing the future in terms of our relationship to him? I do not mean that we do not consider anything else; all I am asking is: Is he the dominating factor here? We look to this unknown future, we think of possibilities, but here is the question: Is he central to all our hopes and plans?

Now the apostle Paul in the Epistle to the Romans shows us the right perspective. This, he says, is how a Christian looks at the future:

*And that, knowing the time, that now it is high time to awake out of sleep: for now is our salvation nearer than when we believed. The night is far spent, the day is at hand: let us therefore cast off the works of darkness, and let us put on the armour of light. Let us walk honestly, as in the day; not in rioting and drunkenness, not in chambering and wantonness, not in strife and envying. But put ye on the Lord Jesus Christ, and make not provision for the flesh, to fulfil the lusts thereof. (Romans 13:11–14)*

So, then, as you look at the future, is it essentially in terms of him?

Now let me put that to you in a number of subsidiary questions. What is your greatest desire as you face the future? We all have desires, we all have wishes, there are certain things we would all like to happen, and we think, as we look at the future: What has it got in store for me? All right, I ask: What do you want? What is your greatest desire? This is a vital test, and the Christian response to that test is this: It is the desire to know him better. 'Come, see a man, which told me all things that ever I did.' Come and listen to him, come and look at him. The woman of Samaria wants to know more and more of him, and she forgets the waterpot, leaves it aside, goes back and fetches the people: this is it!

Mary sits at his feet:

> O that I could for ever sit
> With Mary at the Master's feet!
> Be this my happy choice:
> My only care, delight, and bliss,
> My joy, my heaven on earth, be this,
> To hear the Bridegroom's voice.
>
> *Charles Wesley*

Tell me, can you honestly say, as you face this new year, that your greatest desire is to know him better because of what you have already known of him? Like the apostle Paul, can you say that the greatest desire of all in your life is:

> *That I may know him, and the power of his resurrection, and the fellowship of his sufferings, being made conformable unto his death; if by any means I might attain unto the resurrection of the dead. (Philippians 3:10–11)*

Tell me, my dear friend, is that above everything your supreme desire? Is it your desire to serve him truly, and to please him in all your ways?

Tell me another thing: Above everything else in this coming year, do you desire to see the success of his kingdom? We look at our world, we look at our country, and it is right and good that we should wish for economic improvement and prosperity. We seek health, strength, happiness, wealth – all right, I am not criticizing any of these desires, but I am asking this: Above and beyond all this, do we long for revival, reformation, for his truth to be manifested with power, sin rebuked, men and women converted, falling at his feet, leaving evil? Do we wish to see this country renewed spiritually for his glory's sake? Are we grieved at the blasphemy of this age, and do we long, even beyond the prosperity of the country, to see the prosperity of the kingdom of our God and of our Christ? Is this it? This is inevitably the response of all who are in this true and living relationship to him.

And then I want to ask another question – it is an obvious one, is it not? How do we face the unseen possibilities? What does this year hold for us? Who knows? But the question is: Are you afraid of the future? Are you even afraid to face it? Are you apprehensive? Do you say, 'Don't tell me, I'm afraid'? Does the future hold something of terror from which you shrink so that you try just to enjoy yourself for the moment? This is a vital matter.

At this point, there is a crucial distinction that we must draw. There are two ways of looking at the future. There is a wrong way, a morbid way, which our Lord himself condemned in the Sermon on the Mount:

*Therefore I say unto you, take no thought for your life, what ye shall eat or what ye shall drink; nor yet for your body, what ye shall put on. Is not the life more than meat, and the body than raiment? . . . Wherefore, if God so clothe the grass of the field, which to day is, and to morrow is cast into the oven, shall he not much more clothe you, O ye of little faith? Therefore take no thought, saying, What shall we eat? or, What shall we drink? or, Wherewithal shall we be clothed? (For after all these things do the Gentiles seek:) for your heavenly Father knoweth that ye have need of all these things. But seek ye first the kingdom of God, and his righteousness; and all these things shall be added unto you. Take therefore no thought for the morrow: for the morrow shall take thought for the things of itself. Sufficient unto the day is the evil thereof. (Matthew 6:25, 30–34)*

Now people sometimes misinterpret that by saying that Christianity tells us, 'Never look to the future at all, do not consider the possibilities, just live for the day.' But that is to misunderstand this teaching. Our Lord is saying that we should not be the victims of a morbid care and anxiety; we should not worry about the future. But that does not mean that we should not consider it at all. What, then, is the right way to face the future? It is the way of the apostle Paul. He looks at the future and says:

*For I am persuaded, that neither death, nor life, nor angels, nor principalities, nor powers, nor things present, nor things to come, nor height, nor depth, nor any other creature, shall be able to separate us from the love of God, which is in Christ Jesus our Lord. (Romans 8:38–39)*

That is the right way, and it is very important we should do that. The Christian is not afraid to look to the future. The Christian does look at it, and envisages all the worst possibilities, and then triumphs over them all in Christ Jesus.[2] That is the Christian's response.

So we are unlike the world in every respect; we do face the future, and we face it honestly. It is right that we should do so. We will be a year older – if we are still alive in a year's time. So face it – 10 years, 20 years. Just sit down and remind yourself that ill health, failure of your faculties, these are all bound to come, and eventually death itself.

---

2  For Dr Lloyd-Jones, the coming year was to bring serious illness and the end of his ministry at Westminster Chapel. These pages were certainly true of him.

It is, therefore, of the essence of Christianity that we face these things. We do not just say, 'Well, don't think of them, they will come soon enough.' That is the world! Christian men and women look at them all, but they are able to face them, and to be more than conquerors through him that loved them. This is the way. So apply that in detail. Look at the immediate future: we do not know what may come. We may have a year of great happiness and joy, we may have disappointment and sorrow; we may have abounding health, we may lose it. We may have loss, we may have success; accidents may come, sorrow, bereavement. My dear friends, we are in the midst of life and in the midst of life we are in death. 'Change and decay in all around I see.'

But here is the question: Having looked at these possibilities, these certainties, how do we react to them? And this is where our Lord comes in. Do you rely on him? Do you know that his promises are sure? Do you know that he will always be sufficient, that he will never fail you? That is the question. That is how the apostle faced the future; that is how the first Christians faced it; that is how Christians throughout the centuries have faced it. The Christian is the greatest realist in the world. Christians can afford to face their fears and problems, and believe in facing them. It is the world that tries to forget its problems by entertainment or drink or drugs, by playing and escaping.

Christians are able to face the future because they know him, they have met this man. 'Come, see this man, which told me all things that ever I did: is not this the Christ?' Christians have met him, and they say, 'This one can do everything for me. It matters not what may come to meet me, I am ready for all things because he is the ruler of the universe, the Lord of history, the controller of my destiny. Though I am led as a lamb to the slaughter, whatever may happen to me, I know that nothing shall be able to separate me from the love of

God, which is in Christ Jesus our Lord. This is the test of the Christian. Charles Wesley looks at the Lord and this is what he says:

> Thou hidden source of calm repose,
> Thou all-sufficient love divine,
> My help and refuge from my foes,
> Secure I am if thou art mine;
> And lo! from sin, and grief, and shame,
> I hide me, Jesus, in thy name.
>
> Thy mighty name salvation is,
> And keeps my happy soul above;
> Comfort it brings, and power, and peace,
> And joy and everlasting love:
> To me, with thy dear name are given
> Pardon, and holiness, and heaven.
>
> Jesus, my all in all thou art;
> My rest in toil, mine ease in pain;
> The medicine of my broken heart;

Does he mean this to you? Has he been that to you? And as you look to the unknown future, do you know he is going to be the medicine of your broken heart?

> In war, my peace; in loss, my gain;
> My smile beneath the tyrant's frown;
> In shame, my glory and my crown:
>
> In want, my plentiful supply;
> In weakness, mine almighty power;
> In bonds, my perfect liberty;
> My light in Satan's darkest hour;

Has he been all this to you? Do you know he will be?

> My help and stay whene'er I call;
> My life in death, my heaven, my all.

Has he been that to you? Is he that to you now? Do you know that he will ever be that to you so that whatever may come all is well with your soul? And, ultimately, as you look into the haggard face of death, can you smile and say: 'O death, where is thy sting? O grave, where is thy victory?' (1 Corinthians 15:55). Well, there it is, my friends: What is he to you? Can you say quite honestly:

> Thou, O Christ, art all I want,
> More than all in thee I find.
> *Charles Wesley*

I have found, I find, I know that I ever shall find, for Jesus Christ is 'the same yesterday, today, and for ever'.

52

# The Witness

*The woman then left her waterpot, and went her way into the city, and saith to the men, Come, see a man, which told me all things that ever I did: is not this the Christ? Then they went out of the city, and came unto him. (John 4: 28–30)*

We have been considering together the reaction of the woman of Samaria to our Lord's conversation with her. We have seen that one of the first things that happens to her is a profound conviction of sin, and then that this overwhelming person becomes the dominating factor in her life – that is why she leaves her waterpot. We have seen what this means as it is expounded to us in the pages of the New Testament, as it is confirmed in the lives of the saints in the church throughout the running centuries, and as we know it ourselves.

So now we come to the next step, and these steps follow, I think you will agree, in a kind of logical necessity. They are true psychologically and are true according to the teaching of the word. The next step is that this woman invites her fellow townspeople to come at once and see this person who has made such a difference to her and listen to him. This, again, is something against which we must obviously test ourselves. There is a kind of wholeness about the Christian life or, if you like, the response of the Christian to the Lord Jesus Christ. One step always leads to another; they are indissolubly bound and linked together. So we examine ourselves by each of the particulars, and we also examine ourselves to see if we are manifesting something of the whole. Both are very necessary, otherwise, as we have already seen and as we shall be seeing, we may very well go astray. If we fix on one aspect only, we lack balance, we develop a lopsided Christianity, and we can indeed fall into grievous error.

Let us, then, look at this together. Here is this woman – she has had the experience of meeting this blessed person, and her immediate response is to rush to the city to say to the people there, 'Come, see a man, which told me all things that ever I did: is not this the Christ?' Now the first point that we must notice about her action is that it arose spontaneously. This is most important, and that is why I am starting with it. The way in which this arises is important in and of itself, and particularly, I feel, at the present time.

You will often hear Christian people like ourselves criticized on the grounds that in this matter we contrast unfavourably with the adherents of the cults. We are told how these people give themselves enthusiastically to their work: young men give up their Sunday afternoons to knock at doors and sell their literature. This is a great characteristic of the cults, and it is said of Christians that as long as they can go and enjoy their acts of worship they think they are all right. Then they do these other things when they have time and when nothing more important is calling for their attention. So they spend most of their lives failing to show the concern about other people, and the zeal with this concern, that are so characteristic of the members of the cults.

Now it is not for me or for any preacher to excuse the failure of Christian people, and it is not my purpose to do so now. My comments are not primarily meant for the comfort of the Christian but are intended to bring out certain characteristics of the cults. I want to try to show you that, speaking generally, in this very difference between the behaviour of the adherents of the cults and of Christian people, we see a vital distinction between the two, a distinction that is clearly seen here in the spontaneity of the woman of Samaria.

To describe in general the characteristics of any of the cults, we simply have to use one word: carnality. By that, I mean that they are of the flesh, of the natural man, they are carnal in contradistinction to that which is spiritual, which is ever the characteristic of the true Christian. Let me analyse that a little to show you what I mean. Here is the picture I trust you have in your mind: here is the woman of Samaria rushing back to the city; she typifies Christian people. Then think of what you know to be so true of the followers of the cults at the present time. What is happening today is not new, there have always been cults, but under different names. There were mystery religions in the time of the New Testament and other false, specious teachings that at first seemed to be very Christian but were not Christian at all.

One of the characteristics of the cults is their method of approaching people. First of all, their members have to be urged to go out and do this. The moment they join, they are told that the right thing to do is to get others also. Then a definite scheme or system is always imposed upon them: they all say the same things in the same way. It could really be done almost as well by a gramophone record or tape and, indeed, sometimes is. And this, of course, leads on to the third point, which is that they have to be trained and taught how to go out and speak to people. They are given the formula. It is drummed into them, they are drilled, in order that they may be effective and efficient. I think you will agree that that always marks the way in which the cults operate.

In other words, their method is mechanical. The machine-like element is always very prominent. If you start listening to such people, but then interrupt them and put questions to them, you will find that they are nonplussed because what they have to say is a sort of circle that goes round and round. They are generally taught a certain number of scriptures and they can always produce them, but give them one they have never heard of, or have never been taught to repeat or to expound, and they are lost and fumble, not knowing quite what to say. There is no freedom about their words, but they are learned and repeated parrot-fashion.

And then the other characteristic of cults is a zeal for proselytizing and for gaining adherents; that seems to be their great motive. Now there are fine distinctions here. Obviously, the Christian is anxious that others should become Christians, as I am going to show you, but there is all the difference in the world between being moved by a desire to get adherents to your particular cult or teaching, and the true desire the people should get the blessings of the Lord Jesus Christ. These people are anxious for us to get 'it'. There is always some 'it', some particular thing. And they are very zealous – there is no question about that. The New Testament tells us that the Pharisees 'compass sea and land' to make one proselyte (Matthew 23:15). They were great proselytizers, and the false teachers, the New Testament tells us in many places, have always been characterized by a similar zeal. They know that people have 'itching ears' (2 Timothy 4:3), and they show an enthusiasm and an energy that is quite astonishing until you begin to examine it. But the moment you examine it, you see that it belongs to the flesh rather than to the spirit: it is an imposed system that is carried out in a mechanical manner.

Now, of course, these days this approach is by no means confined to followers of cults and false religions; we see it also in the realm of business. If you listen to the patter of people who want to sell you a cleaning machine or anything else, you can see that they have been trained and that they are repeating parrot-fashion something that they have been told to say. But in contrast to all that, we see this woman of Samaria and what hits us at once as we read this story is the spontaneity of her action. Nobody told her to rush to the city and invite the people to come and see the Lord Jesus Christ. Nobody told her, nobody taught her, nobody urged her. The glorious and remarkable aspect of this story is that she found herself doing it. She did not even have to think; it was done. And this spontaneity is characteristic of the Christian. Now you see the essential difference. That is why I say that this principle is so important. False proselytizing zeal is the characteristic of the spurious rather than of the truth.

Linked with this is the fact that it is obviously the Lord himself who is at the centre of the woman's concern. She is not primarily out to get adherents to the cause to which she is now going to belong, she is not concerned above all else that others should have her experience, though that comes in, but she is motivated by the desire that everybody should come to meet him. This is what is overwhelming her. She wants everybody to listen to him as she has been doing. He is the centre of everything – and this is the most valuable test of all. Even in our Christian work we can quite unconsciously have wrong motives. A minister may be anxious to have more church members or an increase in the collections so that he can boast about it. A congregation, likewise, can be moved by the same desire to show off – 'our church', 'our cause'. But all this is so remote from what we have here. Look at the delightful, glorious simplicity and spontaneity of someone captivated and captured by the Lord. The woman acts as one inevitably acts in such circumstances.

Let me give you further demonstrations of this. My whole purpose is to show that the Christian response is spontaneous and not imposed. Christians witness to others because of something that is working in them. There is one notable example at the end of the first chapter of this Gospel of John. One afternoon, John the Baptist is with two of his disciples when our Lord passes by, and John says, 'Behold, the Lamb of God.' So these two disciples go after him and he speaks to them. Then we are told:

> *[They] abode with him that day: for it was about the tenth hour. One of the two which heard John speak, and followed him, was Andrew, Simon Peter's brother.*

What does Andrew do, having met the Lord and having listened to him?

> *He first findeth his own brother Simon, and saith unto him, We have found the Messias, which is, being interpreted, the Christ. And he brought him to Jesus. . .*

Then we go on:

> *The day following Jesus would go forth into Galilee, and findeth Philip, and saith unto him, Follow me.*

What is Philip's response?

> *Philip findeth Nathanael, and saith unto him, We have found him, of whom Moses in the law, and the prophets, did write, Jesus of Nazareth, the son of Joseph. (John 1:35–45)*

My argument is that it is inevitable. You cannot meet with this person without responding. If it has been suggested to you that this is a duty for which you have to be trained and drilled, there is something wrong and you belong to another realm, it is not the Christian response. We must examine ourselves in the light of this.

Or, again, look what we read in Acts chapter 4 – this is the Christian response:

> *Peter and John answered and said unto them, Whether it be right in the sight of God to hearken unto you more than unto God, judge ye. For we cannot but speak the things which we have seen and heard. (Acts 4:19–20)*

We cannot help it, we cannot stop it, we are bound to, 'we cannot but speak'.

Or take another still more striking example. You may say: that is still about apostles, what about ordinary Christians? But look at Acts chapter 8. We read at the beginning of the chapter:

> *And at that time there was a great persecution against the church which was at Jerusalem; and they were all scattered abroad throughout the regions of Judaea and Samaria, except the apostles.*

What did they do, these people who were scattered abroad? The fourth verse tells us:

> *Therefore they that were scattered abroad went every where preaching the word.*

Then verse 5 goes on to say:

> *Then Philip went down to the city of Samaria, and preached Christ unto them.*

Now in verses 4 and 5, the same English word – 'preaching/preached' – is used to translate two different Greek words. This is a pity because there is an important difference in the meaning of the two Greek words. The difference is this: Philip, who was an evangelist, 'proclaimed', 'heralded' Christ to the people. The suggestion here is of a man standing and addressing a congregation; that is the meaning of the word actually used by Luke. By contrast, it has been very rightly suggested by someone that a very good translation of the word in verse 4, referring to ordinary people, is this: 'Therefore they that were scattered abroad went every where gossiping the word.' They did not stand up in pulpits. The word 'preaching' now carries that connotation for us, and so when we read about the first Christians 'preaching the word', we picture them standing up and addressing congregations. But these people did not do that; they just talked about the gospel. They were 'scattered abroad' because of the persecution and some kind people in Judea and Samaria received them into their homes, and then they just talked to them – it was conversation, it was 'gossip'.

This is the instinctive, characteristic Christian response – Christians cannot help talking about the Lord. These first Christians not only told the people why they were being persecuted and why they had to escape from Jerusalem, they wanted to tell them about this person, and this experience that they had received through him. It was not confined to apostles or to some exceptional people. Here were ordinary members of the church – I use the word 'ordinary' because of the limitation of language. There is no such person as an 'ordinary' Christian, but there are distinctions in offices in the church and these are the people who did not hold any office – they went everywhere, speaking, gossiping, telling people this blessed word of salvation in Christ Jesus.

Now this is so vital that I cannot leave it; let me give you another example. Listen to the apostle Paul writing to the church at Rome and telling the people there about his desire to be with them. This is how he puts it:

*For I long to see you*

– what for? –

*that I may impart unto you some spiritual gift, to the end ye may be established; that is, that I may be comforted together with you by the mutual faith of both you and me. Now I would not have you ignorant, brethren, that oftentimes I purposed to come unto you, (but was let [hindered] hitherto,) that I might have some fruit among you also, even as among other Gentiles. I am debtor both to the Greeks, and to the Barbarians; both to the wise, and to the unwise. So, as much as in me is, I am ready to preach the gospel to you that are at Rome also. (Romans 1:11–15)*

You see the idea? 'I am debtor.' What does the apostle mean by that? He means that he owes it to them. In the word 'debtor' there is the whole idea of compulsion, is there not? The very word conjures up a court, and a man with legal pressure being brought to bear upon him to pay a debt. So Paul is saying, 'I am similar to that man, a kind of pressure is on me. I am a debtor, I owe this. I have the good news and I want to give it, and I feel I must give it.'

This is a concept that Paul returns to in many other places. For instance, he says to the Corinthians, 'Though I preach the gospel, I have nothing to glory of: for *necessity is laid upon me*; yea, woe is unto me, if I preach not the gospel!' (1 Corinthians 9:16). Necessity! 'Woe is unto me if I do not!' 'You ask me why I preach like this,' says Paul, in effect, 'and why I go on in spite of obstacles and persecutions and so on – oh! – that is the answer. I have no choice. I don't sit down and get up and deliberately decide to go out and preach; there is a necessity.' The same necessity sent the woman of Samaria rushing to the city: 'Come, see this man . . .' Spontaneity! You are in a different realm from this drilling and ordering – the mechanics of it all.

Again, in writing to the Corinthians, Paul says, 'Wherefore we labour, that, whether present or absent, we may be accepted of him. For we must all appear before the judgment seat of Christ.' And then he ends with this tremendous statement – the fact is, he says, 'the love of Christ constraineth us' (2 Corinthians 5:9–10, 14). 'Constraineth' is a great word. Apparently the original word, in its root meaning, is this: You put something into a vice and you screw it up and it gets tighter and tighter, and the pressure from the two sides becomes greater and greater. That is the idea – 'the love of Christ' – this constraint, this pressure. Paul is like a man in a vice: I do not decide, I do not get trained, I must, I am bound to . . .

Now that comes out everywhere in all these examples and illustrations in the New Testament, and the big principle, therefore, is this: The difference between the cults and the Christian is the difference between something that is put on from the outside and something that comes from the inside. Adherents of the cults are people who belong to the flesh and behave accordingly. They think after the flesh, they act after the flesh. Not so the Christian. There is in the Christian something compelling, something driving, something urgent, a kind of dynamo. Our words 'dynamo' and 'dynamic' derive from the Greek word for power. There is a dynamism within Christians, something that is operating inside. And this Samaritan woman shows it all to perfection. What is driving her? Oh, it is this inward constraint, this dynamic element; it is this force, and this power of the truth that has become hers.

And as we read the history of the Christian church in general throughout the running centuries, and as we read it in particular in the lives of individuals, we always find this same element: ordinary, simple people talking about the gospel. We are told that Communism spread in a similar way. Communism is not spread by public meetings; it is spread in a more subtle and thorough manner by conversation. A man on a bench talks to his colleagues on the right and on the left, and so it spreads. 'Cellular infiltration' it is called.

And as Christianity spread mainly like that at the beginning, so it has spread many, many times since in periods of revival. Even when the church has been persecuted, people have been born again and they have just talked to one another. And so the gospel has spread from one to the other. In other words, I say again that the whole idea of training people to witness is quite foreign to the New Testament, as it is to the whole history of the Christian church. That belongs to the realm of the cults, the false, the spurious, the human. Of course, human beings by nature have to operate in this way, it is their only way. They always multiply their organizations and institutions; they are bound to. But it is foreign to the church's method; she has something infinitely greater. So the whole idea of 'training' people to witness, giving them the formulae and the phrases, telling them steps and numbers, and especially making them pass an examination afterwards, and then giving them a certificate and commissioning them is ridiculous and laughable from the standpoint of the New Testament and the history of the Christian church.

But even worse, even more serious, is the fact that this approach shows a failure to rely upon the power of the Holy Spirit. There is something ludicrous about this age in which we live. It is astonishing that modern people never ask the most obvious question with regard to all these matters: How did Christianity spread in the past? How did Christian people behave in former ages? If only they asked that question, they would save themselves a lot of trouble, and avoid many serious pitfalls. Instead, we have all become psychologists and must be trained psychologically to talk about Christianity.

Now I have often said this before – the salesman has to pass through a training course. He cannot be a salesman if he has not had the appropriate psychological training. How do you think the people of the last century, and many centuries before, built up their businesses? According to the modern idea, they could never have built up a business, they could never have succeeded. How could they sell goods? They had never been trained in salesmanship, they had never been drilled, they had never been told that if such a question comes, then this is the reply. And the answer is perfectly clear – and if it is clear in the realm of business and of secular affairs, how much more so is it in the realm of these spiritual matters with which we are dealing?

'Are you saying,' says someone, 'that the Christian does not need any training, therefore?'

No, no! But I am saying that he does not need any teaching or training in techniques and methods; he does not need that. The woman of Samaria did not get it, the early Christians did not have it. They were very successful and effective, and their results were more lasting than the modern methods that get you an immediate result that does not last. The early Christians had something more important.

What, then, do we need to be taught? We need to be taught about him; we need to get to know him; we need to be taught the truth as it is in Christ Jesus. That is where the training and the teaching come in. This, again, is the testimony of the New

Testament and of history. The best workers in the Christian church, those who have been greatly used in winning others for Christ, have always been those who have been best, not in techniques, not in a carnal zeal, but in their knowledge and understanding of the truth; they have been those with the profoundest experience.

Experience is of the very essence in this matter. It is the man or woman who has experience who can help others. They can understand, they can sympathize, they can be patient. The life in them enables them. The best workers are, eventually, those who are living the best kind of life. The world soon sees through false Christians, who are glib with their words, perhaps, but whose lives do not bear witness to the words. At first people are taken in – what is offered seems glamorous and wonderful; that is why the cults are successful. But when they apply the test of time, people begin to see through the talk.

Do you know what is the supreme necessity in order to be a witness for Christ and to bring others to him? It is to be filled with the Holy Spirit. That is the secret of the early Christians, as it has been the secret of Christians who have been most used in this respect through the running centuries. It is at times of revival that people always do so magnificently what the woman of Samaria did. The secret, the key, is the Spirit within us, enlightening the mind and moving the heart, giving wisdom and understanding, leading and directing. The New Testament is full of this. For instance, take the case of the evangelist Philip. We read that after he had done his work in Samaria: 'The angel of the Lord spake unto Philip, saying, Arise, and go toward the south . . .' It was an angel who sent him. And then after Philip had arrived on the road, he saw the Ethiopian eunuch, and the Spirit said, 'Go near, and join thyself to this chariot' (Acts 8:26, 29). The Spirit is the teacher. The Spirit is the guide and director. Any drilling that is done is done by the Holy Spirit; it is his constraint. It is always the Holy Spirit.

You see, my friends, if our object were just to get adherents to a cause or a cult or to a teaching, then tabloid training is all right; but we are not dealing with that, we are in the realm of life. This eventually includes being born again and formulae cannot give new birth to anybody. Someone can persuade you to join a movement, logic can get you to buy a commodity on your doorstep or join a political party or a cult. You listen to the arguments. 'Ah, yes,' you say, 'I've never thought of that before,' and you take it up. But that is not Christianity! You do not 'take this up' you are taken up by it. This involves being born again, born of the Spirit. It is the mighty activity of the Holy Spirit of God himself.

So I deduce from all that, this great principle – that anything that attributes results to particular methods is of necessity wrong. It is a very serious statement to make, but it needs to be made in the light of certain modern tendencies. Anything that attributes success to the methods employed is not truly Christian because everything that happens in this realm must be attributed solely to the operation of the Holy Spirit of God. To rely on methods is therefore wrong. Of course, we must have elasticity, we must use all our faculties rightly, we must do all we can, but we must never rely on these things.

Now you see how important this is for you and for me? Do you have the power of the Holy Spirit in you? It is no use our shielding ourselves behind this teaching, and saying, 'Of course, these people who belong to the cults are all wrong, I can see that.' That is all right, but the question then is: What about us? Is there anything moving us? I would sooner, in a sense, the person who witnesses mechanically than the person who does nothing and who is not aware of any compulsion, and has none of this spontaneity that sent the woman hurrying back to the city. Here is the vital and the positive question: Do I know this inward constraint, this 'love of Christ constraining me', that makes me say, 'Woe is unto me, if I preach not the gospel' (1 Corinthians 9:16); necessity is laid upon me, I must, I am bound to?

There, then, is the first great principle – it is a spontaneous action. But that compels us to ask a further question: Why does this action arise spontaneously in this woman? She has lived in that city, leading this wretched kind of life, and everybody knows the sort of woman she is, so why does she now rush back and give this invitation? Why does she act in this manner? There are a number of answers. I cannot deal with them all now, so I will just mention one or two.

The first is this: it is because of what she has found. It is because she is a new woman; she has been changed. We have considered that. But now I want to emphasize that it is because of what she has found. The Christian is not a mere seeker and searcher after the truth. That is the modern idea. You can hear this whenever you like on the television. It is very clever. People discuss theories and ideas, they debate philosophies, they drag in the Russian novelists, of the last century particularly, and it is all so wonderful: we are seeking, searching after the truth. Nonsense! The Christian is not a 'seeker'; the Christian is one who has found. 'Come, see a man . . .' Or, as Andrew and Philip put it: 'We have found' – that is the invitation – 'the Messias, which is, being interpreted, the Christ' (John 1:41). Philip says the same thing: 'We have found him, of whom Moses in the law, and the prophets, did write, Jesus of Nazareth, the son of Joseph' (John 1:45). Oh, my dear friends, here is the great thing; once you have 'found', you want others to know.

I would keep you for a moment with this question: Have you found him? If you have not, of course you have nothing to say.

'Can the blind lead the blind?' asks our Lord on a famous occasion. No, he says, 'shall they not both fall into the ditch?' (Luke 6:39). The blind cannot lead the blind. No, no! Christians are men and women who have found, they have something to give, they are not merely seeking. How can you help others if you do not have anything yourself? What is the use of going to somebody else and saying, 'Well, I see that you're interested in the truth and you're seeking and searching after it; so am I. We must go on, you know. There's a great book coming out next week and I'm hoping to get something out of that . . .' What is the value of that to somebody who is in need and in trouble?

No, by definition, Christians have got something, they have got something to say. The woman of Samaria would not have left her waterpot and rushed into the city and addressed the people unless she had something to say to them; and what she says is: 'Come, see this man: this is the Christ – you are bound to agree with me that he is.' She has found, she has arrived, and this is always the first element. It acts in a dynamic manner in every true Christian. It is inconceivable that anybody who has found in this sense can remain silent. But this does account, does it not, for so much failure in many Christians or in those who regard themselves as Christians.

So the great question we must all ask ourselves is this: Have we got something to give to people who are in need? I may have put it like this to you before but it does not matter if I have – it is worth repeating because it brings this point home to us. I like to think of it like this. Imagine that tonight, when you are in your home, somebody knocks at your door or rings the bell. You go to the door, and there you find a messenger. What is the message? Well, it is a request, an appeal, from a man whom you have known for years, perhaps you have known him since you were children together. Unfortunately, poor fellow, he has gone wrong in life, he has lived a godless life, and yet you somehow liked him. Whenever you met him, you were glad to see him and you always spoke to him, and you often tried to urge him to come with you to listen to the gospel. But he would not come, he laughed it off, as such people so often do.

Now here is the message – this afternoon that poor fellow had a sudden heart attack and he is desperately ill; in fact, he is dying. The doctor can do no more for him. He has told the family, and this man realizes that, he can see it in their faces. And suddenly he has come to himself. He sees that his life is finished and he is going to the unknown and to darkness. He has nothing – nothing to lean on in his past life, nothing to lean on in the present. Nobody can help him, he is absolutely alone, as we all shall be sooner or later, as our soul passes from time to eternity and into the presence of God. He does not know what to do or where to turn, he is in an agony of soul. But suddenly he has thought of you because – well, he thinks of you as a Christian and as a member of a church because you have invited him to go with you to church. So he has sent for you – that is the message. Now then, of course, you have no choice, you must go. And when you arrive in the room, there is your friend lying on his back in bed.

And this is the test as to whether or not we are Christians. Have you got something you can give him that will make all the difference in the world to him? Now I need not waste your time, but what is the point of telling this man that you are also a seeker and a searcher after the truth – he will be dead before midnight? What is the point of saying to him, 'I hope that my sins are going to be forgiven some time, I'm doing my best, I'm living a good life'? Does that help him? That puts him into hell while he is still alive. Or what does it help him if you turn to him and say,

'Well, now, of course, at last you see it. How many times have I told you that the life you were living was wrong? If only you had lived as I live!' What is the value of that? That is sheer cruelty. That, again, is putting him in hell while he is still alive. It is of no value at all.

No, no; that is not the Christian way. Christians are not seeking truth or seeking forgiveness; they are not trying to make themselves Christians by living good lives; they are not merely church members. What are they? Well, in the end, it just comes to this: they are men and women who, like the woman of Samaria, have met Christ, the Son of God. They are able to tell this poor fellow that it is not too late, that it is not hopeless, that no one is justified by their works or by their lives, that we are all sinners and that there is no ultimate difference between us at all, but that this is the message: 'God so loved the world, that he gave his only begotten Son, that whosoever [even he] believeth in him should not perish, but have everlasting life' (John 3:16).

Christians can tell this man, not about their own experience so much, but about Jesus Christ. There is no time to give experiences, there is no time to go through your drill and mechanically quote this or that: all they say is this, 'Jesus Christ'! They just tell the dying man about him, who he is, what he has done. And that is the only way whereby this man can be helped, whereby he can find peace and rest for his soul.

Christians have this knowledge, they have this information, and, as Paul puts it to the Romans, they are able to 'impart' it. 'I long to see you,' he says, 'that I may impart unto you . . .' (Romans 1:11) – pass it on, 'hand it over', 'tell you about', 'gossip it'. So often we are not concerned about others simply because we have nothing to say to them. But if we know this, how can we possibly refrain from telling others about it?

53

# *Rejoicing in Christ*

*The woman then left her waterpot, and went her way into the city, and saith to the men, Come, see a man, which told me all things that ever I did: is not this the Christ? Then they went out of the city, and came unto him. (John 4:28–30)*

We have been considering together the fact that the woman of Samaria does not have to be trained to give her witness, or trained to do 'personal work'; she witnesses automatically, almost instinctively. I am very concerned to stress this principle. This activity of the Christian should always come from within. It should not be imposed upon us as a duty. We should not have to be drilled and then almost dragooned into doing it. If that is our condition, there is something seriously wrong with us. The whole glory of this activity, as we find in the Scriptures, and still more, perhaps, in the subsequent history of the church, is the spontaneity. This is a great principle.

Having dealt with that, we began in our last study to consider a second question, which is this: Why does the Samaritan woman behave in this spontaneous, instinctive manner? I have given one answer, and that is that she patently has something to give. That is the first great reason. But let us continue with this question. What else do you think has moved this woman? Why has she left her waterpot, a deliberate action, to go to the city and say, 'Come, see a man . . .'? Now the very way in which she puts it, of course, gives us our second explanation – it is her realization of the uniqueness and the glory of this person. Here, again, is a most important point. All these points help us to understand what is so wrong with the Christian church at the present time – it is that all our emphases have gone wrong. But here they can be corrected for us.

The woman of Samaria is motivated by the greatness and the glory and the uniqueness of this person she has just met. This is something we can illustrate from the natural level. If ever you are in contact with some great person, you are not only impressed, but you also want everybody to know about your meeting. If ever you have had an audience with the Queen, you will not have had to be trained how to tell people. Nobody will have had to urge you to tell others. The difficulty, in a sense, is to control your telling, and you may become a bore because you keep on repeating the details. That is natural, it is instinctive. Multiply that by infinity and you begin to understand the reaction of the woman of Samaria.

So many of our troubles arise because we forget the objectivity of our faith; we are too subjective. We dwell in the realm of experience, we emphasize experience – I will be doing this myself – we must stress experience. But the order of these matters is what is important, and we must always keep in the forefront the objectivity, the person. This emphasis is characteristic of the great eighteenth-century hymns:

O happy bond, that seals my vows
To him who merits all my love.
*Philip Doddridge*

It is typical, too, of the New Testament. Take, for instance, the apostle Paul's constant exhortation to people to 'rejoice'. But you notice how he always puts it – 'Rejoice in the Lord alway: and again I say, Rejoice' (Philippians 4:4). Paul is not exhorting the Philippian Christians to try to create within themselves some feeling of happiness, quite the opposite. But many people do that; in meetings, they try to work up the congregation with preliminary singing, making a direct assault upon the feelings. That is not the Christian method – 'Rejoice *in the Lord*.'

In other words, you can rejoice at all times, whatever your feelings or mood; whatever your circumstances, you can be a rejoicing Christian. How? By rejoicing 'in the Lord'. You do not look into yourself, you look at him. And if you look at him, and realize who he is and what he has done, then you will be filled, if you are a Christian, with a spirit of rejoicing.

And that is what has happened in the case of this woman. It is the person and her realization of who he is and what he is and the glory of his being that has moved her and created within her the desire that the people in her town should also have the privilege of seeing him and listening to him. I have to stress this because, in many ways, the most important thing of all is the realization that he is who and what he is, and that he is there outside us, beyond us, in the glory. Of course, he is in us, as Christians, as well, but we start with the grand and glorious objective truth. The Christian, ultimately, is a person who realizes that the most important event that has ever happened in this world is the coming of the Son of God into it.

By nature, we human beings are all interested in history, but our history books have tended to be nothing but an account of kings and great generals and captains and so on. There is a sense in which all this is all right. I still maintain that that is true history and that this 'modern history' is not true history at all. The great things in this world have been done by great people and our troubles today are due to the fact that we no longer have such people. So let us try to understand our history anew and afresh, and let us accept, then, that that is a true way of looking at history, and it is right that these great people should stand out. But Christian men and women are people who, while they subscribe to all that, say that the event of events was the birth of the babe at Bethlehem. If you are interested in people, says the Christian, great and glorious people, here is one who stands alone.

Now the uniqueness and glory of our Lord, surely, ought to be self-evident to us. It is everywhere in the New Testament. As is often pointed out, the book of the Acts of the Apostles is merely the book of the acts of the Lord Jesus Christ. 'The former treatise have I made, O Theophilus,' says Luke, 'of all that Jesus began both to do and to teach' (Acts 1:1), and now Luke is going on to tell Theophilus what Jesus continued to do and to teach. Our Lord dominated the life of the apostles. He dominated the thinking of the apostle Paul – 'That I may know him' (Philippians 3:10).

While Christians, therefore, are interested in all secular history, and in all that man has done and can do and has produced, they say that what matters is that our Lord came out of the glory: 'When the fulness of the time was come, God sent forth his Son, made of a woman, made under the law, to redeem them that were under the law' (Galatians 4:4–5). This was the climactic, crucial event in the history of the world and consequently Christian people now see everything in terms of Jesus Christ. They do not say 1968 glibly, they say it in a new way. Everybody says 1968 but not as Christians do; they look back at history. They also look at the present, they look to the future, and they see everything in the light of Christ. Christ has divided history for them, as he has divided everything else. He determines and he controls the whole of life.

Now here is another point against which we must test ourselves and one another. As we talk with people about present circumstances, as we look upon life in the past and as we look to the future, is our Lord prominent in our thinking and do we tell others that here is the sole explanation of our world, here is the guarantee of the future? The Son of God has been in this world, '[God] hath visited and redeemed his people' (Luke 1:68) in the person of his own Son. Nothing else comes anywhere near this momentous event.

The question we must therefore ask ourselves is this: Is the whole of our thinking dominated by the Lord Jesus Christ? Over and above all we have known and experienced, is our chief glory the fact of the Son of God, that Jesus is the Son of God? Are we taken out of ourselves in this respect, and are we amazed and filled with a sense of wonder and of glory at the person of Christ?

Work this out for yourselves. As we have seen, we cannot read the New Testament without being aware that everything is constantly pointing to him. This is where Christianity is essentially different from the cults. They are always turning you in on yourself: 'Are you happy? Are you sleeping? Have you got good health?' It is always *you*. But with Christianity, we start by looking at him, and if we are not doing that, then we must be careful that we are not using the Christian message in a kind of cultic manner. No, we start with the blessed person, this one whom we have met, this one who has entered into history and into our lives, this one who has made everything different and new. 'Come, see a man who has done this amazing thing.'

There, then, is the second great explanation of this woman's actions. But having said that, I come to a more personal experiential level. We must always keep a balance. Some people seem to be almost entirely subjective, others entirely objective, in their thinking and they are both wrong. The Christian truth is both, that is the glory of it. It starts with great objective facts and truths and events – a person. But it is not only that, it is not merely theoretical and academic and intellectual. No, no; Christianity is experiential, it is practical, it is living, it is vital, and if we do not combine these two aspects, then at the very best, we have a poor kind of imbalanced, lopsided Christianity. This must be corrected. We must test ourselves at all these points.

So, then, what has our Lord done for the woman of Samaria? It is for us to analyse her. You can manifest our Lord's work in your life and exemplify it, without fully understanding it, but as you go on in the Christian life, you are able to analyse. You do so in the light of the scriptural teaching, and you very soon see what has really been happening. What has this woman found? Well, first, she has found authority. This is something that everybody is looking for. We are in a world that is full of troubles, full of difficulties and perplexities. We are surrounded by a veritable babble of voices, all of them telling us that they know the answer – we have only to listen to them and to follow them and all will be well with us. But we try them one after the other and never get satisfaction. And we come to realize that we are listening to human voices, and none of them speaks with authority. They have an assumed and spurious authority, which we begin to see through because we realize that they have not found the answer themselves. They are failures in their own lives and do not know it.

Now I need not elaborate too much on this, but the question of authority is a most urgent problem in the world at the present time. Some of the greatest dangers in the world today and some of the greatest disasters in the past, including in the immediate past, have all arisen out of the desire for authority. When there are troubles, people always look for an authoritative statement, an authoritative leader. That is why perhaps the greatest danger at a time like this is the danger of dictatorship. Certainly that was the sole explanation of Hitlerism. Hitler came into power in Germany because of the troubles and the difficulties facing his country. The politicians had been trying; they were honest men and they had done their best, but they could not solve the country's problems. Suddenly a man stood up and said, 'I know! Listen to me. Follow me.' And instinctively they followed him. They wanted authority, they wanted a voice.

Now this need for authority has also largely been the explanation of the success of Roman Catholicism and of the cults. The world is longing for some authoritative statement, someone to listen to, someone to follow who seems to have knowledge. There is nothing wrong in this; it is inevitable because of our whole estate as the result of the Fall. This need is in all of us and when we meet this authoritative word that we are looking for, at once we listen and are ready to follow.

This undoubtedly happened to this poor woman. We have seen the state of her life, it is familiar to you. She has been living a miserable existence and nobody has been able to help her. But at last she meets somebody who seems to understand, who speaks with authority. She is interested in the question of worship and of religion. 'Our father', she says, 'worshipped in this mountain; and ye say, that in Jerusalem . . .' and she goes on talking and arguing. But a point comes when she is silent; here is one who knows and he says so. 'Ye worship ye know not what,' he says, 'we know what we worship: for salvation is of the Jews' (John 4:22). She has met authority, someone whom she feels she can follow.

And as we read the pages of the four Gospels, we find that this note of authority stands out constantly. Have you not been amazed at this? Take the call of the disciples. There are Peter and

Andrew fishing, and James and John with their father in their boat mending the nets, doing their work as usual. Suddenly this person appears and says, 'Follow me,' and they just leave everything and go after him (Mark 1:16–20). And we read, 'As Jesus passed forth from thence, he saw a man, named Matthew, sitting at the receipt of custom' (Matthew 9:9) – a tax collector dong his job, thinking nothing. Suddenly this person comes along and says, 'Follow me,' and Matthew gets up and follows him. What is this? This is authority, this quality that men and women are instinctively drawn to in their lost condition, the authority that they have been looking for.

And, of course, the people recognized our Lord's authority. At the end of the Sermon on the Mount, when our Lord had finished speaking, we are told: 'And it came to pass, when Jesus had ended these sayings, the people were astonished at his doctrine: for he taught them as one having authority, and not as the scribes' (Matthew 7:28–29). This was the inevitable comment. We see there a very interesting contrast. How did the scribes teach? Well, they were always quoting authorities, but here *is* authority. What a difference there is between 'quoting authorities' and 'speaking authoritatively'. One of the troubles in the church today is that people are quoting authorities: What does Tillich say? What does Barth say? And Bultmann? But there is no authority. Humanity longs for this word, this authoritative word, this assured word, and the only person who can give it to us is this blessed person who has met the woman of Samaria. So she now invites her fellow townspeople to come and meet with him and hear what he has to say.

And, thank God, our Lord has given his Holy Spirit, and he can give him in great profusion and power. When he does that, he can cause even a human being to be steeped with authority.

This is what he has done in the people whom he has raised up throughout the centuries in reformation and revival. The world recognized the power of the Holy Spirit in the people, the church recognized it in a measure, and others recognized it, too. A note of authority came from Martin Luther. You can only explain him in that one way. It was the authority that the Lord gave to him through the Holy Spirit.

But here is the next question: Why do we need this authority? What is it in us, in detail, that looks for it and cries out for it? The answers to this question are almost endless. I shall only throw out some suggestions and some hints for you to work out for yourselves. What do we need from authority? First, we need rest of mind, do we not? The mind is restless and curious, the mind seeks satisfaction. That is the whole meaning of philosophy; it is men and women trying to arrive at an understanding of everything, 'arriving at truth', as they put it. Confronted by themselves and the whole problem of life and of the world, of existence and of history, people say, 'Is there any sense in it? Is there any meaning, any explanation? What is it all about? What will it all lead to? The mind is looking and searching, but it cannot find any answers and is restless. But here at last is one who can give rest to the mind and bring the questings to an end. Of course, our Lord was always claiming this. He says: 'I am the light of the world: he that followeth me shall not walk in darkness, but shall have the light of life' (John 8:12). 'I am the way, the truth, and the life: no man cometh unto the Father, but by me' (John 14:6).

What do we want to know? We want to know God. The whole world has been seeking after him. There is not a race of people but that they have this vague sense of some supreme Being. As Paul put it to the Athenians, 'If haply they might feel after him, and find him' (Acts 17:27) – this search for 'the unknown God'. Humanity instinctively feels that there is someone beyond it all. But we cannot find him. 'Canst thou by searching find out God?' asks Job (Job 11:7). No, we cannot. But here is one who can bring us to that very knowledge. We find it in the prologue of this very Gospel: 'No man hath seen God at any time' – so is there no hope? Yes, there is – 'the only begotten Son, which is in the bosom of the Father, he hath declared him' (John 1:18). This is the answer. He alone can do it. We have had speculation, but speculation does not satisfy us because we know it is speculation. And though people may speculate with arrogance and human self-confidence, we know there is nothing in it, it is only their opinion and it will change soon, as all these opinions constantly do. No, there is only one who has authority and John's prologue tells us who he is.

But then our Lord put it still more plainly, you remember, to Nicodemus: 'Jesus answered and said unto him, Art thou a master of Israel, and knowest not these things?' Nicodemus was one of the authorities, a teacher, a very great teacher and a great man, but he did not know. There were limits, as there always are, so our Lord addressed him as 'a master of Israel', but then went on:

> *Verily, verily, I say unto thee, We speak that we do know, and testify that we have seen; and ye receive not our witness. If I have told you earthly things, and ye believe not, how shall ye believe, if I tell you of heavenly things? And no man hath ascended up to heaven, but he that came down from heaven, even the Son of man which is in heaven.*
> *(John 3:10–13)*

Here is authority. Here is an answer about God. Here is one who has looked eternally into the face of God and has come down to tell us about him and to lead us into the blessed knowledge. And

so our Lord gives this immediate rest of mind, and this is one of
the most wonderful things that one can ever receive. You are no
longer bewildered about life, and about yourself, and about your
destiny. You have answers to these great questions – he has given
them. So you say with the writer of the hymn:

> O Christ, in thee my soul hath found,
> And found in thee alone,
> The peace, the rest I sought so long,
> The bliss till now unknown.
>
> *Author unknown*

This is the answer. Or you remember how Charles Wesley puts it
when, just at the time of his own conversion, he cries:

> O! when shall all my strivings cease?

But they did. He found this intellectual peace, this rest of mind,
and the fact is – and this is what we claim – all knowledge is in
him, and it is all here in this book. This does not mean that we
understand it all, but it is all here. There is a complete philosophy
of life here, there is nothing left without explanation. It is all here;
it is in the mind of God. Again, the apostle Paul is able to make
that astounding asseveration, 'We have the mind of Christ' (1
Corinthians 2:16) and we are entering more and more into the full
and complete understanding that he gives.

But, thank God, our Lord does not stop at giving us rest of
mind and peace in the intellect; we find exactly the same peace in
our conscience. The conscience is in even greater trouble, is it not?
The more we know about God, the more our conscience troubles
us, because God knows all things. 'If our heart condemn us,' says
John, 'God is greater than our heart' (1 John 3:20). The writer of
the Epistle to the Hebrews says, 'All things are naked and opened

unto the eyes of him with whom we have to do' (Hebrews 4:13), and every one of us knows this. However ignorant we may be of God, there is a conscience in every one of us. We cannot get rid of it and it goes on troubling us more and more so that we long for peace of conscience, rest of conscience.

The human race has been seeking and striving after peace of conscience. We have a sense of guilt, a sense of unworthiness, a sense of shame, and the great question is: How can this be satisfied? How can this be answered? Much human activity is explained solely in terms of the quest for this peace. The world, of course, has its glib and easy answers, but they do not satisfy us. People try to forget their consciences: they rush into pleasure, or take drugs or turn to the teaching of the cults. In these ways they find a kind of temporary satisfaction, but always the great ultimate question arises, and there they are alone, facing the Judge eternal, and they do not know what they can do about it.

This is the essence of Christianity, is it not? Christian men and women know that they find peace of conscience in one place only, and that is in this one person only, this same blessed person who was speaking to the woman of Samaria. Here is the only one who can say, 'Come unto me, *all ye that labour and are heavy laden*, and I will give you rest' (Matthew 11:28). What are you labouring at? Labouring to make yourself righteous; labouring to atone for your past sins; labouring to make yourself fit to stand in the presence of God? Labouring and heavy laden – the load of your sins. And you are striving and sweating and fasting and praying. You are doing all you can, and the more you do, the more you see his holiness and your own unworthiness. You are at the end of your tether, your conscience is thundering at you and nothing you do can silence it.

But then you meet this blessed Saviour, this blessed person, you hear this sweet invitation, and you feel he is speaking with authority, he knows what he is saying. He says, 'The Son of man came not to be ministered unto, but to minister, and to give his life a ransom for many' (Matthew 20:28). He speaks a parable such as the parable of the Prodigal Son, and there is authority again. He knows, he speaks and acts with assurance and certainty. And the end of it is that believing him and his message, you find that you have peace with God. 'Therefore being justified by faith, we have peace with God' (Romans 5:1). This is the outstanding thing: you know it, you feel it instinctively now, your conscience is cleared, you enjoy peace.

Let me quote another verse from Romans: 'There is therefore now no condemnation to them which are in Christ Jesus' (Romans 8:1). No condemnation! Why? Because we have an explanation, a satisfactory explanation. It is not that God is merely saying, 'I have forgiven you,' but that he has done something. He has made a way of forgiveness. And the Bible tells us how we can be sure. The Scriptures expound to us the whole blessed doctrine of the atonement. This is argued out by Paul in the third chapter of Romans. God is just, says Paul, 'and the justifier of him which believeth in Jesus' (Romans 3:26). God does not set aside the Law, he honours the Law, he fulfils it. God's own Son 'his own self bare our sins in his own body on the tree' (1 Peter 2:24). God 'has made him to be sin for us, who knew no sin; that we might be made the righteousness of God in him' (2 Corinthians 5:21). So we know that our sins are forgiven, and knowing that, we have peace and rest in our consciences. This is the most blessed knowledge that we can ever have. It is only the Christian who knows it. This woman of Samaria has felt it. She does not fully understand it, but our Lord has not only revealed to her every sin 'that ever I did', but she knows he is also able to deal with her sins. Though he condemns, he heals.

And then we go on to the next point, which is this: beyond any question, this woman is aware of new life within herself.

Forgiveness alone is not enough; we need new life. Look at her; look at the kind of life she has been living, that has produced the misery, the social ostracism, probably. But having met this person, she not only knows she is forgiven, she is aware of a new kind of life. This is it, is it not? You cannot be a Christian without this new life. A Christian is someone who is born again – born of the Spirit, born from above. This woman is aware that she has new desires within her, a desire for a new type of life, not that old life she has been living. She did not know any better then, and she did not have the desire for anything better. But now she has looked into the face of purity, everlasting purity, the holiness of God in the face of Jesus Christ, and she has a desire within her for purity and cleanliness, chastity, a holiness that she has never known of before. And, still more important, she is aware of the fact that this is possible for her.

It is very difficult for us, is it not, to realize the fullness of this woman's feelings at this point, but this is Christian testimony, this is the experience of the saints throughout the centuries. The miracle is that a woman who has lived this kind of life, who has had five husbands and is now living with someone who is not her husband, as she confessed to our Lord, that such a woman not only wants to be out of all that and to live a new life, but knows it can be done. It does not need much imagination to know that she has often become so miserable in that old life that she has longed to get out of it. She has tried, she has made resolutions, she has made efforts, but she has always gone back. Try to extricate yourself from any one of the things that grip you, and you cannot do it.

Now the amazing truth is that the effect of meeting Jesus Christ is that he not only creates within you the desire to be different, but he also gives you the feeling that you can be. He transmits something of his own purity and his own strength and his own power to you so that you have the blessed feeling that it can be done. And so you feel you can trust him, you can trust to his protection and to his guardian care. He puts into you, somehow, unconsciously, this feeling of a new strength, a new understanding, and a new power that will enable you to live this new and glorious life to which he has opened your eyes.

But our Lord goes beyond that; he gives you a new view of life itself and of your own future. You see opening before you a new kind of existence. You are no longer dependent upon the world, its excitements, its pleasures, its opinions and its comings and goings. You are aware that though you are still in this world, you do not belong to it; you see through it and beyond it. You find you are living as a stranger, your citizenship is in heaven. You feel at once that you belong to a new realm, that God has delivered you 'from the power of darkness, and hath translated [us] into the kingdom of his dear Son' (Colossians 1:13), you know this.

Now you do not fully understand all this – you go on to understand it. He has cleansed your past, you have certainty in the present, and now you look to the future without terror, without alarm. And, remember, this includes death and the grave, the last enemy. Christians already have their conquest; they are no longer terrified of illness or of death or of the grave. They can look at it and say:

> *O death, where is thy sting? O grave, where is thy victory? The sting of death is sin; and the strength of sin is the law. But thanks be to God, which giveth us the victory through our Lord Jesus Christ. (1 Corinthians 13:55–57)*

Read for yourselves the fifteenth chapter of the Gospel according to St Luke because three times over our Lord makes this very point. You see there, in a sense, the difference between the Christian and the Pharisee. Both the Christian and the religious person can be measured entirely by this note of joy. You may be religious, but if you are, it will be self-contained, there will not be much joy about it. Like the Pharisees, you have to spend the whole of your time in 'being religious', trying to please God, hemming yourself around. You have no contact with other people, you have nothing to tell them. You are so busy putting yourself right and safeguarding what you have, that you have nothing to give, and so you do not give. You are not happy yourself and you do not want to make other people happy. That is very different from the woman of Samaria and from the true Christian, always.

In Luke 15, by contrast, we read how the woman lost her coin and then found it: 'Come,' she says – she invites her neighbours. 'Rejoice with me.' The shepherd who loses his sheep. He searches for it and finds it. Back he goes and says, 'Come. Rejoice with me.' And the father who has found his son again – or whose son has come back to him – says, 'Put the best robe on him, kill the fatted calf, invite the neighbours, let's have a feast. Come.' Of course, the elder brother, the religious man, does not approve of this. He has no joy, and he sees no occasion for rejoicing. But the moment one really understands these things there is this dynamic element. Those who are truly Christian must rejoice, and they want everybody to rejoice with them. That is what happens to this woman.

And so the final test we apply to ourselves in this connection is just that: Has the Lord Jesus Christ made you rejoice? Has he filled you with a spirit of praise? You can be a great theologian but have no joy. You can be very religious but without joy. You can be very moral but is there joy? Joy is the particular mark of the Christian. 'Rejoice in the Lord alway: and again I say, Rejoice' (Philippians 4:4). There is no better test of our knowledge of our Lord, and of what we claim he has done for us, than the extent of our joy and our rejoicing in him and in what he has done for our souls.

## 54

# *The Need and the Cure*

*The woman then left her waterpot, and went her way into the city, and saith to the men, Come, see a man, which told me all things that ever I did: is not this the Christ? Then they went out of the city, and came unto him. (John 4:28–30)*

In these verses, we have seen how the woman of Samaria was moved spontaneously to fetch her fellow townspeople to come and see the Lord. We have shown that it was the person of our Lord himself and her joy in her encounter with him that made her do this. But that is not all, there are still further reasons, further motives, that impel her to behave in this way, and we must examine ourselves in their light.

But first I want once more to put my general question: Do you find yourself like this woman? That is the point. We are not just looking at her in some kind of detached manner, interested in psychology, in phenomena. No, no; the whole point of this incident is that it examines us and searches us. Are we behaving as this woman behaved? Is the response that she made to the Lord also our response? Do we know something of her spontaneity? Are we moved by her motives?

So I come to the next characteristic of the woman of Samaria, which is that she obviously has a great concern for the people of her town. Her first reaction, once she is aware of all this within herself, is immediately to think of them. Once more, you will all agree, this is always true in the natural realm. When we derive some great benefit, this is the way we tend to behave – we do not even think about it. We saw this kind of response in the three parables in Luke 15. But, now, not only do we want people to rejoice with us, it goes beyond that and we have a concern for others. Our natural concern for one another is greatly heightened when we become Christians because, as I shall show you, one of the first things that happens to us is that we cease to be entirely self-centred. We are more or less self-centred until we become Christians. The great trouble in the world is selfishness, self-centredness – *I*. It does not matter about anybody or anything else, it does not matter about your country, as long as you are all right. But the Christian is not like that.

There are two elements, I think, to the concern that the woman of Samaria feels, and that any Christian must feel about those who are not Christians. But, again, before I come to this double analysis, let me ask a question: Are you concerned about other people, about those who are not Christians? I am not asking if you denounce them or condemn them. The world can condemn, and it does. I am not asking if you are irritated by them, or horrified by the immorality and the vice and the slackness and all that is portrayed to us in the newspapers and on the television. That is not it. I am asking: Are you concerned about it? Does it trouble you? Are you concerned about the people who are in that condition?

Now this concern divides itself up into two elements. The first is that this woman has undoubtedly become concerned about the utter superficiality and the final futility of the lives of non-Christians. Here she is. We know the kind of life she has been living, a life of immorality. Now the world thinks that is wonderful. That is what it is boasting of today, is it not? This is the thing to do. You are a back number – what they call today a 'square', whatever that is – if you do not do these things. The world says that this is life. And I am not only talking about the life of the world when it lives as this poor woman has been living, I am thinking of the world at its very best, its highest. The Christian immediately sees the superficiality and the emptiness of it all in a final sense.

Now this is established and emphasized in many places in the teaching of the Scriptures. One of the first signs that one has become a Christian is that one sees through the world. Having been born into the world, we had been dominated by it, by its mind and outlook. Paul says in Ephesians 2:2: 'Wherein in time past ye walked according to the course of this world' – the worldly round, the 'thing to do', all that the world regards as thrilling, the reason why people brought up in the country long to get to London – 'the life of London'. Marvellous! If, as a Christian, you do not see through all this, then you had better examine your foundations again. You cannot be a Christian and go on regarding the world and its life as people of the world do; it is impossible. The Bible tells us:

*Love not the world, neither the things that are in the world. If any man love the world, the love of the Father is not in him. For all that is in the world, the lust of the flesh, and the lust of the eyes, and the pride of life, is not of the Father, but is of the world. And the world passeth away, and the lust thereof: but he that doeth the will of God abideth for ever. Little children, it is the last time . . . (1 John 2:15–18)*

Read those verses, study them and examine yourselves in their light. The Christian has seen through it all – the vanity, the emptiness. John was very concerned about this, so later in his epistle he says it again: 'For whatsoever is born of God overcometh the world: and this is the victory that overcometh the world, even our faith' (1 John 5:4). You see the contrast? These are opposites. The life of the Christian and the life of the world are opposed. The world is so organized as to be inimical to us and to our best interests. If you have not discovered that, you are not a Christian at all. The world does not even believe in the soul, it does not believe in God, it does not believe in an after life. Its sole concern is the present life, and people and what they do – their thrilling wonderful activities, which the world judges by its own standards.

Now I am anxious to make this clear, so I repeat that I am not only thinking of life as lived by this poor woman of Samaria, but am also thinking of it in its most cultivated and cultured aspects, all that the world regards as glittering. The kind of people who call themselves intellectual are sorry for us meeting like this on a Sunday morning. We ought to be reading the Sunday supplements, the criticisms of the books and the music. But Christian men and women see through the artificiality of all that. They see that even at its best there is no depth in it, no satisfaction; there is nothing for the soul.

Oh, you can have intellectual interests, you can be moved emotionally and in other respects, but it is all rather like an iridescent bubble. It looks very beautiful but you have to keep it going, and it demands energy. You are fascinated by it, but at any moment it can burst and you have nothing left. The world is all very largely a pose, an affectation. What is so pathetic is its superficiality. You see people affecting an interest in things that they do not really care about at all, putting on interest like a cloak or a mask in order to be able to have a wonderful conversation. That is what I mean by the superficiality of it all. It does not answer the profundities that are in human nature, for human beings, after all, have souls and cry out for something bigger, something deeper.

But you really see through the world when you come to a time of need or a crisis, and all that the world has does not help you at all. The sophistication will never give you comfort or ease, it will never give you rest, it always leaves you. The world always does that to us if we belong to it – you remember what it did to poor Judas Iscariot. He was a traitor to our Lord and he plotted with our Lord's enemies, and they were very kind and ingratiating. Then Judas, when he had betrayed our Lord, suddenly realized what he had done. He was sorry and went to them to tell them about it. But they said, 'What has that got to do with us? That's your business.' They abandoned him, left him to himself, and he committed suicide (Matthew 27:3–5). That is the world always. The world never gives you anything when you really need it.

That is what the poor Prodigal Son found, was it not? While he had his pockets full of money in that strange 'far country', of course, he had any number of friends. As long as you pay, the world will fawn upon you and praise you. But the famine came, his money was all spent, and he 'began to be in need'. You remember the pregnant phrase, 'and no man gave unto him' (Luke 15:16). Of course not! They were all out for themselves, those supposed friends, those well-wishers. And the world always does that. When you need it most, it has nothing to give you, it abandons you.

Now the Christian realizes this at once. The apostle Paul talks about 'the unfruitful works of darkness' (Ephesians 5:11) – and what a wonderful phrase that is. That kind of life is unprofitable, it never produces fruit. It has its immediate results but, as with drink and all these things, the effects wear off. The writer of the Epistle to the Hebrews talks about 'dead works' (Hebrews 6:1) and, again, what a marvellous phrase. Dead works; there is no life in them. It is all mechanical, it all has to be kept going, so you need money and organization.

But the Christian sees through that immediately. Our Lord says, 'For what shall it profit a man, if he shall gain the whole world, and lose his own soul? Or what shall a man give in exchange for his soul?' (Mark 8:36–37). That is the very essence of the Christian outlook. Christians look at the world as it is, at its best and highest as well as in the gutters where this poor woman lived. They look at it all and that is their question: 'What shall it profit a man, if he shall gain the whole world' – the wealth and the knowledge, the sophistication and the applause, everything the world prizes – 'and lose his own soul?' – this imperishable thing, this thing that belongs to God and is bigger than the whole universe; this thing that nothing but God can finally satisfy.

Our Lord puts this in another way, which shows us still more clearly the kind of feeling that this woman felt instinctively. We are told:

> *But when he saw the multitudes, he was moved with compassion on them, because they fainted, and were scattered abroad, as sheep having no shepherd. Then saith he unto his disciples, The harvest truly is plenteous, but the labourers are few; pray ye therefore the Lord of the harvest, that he will send forth labourers into his harvest.* (Matthew 9:36–38)

You see the picture; that was our Lord's view of humanity apart from him – fainting and as sheep without a shepherd. Now that description of sheep means the two things I have been mentioning. It means, first, that the people were not getting proper sustenance. One of the main functions of the shepherd is to lead the sheep into the green pastures. He knows where there is food, where there is pasture, so he leads them there and they follow him. But these people were fainting because they were not having proper food, like sheep without a shepherd. And that is the truth about the world today. All that it has to offer and of which it is so proud does not feed the soul, it leaves us fainting.

The second point is that a shepherd protected his sheep. There were dogs, marauding dogs, that came and attacked and harassed the sheep, and would even kill them at times. Having no shepherd, the sheep had no protection. In the same way, when life begins to attack you – illness or disease or old age – you are left on the scrapheap, you are left to yourself: 'No man gave unto him.'

So Christians see this; they see that this supposed marvellous life is the emptiest thing, it is just a bubble. 'For what is your life? It is even a vapour' (James 4:14). The same idea exactly. This is what this woman sees in a flash, as it were. She sees through the futility, the vanity of the life she used to live, and others are still living, and she wants them to see through it, too. We find this expressed constantly in our hymns:

> Fading is the worldling's pleasure
> All his boasted pomp and show;
> Solid joys and lasting treasure
> None but Zion's children know.
>
> *John Newton*

My dear friends, before we go any further, let me ask: Have you seen through the world? Have you really seen through what it offers and glories in? Have you seen its emptiness, its shallowness, its final futility? For the Christian, this is inevitable. Everywhere in the Bible there is the great contrast between the world and the people of God. That is the whole secret of the Old Testament saints, those mighty giants. That is the great argument, is it not, of Hebrews chapter 11. Why did those people live as they did? And the answer is that they saw through the world and were looking for 'a city which hath foundations, whose builder and maker is God' (Hebrews 11:10). That is why they forsook the world; that is why they became pilgrims and strangers, and travellers and sojourners; that is what made Abraham obey the call of God in Ur of the Chaldees; that is what made Moses renounce it all, at that critical point when, having been adopted by Pharaoh's daughter, he might have become the greatest man in Egypt. Instead, he joined himself to these slave people, the Hebrews, to whom he belonged. 'He had respect unto the recompence of the reward . . . as seeing him who is invisible' (Hebrews 11:26–27). He saw through all that the world had to offer because he saw it in the light of that which belongs to God.

There, then, is the first element in this woman's concern about these other people. But there is another factor that in a way is still more important – she not only sees through the emptiness and the futility of their lives, she sees the danger of their position, and this is where the element of urgency always comes in. You cannot become a Christian without realizing at once that the non-Christian is in a very dangerous position. Again, this applies on a natural level. As soon as you realize that somebody is unknowingly in danger, you warn them. You give them the necessary information. You say, 'Look here, perhaps I shouldn't be doing this but I must tell you, I'm concerned about you. I'm warning you – be careful.' And you tell them that this and this and that is happening or is going to take place. It is quite natural, is it not?

How much greater should be our concern about the precariousness, indeed, the extreme danger, of people's situation in the spiritual realm! Read the sixteenth chapter of Luke in order to see this put to us in a plain and alarming manner. Dives was a rich man who lived the life of the world. Dressed in gorgeous robes, he 'fared sumptuously every day'. And all his family were living in the same way. But he died and now here he is in hell. His chief desire is that he may escape from there and go to be in Abraham's bosom with the poor beggar, Lazarus, whom he ignored while he was still alive. But that cannot be granted. Then he asks: 'I pray thee therefore, father, that thou wouldest send him [Lazarus] to my father's house: for I have five brethren; that he may testify unto them, lest they also come into this place of torment' (Luke 16:27–28). Dives has realized it now. He has not only seen through the vanity of the world, he sees that he is where he is because he had lived a worldly life and did not know, did not realize, what he was doing. So he says, in effect, 'Send to my five brothers. They are still in the ignorance that I was in. Send Lazarus to warn them so that they may not arrive in this same place and suffer this same horrible fate that has overcome me.'

Now this is the very thing that the woman of Samaria has realized. 'Come, see a man, which told me all things that ever I did.' We have emphasized this – her sense of sin, her conviction, the guilt of sin, realizing something of what sin is in the sight of God. This is the very centre of her experience. Christians are first of all convicted of the fact that they are sinners in the sight of God, that they are in a dangerous position. Having realized this, the woman of Samaria rushes to tell the people in her town because they have no idea. Not only the people who have lived as she has, but even the best people in the city are quite unaware of their position. This is the whole tragedy with men and women as they are by nature, unenlightened by the Scriptures and the Holy Spirit. They think that this world is everything, they are proud of it and never consider their death and the judgement beyond it. They regard such thoughts as morbid, and try to explain them away – you are familiar with all this. So this woman, realizing that the other people are in this appalling ignorance, inevitably wants to tell them, or, at any rate, wants to bring them to the one who can make it all plain and clear to them.

Now we have come to a very important point, a point that I think is the key to many of our troubles in the Christian church at the present time, perhaps especially among those of us who are evangelical. I ask once more: Are we, or are we not, like this woman? If we are not, if we do not feel this concern for others, and if we are not doing anything about them, the question is: Why not? I suggest that probably the main explanation is our failure to realize the danger people are in when they are outside Christ.

Why do we fail here? I feel it is largely because we have a defective sense of sin in ourselves. That is why I started with conviction of sin and emphasized it in earlier sermons. The danger of the soul outside Christ has not been emphasized in this century, in fact, we have not liked this teaching. We have said we must tell people to come to Jesus, we must always be positive. We do not like preaching the Law, we do not like the thunderings of the Law, we do not like the Old Testament. No, no; the gospel, we say, is a matter of love. And, of course, after a while this omission becomes so common, and something we are so accustomed to, that we even forget all about it. But there is only one thing that keeps us right individually, there is only one thing, ultimately, that will make us be concerned about others, and that is that we know something about the fear of hell.

There is no question about the necessity for a real conviction of sin. It must always come first, it must always be emphasized, because, I repeat, it is this that always keeps us right ourselves. I have heard so many people say, 'Oh, I wish I could go back again and get the thrill and the enjoyment of that time when I was converted, when I began to be a Christian.' They say that they no longer feel the same enthusiasm, that they have become humdrum Christians, living a humdrum kind of Christian life, and they add that they cannot understand it.

And then, of course, in order to try to correct this dullness, they try to work up some sort of excitement. And they organize this or that, something to bring a bit of life back into the church. The church as a whole, as well as the individual, behaves in this way. But you see the fallacy? It is really like someone who is not feeling very well taking to drink; it is the dangerous argument for taking a stimulant. No, first, find out why you are lacking in spiritual life. Think of a person beginning to feel loss of energy, lack of interest and so on. Now the bad doctor is the one who does not really try to find out the cause but says, 'What you need is a tonic,' and writes out a prescription. That is very bad medical practice; the doctor should first try to discover why this person who was so full of life and energy is now so low. What is the matter?

And we must do the same in the spiritual realm. The Christian's joy should not only not decrease as time goes on, it should become greater and greater. People do not like to be told this. They say, 'No, no; of course you cannot expect to go on like that through your life. The child is full of exuberance and enthusiasm and gets joy over things. But as children grow up, they become more staid and more settled, and then in middle age they probably become cynical and peter out.' But, my dear friends, that is not true of the Christian life. The joy of the Christian life, as I have been trying to show you, is a joy that is based upon knowledge and upon understanding. The joy of the apostle Paul and the other New Testament writers became greater and greater, and the nearer we get to the glory, the greater should be our joy, too.

But if it is not, why not? I suggest that the answer is that we have paid far too much attention to experiences, far too much attention to the initial decision – and, of course, this all belongs to the past, and cannot be repeated. You have taken your decision or you have had your experience, now you must go on with the Christian life, it is a matter of duty. Or perhaps when you were young, you belonged to some union or society, and that kept you going, but then you had to go out into the world and you got married and the problems of life came. The stimulus that kept you going in those early days has gone, and you flag, and say, 'I don't seem to have much experience of joy. It was there, I did have it' – and so you just keep going and trudge along.

How wrong that is, how tragically wrong! What is the matter? It is the failure to realize the truth about yourself at all stages and at every point in the Christian life. By nature, you are a hell-bound sinner – if you are not as moved and as concerned about that today as you were 20 years ago, then there is something radically wrong with you. The Christian should never get over this fact. I do not care how long you have been a Christian, you are nothing but a sinner saved by the grace of God.

There is a story of Daniel Rowland, that great preacher of 200 years ago, a man who knew what it was to be transported up into the heights in preaching and in private, a man who had great experiences from God and who under God had been the means of leading so many thousands to Christ in the amazing Evangelical Awakening in Wales. He was dying at last and somebody, one of the other preachers, went to him and said, 'How are you,

Mr Rowland, what is your experience?' And this is what he said: 'I am still nothing but an old sinner saved by the grace of God.' That is it! That was his secret. He never forgot that.

And you and I must never forget, we should always be aware of it. Every day when you wake up, you should say to yourself, 'I am what I am by the grace of God.' Why are you a Christian? Why are you getting on your knees to pray by the side of your bed? Why do you read your Scriptures? Do not just go on mechanically, but ask yourself: 'Why am I doing this?' And then say, 'It's because God in his infinite grace awakened me, opened my eyes, showed me myself as a guilty sinner bound for hell and eternal destruction, and then showed me what his Son had done for me' – and you will be up on your feet rejoicing. You should do that daily. That is how you 'rejoice in the Lord alway' (Philippians 4:4). You rejoice *in the Lord*, not in your experiences, not in what has happened to you, not in what you are doing, but 'in the Lord', and that means, at once, that you will be reminded of where you were, the precariousness, the hopelessness of your situation, and how you are saved, in one way and in one way only.

And if you do that, you will at the same time be reminding yourself immediately, automatically, that all those other poor people are still in that hopeless condition. You have relatives in that condition, you have friends, acquaintances, in that position; the people you have worked with, the world around you – that is still its condition. That is the way to be like the woman of Samaria. 'Come, see a man, which told me all things that ever I did.'

> Men die in darkness at thy side,
> Without a hope to cheer the tomb;
> Take up the torch and wave it wide.
> *Horatius Bonar*

This is it. They do not know it. 'Men die in darkness at thy side.' They are round and about us and they do not know it. My dear friends, if you realize this, you cannot be silent, you are bound to tell them. It is inevitable. But this is the way to go about it – not by numbers, not because it is the right thing to do, but because you are sorry for them, you are alarmed about them, and you feel that you would be a cad if you did not warn them.

But let me give you one further point. I want to put this positively as I close. This woman's concern for her people has a positive aspect and it is this: she rushes back out of her desire that the people of her town might also share in the benefits that she is enjoying. She does not stop at a negative concern – she is moved by the fact that they are missing what she now has when it is possible for them to enjoy it, too. She is sorry for them, sorry that they should go on eating the husks that are put out for the swine – and, in the last analysis, that is what civilization is – and she is anxious that they should begin to enjoy the riches, the food, that God has already provided. Was it Samuel Rutherford who said that he had lost his taste for the stale brown bread of this world since he started tasting of the heavenly manna? That is it; she wants everybody else to taste it also.

In other words, when you come to know the joy of the Christian life, then you feel you cannot keep it to yourself, you cannot be selfish. There is a great story in 2 Kings 7. The city of Samaria – at that time the capital of Israel – was besieged by the mighty army of the Syrians. Inside the city, all the food had been eaten and the people were dying of starvation. But then we read of four poor lepers. Because they were lepers, they could not go into the city, and they were outside the city gate. They also had no food, and did not know what to do. They said, 'If we try to get into the city, we'll die there. We might as well try the Syrians.

If they receive us and give us some food, then we'll live; if they put us to death, then we'll die, but we were going to die anyway.'

So that evening, these lepers took the risk of going to the Syrians' camp. When they got there, they found the camp deserted. The horses, the camels and the food and everything else were all there, but there were no people. This was because as darkness was falling, God had made the Syrians hear the noise of a vast approaching army, and thinking that this army was coming to the rescue of Samaria, the Syrians had fled in terror. So these lepers suddenly found themselves in the midst of wealth and abundance. They at once began to enjoy the food and drink and to hide the clothes and the silver and gold. It was an instinctive reaction – 'I'm alone. I'm on to a good thing. I'll keep it to myself and not let anybody know.'

But then the lepers came to themselves and said, 'We do not do well: this day is a day of good tidings, and we hold our peace' (2 Kings 7:9). All those people in the city were starving. Could these four go on enjoying themselves in selfishness and allow them to die? Could they keep silent when they had discovered riches? No, no; it was wrong. So they rushed back to the city and told everyone the good news.

That is exactly what the woman of Samaria did. When you have come across this 'good thing' you cannot keep it to yourself. The Christian is not selfish. One of the great changes that takes place is that we cease to be self-centred and to hold it all in to ourselves. We want to share it, we want everybody to enjoy it. Why? Well, we are in a common salvation! This is what moved the apostle Paul, as we have seen. This is why he felt he was a 'debtor'. This is why he says, 'The love of Christ constraineth us' (2 Corinthians 5:14).

Shall I put it to you in this way – trusting that this will bring it right home to all of us? I may have told you this before, but it is worth repeating. Look at that great verse, Romans 1:16: 'I am not ashamed of the gospel of Christ: for it is the power of God unto salvation to every one that believeth.' A man working in Egypt in the early years of this present century found a fragment of papyrus on which was written the words of Romans 1:16, and it gave him most wonderful information. It was written in koine Greek – the common Greek that was spoken in the first century – and he found that instead of the usual Greek word for 'power', a word had been used that also meant 'prescription'. So Romans 1:16 could be translated like this: 'I am not ashamed of the gospel of Christ: for it is the prescription of God unto salvation to every one that believeth.' Now you see what that tells us? Why was Paul longing to come to Rome? Because he had a prescription.

Can you not see the analogy? Imagine a man who for many years had suffered from some very painful and crippling disease, say, in his joints. He was in agony; he could not move and had almost become a cripple. He had tried his doctor, who had done his best, but the man was no better. So he had tried another doctor, but to no avail. He had tried all the great doctors who had been recommended to him, but not one of them had been able to cure him – at best there had only been a temporary improvement. He was almost at the point of despair.

But, at last, he heard of a great physician somewhere in another country who seemed to cure people suffering from this ailment. He said, 'I must see this doctor,' and he travelled to this country. The moment he met this physician, he realized that this man was different, he seemed to understand him. 'Yes,' said the physician, 'I do understand your condition and not only that, I can cure you.' He sat at his desk and wrote out a prescription. 'Take this,' he said. 'You will lose your pains, your joints will become supple, and you will be perfectly well.' So the man went to the chemist with the prescription, got it dispensed, and began taking the medicine. He kept on taking it, and the pain did indeed begin to go, the joints became free and he was cured.

Now that man walks up and down the streets of life. One afternoon he sees a man coming up on the other side of the street. He does not know the man, but he knows exactly what that man's trouble is – he can tell by the way the poor man is holding himself and shuffling along. He says, 'That man has my old complaint.' In his breast pocket is the prescription given by that great physician. What does he do? There is no question, there is no argument, he does not need to be trained or persuaded. He says to himself, 'If I don't cross the street and accost that man, I'm a cad.'

So he crosses the street. He does not wait for an introduction, he is not interested in etiquette and formalities. That other man is suffering and he has the cure. He is bound to speak. He says, 'Excuse me, sir, I don't know you and you don't know me, but I do know what is the matter with you. You have a complaint that I once had; tell me, have you ever heard of this?' and he produces his prescription. 'Take it and it will cure you as it cured me.'

'I am a debtor.' 'The love of Christ constraineth me.' I know. The woman of Samaria knows that the one who has cured her of her terrible disease can also cure her people, and all that is necessary is that she should bring them to him: and that is what she does. At the present time, your friends, relatives, associates and neighbours are dying because of the lack of a cure. Do you have this cure? If you have, and you realize the truth about them, you will feel that you are bound to tell them. You will feel that you are a 'debtor' to them, and that, indeed, you are a cad if you do not tell them.

55

# The Pre-eminence of Christ – Telling Others

*The woman then left her waterpot, and went her way into the city, and saith to the men, Come, see a man, which told me all things that ever I did: is not this the Christ? Then they went out of the city, and came unto him. (John 4:28–30)*

It is very important at this present time that we should all know the difference between being religious and being Christian. The failure to understand this difference is certainly the major problem in the church and, therefore, of course, it becomes a major problem in the world. Men and women are outside the church and they are not interested in it, and I suggest it is largely because they are not interested in a dead, formal religion. I still believe that when they are confronted by the true Christian faith and message as they see it exemplified in Christian lives, they will respond as these people in this city of Samaria did. If you are concerned about the state of the world and of this country, morally and in every other respect, and if you believe that the message of the gospel is the only hope for any individual in the world, and for the world itself in general, then this is a very urgent question for you.

This issue becomes particularly urgent for the individual Christian for this additional reason: we are living in days when it is no longer the custom for people to go to churches and chapels to listen to the preaching of the gospel; the responsibility of the individual Christian therefore becomes correspondingly greater. As at similar times in the past, there is no doubt but that it is largely through the personal witness of Christian people that the gospel will be spread in this our day and generation.

If only everybody in the church acted as this woman did, the situation would be transformed in a very short time. We are therefore analysing her motives, the things that produce this spontaneous impulse in her, and we have noted some of them. She has something to give. She has found the uniqueness of the person. She knows what he has done for her. And then she is concerned for the people in her town. She longs that they should share what has now come to her.

There is just one other motive that I must mention, and it is, indeed, a kind of climax to everything that I have been saying. This is her desire that all might come to glory in this person, that all might come to praise him. Or, putting it in another way, it is her desire that he might have the glory. As Paul puts it in writing to the Colossians, 'That in all things he might have the preeminence' (Colossians 1:18).

This, again, is a most delicate and sensitive test, and it can also be illustrated very simply by a human analogy. I have already used the very good analogy of doctor and patient. Our Lord is the great Physician, he is the Healer. Salvation means health, spiritual health, total health. So this is the obvious analogy and it works very well at this particular point. Whenever people have had experiences of being in trouble with regard to health, they try their physicians or seek specialist advice – and keep on trying until at last they find somebody who can help them. And I pointed out last time that when you are better again, your first impulse is to let everybody know about the cure.

But, of course, it does not stop at that. There is another element that comes in – you are concerned that this particular doctor should have the glory and the praise. You want everybody to feel the same wonder that you feel, and so you are anxious to send everybody to your doctor. Now there is an important double motive here. It is not simply that you are anxious that other suffering people should benefit, though, of course, you are. This desire is instinctive, as we have seen. If you have discovered something good, you want to share it. That is why I have put this first. But over and above that, you are anxious to show your gratitude to the one who has helped you, and the best way of doing that is to send everybody to him or her; you cannot give greater praise. 'Oh,' you say, 'you must go to so-and-so! Don't waste your time anywhere else.'

Now this is clearly seen in the woman of Samaria. She is so thrilled by this person and what he has done for her that she wants everybody else to come and admire him, and praise him and be astonished at him. And, again, she is no exception. As we read the four Gospels, we find that people were constantly talking about what he had done for them, spreading the news to such an extent that it even became an embarrassment to our Lord and at times he told them not to do this because his work was being hindered. He could have been kept in any one village, as it were, by everybody coming to him, but he said that he had to go to other places to preach the gospel. So he had to extricate himself from them. But it is emphasized everywhere in the Gospels that this was the inevitable reaction. The Christian is anxious that the Lord should have the praise and the honour and the glory, that everybody should go to him and that everybody should be filled with the same admiration.

To put it in more theological language, Christians are people who make their boast in the Lord Jesus Christ. And that is why I say that this is a very delicate and sensitive test. 'He that glorieth,' says the apostle Paul, 'let him glory in the Lord' (1 Corinthians 1:31). This is the test of Christian men and women. They see that this person is the only one who matters, he is the object of their affection and their desire, and of everything else, and they make their boast in him, they glory in him. Watch that word 'glory' as you read the Epistles, particularly of the apostle Paul. It is said, and I tend to agree, that it is the word that he uses so frequently because it really means 'to make your boast'. Paul, as a Pharisee, had boasted of his knowledge of the Law, his correctness, in a mechanical sense, his morality and his religion. He shows us that in Philippians 3, in that little bit of autobiography where he is really saying: 'I no longer boast in myself, or in the fact that I am a Jew of the tribe of Benjamin, or in any of these things. I make my boast in him.' He glories in the Lord, and he wants everybody else to do the same.

We can look at it like this: the Christian is one who talks about the Lord. 'Come, see a man, which told me everything that ever I did.' You notice that the woman of Samaria does not speak about herself primarily, she does not speak about the benefits that she has received, though she has received them, and we considered them in looking at her motives. But she talks about the Lord Jesus Christ. That does not mean that we never give our experience of the benefits of the Christian life, but the order here is extremely important. And, again, it is important because we are so anxious to contrast the Christian message, the Christian faith, and the Christian experience with that which belongs to the cults – these counterfeits that the devil introduces to keep people from Christ and from God – and this is one of the ways in which you can see the difference. The adherents of the cults generally talk about themselves and the benefits that they have derived. Of course, they then tell you that you can enjoy the same benefits if you adopt this teaching, but that is their method. But here is something quite different: the Christian talks first and foremost about this blessed person. The benefits are secondary.

Take the exhortation in the New Testament about rejoicing and notice the way in which it is put: 'Rejoice *in the Lord* alway: and again I say, Rejoice' (Philippians 4:4). There are times when circumstances are adverse and are inimical to your joy. If you are relying upon nothing but some happy inward sensations, you will not receive the support you need, as feelings are always variable and you cannot rely on them. The writer of the hymn says:

> I dare not trust the sweetest frame,
> But wholly lean on Jesus' name.
> On Christ, the solid Rock, I stand;
> All other ground is sinking sand.
> *Edward Mote*

And that is perfectly true. If you start with your experiences and with yourself, you will find there will be times when you really have nothing to say. And if you have followed one of the cults and say there is no such thing as disease and then you become ill, you are in a bit of trouble, are you not? But this is not the Christian position at all. Christians start with the Lord. Whatever I may feel, whatever my position may be, he abides ever always the same, and so I can always speak of him.

> In every high and stormy gale
> My anchor holds within the veil.
> *Edward Mote*

It is always Christ, everything that is true of him. So you speak of him as the woman does, and you yourself and your experiences and benefits come afterwards.

Now this is such an important point that I really must establish it for you. Take, for instance, what we are told in the second chapter of the book of Acts. Here are these disciples. They have been waiting ten days, as our Lord instructed them, for the coming baptism of the Holy Spirit. And then the great day comes and the Spirit is poured forth upon them. They are all filled with the Spirit, and they begin to speak with other tongues. They have an amazing experience, which obviously has a vital effect upon them, filling them with joy and with ecstasy, with praise and thanksgiving.

And then the crowd comes together and can see at once that something has happened to these people; some of the crowd even suggest that they are filled with new wine. But this is what is interesting: Peter now gets up to speak, and what does he do? He does not speak about the experience. He starts off by saying, 'This is that which was spoken by the prophet Joel' (Acts 2:16). Yes, but he says that in order to speak about something else. This, he says, is entirely due to this person whom you and your rulers crucified but who rose again. Peter's sermon is about the Lord Jesus Christ. This is what is remarkable. Here the disciples are, filled with the Spirit, with the accompanying phenomena, but they do not talk about that, they talk about him. Of course, our Lord had prophesied that this would be the case. He said that when the Spirit came, he would glorify him (John 16:14) and immediately the Spirit began to do that. The whole emphasis is upon the Lord, his person and work.

And there is another equally interesting example in the very next chapter. Peter and John are going up to the Temple at the hour of prayer in order to pray and they are accosted by a lame man sitting at the Beautiful Gate of the Temple. Then they are given authority and power to help him and there is great excitement, a phenomenon, something has happened, a fact. Again the crowd gathers together and once more Peter begins to preach. Does he say, 'Now, look here, you can all be healed, if you like, all of you can get the experience that this man has just had'? No, he says:

> *Ye men of Israel, why marvel ye at this? or why look ye so earnestly on us, as though by our own power or holiness we had made this man to walk? The God of Abraham, and of Isaac, and of Jacob, the God of our fathers, hath glorified his Son Jesus; whom ye delivered up, and denied him in the presence of Pilate . . . (Acts 3:12–13)*

It is again a sermon on the Lord Jesus Christ. Go through the book of the Acts of the Apostles. You will find this same emphasis everywhere. We see it when Peter is preaching in the household of Cornelius. And when we come to the section of Acts that deals primarily with Paul, all along we find that Paul is not telling the people about what has happened to him and how that can happen to them, but he is recounting the facts about Jesus – he is preaching Christ.

It is equally clear in the Epistles: 'We preach not ourselves, but Christ Jesus the Lord' (2 Corinthians 4:5). The people are always reminded of this great doctrine concerning the Lord. This is what matters; this always comes first. And when we come to the book of Revelation, it is the same. He is there: what he has done, what he is doing, what he is going to do. The entire book of Revelation concentrates on him and finishes by saying, 'Even so, come, Lord Jesus.'

Now these early Christians were passing through terrible times – persecutions and trials and tribulations – but their message was always a message that glorified him, gloried in him and wanted others to do the same. As Paul puts it in Colossians 1 (here he is, preaching the gospel to the Gentiles, he is indefatigable, and he explains his teaching, he divides it up and tells us exactly what he is doing): 'whom we preach' – that is it, that is his work, 'Christ in you, the hope of glory' (verse 27) – 'warning every man, and teaching every man in all wisdom; that we may present every man perfect in Christ Jesus' (verse 28).

It is always the same, and therefore this is something to which we must pay very great attention. Paul says: 'He that glorieth, let him glory in the Lord' (1 Corinthians 1:31). And again: 'God forbid that I should glory' – he is contrasting himself with false Judaizing teachers who gloried in the flesh, in legalistic details and in themselves and their converts – 'save in the cross of our Lord Jesus Christ' (Galatians 6:14). 'From henceforth let no man trouble me,' he goes on to say in verse 17. In verses 14 to 17, he is saying, in effect: 'Leave me alone: nothing matters to me except that this person may receive all the honour and the glory and praise.'

Have you not noticed, as you read, how Paul will suddenly seem to go off at a tangent? The literary pedants, of course, are upset by this. He interrupts his sentences, they say. Sometimes he does not complete them and he seems to have forgotten what he started saying. But what makes him do this? Oh, it is that he has mentioned the Lord's name and off he goes to some great apostrophe of praise. What matters to Paul over and above even the doctrine and all that we get by way of experience, is the Lord himself. Paul is anxious that Christ should have the pre-eminence, that he should stand out.

And, then, when we come to our hymn books, we find that the great hymns, especially the great hymns of the great periods of revival, likewise always glorify Christ.

All hail the power of Jesus' name . . .

This is the note. The desire is this:

> Let every kindred, every tribe
> On this terrestrial ball
> To him all majesty ascribe,
> And crown him Lord of all.
> *Edward Perronet*

> O for a thousand tongues to sing
> My great Redeemer's praise.
> *Charles Wesley*

That is Charles Wesley's desire. It is the desire of all true Christians. They want the whole world to come to him, to go to him. Once people see him, they will admire him and take glory in him and in him alone. And, incidentally, it is interesting to notice where those hymns I have just quoted come in the hymn book. They do not come under the section headed 'Christian ministry' because they are not only for preachers. The danger is to think, 'Ah, well, that is an appropriate hymn for an ordination or just before a sermon. No, no; they are for all Christians. This glorying in the Lord Jesus should be true of every Christian, as it is true of this woman of Samaria. If I am a Christian, surely this is my inevitable reaction. The Christian talks about him, the Christian wants everybody to see him, the Christian wants everybody to know him, the

Christian wants everybody to praise him, the Christian wants everybody to follow him. He is the centre of the Christian's life.

The reasons, of course, are perfectly clear. Christians alone realize who the Lord is. That is why the apostle Paul writes all about the Lord Jesus Christ in that first chapter of the Epistle to the Colossians. Those foolish people had been listening to some false teachers who were going round the churches. They tended to follow the great apostle round and they had a hotchpotch of teachings, a specious mixture of philosophy and Jewish practices. Paul deals with their teaching still more specifically in the second chapter of Colossians – that is his purpose in writing this letter. They talked about experiences and thrills, and the foolish Colossians were listening to all this – it seemed so wonderful. People are always ready to make sacrifices and to become ascetics; they will fast and sweat and pray; if necessary, they will mutilate their bodies. People have done this throughout the centuries. Anything that panders to the flesh gives this idea of 'will worship', as the apostle says (2:23).

By contrast, Paul brings in his great message and he says: 'What are you talking about?' These teachers said that there was a whole series of angels, a gradation of angels and intermediaries, between God and man. It all sounded so intellectual, and yet at the same time so thrilling to the emotions. But Paul brushes it all aside. He says, in effect, 'You would never have looked at that teaching if you had but realized the truth about him. If you had understood this, you would always have given him, and him alone, the pre-eminence.' Why? Because, says Paul, he is who he is: 'the firstborn of every creature' (Colossians 1:15). He is the one through whom and for whom the world was made. The glory of the person!

This is what is lacking in us. We are all so subjective, we keep taking our spiritual pulses, and are concerned about these little aches and pains. We even tend to think of the church as a kind of dispensary where soporifics are dispensed to make us feel a little bit better and more comfortable. Tell me, what brought you to this church this morning? Did you come to praise him, to consider him? Did you come to get more knowledge of him and a better understanding of him so that you can go and tell people about him, or did you just come for something you want?

Now do not misunderstand me. I must put it in this extreme form in order to correct the tendency that is in all of us to regard church as here for us, as it were. It is not primarily. The church is 'the pillar and ground of the truth' (1 Timothy 3:15), and today's church is as she is because she has forgotten all this. The church is afraid, so she is modifying everything, even her message, in order to attract and to interest and to hold people. What a travesty! The business of the church is to hold Christ forth. She is 'the pillar and ground of the truth', this great pillar that is displayed, 'that in all things he might have the preeminence' (Colossians 1:18). It is when the church fails to realize this that we go wrong and, of course, the apostle is never tired of showing this.

This is the way, incidentally, to deal with our personal problems. Have you often found that? I have found it many a time, thank God, thank the Lord Jesus Christ. My little problems! When I have met him again, they have gone, I have forgotten all about them. When he comes in, it is like lifting up the blinds and the sun coming in. That is the effect he has. If we only knew him better and realized these truths concerning him, all these other specious false doctrines would be seen for the nonsense that they are and would vanish. All the cleverness of the world – what is the value of it? There is nothing in it. And fancy giving our time and attention to things like that, being misled by them, being troubled by them, when he is here in the midst and we are to look at him, the glory and the wonder of his very person! At this very moment, he is 'upholding all things by the word of his power' (Hebrews 1:3). That is who he is.

And then the apostle goes on to point out what the Lord has done. Here we are with the Communion Table before us, the bread and the wine. How can we talk about anything else? How can we be interested in anything else? Read again Philippians 2:4–11. Think of him, 'who, being in the form of God, thought it not robbery to be equal with God: but made himself of no reputation'. Is there anybody else worth talking about? We glory in people; it is pathetic, is it not? There has never been a man or woman who is worthy of our glory. Everything we have, we have received, we have not created it, we have not produced it. 'What hast thou that thou didst not receive?' says Paul to the Corinthians (1 Corinthians 4:7). Foolish people, he says, glorying in men. Here is the only one. He is and he has given every man and woman all they have. All abilities, everything, have come from him. Here is one to glory in because he is who and what he is. He is 'the brightness of his [God's] glory, and the express image of his person' (Hebrews 1:3).

So you see that this woman of Samaria was saying, 'Come and see him; come and see this person. Come and see him that you may fall at his feet' – and that is what we are to do. That is our business as Christians. 'Tis all my business here below', says Charles Wesley, 'to cry, Behold the Lamb!' So there it is, the incarnation, the self humiliation of the Son of God, born as a man in the likeness of men – yes, 'in the likeness of sinful flesh' (Romans 8:3). That is what he has done.

Now who do *you* speak of? I have given you the human analogy, this doctor, some great statesman, politician, scientist; all right, you admire them because of what they have done. But as you tell the world about what these other people have done, you must speak to them of what he has done. And you go on to tell them about how he not only took the form of a servant, but also humbled himself even to 'the death of the cross' (Philippians 2:8), and you tell them about the cross. You look at it:

When I survey the wondrous cross
On which the Prince of glory died,
My richest gain I count but loss,
And pour contempt on all my pride.

*Isaac Watts*

You do not talk about yourself any longer, you talk about 'the Prince of glory', this paradox, as Peter puts it in that sermon recorded in Acts 3: '[You] killed the Prince [author] of life' (verse 15). The author of life is put to death. You can tell people about that – that you are not interested in any other drama because this is *the* drama and everything else is a pale imitation. So you tell them about what he has done.

There in that Epistle to the Philippians, Paul is dealing with a most practical matter – a lack of co-operation among certain people in the church. 'Look not every man on his own things,' Paul says, 'but every man also on the things of others' (Philippians 2:4). Do not be selfish, he says, share with one another. But Paul cannot even talk about that without going off at once – the person! Oh, he says, what am I talking about? 'Let this mind be in you, which was also in Christ Jesus' (verse 5). Here is the solution.

A friend was asking me the other day, 'How can I be humble?' He felt there was pride in him and he wanted to know how to get rid of it. He seemed to think that I had some patent remedy and could tell him, 'Do this, that and the other and you will be humble.'

I said, 'No, I have no method or technique. I can't tell you to get down on your knees and believe in prayer because I know you will soon be proud of that. There's only one way to be humble and that is to look into the face of Jesus Christ; you cannot be anything else when you see him.' It is the only way. Humility is not something you can create within yourself; rather, you look at him, you realize who he is and what he has done, and you are humbled.

> My richest gain I count but loss,
> And pour contempt on all my pride.

The only way to get rid of pride is to regard it with contempt, and he alone will enable you to do this. He humbled himself, his body was broken, his blood was shed. This is an actual fact.

Why did he do it? He did it that you and I might be forgiven. He did it that you and I might become the children of God. He did it to redeem us, that we might be 'delivered from the power of darkness' to which we all belong by nature, and be brought into 'the kingdom of his dear Son', the Son of God (Colossians 1:13). This is all fact, and once we see it, what else can we talk about?

And then there is his glorious rising, his conquering of death and the grave, the last enemy (1 Corinthians 15:26). So Christians begin to look to the future. They make that grand leap that the apostle makes there in Philippians 2:

> *Wherefore God also hath highly exalted him, and given him a name which is above every name: that at the name of Jesus every knee should bow, of things in heaven, and things in earth, and things under the earth; and that every tongue should confess that Jesus Christ is Lord, to the glory of God the Father. (Philippians 2:9–11)*

It is all there. And what do Christians want? They want to see the whole world falling at the feet of this blessed person. This is the height of their ambition, this is their greatest desire. They are 'looking for and hasting unto the coming of the day of God' (2 Peter 3:12). They are looking forward to this great day when every tongue shall confess and every knee shall bow. The greatest people the world has ever known, and all the potentates and principalities and powers in the heavenly places and on earth and under the earth, shall all humble themselves before him and look up in admiration at him and glory in him and 'confess that Jesus Christ is Lord, to the glory of God the Father' (Philippians 2:11).

Knowing all these things about him, Christians are inevitably bound to talk about them. They are anxious that everybody else should know this and should bow before him. They realize that people are in ignorance and are rebellious and that their only hope is to get to know him. The Christian's great concern is not simply that other people should get the benefits of knowing him – I have already dealt with that – but that others may see his glory and worship him. It should be intolerable to contemplate that there is anybody who does not acknowledge him – not primarily because they are wrong and are in a state of misery, but because they are not 'bowing the knee' to this King immortal, invisible, the Son of God, the Saviour of the world. That is the motive, as it clearly is in the case of the woman of Samaria. She longs that these people should come, and she delights in the anticipation of seeing the expression on their faces when they see him and hear what he has to say.

There, then, are the leading motives that urge this woman to leave her waterpot and go and bring the people to see him; and these are the motives that should impel every one of us to do this in our own way and in our own time and generation.

But this leads me to the next question, which is this: How is this work done? I want to be very practical because this is an important and urgent question for every Christian at this hour. I repeat that it is no use your bemoaning the times, the increasing immorality and vice, the war in Vietnam and the whole horror of the state of the world, there is no point if you do nothing about it. Negative condemnation is utterly useless. The world is ignorant, it needs the gospel message, it needs the truth about this blessed person and you and I alone can give it. How are we to do it? Well here in the Bible we are given vital instruction.

Now we cannot do precisely what the woman of Samaria does. Our Lord is no longer here as he was in the days of his flesh. What, then, do we do? Thank God, he himself and his disciples, his apostles, the writers of these books, have given us the knowledge and instruction that we stand in need of. I will try to summarize it for you.

Before we come down to the particulars, let us look at this question in general and, again, I must remind you hurriedly of the negatives. How is this work to be done? The answer is, first, never mechanically. If it is done mechanically, it will probably do more harm than good. We must never witness to the glory of our Lord merely because we feel it is our duty, that we ought to be doing it and, if we have not, will feel a bit unhappy when we go to bed at night and pray to God. I hope that all I have been saying gets rid of such notions. Obviously, also, it is not a question of behaving more or less like a parrot and just repeating clichés and formulae. That is inconceivable when you put this into the context that we have been dealing with. There have been books written on this subject and it is pathetic to notice the tendency to adopt a mechanical approach.

How, then, do you do this work? Well, positively, first, you prepare yourself. This is of the utmost importance. What you are is infinitely more important than what you do, and what you do ultimately depends upon what you are. The danger is that you pick up the manuals and rush off into the details. No, the Christian always has to prepare himself or herself. I have often illustrated this. This is my experience, my testimony, as a preacher of the gospel. The most important thing for a preacher is to prepare himself. It takes us quite a long time to learn that. The young man prepares his sermon and feels, when he has finished preparing it, that he is right. What a fallacy! I have been very guilty of it, we all have; it takes a man years to learn this lesson. You can have an almost perfect sermon, but if you are not right, it will be no good, it will be 'as sounding brass, or a tinkling cymbal': great knowledge, great learning, polished phrases and sentences. Rubbish! Nonsense! Oh, you will get admiration, 'Verily I say unto you, They have their reward' (Matthew 6:2) – but what a reward! No, no; the preparation of the man is the important thing; nothing is so important.

After putting it like that in general, I move on to the next point – the first detail – which is that we bring ourselves to a realization of the seriousness of the task. The seriousness! What do I mean? I am not talking about preaching only. It is true of preaching – preaching is the most serious thing in the world. You see, that is why, if one did not believe in the Holy Spirit and the power that he can give, one would never dare enter a pulpit – 'Who is sufficient for these things?' (2 Corinthians 2:16). But it is equally true of anybody who talks to an individual about these matters.

First, then, we realize the possibility of our doing great harm and antagonizing people. That is the place to start. Do not rush into this and say it is quite simple, you have this verse and that, and there you are, a ready reckoner kind of evangelism. What a terrible thing it is! You must start by realizing the harm you can do. I have had to deal with near tragedies in this respect, harm done to people by injudicious Christian people whose motives were excellent, who wanted to do good and to warn their relatives or friends, but who were speaking mechanically, superficially, and had never realized the seriousness of what they were doing.

Now it sounds as if I am discouraging you, does it not? No, no; I am not discouraging you, I am encouraging you to do this work in the right way. Then you will have fruit and you will have glory with God. So we start by realizing that we are dealing with souls, with immortal souls; we are dealing with people not only as regards their life in this world, but their eternal destiny. We are not trying to get people to join a club or an institution, or to take up a theory that we are interested in. No, no; we are dealing with immortal souls and their everlasting destiny. It is the most serious and responsible work in the world.

And then you realize – and to me this is, perhaps, the most important point of all – you must always start by realizing that the work you are attempting to do can only be done, finally, by the Holy Spirit. You can never make anybody a Christian – never. You can make them church members but you never make them Christians. It is impossible. The Holy Spirit alone can do this, and, therefore, we must always be afraid of spurious results, temporary results, something that people have done rather than the Holy Spirit.

To conclude this point, let me put it to you in the words of the great apostle, the man who probably knew more about this work, both in public and in private, than he knew about anything else. This, he tells us, is how he approached it:

> *I was with you in weakness, and in fear, and in much trembling. And my speech and my preaching was not with enticing words of man's wisdom, but in demonstration of the Spirit and of power. (1 Corinthians 2:3–4)*

Now why the fear and the much trembling? For the reasons I have already given you. Paul knew what he was doing. He knew the danger, the responsibility, the possibility of harm – 'in weakness, and in fear, and in much trembling' – this authority, this genius! But he knew that he was dealing with the human soul.

Or listen to the apostle saying this again in a very striking way:

*Now thanks be unto God, which always causes us to triumph in Christ, and maketh manifest the savour of his knowledge by us in every place.*

That is what you are doing, for, Paul says, the fact is this:

*For we are unto God a sweet savour of Christ, in them that are saved, and in them that perish: to the one we are the savour of death unto death; and to the other the savour of life unto life.*

And then Paul asks a question:

*And who is sufficient for these things? (2 Corinthians 2:14–16)*

And that is the position of every Christian who speaks to another about the Lord Jesus Christ. You can be 'a savour of death unto death' or 'of life unto life' – 'Who is sufficient for these things?' And once you ask that, you have avoided and evaded most of the terrible dangers, for you are humbled, you realize the seriousness of what you are doing, the tremendous responsibility and the necessity of the presence and power of the Holy Spirit. And that, as I hope to show you, will also be essential for the other practical aspects of the carrying out of this great desire to bring everybody to him: That in all things and by all people he, and he alone, may have the pre-eminence.

56

# *More than Conquerors*

*The woman then left her waterpot, and went her way into the city, and saith to the men, Come, see a man, which told me all things that ever I did: is not this the Christ? Then they went out of the city, and came unto him. (John 4:28–30)*[1]

There have been various periods in our history when the masses have been outside the church and indifferent to her message. It is at such times that the witness of the individual Christian is greatly enhanced. Today, we are living at such a time. But why are people today largely outside the church? Is it that we are failing in our witness as individual Christians? Is it that we are somehow or another different from the woman of Samaria so that those who know us are not attracted, not interested, not concerned, even, to listen to the gospel? This is a very important matter. It is not merely a matter of duty that we should consider this question – it

---

[1] This was Dr Lloyd-Jones' last Sunday morning service as the Minister of Westminster Chapel.

becomes a very thorough test of our whole position as Christians. There is something wrong with the Christian who cares simply about himself or herself and has no concern whatsoever about those who are outside.

That is the background to our consideration of verses 28 to 30, which we are dealing with in a very practical way. Having considered the motives that impelled the woman of Samaria to fetch her fellow townspeople – motives that have always impelled Christian men and women – we are now considering the way in which we bring people to our Lord, and this, again, is all important. Now in the case of this woman, all she had to do was invite people to come out of the city to meet our Lord as he was there by the side of the well. We cannot do that, but the principles are perfectly clear and there are many guidelines in the Scriptures. Once we leave the four Gospels and go on to the book of Acts and the Epistles, we find the people in the position that we are in today, and there is abundant teaching with regard to this whole matter.

We have been emphasizing the importance of what we are. We are bound to start here because what we are is altogether more significant than what we do. We are in a century that is activist, and part of its trouble is that, forgetting principles, people rush off into action. So it is essential that we should remind ourselves that though we may do this, that and the other, if we ourselves are not right, we are wasting our time and people will not listen to us. 'What you are,' they say, 'speaks louder than what you say.' And they are interested in what we are.

So we are considering the kind of impact that we as Christians should be making upon others. As we have seen, the book of Acts records that it was ordinary Christians, scattered abroad by persecution, who spread the gospel. They were in contact with other people, and it was what these others saw in the Christians that aroused the desire to be like them. This is the way that God has always used so strikingly for the extension of his kingdom. What staggered the ancient world was the quality of life of the Christians. Therefore this is a subject that we should consider very carefully.

So what are the characteristics of the Christian? Christian men and women are serious people. They are followers of one who was 'a man of sorrows' (Isaiah 53:3). They do not take the superficial, giddy view of life that so many have in the midst of tragedy. They are bound to be serious, they cannot help themselves, and they realize the seriousness of what they are doing. They know something of what the apostle Paul experienced when he went to Corinth 'in weakness, and in fear, and in much trembling' (1 Corinthians 2:3). The days are evil and it is only Christians who really have an understanding of the times.

But we must hasten to say that Christians also have joy, a joy that no one else has. The seriousness and the joy are not incompatible; they go together. It is a serious joy or a joyful seriousness. It is not solemnity; it is not dullness. The last thing the Christian should ever be is dull. A dull Christian is a contradiction in terms.

But let me suggest some further qualities that, it seems to me, are particularly important at a time such as this. The Christian is one who always conveys a sense of peace. We can use many other words for this – a sense of tranquillity; a heart that is at rest. You see the relevance of this at the present time. The word that really describes the world as it is today is that word of the prophet Isaiah: 'But the wicked are like the troubled sea, when it cannot rest, whose waters cast up mire and dirt' (Isaiah 57:20). Is not that the modern world? Oh, the restlessness of this age! The hurry, the tension, the excitement, the lack of stability. It is a time of trouble, a time of confusion, a time of uncertainty. Its waters cast up mire and dirt, and we see that in our newspapers and on our televisions. It is a part of the restlessness.

That is the world in which we live, and that is the description of the wicked. Now we give that word 'wicked' much too restricted a meaning. The term means all those who are not Christians. And they are 'like the troubled sea', carried about hither and thither, having no centre, no central stability, and at the same time, of course, troubled in mind and troubled in spirit.

I need not keep you with this. It has been talked about at great length. This restlessness is the outstanding characteristic of the present age. It is an age that has to live on drugs, tranquillizers and soporifics, and depends on artificial means to get to sleep. The commonly used words in our vocabulary today are the words 'tension' and 'stresses and strains'. And then, on top of that, there is the mania for pleasure. It is all because of this restlessness, the turmoil of life, and the complete failure to deal with it and to understand it.

Now that being the state and condition of the world, it is obvious that the Christian is to be the exact opposite. The sense of peace that Christians have is one of the most wonderful proofs of the Christian faith, and it is this, when it is seen in us, that attracts others, because, I say again, the world is always more ready to listen when it sees an example than when it hears mere talk. It is familiar with the talk.

The cults, of course, thrive on the condition of the modern world, and are always offering easy remedies. But people have tried them, and the philosophies, and are tired of it all. They just find that it does not work. This is what is so significant today. People have only turned to drugs and other forms of escapism because they have lost hope in what the world has to offer them and have lost confidence in human reason and understanding.

They have got to escape, they say. The world cannot help. There is nothing there. This is a very serious matter. As we said earlier, politically, the world tends to turn to dictatorship in a time of restlessness and uncertainty.

All this gives us as Christians an exceptional opportunity. We have the opportunity to show that though we are in the same world and subject to the same pressures, yet we are essentially different, and the big difference is expressed in a line from the hymn by Anna L. Waring: 'a heart at leisure from itself'. That sense of tranquillity, of peace, of being at rest, is the greatest thing of all.

Now it is my contention that it is the Christian alone who is capable of this. I do not want to weary you with an analysis of all this, but we are aware of the teaching of the Stoics. As in the days when our Lord was here, so now and in every time of strain and stress, this philosophy tends to come in. But Stoicism does not teach a heart at rest, it is mere resignation, a mere refusal to face things. That is not true rest, it is a form of repression. If you have the will power and the health to follow this philosophy, you may give the impression of having a kind of 'rest' in your life, but you do not really have it. Merely to hold things down is not to be at peace. There is no solution there, only grim determination just to go on in spite of everything. I grant you that there may be something quite noble about it, something that at times can even appear to be heroic, but it is always negative and, in any case, it is of no value to others because it is entirely dependent upon the will power and ability of the person concerned.

Or there are some people who are born with a phlegmatic kind of temperament; they do not react as others do, they seem to be rendered more insensitive to things that happen. 'All right,' says someone else, who is very different. 'But I was not born like that.'

Like the Stoic, the phlegmatic person has nothing to give to anyone else.

But that is not the position of Christians. The reason for their peace, of course, is that they have a solution, an understanding of life. This has not come from anything in themselves, they have received it from the word of the Lord. To quote Matthew Arnold, the Christian is someone who is able to 'see life steadily and see it whole', and that is the only thing that gives inward peace and rest. The Christian is no longer frantically looking for some solution or for some understanding. It is the search for understanding that causes the restlessness. The book of Acts describes this perfectly. One of the most sophisticated cities and societies in the ancient world was Athens, the Mecca of philosophy, where all the philosophers went. It was the seat of learning and of understanding, and, of course, the great object there was, as the book of Acts tells us, 'either to tell, or to hear some new thing' (Acts 17:21).

Now why was that the characteristic of the life of Athens? It was because of the perplexities created by the whole problem of life and living. They were trying to understand and they could not. The philosophers were cancelling one another out, and none of them was really satisfactory. And as the secular historians tell us, the rate of suicide among the philosophers was higher proportionately than in any other section of the community. So, you see, the whole society was restless – and it is, I repeat, just the same today. People are on edge, they are tense and under a tremendous strain. You see it in their faces.

So here is our opportunity and here is the test for us. Do we have hearts at leisure from themselves? Have we an inward peace? If we have, it inevitably shows itself. We read of our blessed Lord that 'he could not be hid' (Mark 7:24), and this peace simply cannot be hid. This is a great psychological point, of course.

What we are inside always shows itself. It shows itself in our faces, in our eyes, in the very atmosphere that we carry with us. There are certain people whom we cannot meet without immediately feeling at rest. We cannot analyse it, we just know it, we are at once conscious of it. Of course, we can all put on appearances, can we not? We can smile and appear to be very wonderful when everything is wrong inside. But here is something different, this peace is not playacting, it is not all on the surface.

People of the world see through all the playacting because that is how they live themselves, but when they come across these Christian people, they know at once that they are different. They see this inward peace, they recognize that Christians have what is called 'the quiet heart'. This is what the Quakers, in particular, have always been concerned about, and to that extent, of course, they are absolutely right. They have tended to turn this into a philosophy and into a cult, and, in a very subtle way, because of their departure from the orthodox Christian faith, it becomes for them just a refined form of Stoicism. But the quiet heart itself, the tranquil heart, the 'heart at leisure from itself', that they are seeking, is always right.

And there is nothing that so opens the door of opportunity as that you and I should have this sense of inward peace and rest. In this way, we can influence others and bring them to the Lord Jesus Christ, for our whole testimony is that we are not like this by nature, that some of us were as far removed from this as it is possible for a human being to be. We do not have some sort of bovine stolidity. No, we have been given this peace by the grace of God. Our Lord said, 'Peace I leave with you, my peace I give unto you: not as the world giveth, give I unto you. Let not your heart by troubled, neither let it be afraid' (John 14:27). This is the peace of God. And what he has done for us he can do for others.

Then there is something further, which leads logically and directly from that, and is an extension of it, but I put it separately because I think one must. People must be able to see that we have inner reserves. I draw the distinction because they must first see that we are at peace. After that, they see that we continue to be at peace in spite of what happens to us. This is an important distinction because the great test of life is what we are like when things go wrong.

Very many people give the impression of having inward peace and tranquillity when everything is going well. We can, most of us, put up a very good show when we are well and hale and hearty and young, and everything is prospering and the sun is shining in the heavens; most of us are fairly good under such conditions. We have wonderful theories and say we will do this, that and the other. But the test comes when everything goes wrong. Then people find that they have nothing at all, and they break down. And that is where the opportunity for the Christian comes in at the present time because never have the outward stresses and strains been greater than they are just at this moment.

Our Lord dealt with that once and for ever at the end of the Sermon on the Mount in the parable of the two houses. Here is a man who rushes up his house without a foundation, and he is very amused that that other fellow is so slow. He has got his house up before the other man has dug his foundations. What a fool! 'This is marvellous! Solves all my problems.' Short cuts! But then the rain descends and the floods come and the wind blows, and the whole building collapses. That is so typical of the world: its theories and ideas cannot stand up to the test.

And here, again, the Christian is essentially different. Now this is one of the profoundest tests that we can ever apply to ourselves. It is the great test between believism and faith, between taking up religion and being taken up by it, between having it in your head and having it in your heart, in your spirit, at the centre of your life. The whole point about Christian men and women is that they are not easily disturbed or shaken by what happens; they are no longer dependent upon circumstances for their happiness and for their joy. This is absolutely basic. What has happened to us as Christians is, as is put so frequently in the New Testament, that we have been delivered from 'this present evil world' (Galatians 1:4) and translated 'into the kingdom of his [God's] dear Son' (Colossians 1:13). Now when Paul says that we have been delivered from this present evil world, he does not merely mean that we are delivered from its practices, from its habits and customs. These words mean much more. They mean that we have been delivered from the world's way of thinking, from its outlook, from its whole understanding of life and living and the purpose of it all. This is one of the things that is most striking about the Christian. Those who are not Christians, by contrast, are dependent upon what happens to them, they are dependent upon their surroundings and circumstances.

Now there is no need to prove this, it is shouting at us. Why do people spend so much money on drinking and on smoking and on pleasure? It is obvious, is it not? They cannot live without it. They are dependent upon it. They are dependent upon other people, they are dependent upon the state of their health, they are dependent upon success. They are in the hands of circumstances and conditions and the things that are happening round and about them. The result is that when there is a change, an adverse change, in their circumstances, and everything is collapsing, they have nothing to fall back on. There is no sense of having an inward reserve; there is no satisfaction within. They have been kept going by the things outside. The life of the unbeliever is indeed like a bubble – you keep it going, you go on blowing, and then, if you cannot for some reason, it collapses and is gone.

Here is one of the greatest and most glorious differences between the Christian and the non-Christian. Indeed, here is one of the great differences between the child of God and the one who is not a child of God. The psalmist says:

*Unto the upright there ariseth light in the darkness: he is gracious, and full of compassion, and righteous. A good man sheweth favour, and lendeth: he will guide his affairs with discretion.*

Now then:

*Surely he shall not be moved for ever: the righteous shall be in everlasting remembrance. He shall not be afraid of evil tidings*

– are you afraid of evil tidings? This man, this righteous man –

*his heart is fixed, trusting in the LORD. His heart is established, he shall not be afraid. (Psalm 112:4–8)*

Now that is the Old Testament. Here is a man writing at least a thousand years before the coming of the Son of God into this world and yet he is able to say that; and it was true. That is the secret of those great men of the Old Testament, the patriarchs, the psalmists, the prophets and others, it was true of them. And yet we know that we are in a superior position. They were children of God, yes, but they had not the knowledge that we have. 'He that is least in the kingdom of heaven is greater than he [John the Baptist]' – in position and in understanding (Matthew 11:11); and yet there it is in the Old Testament. And so we ask ourselves this question: Are we afraid of evil tidings? The world is because its heart is not fixed, because it is not established in the very centre.

Or let me put it in another way. The book of Proverbs says this: 'The name of the LORD is a strong tower: the righteous runneth into it, and is safe' (Proverbs 18:10). In other words, the righteous have a place to retreat into. When the enemy is attacking powerfully outside and they feel their defences are being penetrated and they are tending to lose ground, they are all right, there is no panic – 'the strong tower'. Here is this tower that is impregnable, 'the righteous runneth into it, and is safe'. He enters into his keep, and he knows that here there is something that no enemy can ever penetrate.

That, again, is Old Testament, but this is obviously so true of Christian men and women: it differentiates them from non-Christians; they have inner resources. And is there anything more glorious and more wonderful about this life than just this very fact that there is within us a place that is absolutely impregnable no matter what the world may think or do? And does it not become obvious that the real reason why so many are outside the church is that they do not see people like this inside the church? They say, 'Ah, these people, they go to this place on a Sunday and they affect an interest, but I have watched them when things go wrong and when troubles come and they are no different from the rest of us, they are just as panicky and they obviously do not know what to do.' Those are the words that are used. They say, 'What's the value of all their church-going?' And it is a perfectly fair criticism. It is no use your talking about the Christian faith if that is how you behave? They say, 'What's the value of your faith if it can't help you at the time of trial?'

The New Testament is full of this teaching. Let me give one or two of these glorious examples in order that we may all examine ourselves and, I trust, be filled with a sense of shame and realize that the first thing we must do is put ourselves right and become the sort of people about whom anyone meeting us will say, 'I would give the whole world if only I could be like you!'

Let me give you this great example: look at the apostle Paul. Here he is in prison. First-century prisons were dank, damp, horrible in every sense, and Paul is suffering. But one afternoon he is brought out of prison to give a little bit of entertainment to a king and a queen and a Roman governor. They ask him about the Christian faith and Paul gives them the account of his conversion. Then Paul says: 'King Agrippa, believest thou the prophets? I know that thou believest,' at which Agrippa says to Paul, 'Almost thou persuadest me to be a Christian.' Do not misunderstand that. Perhaps a better translation is: 'Do you think that with such a little talk you can make me a Christian?' But here is the important point. Paul then says, 'I would to God, that not only thou, but also all that hear me this day, were both almost, and altogether such as I am, except these bonds' (Acts 26:27–29).

I think that is one of the greatest statements ever made. Think of the position: here is a man, a prisoner with the chains hanging from his wrists, and he is addressing the King and the Queen and the Roman Governor. They are at liberty, enjoying life, while he is in a prison. And yet this prisoner is able to say: I would give anything if only you people could be as I am. Oh, I wish you had the inward peace and the rest that I am enjoying! I wish that you could have the experience that I am having in that prison cell! Oh, that you were as I am!

Here is a man who is entirely independent of his circumstances – they make no difference to him. He has inner reserves, he has something here that is bigger than the whole universe. It does not matter what man may do to him and he would that all others should be as he is. He does not want them to be in bonds, he does not want them to suffer, but what he does want them to have is the rest, the peace, the quiet, the satisfaction, that he has. He wants them to discover that the truth is that whatever happens to Christian people, it all ministers to this life that they have been given through the Lord Jesus Christ by the Holy Spirit.

Now let the apostle himself teach you. He himself gives us the explanation. He tells us why he was able to speak as he did on that occasion to Agrippa and Festus. In a passage in 2 Corinthians 4 he quite honestly and frankly gives us an account of the difficulties that he has been going through. Yet he says this:

> *We have this treasure in earthen vessels, that the excellency of the power may be of God, and not of us. We are troubled on every side, yet not distressed; we are perplexed, but not in despair; persecuted, but not forsaken; cast down, but not destroyed; always bearing about in the body the dying of the Lord Jesus that the life also of Jesus might be made manifest in our body. For we which live are alway delivered unto death for Jesus' sake*

– those were the things that were happening to him, but notice the great contrasts. What is the explanation? Well, here it is –

> *For which cause we faint not; but though our outward man perish, yet the inward man is renewed day by day.*

My dear friends, this is the question: Do you know the difference between the 'outward man' and the 'inward man'? Are you living your life entirely on the outward level? So many people are. They live on talk and gossip and excitement and pleasure. It is all outside, and inside there is an emptiness. That is not Christianity. What makes a Christian a Christian is the inward life, new life from God, 'the life of God in the soul of man'. Christians are 'partakers of the divine nature' (2 Peter 1:4). There is an 'inward man' and this 'inward man' is entirely independent of the 'outward man' and is being renewed day by day.

And then Paul continues:

*For our light affliction*

– all that has been happening to him, all that he has been describing, he calls a 'light affliction' –

*which is but for a moment*

– what does he mean by 'but for a moment'? Does he know that the persecutions are going to stop? Has he got second sight? Is this sympathetic understanding? Does he know that all his circumstances are suddenly going to change and all is going to be well? Is that what he means? Of course not! No, that is his view of life in this world. For the Christian, it is only 'a moment'. Of course, for the non-Christian, life in this world is everything. And when physical death comes, that is terrible. It is the end of all things: 'Death! I'm getting older. No, I'm not! I must do everything to keep young – rejuvenation! I'll go to the end of the earth, get an operation, a new heart. Life!'

What a tragedy! That shows the emptiness of the heart. But what about this 'light affliction, which is but for a moment'? What does it do? It –

*worketh for us a far more exceeding and eternal weight of glory*

– this word 'worketh' is most important. It means 'produces', 'creates', 'stimulates'. The 'light affliction, which is but for a moment', all these terrible things that are happening, are creating within the apostle, and increasing and enhancing within him, 'a far more exceeding and eternal weight of glory'. How do they do it? Well, Paul says, the secret is –

> *while we look not at the things which are seen, but at the things which*
> *are not seen*

– what another vital distinction this is! What do you spend your time looking at? Are you always looking at something outside? Do you live through the winter by thinking of your summer holidays: is that how you get through? Many people are like that. Now let us be reasonable about these things. I am not saying that you should not plan your summer holidays, but what I am saying is that you should not live on that. Some people are always talking about their schemes and plans and proposals, as if they cannot enjoy the present moment. They have nothing within them. 'We look not at the things which are seen, but at the things which are not seen.' The whole secret of Christian men and women is that they see 'the things which are not seen', and they can see them wherever they are. Within a prison cell they see them: they are not outside, they are inside.

And so the more adverse and cruel and trying the circumstances, the more they remind Christian people of their imperishable souls and of the Lord Jesus Christ, who had similar experiences when he was in this world. They remind Christians that the Lord has gone on to prepare a place for them and will come again and receive them unto himself. The apostle goes on to put it like this:

> *For we know that if our earthly house of this tabernacle were dissolved,*
> *we have a building of God, an house not made with hands, eternal in*
> *the heavens. (2 Corinthians 4:7–11, 16 – 5:1)*

So the more you are afflicted and tried by things that happen to you from the outside, and the malignity of men, the more it drives you to realize that you do not belong to the world, that you are bigger than it, that you belong to Christ, you belong to heaven, you belong to glory – 'a far more exceeding and eternal weight of glory'.

The trouble with all of us is that we think so little about that glory; we are looking so much at the outside, at the seen, the visible, that we do not gaze upon the unseen, the eternal, the glorious, that God in Christ is preparing for us. We do not heed the exhortation of Paul to the Colossians, 'Set your affection on things above, not on things on the earth' (Colossians 3:2). So it works like this: when afflictions and trials come, they force us to do what we had foolishly not been doing. We cannot enjoy the outside because it is all against us at the moment, and that, therefore, reminds us of the 'inside', the unseen, the eternal, the spiritual. And the moment we begin to think in that way, we are immune to what happens outside. This builds up and we see the eternal more and more gloriously, and we know we are going on to it. So even if they kill us, what have they done? They have simply introduced us to that glory at an earlier point than we had expected. 'Though our outward man perish, yet the inward man is renewed day by day.'

Now, my dear friends, it is the people who give this impression who conquer the world. These are the people who act as magnets, drawing others to the Lord Jesus Christ. The apostle Paul was full of this; clearly it was one of the most important things of all to him. For your encouragement, let me remind you of what he wrote to Timothy. Timothy was so like us. He was nervous, apprehensive, troubled, anxious about the care of the churches, and now he gets a message to say that Paul is not only in prison but is likely to be put to death at any moment. So as well as being worried about himself, Timothy is worried about Paul, and the apostle has to write to him. Look here, says Paul:

*For God hath not given us the spirit of fear*

– that is what we have by nature, and the world is in the grip of the spirit of fear this morning. What has God given us? –

*but of power, and of love, and of a sound mind [discipline].*

So Paul goes on to say:

*Be not therefore ashamed of the testimony of our Lord, nor of me his prisoner: but be thou partaker of the afflictions of the gospel according to the power of God; who hath saved us, and called us with an holy calling, not according to our works, but according to his own purpose and grace, which was given us in Christ Jesus before the world began, but is now made manifest by the appearing of our Saviour Jesus Christ, who hath abolished death, and hath brought life and immortality to light through the gospel: whereunto I am appointed a preacher, and an apostle, and a teacher of the Gentiles. For the which cause I also suffer [I am suffering] these things*

– I am in prison and I have been treated very cruelly, and in a most unjust manner. Then that blessed word 'nevertheless' –

*nevertheless I am not ashamed*

– I am not troubled, I am not taken unawares, I am not grumbling and complaining, and you must not. Why not? –

*for I know whom I have believed, and am persuaded that he is able to keep that which I have committed unto him against that day. (2 Timothy 1:7–12)*

Well, there it is, my dear friends. To use again the language of the great apostle, the Christian does not merely manage just to get through; that is what the Stoic does. Here is the Christian:

*Who shall separate us from the love of Christ? shall tribulation, or distress, or persecution, or famine, or nakedness, or peril, or sword?*

*As it is written, For thy sake we are killed all the day long; we are accounted as sheep for the slaughter. Nay*

– this blessed protest, the inner man begins to speak –

*in all these things we are more than conquerors through him that loved us. For I am persuaded, that neither death, nor life, nor angels, nor principalities, nor powers, nor things present, nor things to come, nor height, nor depth, nor any other creature, shall be able to separate us from the love of God, which is in Christ Jesus our Lord. (Romans 8:35–39)*

Oh, beloved Christian, are you giving everyone the impression that you have inner reserves, that your 'inner man' is growing day by day and is independent of circumstances – of chance, of war, it does not matter what it is – and that all they do is increase this 'far more exceeding and eternal weight of glory'? Believe me, when the Christian church, oh, as insignificant as she is today, is filled with people who give that impression, the world will come streaming in, for it is the one thing that it cannot discover, because it is only to be found in our blessed Lord and Saviour Jesus Christ.